Literacy and Learning

Literacy and Learning in the Content Areas:
Strategies for Middle and Secondary School Teachers

SECOND EDITION

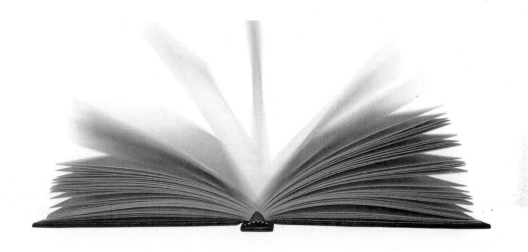

Karen Kuelthau Allan
Lesley University

Margery Staman Miller
Lesley University

Houghton Mifflin Company   New York   Boston

Publisher: Patricial Coryell
Senior Sponsoring Editor: Sue Pulvermacher-Alt
Senior Development Editor: Lisa Mafrici
Associate Project Editor: Reba Libby
Editorial Assistant: Rachel Zanders
Senior Manufacturing Coordinator: Priscilla Bailey
Marketing Manager: Jane Potter
Senior Designer: Henry Rachlin
Cover Image: © Tristan Paviot/Getty Images/Stone

Printed in the U.S.A.

Library of Congress Catalog Card Number: 2003109888

ISBN 0-618-33277-4

123456789-DOC-08 07 06 05 04

Brief Contents

Contents

PART TWO
Teaching Tools for Strategic Learning 79

Preface

As we worked on *Literacy and Learning in the Content Areas: Strategies for Middle and Secondary School Teachers,* Second Edition, literacy was once again at the forefront of the nation's educational agenda. With "Reading First," the federal government and the nation focused on teaching all students to read by fourth grade. What policymakers and the general public have not recognized is that literacy learning continues throughout the grades, especially when students read content-area texts that contain new technical information. All of us who work with middle- and secondary-school students and their teachers know that struggling readers, as well as average and above average students, can meet difficult texts in the content areas. Many students can benefit from strategy instruction and from teaching tools that support their learning of content.

Therefore, when we revised *Literacy and Learning in the Content Areas,* we maintained the overall goal of showing content-area teachers how literacy strategies and teaching tools will support their students' construction of meaning in their specific subject area.

Our Approach

First and foremost, our design of this book emphasizes literacy strategies. Our goal is for preservice teachers to become aware of their own literacy strategies so that they can nourish their students' strategic learning. To build their metacognitive awareness of literacy strategies, we provide modeling and explaining scripts that exhibit how and why strategies can be applied to content-area texts. We explain strategies used before reading (such as activating prior knowledge), during reading (such as text and schema connections), and after reading (such as reviewing and evaluating knowledge). The scripts also are specific examples of how they could model and explain strategies to their future students.

Second, we emphasize teaching tools that support students' learning of strategies and content. Sequenced by when teachers use the teaching tool, we present teaching tools for before reading (such as brainstorming, word map), during reading (such as DRA, comprehension guides, and vocabulary in context), and after reading (such as summaries and post-reading guides). Furthermore, we interweave assessment with instruction by describing how teaching tools can be used concurrently to instruct and to assess learning and by presenting assessment-only tools, such as retelling. We also integrate writing teaching tools (such as journals and revising drafts) to complement the reading teaching tools.

Third, we show preservice teachers how to incorporate literacy strategies and teaching tools into content-area curriculum units. We demonstrate how a teacher supports students in the beginning, during, and at the end of a women's history research project. We also provide specific examples of middle and high school units that respond to the standards in their respective content areas: a geology unit, a math and language arts unit, and an immigration and cultural diversity unit.

While this book continues to appeal to novice teachers in particular, experienced teachers and reading specialists have found that our focus on students' literacy strategies has enhanced their professional development.

Key Revisions in the Second Edition

Although we've maintained the text's overall philosophy and approach, we have made a number of changes that we think make *Literacy and Learning in the Content Areas*, Second Edition a better, more accessible text. We have:

- **Reorganized and streamlined the chapters** to better highlight the literacy strategies and tools while keeping the "before, during, and after reading" approach. (See the section on "Content and Organization" in this preface for details.)

- **Expanded and highlighted coverage of diversity** in Chapter 2, "Students as Learners," to include a section on teaching diverse students, and throughout the text with new content on the needs of diverse students, which is called out with **new diversity icons** in the margins.

- **Emphasized coverage of key national and state standards**, which is now identified by **new standards icons** in the margins. As standards play an increasing role in teaching today, this important coverage is better highlighted throughout the text.

- **Increased coverage of technology**, in particular electronic texts and use of the Internet, with concentrated coverage on electronic texts in Chapter 3 and conducting research in Chapter 9, examples of using technology in lessons and units, plus **new Web Site Resources** at the end of each chapter.

- **Added a list of Key Concepts to the beginning of each chapter** to help readers learn new vocabulary, and then defined those concepts in the margins next to where the concepts appear in the text.

- **Added and updated relevant, practical resources**—books, journal articles, and web sites—to the end of each chapter.

Content and Organization

As mentioned, this edition of *Literacy and Learning in the Content Areas* has been streamlined and reorganized so that the content is more accessible and the literacy strategies stand out better. This involved combining some chapters, and splitting others apart.

Part One, "The Contexts of Teaching and Learning," presents the facets of teaching and challenges preservice teachers to be responsive in teaching their students.

- Chapter 1, "Teacher as Learner," defines content-area teaching and the concepts of literacy, learning, and strategies; integrates those concepts by discussing teaching strategies and content learning; and concludes with a discussion of adolescents' literacy and learning out of school and its implications for in-school literacy and learning.

- Chapter 2, "Students as Learners," describes student diversity; discusses students' schemata knowledge, strategies, and motivation; and offers guidelines and suggestions for teaching diverse students.

- Chapter 3, "Choices and Decisions for Content Learning," describes the variety of texts and selection criteria; discusses pedagogy choices; defines the types of teaching and assessment tools discussed in Parts Two and Three; and offers a sample lesson for teaching strategies and tools in tandem.

Part Two, "Teaching Tools for Strategic Learning," emphasizes when learners use strategies to learn and when teachers use teaching/assessing tools to support students' learning of content.

- Chapter 4, "Building on Your Students' Prior Knowledge," focuses on "before reading"; models the two strategies of activating prior knowledge and previewing and predicting; explains tools like brainstorming, graphic organizers and anticipation guides; and concludes with using journals for brainstorming ideas for writing.

- Chapter 5, "Building Students' Vocabulary," discusses selecting vocabulary to teach before reading; models learning new vocabulary; explains tools such as student self-rating, word map, and morphemic analysis; and ends with writing new words in journals.

- Chapter 6, "Comprehending and Constructing Knowledge," focuses on the core of the reading process that occurs during reading; explains text-based and schema-based connections and types of questions; models strategies for finding and interpreting information; describes teaching tools such as DRA, comprehension guides, and peer-led discussions; and concludes with describing types of journal writing for learning content.

- Chapter 7, "Supporting Strategies for Comprehension," presents three strategies that help students comprehend: capitalizing on text organization, making notes, and defining vocabulary in context; explains narrative and expository text organizations and teaching tools like text pattern guides; describes teaching tools for making notes, like graphic organizers; models defining vocabulary in context and explains teaching tools like semantic feature charts and using context clues; and concludes with writing first drafts.

- Chapter 8, "Studying: Reviewing and Evaluating Knowledge," provides a lesson on strategies that leads to modeling summarizing an article with students; includes teaching/assessing tools, such as post reading guides, PORPE, and reinforcing vocabulary; discusses tests, essays, and portfolios; and concludes with revising first drafts.

- Chapter 9, "Researching with Multiple Sources," melds the previous chapters and foretells the units in Part Three; discusses the different purposes for research projects—extending knowledge and learning to conduct research, particularly with print and Internet sources; describes different end products like communication projects and term papers; and presents a middle school research project in which the teacher focuses on teaching students to evaluate and synthesize information from print and Internet sources.

Part Three, "Enhancing Learning Through the Disciplines," embeds literacy strategies and teaching tools within curriculum development of content-area units. This part also presents the range of curriculum units that teachers may choose to embark upon at different times in the year or in their career.

- Chapter 10, "Designing Curriculum for Learning: Teaching for Major Understandings," compares the curriculum standards in the major disciplines; defines three curriculum models—single discipline, coordinated, and integrated; and outlines a unit plan useful across the disciplines.

- Chapter 11, "Enhancing Literacy and Learning In and Among the Disciplines," outlines an overview of single discipline and coordinated curricula; discusses common and specific concerns among the disciplines; and presents a single discipline unit on geology for high school and a coordinated unit between math and language arts for middle school.

- Chapter 12, "Integrated Curriculum," defines interdisciplinary, integrated, and thematic study; describes the rationale for as well as the planning and coordination necessary to create integrated units; and presents an integrated unit on immigration and cultural diversity for high school students.

- Chapter 13, "Continuing to Grow as a Reflective Professional," describes taking an inquiring stance toward one's teaching; presents an example of an inquiry project completed by a preservice middle school teacher; and concludes with suggestions for joining the profession and a discussion of professional standards for teachers.

Study Aid Pedagogy

In addition to the aforementioned special features, we have included the following learning pedagogy and resources to assist readers' comprehension of the chapters:

- **Chapter-Opening Graphic Organizers** are designed to give readers an overview of the chapter's content and to encourage readers to use previewing strategies.

- **Purpose-Setting Questions** are designed to help readers predict the context of the chapter, activate their own prior knowledge about the content of the chapter, and guide their comprehension of the chapter.

- *New* **Key Concepts** are listed at the beginning of each chapter so that readers have a better idea of the important concepts in the chapter. These key concepts are now highlighted in blue in the text and defined in the margins.

- *New* **Diversity and Standards Icons** now appear in the margins and indicate where you'll find either diversity information or information on national and state standards.

- **Summaries** appear at the end of each chapter and highlight the key points of the chapter.

- **Inquiry into Your Learning and Inquiry into Your Students' Learning** features appear at the end of each chapter and provide ideas for field-based activities. For additional field-based activities, the **Teacher as Inquiring Learner** feature suggestions are inserted into chapters.

- **Resources** now appear at the end of every chapter and are designed to encourage readers to continue their learning about specific topics. The resources are divided by books, articles from professional journals, and Internet web sites.

- **References** appear at the end of the text and show a complete reference for all of the sources used in the text.

Accompanying Resources for Instructors and Students

- An **Instructor's Resource Manual** is offered to provide instructors with additional teaching and assessment support materials. Features include model syllabi, activities and discussion topics, and test items for each chapter.

- A **NEW companion web site** contains a variety of resources and tools for students and instructors, including an electronic version of the IRM with transparency masters for instructors, additional literacy examples and strategies for different content areas, additional examples of unit plans for different curriculum models, web links for URLs that appear in the text, interactive flashcards for vocabulary study, and more.

Acknowledgments

Writing, like teaching, is a collaborative process. We have many people to thank. First, we thank our students who, in becoming teachers, brought literacy strategies and tools into their teaching and their classrooms. Many students understood that metacognition and strategy instruction could be transferred from literacy into math, science, and social studies. We also thank experienced teachers who refined our strategy instruction with their students and supplied us with curriculum ideas and classroom examples.

Second, we thank our colleagues at Lesley University, particularly those in the School of Education. Our faculty colleagues participated in conversations about teaching, learning, and literacy and encouraged us throughout the project. Our Ludke Library colleagues assisted us in our varied searches. Our graduate student, Rachel Sandrew, assisted us in the chapter resources sections. Dean William Dandridge kept his watchful eye on our progress and encouraged us.

Third, we thank the following reviewers:

Nancy S. Bailey, Metropolitan State College of Denver

Lee A. Dubert, Boise State University

Mychael Irwin, Texas Tech University

Diane L. Lowe, Framingham State College

Alan M. Weber, Central Michigan University

Kenneth J. Weiss, Nazareth College of Rochester

They thoughtfully and thoroughly challenged our thinking and so strengthened the book. We thank them for the time they willingly gave, their thorough comments, and their knowledge of literacy, teachers, and college students.

Fourth, we thank the people associated with the Houghton Mifflin Company. We thank Sue Pulvermacher-Alt, Senior Sponsoring Editor, who supported the revision of the book. We also could not have brought this book to fruition without Kassi Radonski, Development Editor, who helped us incorporate our revisions within our original version, Lisa Mafrici, Senior Development Editor, who steered us carefully throughout the publishing process, Reba Libby, Associate Project Editor, and Rachel Zanders, Editorial Assistant, who skillfully shepherded us and the book through the details and deadlines of production, and Sara Hauschildt, Editorial Associate, who helped produce the IRM and website materials.

Finally, we thank our extended families and close friends who have experienced this project with us. Margery expresses deep gratitude to her parents who have always encouraged her to pursue new challenges and to her husband, Lee, who has offered his understanding throughout this project. Karen dedicates this book to the memory of her late husband, Andrew A. Allan, who celebrated the initial endeavors and drafts of this book and who devoted his life to students' and teachers' learning.

Karen Kuelthau Allan
Margery Staman Miller

Literacy and Learning

PART ONE

The Contexts of Teaching and Learning

© Susie Fitzhugh

CHAPTER 1

Teacher as Learner

KEY CONCEPTS

- **construct knowledge,** p. 14
- **metacognitive awareness,** p. 15
- **strategy,** p. 15
- **skill,** p. 16
- **teaching tools,** p. 17
- **model and explain,** p. 18

PURPOSE-SETTING QUESTIONS

1 Why did you choose to become a content-area teacher? What topics in your content area do you feel knowledgeable about, and what areas do you need to learn more about?

2 Think about what you have learned about students, pedagogy or teaching practices, and curriculum materials in your college program. In what areas would you like to learn more?

3 How do you use literacy (that is, speaking, listening, reading, and writing) to learn in your content area? What have you read that has intrigued you? How do you use writing to help you understand your thinking in your content area?

4 What out-of-school literacy actions do you engage in? Do you read printed text, electronic text and graphics, view movies, and listen to CDs? Why do you engage in those activities? What do you learn from them? What strategies do you use when you're engaged in them? Do you think you could use any of those activities to inform your teaching?

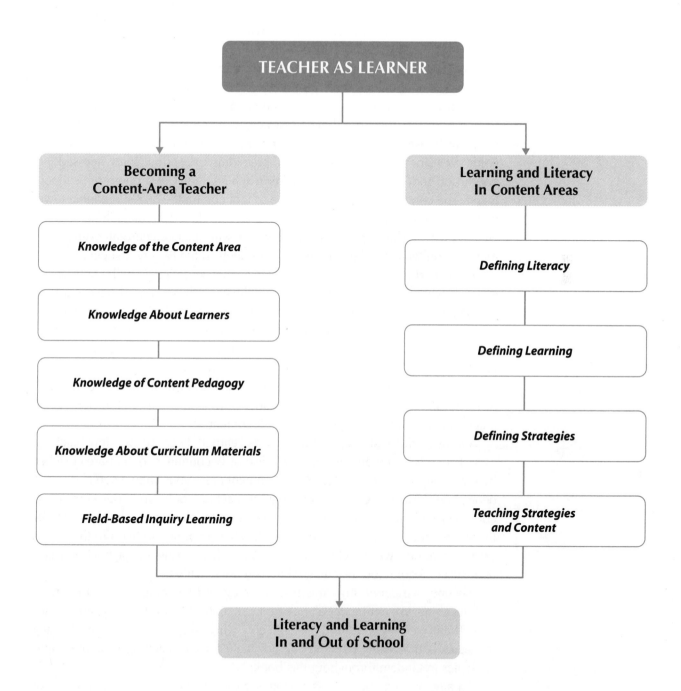

TEACHER AS LEARNER

Becoming a
Content-Area Teacher

Knowledge of the Content Area

Knowledge About Learners

Knowledge of Content Pedagogy

Knowledge About Curriculum Materials

Field-Based Inquiry Learning

Learning and Literacy
In Content Areas

Defining Literacy

Defining Learning

Defining Strategies

Teaching Strategies
and Content

Literacy and Learning
In and Out of School

Congratulations! You have decided to become a teacher! Although you were born in the twentieth century, you will spend your teaching career in the twenty-first century. What changes will you experience and witness in the next century? Like you, Louise Kuehlthau (the grandmother of one of the authors) had a teaching career that crossed two centuries; born in the nineteenth century, she taught in the twentieth. Think about the changes she experienced. Born when horses drew carriages, she drove a car across the country. Born when kerosene lamps lit houses, she watched Neil Armstrong walk on the moon on her new color television set. Born during the Impressionist art period, she witnessed the pop art of Andy Warhol. Beginning her teaching career in a one-room school-house, she concluded it by chairing the school committee of a burgeoning town with a large high school. She never would have predicted the magnitude of those changes when she began teaching. Where will science, current events, art, music, and literature take you and your students in the twenty-first century?

One prediction that you can make is that knowledge will continue to expand exponentially. Grandmother Kuehlthau probably could have made a reasonable attempt to cover a content area; now we hold no such expectations. The curriculum has become increasingly packed as more and more topics have been added; teaching has become more swiftly paced and learning more superficial. The result is that teachers can no longer pretend to cover a content area. Instead, teaching must focus on strategies that will allow people to continue to learn beyond the time when they are students. Thus, the heart of this book is literacy strategies for lifelong learning in all content areas.

We titled this first chapter "Teacher as Learner" because we view teaching as a lifelong learning process. First, we discuss becoming a content-area teacher by increasing your knowledge of your content area, your knowledge about students, your knowledge about pedagogy or teaching tools, and your knowledge about curriculum materials. Although you want to learn as much as you can in these four areas now, even experienced teachers continue to learn in these four areas. Therefore, we conclude this section with a discussion of how you can realistically learn about teaching while you are teaching.

Second, we define how this text, *Literacy and Learning,* fits with content-area teaching. We define three important concepts: literacy, learning, and strategies. Then we integrate the three concepts when we discuss teaching literacy strategies and learning content. We advocate for the teaching of content and strategies in tandem throughout this book.

Finally, we conclude by discussing adolescents' literacy and learning out of school and how teachers can learn from out-of-school literacy actions to engage students' in-school literacy and learning actions.

Becoming a Content-Area Teacher

You have decided to become a teacher because you enjoy your content area; maybe you are even passionate about it. You like investigating and predicting weather, enjoy reading and discussing Jamaica Kincaid's books, find mathematics in everyday situations, or carry a sketchbook with you everywhere. But more than being engrossed in your content area, you want to communicate that content to young people. You hope to interest students in applying your content area to their everyday lives and to interest at least a few of them in pursuing the subject in a career.

Your combined interest in your content area and your students sets you apart from other people majoring in your field. In many jobs and professions, workers are continually updating their knowledge; anthropologists continue to study their cultures, economists the theories of the marketplace, poets poetry. Unlike these and other workers, middle school and high school teachers not only continue to learn in their subject area, they also study teaching-learning events in their own classrooms. Recognizing the need for knowledge in subject matter and in teaching the subject matter, the Carnegie Commission states:

> Teachers must think for themselves if they are able to help others think for themselves, be able to act independently and collaborate with others, and render critical judgment. They must be people whose knowledge is wide-ranging and whose understanding runs deep. . . . They must be able to learn all the time. . . . Teachers will not come to school knowing all that they have to know, but knowing how to figure out what they need to know, where to get it, and how to help others make meaning out of it. (Carnegie Commission, 1986, p. 25)

Since both the knowledge in your content area and the students in your classes continually change, teaching is a continuous and career-long learning experience. We agree with Shulman (1986, 1987) and Cochran, De Ruiter, and King (1993) that teaching requires learning in four areas:

- Knowledge of the content area: Content, strategies, and attitudes of the subject area and connections to other subject areas

- Knowledge of learners: Cognitive and affective development of students as well as their cultural environments

- Knowledge of content pedagogy: Teaching tools at the confluence between content and students

- Knowledge of curriculum materials: Textbooks, curriculum guides, computer programs, and primary sources, among others

Educators in different content areas have also described teaching as learning four areas (for example, mathematics—Ball, 1991; English—Grossman ence—Hollon, Roth, & Anderson, 1991; and history—Wineburg & Wil have begun learning in the four areas in your college preparation, but e experience, you will continue to learn in each of these same areas.

■ Knowledge of the Content Area

In preparing to be a middle school or high school teacher, you have been majoring in a field and probably specializing in a specific area. When you teach, you may have studied some of the topics in the curriculum but not others. For example, suppose you are a political science major or an American Revolution specialist. As a social studies teacher, you will need to broaden your knowledge of American history. Or perhaps you decide to teach a new topic, like asteroids, because you're interested in it, your students are interested in it, or the topic is in the news or movies now. You will need to update your knowledge about asteroids. Becoming a continuous learner in your content area may require you to learn new topics, build on your current knowledge, and learn about new ideas and theories in your field.

Rather than communicating a list of isolated facts as a content-area teacher, you want to communicate the major ideas in your content area as well as the strategies to learn in your area (McDiarmid, Ball, & Anderson, 1989). What are the major themes in history, styles and media in art, or theories in earth science? How are the major ideas in your content area related to each other? In addition, think about what "doing" or learning your content area means—what a mathematician does or what a historian does. Does mathematics consist of algorithms and theorems to be solved or is it a means for describing different patterns in the world? Is history the interpretation of people's actions, the chronological representation of factual events, or a framework for understanding current policy and social issues? Is literary analysis one absolute interpretation of a book or one individual's response to the book among other possible responses?

We do not mean to imply that there is necessarily one way to view your content area. In some content areas, experts disagree about "knowing and doing" their domain; in others experts generally agree. Furthermore, views change as new theories are considered. To help teachers think about "knowing and doing" in their content area, professional organizations have followed the lead of the National Council of Teachers of Mathematics and developed curriculum standards for their respective content areas. The curriculum standards are meant to be general guidelines for teachers to use when they are deciding what students should know (content) and how students might learn (or do math as a mathematician would). You might want to go to the web site of the organization for your content area and read the curriculum standards. (Refer to Resources at the end of the chapter.) Building on the professional organizations' standards, individual states have developed curriculum standards or frameworks to guide curriculum development in that state. Furthermore, in some states, the state standards are aligned with the state assessments of students' learning. However, none of the standards tell you exactly what to teach or how to teach; they are broad guidelines. We recommend that you investigate both your professional organization's and your state's curriculum standards. (We return to standards in Part Three.) Furthermore, we recommend that you think about how you view your content area. For although you will have curriculum mandates to meet, we think that how you view your content area will influence the ideas and concepts you teach, how you teach those ideas, and the learning you impart.

TEACHER AS INQUIRING LEARNER

Find a partner whose field is the same as yours, and together discuss and take notes about the views each of you holds about your content area.

- What are the major topics, ideas, and theories in your content area? How do they relate to one another and extend into the everyday world? How do experts tackle questions or problems in your field? What strategies do they use to investigate or learn? How do new ideas or theories become accepted in your field? How do experts "do" your content area?

After you have listed your ideas, describe your view of your content area to partners in a different field.

- How is your description of your content area different from and similar to their descriptions of theirs? Do you have any revisions to your own description?

Compare your ideas to the standards on your professional organization's web site. Under which standards can you place your ideas? Do the standards give you other ideas to include in your view?

■ Knowledge About Learners

In your teacher preparation program, you probably have taken a course on adolescent psychology and read research and theories of cognitive and emotional development. Maybe you have had the opportunity to take a multicultural course and recognize that students bring diverse cultural heritages to schools. Although you have learned general information about development and diversity, you will be continually learning specifically who your students are and what previous learning they bring to classrooms (see Chapter 2, "Students as Learners").

Knowing his subject matter, his students, and curriculum materials, the teacher created a problem-solving activity for these students.

© Susie Fitzhugh

Your students may look similar, but in fact they have diverse characteristics, such as race or ethnicity, language, income level, gender, and special needs, and in unique combinations. In addition to their previous learning in and out of school, they bring unique knowledge, strategies, and attitudes to your classroom. You will want to discover what information (or even misconceptions) your students have before you teach a topic. You will also want to discover what typical strategies they use for tasks, such as solving algebra problems or writing a persuasive letter to the editor. If you teach in the same school for a number of years, you will become adept at predicting your current students' diverse characteristics and background knowledge. Even so, you will continue to learn about your students because students are different and unique, and they are always changing.

Our major focus in this book is on literacy strategies that help students learn content (we discuss them in Part Two). Most middle school and high school students use some strategies, but they may not be aware of how they use them. Less successful students do not use effective strategies and usually are unaware that strategies even exist (Garner, 1987; Garner & Alexander, 1989). You will want to learn what strategies your students use and what strategies can help them learn better.

Thus, a second area for your continuous learning is learning how diverse your students are. Even though you may teach 125 students, you can learn how each one is a unique combination of race or ethnicity, language, income level, gender, and special needs, for example. In addition, your students are unique in the knowledge, strategies, and motivation they bring to your classroom. Since students are why all teachers teach, we discuss students as learners in Chapter 2.

■ Knowledge of Content Pedagogy

Content pedagogy is the area that makes you a teacher. Positioned at the confluence between knowledge of content and knowledge of students, teachers make decisions about teaching-learning events: the teaching tools, student activities, and curricular materials to use. For example, all teachers, but especially history teachers, figured out how to put the events of "9/11" and the United States government's subsequent policies and actions into context for their particular students. Teachers in New York City made different decisions than teachers in Reno, Nevada, but both were at the confluence between content and students.

Another example is that both an English major and an English teaching major study Shakespeare, but only an English teacher decides how to communicate to students the universal themes of Shakespeare. Unlike a Shakespeare professor who begins with Act I, scene 1 of Romeo and Juliet, an English teacher might bring to class news articles about Serb and Croat lovers in Sarajevo to discuss before reading the play. And finally, although both history majors and history teaching majors study the Civil War from primary source materials, a history teacher selects sources that project clearly either a Northern or a Southern point of view. After studying the sources, the students would role-play both Union and Confederate people to interpret the effect of the war on our nation and to learn what "doing" history means.

In bridging content and students, teachers make instructional decisions about teaching tools and student activities that support and enhance students' learning. In our examples above, the teachers chose discussion and role play. You have probably learned about teaching methods in your own content area. In Part Two, we focus on teaching tools for literacy strategies that support learning your content area.

When teachers think about bridging content and students, they also make decisions about the communication roles students and teachers play in the social environment of the classroom (see Chapter 3). Teachers decide when to lecture and when to have the students work in small groups. They think about when student-to-student exchanges of ideas will enable students to clarify, evaluate, and revise their thoughts and positions about the content under study. In our examples above, what decisions about communication roles do you think the teachers made?

Beginning teachers usually focus on their own teaching actions—what they are doing in the classroom. We encourage you to focus as quickly as possible on students' actions—what particular students are doing—because knowledge about your students' learning will inform you about your teaching. Studying specific teaching-learning events and particular students will become an absorbing learning experience that will last all of your career.

■ Knowledge About Curriculum Materials

Learning about curriculum materials, one aspect of content pedagogy, is a continuous pursuit of teachers. The availability of suitable materials is often the deciding factor about whether to teach a particular topic. Even in their "leisure" time, teachers serendipitously search for a more current article, a more accessible primary source, or a new author that will better support teaching-learning in their classrooms.

In your subject-area methods courses, you probably examined specific materials. Although beginning teachers usually rely on textbooks, we encourage you to incorporate other sources, such as library books, primary sources, and on-line texts. You may have students who read a variety of materials outside of school—newspapers, magazines, web sites. As you expand your knowledge of the variety of materials available, you will need to evaluate their contents and usefulness carefully (see Chapter 3).

■ Field-Based Inquiry

As you begin teaching, we expect you to work on becoming a reflective practitioner about your teaching, your students, and your classroom. You can observe your students, analyze how they are learning and how you are teaching, and reflect on how your practice can improve.

To start you on becoming an observant and reflective teacher, we offer three types of field-based inquiry activities throughout the book: Teacher as Inquiring Learner, Inquiry into Your Learning, and Inquiry into Your Students' Learning. These activities will give you opportunities to examine content-area teaching, specific teaching-learning events, your learning and literacy strategies, and your students' learning and literacy strategies. As you engage in those activities, we recommend keeping a field notebook in which you record what you do and what you observe, the data you collect, as well as your thoughts, analysis, and reflections about what you're learning. For example, look ahead to the Teacher as Inquiring Learner activity on page 15. If you choose to do that activity, your field notebook might look like Figure 1.1.

FIGURE 1.1 Sample Field Notebook for Inquiry Activities

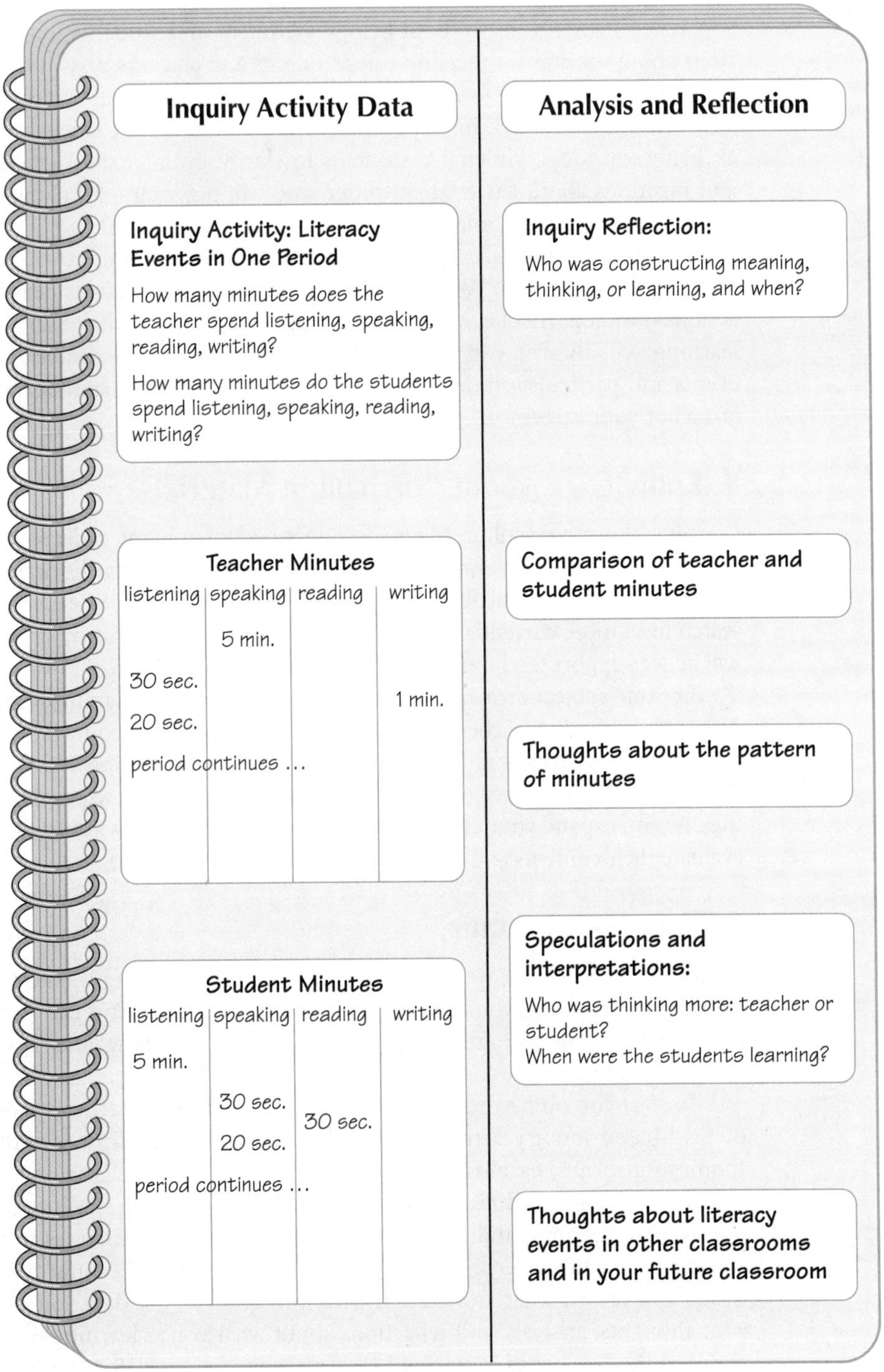

Inquiry Activity Data

Analysis and Reflection

Inquiry Activity: Literacy Events in One Period

How many minutes does the teacher spend listening, speaking, reading, writing?

How many minutes do the students spend listening, speaking, reading, writing?

Inquiry Reflection:

Who was constructing meaning, thinking, or learning, and when?

Teacher Minutes

listening	speaking	reading	writing
	5 min.		
30 sec.			
			1 min.
20 sec.			
period continues ...			

Comparison of teacher and student minutes

Thoughts about the pattern of minutes

Student Minutes

listening	speaking	reading	writing
5 min.			
	30 sec.		
		30 sec.	
	20 sec.		
period continues ...			

Speculations and interpretations:

Who was thinking more: teacher or student?
When were the students learning?

Thoughts about literacy events in other classrooms and in your future classroom

We offer you the inquiry activities so that you begin your career-long search to understand your teaching, your students' learning, and events in your classroom better. Teaching is an uncertain craft (McDonald, 1992) at which teachers first apprentice and then spend their careers practicing.

Learning and Literacy in Content Areas

We have joined learning and literacy because in every field ideas are communicated through literacy actions—speaking, listening, viewing, reading, and writing. Your students will use literacy actions in school to learn content and to express what they have learned. They will also engage in literacy actions out of school for their own goals. Today, many students use multiple literacy actions (New London Group, 1996). Especially in the electronic context, they merge print, visual images, and audio sound. In this section, we first define literacy, learning, and strategies. Then, we conclude with an overview of teaching strategies and content.

Defining Literacy

In every field, powerful ideas are communicated to others through a literacy action. Listen to Martin Luther King Jr.'s "I Have a Dream" speech, and you will be persuaded by the truth of his words. Read Rachel Carson's *Silent Spring*, and you will be motivated to take action against DDT or Agent Orange. Debate war and peace issues with friends and you will hone your own ideas about the controversies in public policy. In taking literacy actions, Martin Luther King, Jr., Rachel Carson, and you and your friends think about the ideas, the purposes for communicating, and the audiences to receive the ideas. Literacy actions are social actions in which the speaker or writer of the ideas and the listener, viewer, or reader of the ideas interact through the message or content ideas (Moffett, 1983; Barnes & Todd, 1995). Without literacy actions, ideas would lay dormant and inert. People pursue literacy actions to explore their own ideas and to communicate ideas to others in society.

As social actions, literacy actions communicate not only ideas but also identify the social group one is part of and communicating to (Gee, 1996). For example, Martin Luther King Jr.'s speech was delivered as a sermon identifying him as a preacher and civil rights leader. Furthermore, if you listen to the speech, you can hear not only the cadence of a preacher speaking but the audience responding—agreeing with him and encouraging him to preach more. The literacy actions of a sermon and response fit the moral cause that the preacher is admonishing his followers (and the nation) to act upon. In communicating with particular social groups, we show our identity with each group by using the words, forms, actions, and behaviors acceptable to that group. You communicate differently to professors than to friends, taking on the identities of industrious student and trusted confidant respectively. You choose the manner of communication that fits the social situation.

Your classroom is a social community in which students are engaged in literacy actions (speaking, listening, viewing, reading, writing) and so are communicating not only their ideas but also their identities—their home background identity and their adolescent identity. (We discuss students more in Chapter 2.) Your students recognize that they are communicating their adolescent identity and their identity with other teenagers by their dress, their hairstyles, and their walk. They also have particular literacy actions, ways of speaking, listening, viewing, reading, and writing, that express their membership in various groups—the rapper group, the budding poets group, or the jocks, for example. They may adopt different literacy actions (and identities) when in different social communities, such as when they move from home to school or from the jock to poet group.

Since students bring their different home and adolescent identities into your classroom, you will want to learn to recognize and honor those identities and the literacy actions associated with them. In addition, your discipline community has particular literacy actions that communicate both ideas and identity. Your students may be more or less familiar with how your discipline community communicates ideas to each other and to the general public. As a content-area teacher, your aim is for your students to add to their repertoire the ideas and the forms of communication your discipline community uses. For example, you could have students interview community members, experts or other students either in person or on-line. You could incorporate a variety of texts—primary documents, newspaper articles, web sites—for students to read. You could have students write data in field notebooks, email in Spanish to students in Mexico, or present an oral argument to the school committee. In Part Two, we present literacy strategies and actions that will support your students learning to "know and do" your content area.

◼ Defining Learning

construct knowledge
Actively build and rebuild what one knows.

The old adage, "You can lead a horse to water but you can't make him drink," applies to learning, too. We can present information to people but we can't make them learn. That is why we subscribe to the theory that people *construct knowledge*, actively build and rebuild their knowledge, when they learn. In constructing their knowledge, they use strategies to remember, incorporate, and apply knowledge to situations, problems, and issues. In every field, experts have both a large knowledge base and a range of strategies that they use in tandem as they learn or create new information (Alexander & Judy, 1988). Some people figure out learning strategies on their own; others do not and could benefit from instruction. Therefore, our emphasis in this book is on the tandem teaching of both content knowledge and strategies.

We also think learning is often constructed with others in social situations. Students learn what they think through a discussion with peers; they lay out their evidence for their conclusions and learn to debate the different results. Students learn by writing their reactions to a newspaper article in a letter to the editor. When they send it to the local paper or the school newspaper, they may learn from the other letters sent in. Students even learn by conducting an internal dialogue with the author of a novel. When writing in a journal, they react to the author's craft and explore how the author created reactions in readers. In each of these examples, learning is constructed by using a literacy action in a social context or by interacting with others. In this book, we present teaching tools that support learning of content within the social situation in your classroom. We also encourage you and your students to communicate learning to audiences beyond your classroom—the community, other schools, or even national figures.

TEACHER AS INQUIRING LEARNER

Observe a classroom in your content area, and record your observations of the types of literacy events that occur and their participants. Within one period, track the number of minutes the teacher spends listening, speaking, reading, and writing. Also track the number of minutes the students spend listening, speaking, reading, and writing. See Figure 1.1. Think about the learning goals and objectives you think the teacher had for the period.

- How would you assess who was constructing meaning and when was it occurring?

■ Defining Strategies

In this book, we ask you to think about what strategies you use to learn in your content area, and especially what literacy strategies you use. We think that if you are aware of your own learning and literacy strategies, you will be better able to teach strategies to your students. You also will be better able to decide when a particular strategy would be appropriate and how it is used in a specific situation. In essence, you will be able to make your invisible strategies visible to your students in the context of learning content knowledge.

model + identify strategies used. (handwritten)

metacognitive awareness Being conscious of one's thinking.

Strategic learners are conscious of what they know, how they learn, what tasks require, and how they are progressing. Educators call this consciousness *metacognitive awareness*, or thinking about thinking (Flavell, Miller, & Miller, 1993; Garner, 1987). We picture metacognitive awareness as working like the control panels in a computer that oversee how programs function. Think back to a time when you were confused about what was required for an assignment. In metacognitive terms, you monitored your thinking: you recognized what you did not know and determined what strategies were necessary to do the assignment. In contrast, think about a time when you were completely absorbed in a novel or were solving a problem smoothly. In metacognitive terms, you monitored your progress or recognized that you were progressing well and need not change strategies.

Not all students are metacognitively aware, although the older the students are, the more likely it is that they are aware (Garner & Alexander, 1989). Teachers often assume that students are aware of what they know and don't know—their content knowledge. In fact, poor students often do not recognize that they do not understand a text, and not all students recognize when they are confused or need to study more. Furthermore, we think that many students are unaware of their strategy knowledge—in other words, how they learn. For some students, learning has come so easily that they have not considered how they learn. For others, learning has been so difficult that they attribute any learning success to luck rather than to their own efforts. Certainly some students are aware of how they learn, but we think that most students do not think strategically about how to accomplish a learning task or use a small repertoire of strategies for every task without regard to the different requirements of each specific task.

strategy Conscious plan of action to fit a situation.

Let's define what we mean by *strategy*: a conscious plan of action for achieving an activity or goal (Dole, Duffy, Roehler, & Pearson, 1991; Duffy & Roehler, 1989; Paris, Lipson, & Wixson, 1994; Pressley, Goodchild, Zajchowski, & Evans, 1989). People choose a strategy to use based on their assessment of what the task requires and their purposes for completing the task. Rather than just plunging ahead, strategic learners stop and think about how to proceed. Sometimes they invent a new strategy, at least for them, or adapt a strategy they already know to fit the task better. Thus, the key words for describing strategies are *conscious, selective, useful for the situation,* and *adaptive.*

We think that metacognitively aware learners are conscious of their strategies when they encounter a new or a difficult task. But when they face a familiar or easy task, we think they routinely apply strategies that have been successful for them in the past (Pressley et al., 1989) and consider adapting those strategies only when problems arise. For example, chess players have familiar strategies that they successfully use, especially when facing an easy opponent. They make their moves routinely until, by luck, the easy mark makes a challenging response. Then they must reconsider more consciously and deliberately their strategies to achieve checkmate.

In the research on strategies, two recurring questions arise: (1) What is the difference between strategies and skills? and (2) Are strategies general and applicable across all disciplines or specific and applicable to only a particular discipline? Neither of these questions is easily or definitively answered. Let's outline our position on each question.

First, *what is the difference between strategies and skills?* You have probably heard the term *skills* applied regularly—for example, to arithmetic skills, reading skills, soccer skills, basic skills. Educators and researchers used the term *skills* before they used the term *strategies,* and in some cases people have just substituted the term *strategy* for *skills* (such as *reading strategies* for *reading skills*). We, however, define a *skill* as a discrete action in isolation (Dole et al., 1991; Duffy & Roehler, 1989; Paris et al., 1994). For example, knowing addition facts is an arithmetic skill. But you need a problem-solving strategy to know when using addition would be appropriate to solve a problem. Thus, for us, the key words that describe "skill" are *discrete* and *isolated action* and for "strategy," *planned* and *useful action in context.*

skill Isolated action not tied to a situation.

Second, *are strategies general and applicable across all disciplines, or specific and applicable to only a particular discipline?* This discussion has been swinging back and forth for decades (Perkins & Salomon, 1989). As an example, physics experts use specific strategies, and yet when they come upon an unfamiliar problem, they may use a general strategy, like thinking of an analogy. Recognizing what information is relevant to the problem—content knowledge—makes both general and specific strategies effective. Therefore, Perkins and Salomon argue for a consensus position of general strategies applied in specific contexts. We agree.

We think that literacy strategies are general strategies for use in specific contexts. As a content-area teacher, you will want to teach literacy strategies in tandem with your content-area texts. Therefore, you will use strategies in a specific, contextual setting and concentrate on the strategies that are useful to your students' doing learning and literacy tasks in your content area.

When you work with a teacher in another content area, you both may discover that a general strategy is useful in both content areas, although you each apply the strategy in a discipline-specific manner. For example, a general literacy strategy is to preview or get an overview of the text (see Chapter 4). Mathematicians preview or quickly read the entire problem through before deciding how to solve it. Poets preview or read aloud a poem in its entirety before they read to interpret it. When the mathematician and the poet preview their respective texts, both are striving to get a general sense of their texts. However, they notice different aspects or features about their texts, based on their knowledge of their respective fields. Since the particular features significantly contribute to their understanding, the strategy of previewing is specifically applied, in a very contextual manner, to their respective texts. Thus, content knowledge and strategy knowledge are intertwined, one reinforcing the other.

By the way, both teachers will need to apply the strategy because students will rarely independently transfer the previewing strategy from a math class to an English class. Both teachers need to remind the students of the other teacher's application of the strategy.

In this book, we emphasize general literacy strategies that can be specifically applied across different content areas. The literacy strategies function to support learning in specific contexts—your content area—and so we have included examples from different content areas. We expect you to construct your knowledge of strategies—both literacy strategies and strategies more specific to your content area—and to select or adapt useful ones.

■ Teaching Strategies and Content

We are interested in your becoming an effective content-area teacher. Thus, we focus on content pedagogy, the *teaching tools* that use literacy to support learning content. We use the term *tool* to refer to the instructional activities that constitute the teaching-learning events in classrooms.

As a content-area teacher, you concentrate on the content you want your students to learn. Concurrently, you need to think about the literacy and learning strategies your students need to use to learn that content. Once you have decided what content and what strategies will be in your lesson, you need to choose the tools you will use to teach. As you can see in Figure 1.2, the tool should fit your purposes and your students because each tool has different purposes. In Chapter 3, we fully define each tool, and in Part Two we present specific tools in each category. Now, because the major focus of this book is literacy strategies in the context of learning, we want to explain the teaching tool of modeling and explaining, which we highlight with specific examples or scripts in Part Two.

Athletes, carpenters' apprentices, and chefs' assistants have been instructed through modeling and explaining for a long time, but the academic areas have only recently begun to incorporate the coaching or apprenticeship type of instruction (Collins, Brown, & Newman, 1989). When you choose the teaching tool of modeling and explaining, you aim to make your invisible literacy strategies visible to your students by using a book or an article they will read—a specific, contextual setting (Duffy et al., 1987). Becoming metacognitively aware of your use of learning and literacy strategies will help you model and explain, discuss, and even trade strategies with your students. To teach students how to use strategies, you would read their text and demonstrate how you use strategies (called modeling). You would also interrupt your reading to explain your thinking and your strategies. You explicitly discuss with your students:

- What the strategy is and does (declarative knowledge)
- When and why to use the strategy (conditional knowledge)
- How to use the strategy (procedural knowledge)

teaching tools
Instructional activities that support students' learning.

FIGURE 1.2 Choices of Pedagogical Tools

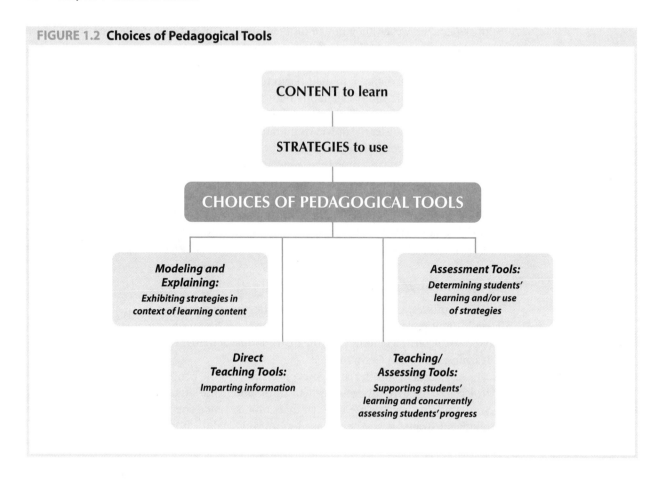

model and explain A
teaching tool that
demonstrates a strategy
and explains why, when,
and how to use it.

If you modeled strategies without explaining, you would exhibit their use with a specific text. But the students would have to infer from your model what strategies were used, how they were used, and why they were used. Because the strategies are embedded in your reading (modeling), they may not recognize that you are using strategies. Therefore, you should both *model and explain* specific strategies you use with particular texts. (We provide example scripts in Part Two.)

After modeling and explaining a strategy, you need to coach students as they try out using the strategy in a similar contextual situation. As they practice the strategy (often with partners at first), you and their peers can offer suggestions or pointers. Finally, students independently recognize when and where to incorporate the strategy (Pearson & Gallagher, 1983).

When teachers (or even students) model and explain their literacy strategies, they are demystifying their processes by making their strategies visible. Let's consider an example of modeling and explaining from physical education: learning the lob shot in tennis. The tennis coach begins by explaining what a lob is; this is *declarative knowledge.* She then sets up game scenarios and explains the purpose of the lob and when and why to use it—*conditional knowledge.* Next, she describes how to execute a lob—*procedural knowledge*—by elaborating on how to stand, hold the racket, and hit the ball. As she does so, she demonstrates (or models) the lob by actually executing a few lobs. (Note that hitting a lob in isolation is a skill. When the player knows not only how to lob but selects when and where to use the lob in a particular situation, then the lob can be called a strategy.)

If the tennis coach just modeled the lob in a game, the players would have to figure out the hidden or implicit techniques that the coach used. They would have to infer how to execute the lob and when to use the lob in a game. Some players would figure out the techniques. Others would not.

When content-area teachers use modeling and explaining, they need to select which literacy strategies fit the text. What strategies will be most useful for the texts that students read? What strategies will expand the students' repertoire of literacy strategies? What literacy strategies are most important for the goals and objectives in the unit of study?

In conclusion, literacy and learning in the content areas merges literacy actions and literacy strategies with your content area knowledge and learning strategies. Specifically, we emphasize three aspects of learning in this book: (1) your learning with literacy in your content area, (2) your students' learning with literacy in this content area, and (3) your learning to become a content-area teacher. In Part Two, we present literacy strategies and teaching tools to support learning in your content area. To end this chapter, we discuss adolescents' literacy and learning out of school and how that could inform in-school literacy and learning.

 TEACHER AS INQUIRING LEARNER

The purpose of this activity is to help you become metacognitively aware of your literacy strategies so that you can model and explain them to your students. (At this point, we do not expect you to name specific literacy strategies. In Part Two, we present literacy strategies, but don't peek ahead. This is an exploration activity—not a test!)

To complete a think-aloud activity, select an easy text and a hard text in your content area. First read the easy text aloud for fifteen minutes. As you read, stop and voice your thoughts into a tape recorder, or jot your thoughts in the margins of the text.

• What are you thinking about as you interact with the text? For example, what did you think when you read the title?

Repeat the think-aloud activity with the hard text. Then analyze your reading and thinking with the easy text and the hard text.

• What strategies did you use with each text? Were your strategies different with the hard text than the easier text? Why?

Literacy and Learning In and Out of School

Your students engage in literacy actions both in and out of school. However, often those two social situations entail very different literacy actions. Out of school, students engage literacy actions purposefully and socially. They decide upon the literacy action because they have a specific goal—a learning goal, a social goal, or both. Because they have chosen the literacy action, they are engaged, interested, and motivated. The girls dubbed the "social queens" read teen magazines for the latest fashions, want to be the first one to get the latest issue, and call their friends to discuss the new issues (Finders, 1997). Boys go on-line for NASCAR and hockey results because their friends at school expect them to know and discuss those results (Smith & Wilhelm, 2002). Urban taggers write artistic renditions of their names or identities on transit stations and local buildings so that people can see that they are in this territory (Weinstein, 2002). Secret poets seek out like peers to share new poems with and get reactions from them (Weinstein, 2002). Students with computers at home are engaging in many literacy actions like web browsing, emailing or instant messaging, and media viewing or listening (Leu, 2002). A middle school student may visit the web site of a hot new singer and then go to her instant messaging group to see who's on-line and discuss the web site, among other things.

In each of these out-of-school examples, the students first have chosen a reason or purpose for the literacy action. Second, they have learned content—even the tagger is learning visual content and form from his own and other's renditions. Third, they chose the literacy action because they wanted to communicate with and show membership in a specific group. The "social queens" read and discussed fashion magazines to maintain social group identity. Boys found scores on-line so they could discuss with friends. Urban taggers wanted to communicate with other taggers and neighborhood people.

These adolescents engage in these learning and literacy actions because the actions are a combination of social interaction and learning content of choice. Like these adolescent out-of-school literacy actions, you probably engage in multiple literacy actions that merge speaking, listening, viewing, reading, and writing and that have purposeful and social reasons. How can we similarly engage students in school?

We are not arguing for abandoning the content you need to teach for teen magazines, pop artists' web sites, or graffiti. We think the popular culture literacy actions should remain within the teen culture. Students may not choose to share their out-of-school lives and literacies in school. However, we do think that in-school learning and literacy could resemble more closely aspects of out-of-school learning and literacy actions.

To be more explicit in communicating the purposes for learning content, we can tie that content to issues, problems, themes in our communities, the nation, and the world. In fact, professional organizations have explicitly or implicitly related their standards to the world beyond the classroom.

We can incorporate a variety of literacy actions and forms that occur in the world. Students can read a variety of texts (Chapter 3) and communicate ideas in a variety of forms of speaking (debates with classmates, speeches to local organizations) and writing (letters to senators, short stories to publications). The audiences could be other classmates, community people, national officials, or on-line students in other states or countries.

We can recognize that students are engaged in literacy actions appropriate for their own reasons and social goals (Weinstein, 2002). We could investigate with the students if they use literacy strategies or actions that might resemble school literacy strategies or actions. For example, how signifying by African-American adolescents compares to simile and metaphor (Lee, 1993) or what are the advantages and disadvantages to adding Standard English to my neighborhood version (Fecho, 2000).

In this way, we can build on students' backgrounds and lead them into learning and literacy in the content areas. For in both literacy and learning, we aim to take students from where they are to places they had never thought of going.

Summary

One goal for this chapter was for you to begin thinking about teaching in the twenty-first century. We also wanted to introduce you to what you will learn about in this book and your course.

We discussed that to become a content-area teacher now and in the future, you want to learn continually in four areas:

- **Knowledge of your content area**
- **Knowledge of learners**
- **Knowledge of content pedagogy**
- **Knowledge of curriculum materials**

We encouraged you to begin reflecting on teaching through the inquiry activities in this chapter. Inquiry activities will be in every chapter and at the end of each chapter.

Next we discussed literacy and learning in the content areas:

- **Our definition of *literacy*—speaking, listening, viewing, reading, and writing in a social context**
- **Our definition of *learning*—constructive and often social**
- **Our definition of *strategies*—conscious plans of action**
- **Teaching strategies and content**

Finally, we discussed how adolescents are engaged in literacy out of school and how we could engage them in literacy and learning in school. We advocated for purposeful learning in a social context, for a variety of literacy texts to read, and for a variety of literacy actions to express learning to different audiences.

As you begin your career in teaching, we aim to support your learning by presenting literacy strategies and teaching tools that will help your students learn the important ideas in your content area (Part Two) and discuss how to incorporate literacy and learning into content area units (Part Three).

Inquiry into Your Learning

1. Interview an experienced teacher in your content area. How does the teacher want his or her students to view the content area? What are his or her major goals for the students that underlie his or her teaching? What does the teacher consider the major themes or ideas in the content area? How do those major ideas relate to one another and to the everyday world? Can the teacher sketch a diagram or model of the essence of the content area, the relationships among the major ideas, or what it means to "do" the content area?

2. Write your literacy autobiography. How did you learn to read and write? Both in school and out of school, what texts have you enjoyed reading or shared with your peers as you've grown up? What types of writing do you do in school and out of school? In school, were you taught strategies for reading, writing, and studying? Describe what you remember about learning literacy strategies.

Inquiry into Your Students' Learning

1. Interview a student about his or her literacy activities in and out of school. What does the student read and write in school? What speaking and listening activities does the student engage in during school? Outside school, what reading and writing, speaking, and listening does the student engage in? Does the student use literacy to accomplish everyday activities, like ordering a hamburger or using a computer program? Does the student use literacy as a hobby, such as reading a book for pleasure or keeping a diary? How would the student assess the importance of literacy to his or her everyday life and to his or her learning in school?

2. Interview a student about his or her favorite, most challenging, most fun, and/or most important class. How does the student define each of those classes? Why does he or she define the class that way? What does the teacher do in that class? What do the students do in that class? Does the student have other adjectives or descriptors for a particular class? Why does the student describe the class in that manner? What would the student suggest to a new teacher in his or her school? What does the student see as the best part of teaching? What is the hardest part?

Resources

Books

Commission on Adolescent Literacy. (1999). *Adolescent literacy: A position statement.* Newark, DE: International Reading Association. Advocates for literacy instruction during adolescence and lists resources and references.

Finders, M.J. (1997). *Just girls: Hidden literacies and life in junior high.* New York: Teachers College. Describes the in-school and out-of-school literacy practices of two groups of Midwestern girls—"the social queens" and "the tough cookies."

Smith, M. W. & Wilhelm, J. D. (2002). *Reading don't fix no Chevys: Literacy in the lives of young men.* Portsmouth, NH: Heinemann. Describes the in-school and out-of-school literacy practices of 49 boys from different types of schools and neighborhoods.

Journals

Case, E. (2003). Symbiosis: An evolutionary innovator. *The Science Teacher, 70* (4), 30–33. Describes a study of symbiosis in relation to science curriculum standards.

Oldfather, P. & Thomas, S. (2000). What does it mean when high school teachers participate in collaborative research with students on literacy motivations? *Teachers College Record, 99* (4), 647–691. High school students and their respective teachers investigated the students' motivation for learning and the qualities of their classrooms that supported their learning.

Weinstein, S. (2002). The writing on the wall: Attending to self-motivated student literacies. *English Education, 35* (1), 21–45. Primarily describes the literacy actions and meanings of tagging urban boys but also includes other literacy actions of urban boys and girls in an alternative high school.

Web Sites

American Council on the Teaching of Foreign Languages, **www.actfl.org.** Has information on publications, standards, workshops and conferences, jobs, and useful links to sites around the world.

International Reading Association, **www.reading.org.** Offers literacy publications including the English/Language Arts (K–12) standards, calendar of conferences around the world, and many on-line resources, such as Reading On-line (for K–12 teachers) and On-line Communities.

National Council for the Social Studies, **www.ncss.org.** Has a publication of the social studies standards, information on conferences and publications, and Teaching Resources section with a Databank and Teachable Moments (teaching current events suggestions).

National Council of Teachers of English, **www.ncte.org.** Provides an overview of the English/Language Arts standards as well as the publication, a free inbox with views and ideas for the classroom, and special resources such as Langston Hughes Poetry Circle that teachers can join, in addition to information on conferences and publications.

National Council of Teachers of Mathematics, **www.nctm.org.** Contains elementary, middle school, and secondary sections, offering standards, a weekly problem, lesson plans, as well as information on journals, publications and conferences.

National Science Teachers Association, **www.nsta.org.** Has the standards among its publications and provides current science and teaching news, Today in Science History, and grade level sections with on-line resources, lesson suggestions, and a teacher interaction.

CHAPTER 2

Students as Learners

KEY CONCEPTS

- **diversity, p. 27**
- **culture, p. 27**
- **English language learners (ELL), p. 31**
- **socioeconomic status (SES), p. 32**
- **learning disability (LD), p. 34**
- **schema (plural: schemata), p. 35**

PURPOSE-SETTING QUESTIONS

1 What is your cultural background? How do you define yourself in terms of race, ethnicity, language, socioeconomic status, gender, and special needs? How has your background influenced your views, interests, values, choice of college, and decision to be a teacher?

2 Whom have you met in college who is different from you? How has that person's school experiences been different from and similar to yours? Do you hold different or similar views about the opportunities that schools offer students? Can you explain how those differences or similarities originated?

3 Can you remember what background knowledge you brought to your high school or college classes in your content area? For example, can you remember what elementary geometry knowledge helped you understand geometry in secondary school or college? Do you remember how your teachers built on your previous learning?

4 Think back to your high school days. Was the diversity in your school population acknowledged by students and teachers? Did the school welcome diversity in the school population? How will you welcome diverse students and provide equal opportunity for all students?

STUDENTS AS LEARNERS

Who Are the Students in Classrooms?

- *Diversity of Race, Ethnicity, and Religion*
- *Diversity of Language*
- *Diversity of Socioeconomic Class*
- *Diversity of Gender and Sexual Orientation*
- *Diversity of Special Needs*

What Do Students Bring to Classrooms?

- *Content Knowledge in Schemata*
- *Strategies for Learning*
- *Motivation for Learning*

Teaching Diverse Students

- *Build Your Knowledge*
- *Create Your Classroom*
- *Adjust Your Communication*

As a Native American friend of mine says, you will be the children's teacher when you learn to accept their gifts.

(Featherstone, 1995, p. 18)

Your students' gifts are their identities, cultures, knowledge, strategies, and attitudes for learning that they bring to your classroom and develop within it. As their teacher, you can gain the understanding to be able to respond to the unique gifts and needs of your students, even when you have 100 or 125 students. When you are able to "see students individually," you will have become a responsive and reflective teacher. This will not happen on the first day or in the first month. Teaching is not a recipe or a "one size fits all" formula (Reyes, 1992). Teaching is learning about and with students.

In this chapter, we present three major aspects of Students as Learners (see the chapter graphic). First, we focus on who the students are in classrooms today and who they will be in the future, because understanding the diversity characteristics of your students will help you teach your content. We will discuss five categories of diversity—race, ethnicity, and religion; language; income levels or socioeconomic status; gender and sexual orientation; and special needs— because you are likely to teach students who represent these diversity characteristics. As we will repeat throughout the chapter, we want you to remember that not everyone with the same diversity characteristic is alike. Students are individuals with unique combinations of characteristics.

DIVERSITY

Second, we define what students bring to classrooms from their previous learning. Educators no longer view students as blank slates on which to write new knowledge; now educators recognize that students enter their classrooms with previous knowledge, strategies, and motivations. As a content-area teacher, you need to think about what students bring so that you can build on the content they have already learned, the strategies they use to learn, and their motivation toward learning.

DIVERSITY

And finally, we discuss teaching and learning with diverse students, offering you guidelines and practical suggestions. If all the population predictions hold true, you may be teaching students who are not like yourself. Our guidelines and suggestions will help you learn about your individual students. For even if they look similar, every student is unique.

Who Are the Students in Classrooms?

ELL populations are growing

The population in the United States is becoming more diverse racially and ethnically. If you look at the public school enrollment data for 1986 and 2000 (see Table 2.1), you will see that the White student population has decreased while the other racial/ethnic student populations have increased. While California leads the nation in immigrant students, even in Dodge City, Kansas, nearly 40 percent of the school children have immigrant backgrounds (Suáres-Orozco, 2001). Because these trends are expected to continue, more classrooms will have students from diverse backgrounds.

Students are diverse in characteristics other than race, and ethnicity, and religion. Students speak different languages, come from families with different income levels or socioeconomic status (SES), have gender and sexual orientation differences, and may have special learning needs. Each of these diversity characteristics brings challenges and gifts to teaching and learning in content-area classrooms.

Although some people use the term *multicultural*, we prefer the word *diversity* to refer to the broad range of differences among students in classrooms. We begin by presenting an overview of diversity in regard to only five categories—race, ethnicity, and religion; language; SES; gender and sexual orientation; and special needs—although we recognize that people have these characteristics in combination as well as other characteristics we do not address. You also know that people are individuals, and so although we discuss groups, we do not mean to stereotype any individual.

DIVERSITY

diversity Broad range of characteristics or differences among students, such as race, ethnicity, and religion; language; socioeconomic status; gender and sexual orientation; and special needs.

culture Behavior, values, beliefs, and views of the world of people in the same group.

■ Diversity of Race, Ethnicity, and Religion

Everyone belongs to several cultural groups (Gollnick & Chinn, 2001). Our various *cultures* define the ways we perceive and behave in the world, as well as our beliefs and values. People define themselves in terms of the microcultures—different cultural groups—with which they identify, such as race, ethnicity, religion, language, gender, class, occupation, age, learning ability or achievement, personal hobbies and interests,

	White	Black	Hispanic	Asian or Pacific Islander	American Indian/ Alaskan Native
% in 1986	70.4	16.1	9.9	2.8	0.9
% in 2000	62.1	17.2	15.6	4.0	1.2

TABLE 2.1 **Enrollment in Public Elementary and Secondary Schools, by Race or Ethnicity**

Source: National Center for Education Statistics (1996 & 2002).

or personality traits. People with different cultural group identities can experience the same situation differently. For example, males and females (gender culture) often experience events in the workplace differently (the business culture).

If you are a White American of European descent, you may not think much about your race or ethnic culture's characteristics because it has been the dominant culture in the United States. If you are an African American, Asian American, Hispanic American, Middle Eastern or Muslim American, or Native American, you probably do realize that you participate in two cultures: your ethnic culture as well as aspects of the dominant culture. However, even those panethnic terms do not describe your ethnic culture. You may refer to yourself as Cape Verdean rather than African American, Chinese rather than Asian American, Salvadoran rather than Hispanic, Yemeni rather than Middle Eastern American or Navajo rather than Native American.

A simple example of a dominant perspective is the Mercator map projection of the world. You have probably seen Mercator's map with the Americas and Europe near the center and Asia split between the right and left sides. Because a map projects the mapmaker's concept of the world, Mercator must have believed that North America and Europe were more important than Asia. Have you ever seen a map with Australia at the top instead of the bottom? We have, and it surely communicates Australia's "cultural" perspective!

In addition to race and ethnicity, religion is a large part of culture, shaping one's view of life and one's behavior. You may know Jewish or Greek Orthodox students who are absent for religious observances. Schools now need to acknowledge the variety of religions their students practice and make appropriate accommodations. For example, gym requirements need to be changed for Muslim Yemeni girls who choose to be fully covered (Sarroub, 2001). Thus, schools need to go beyond just excusing a student's absence for a holy day and consider how to accommodate religious tenets that affect teaching and learning.

TEACHER AS INQUIRING LEARNER

List the specific cultural groups that define you—for example, "White, male, student teacher, musician." Think about the characteristics we will discuss—race, ethnicity, and religion; language; socioeconomic status (SES); gender and sexual orientation; and special needs—as well as others that may define you, such as career choice, age, interests, or hobbies. Draw a circle or pie chart. Allocate sections of the pie chart to each cultural identity.

- Which of these cultures are most important to defining you?

Our country has struggled with the ideal of equality and the reality of a diverse, immigrant population since its beginnings. Remember that the framers of the U.S. Constitution struck a notorious compromise that allotted seats in the House of Representatives by counting "free Persons" and "three-fifths of all other Persons," or slaves. Although education is meant to provide equal opportunity and immigrant students aspire to a high school diploma (Olsen, 1997), ethnic culture students, who are often also poor, dominate the lowest track in high schools, are numerous in special education classes, are scarce in advanced placement courses, and have high dropout rates (Oakes, 1992; Olsen, 1997).

Why do some minority culture populations succeed in school while others fail? Ogbu (1993) argues for a theory that contrasts the identities of voluntary and involuntary immigrants. Voluntary minority people (for example, some Europeans and Central Americans) have come to the United States to try to be more successful than they were in their homeland. Keeping their original identity, they add a second identity of the dominant culture that helps them succeed in school. In contrast, involuntary minority people (for example, Native Americans and African Americans) create their identity in opposition to the White American identity. When they view school success as part of the White identity but not part of their own ethnic identity, they may decide not to excel in school.

We see parallels to Obgu's theory in the research on different generations of immigrants (Lee, 2001; Rong & Brown, 2001; Suárez-Orozco & Suárez-Orozco, 2001). Many voluntary immigrants come to find a better life for their children, if not for themselves. Those immigrant children that are foreign-born remember the trials of their former country and view school as the way to improve their lives. However, the children born in the United States learn the dominant culture, do not achieve as well in school, and therefore see no benefit in working hard in school. Unlike the foreign-born students who may ignore the racism they encounter, U.S.-born students may react to the racism they experience. Some urban high school students view dropping out as political action against the school and see no benefits in continuing their education (Fine, 1991). Thus, contrary to the general belief that each generation will be better off, researchers are finding that subsequent generations are not necessarily more successful.

An ongoing goal of every teacher is to learn about the individuality of each student in his or her diverse student population.
© Susie Fitzhugh

Nevertheless, we caution against automatically applying the theory to groups and especially to individuals. Voluntary minority students can struggle in school, and involuntary minority students can thrive there (Nieto, 1996). School success or failure is probably a combination of "personal, cultural, political and societal processes in which all of these factors affect one another in sometimes competing and contradictory ways" (Nieto, 1996, p. 246).

To ignore race and ethnicity is to deny a person's heritage or identity. As the student population becomes increasingly diverse, all educators need to strive to understand their own culture and their students' cultures and how these identities can affect teaching and learning. Remember that culture is dynamic, multifaceted, and embedded in specific contexts (Nieto, 2002). Some students may create a hybrid or transcultural identity (Nieto, 2002; Suárez-Orozco & Suárez-Orozco, 2001). As a teacher of diverse students, you will want to learn not just their panethnic cultures but the specific racial, ethnic, and religious cultures of your students and how they prefer to identify themselves. For example, do they prefer Chicano/Chicana, Mexican American, or Latino/Latina? Maybe they prefer an original term like Tiger Woods does "Caublinasian" (Caucasian, Black, Indian, Asian heritage). The only way to find out is to ask.

Teaching diverse students is complicated and requires sensitivity on the part of teachers. You will stumble, most likely, but you will also learn if you listen to your students. For example, McDiarmid recalls his scientific discussion with Yup'ik Eskimo students in which they analyzed how the refrigeration system worked and why it was broken. At the end of the discussion when McDiarmid asked why the cooler broke, "one of the students who had been most involved in the conversation replied, 'Ghosts'" (1991, p. 257). Recognizing the clash between the scientific, dominant culture and a spiritual, ethnic culture did not solve McDiarmid's teaching dilemma, but at least he understood the cultural clash he faced.

■ Diversity of Language

Even though bilingualism is pervasive throughout the world and even though we are living in a global society, bilingualism is a hot political debate in the United States. Usually because dominant culture people have immigrant ancestors who learned English on their own, they think recent immigrants need only to be surrounded by English speakers to learn English. Immigrant students are learning English as quickly and as well as they always have (Suárez-Orozco & Suárez-Orozco, 2001). They want to learn English to participate in the academic and social life of the school (Olsen, 1997). However, both in the past and now, language-minority students are more likely to drop out of school; in fact, Hispanic youth have the highest drop out rate—28 percent (National Center for Education Statistics, 2002).

You may have met different terms describing various second-language programs and students. In transitional bilingual programs with bilingual teachers, the students read, write, and learn content in their first language as they begin to learn English; then they use both languages to learn and finally use primarily English. In English as a Second Language (ESL) classes, the teacher speaks only English, and the students learn content and literacy in English. In a sheltered English program or sheltered content classes, only English is spoken, like ESL, but the teacher uses simpler vocabulary and materials to foster understanding of the content. In California with Proposition 227, the program lasts only one year. When many students speak the same first language, schools often establish transitional bilingual programs. When only a few students speak one language or when many students speak different languages, schools usually establish ESL classes.

Different terms have been used to describe students learning English. The term *limited English proficiency* describes the amount of English language that students speak, not their ability to learn English. The term *English language learner (ELL)* is the preferred term because it does not imply a deficit. Throughout this book we will use ELL to refer to these students.

English language learner (ELL) A student who adds the English language to their native language knowledge.

The research evaluating programs is fraught with both design problems and political agendas (August & Hakuta, 1998). Therefore, some researchers are investigating classroom-based questions about teaching and learning (Moll, 1992; Minami & Ovando, 1995). For example, researchers have found that Spanish/English bilingual students who are successful English readers use strategies in both languages and use their Spanish knowledge to support their English (Langer, Bartolome, Vasquez, & Lucas, 1990; Jiménez, García, & Pearson, 1996). Accepting ELL students' use of both languages in mainstream classrooms may help reduce their anxiety toward speaking English and reduce their coping strategy of avoiding speaking (Pappamihiel, 2002). We think this recent research supports our focus on strategies in Part Two.

As you think about language diversity, consider several factors that are involved in learning a second language (García, 2002). To start, students' first language is a part of their cultural identity. Second, students learn conversational language for specific situations (such as ordering a hamburger) more easily than the abstract academic language of content areas (such as studying ions). Third, students usually understand more of what they hear and read in English than they can express in speaking and writing. And last, if students have studied the content and learned to read and write in their first language, then learning in the second language can be easier. Refugee ELL students who have had little continuous schooling will face the challenge of learning both English and content—a six-to seven-year endeavor.

Diversity of Dialect. Most languages have different dialects or versions of the language that have small differences in pronunciation, vocabulary, and grammar. In language terms, different dialect speakers can express ideas equally well and understand each other. However, in many languages, one dialect has acquired more social prestige than the others. Standard American English is the dialect the dominant culture has accepted for public oral and written communication. Therefore, schools and textbooks use Standard American English. Among the dialects in the United States, Black English dialect (most recently called Ebonics) and Appalachian English have not been attributed social prestige, even though their linguistic differences with Standard English are small (Warren & McCloskey, 1997). Many dialect speakers can express and read a variety of dialect styles from literary (poetry by Langston Hughes) to vernacular to Standard English (Perry & Delpit, 1998).

Dialect, like language, communicates home culture and is a part of our individual identity. Some teachers differentiate between home language or code and school language or power code and teach their students appropriate usage for specific situations (Delpit, 1995). After studying home language, peer language, and Standard English,

Baker's technical school students learned that Standard English is a choice that students can make and they have options for different settings (Baker 2002). In investigating home codes and power codes, Fecho's African- and Caribbean-American students found code switching to have both positive and negative ramifications for their identity. For some students learning the power code of Standard English is not just learning a grammar; identity is involved (Fecho, 2000). Like cultural diversity, educators need to be sensitive to their perspectives of language and dialect differences and assist students in adding, not eliminating, the languages or dialects that are appropriate for various social situations.

■ Diversity of Socioeconomic Class

Americans, and especially educators, want to believe our society is a meritocracy: If students study and work hard, they can succeed. In fact, educational success can often be predicted by *socioeconomic status (SES)*, and low SES students are more likely to drop out (Committee for Economic Development, 1987).

Although society as a whole has a range of SES levels, many residential communities are not economically diverse. Wealthy suburbs have public schools with more resources; poor cities have schools with fewer resources (Committee for Economic Development, 1987). Middle-class immigrants with skills move into neighborhoods that have schools with resources; while unskilled or semiskilled immigrants move into poor, urban neighborhoods that have schools with few resources (Suárez-Orozco & Suárez-Orozco, 2001). Affluent schools promote students' languages, such as Cantonese and Mandarin, through language programs for all students, while poor schools forbid students to use their primary language and employ more inexperienced teachers or a series of substitutes (Chang, 2003). These resource differences have resulted in differing educational opportunities (described as *Savage Inequalities* by Kozol, 1991) and lawsuits about educational financing in several states.

Within a school population, the low SES students (often also diverse in race and ethnicity, and English language learners (ELL)) dominate the low groups in elementary schools, the low tracks in secondary schools, and the special education or compensatory programs throughout the grades. Although the tracks or programs were established to meet student needs, these instructional differences result in different educational experiences. In the high tracks, the teacher's instruction focuses on conceptual understandings, includes a variety of academic tasks and less lecturing (although still plenty), and communicates respect and self-worth to the students. In the low tracks, the teacher's instruction focuses on basic skills, isolated facts, and fewer topics; includes more repetition and lecturing; and communicates disrespect and low expectations to the students (Knapp & Woolverton, 1995; Rubinstein-Ávila, 2003). Some teachers of low SES students use standardized tests to determine their instruction and curriculum (Center for Study of Testing, Evaluation and Educational Policy in García & Pearson, 1994). The teachers in Olsen's research (1997) did not recognize that the tracks in their high school were segregated by race and language. Educators at all levels need to examine their good intentions for meeting student needs and determine if their instruction expands, rather than limits, students' opportunities.

---

socioeconomic status (SES) A combination of economic factors (such as income level or subsidized school lunch) and social factors (such as type of job) that determine high, middle, or low class in society.

■ Diversity of Gender and Sexual Orientation

Many educators began to examine their classrooms and their teaching for gender patterns when *The AAUW Report: How Schools Shortchange Girls* (American Association of University Women, 1992) and *Failing at Fairness: How America's Schools Cheat Girls* (Sadker & Sadker, 1994) were published. Most educators believe they are fair until they look closely; ourselves included. When we examined our college classrooms, we found that the male students talked and asked questions proportionately more, thereby dominating the class conversation. Although schools have made progress toward equity (American Institutes of Research, 1998), teachers at every level need to examine the gender patterns in their classrooms and how those patterns influence communication roles and grouping decisions.

Although gender achievement differences are narrowing, enrollment differences still occur. Girls are more likely to take advanced placement biology but less likely to take physics or calculus which they need for math, science, or computer careers (American Institutes of Research, 1998). And often even high-achieving young women do not elect to pursue math or science majors or careers unless they have a parent's or teacher's encouragement (American Association of University Women, 1992). In contrast, reading/language arts or verbal achievement has been touted as the area where women achieve more than men. More girls than boys take courses in English, foreign languages (French and Spanish), and the Fine Arts (American Institute of Research, 1998).

Racial, ethnic, and religious culture affects gender roles, especially girls' opportunities for education (Lee, 2001; Sarroub, 2001). Hmong and Yemeni girls may have arranged marriages, choose to hide their marital status, and may have to negotiate with their families to continue their education. Lee reports that a high school Yemeni girl negotiated with her parents to delay arranging a marriage and to allow her to continue her education. Some girls maintain their high academic achievement as an avenue to more freedom. These girls are discovering how to create dual identities.

Sexual Orientation. Schools are often hostile environments for gay, lesbian, bisexual, and questioning adolescents. Estimates show that from three to ten percent of the school population are homosexual or bisexual (Munoz-Plaza, Quinn, & Rounds, 2002). These students are at risk for verbal and physical abuse, truancy or dropping out, suicide, and substance abuse (Nichols, 1999). At a time when adolescents are forming their identities, schools need to prevent the harassment of every student or face court cases (Henning-Stout, James, & Macintosh, 2000). First, schools need to include sexual orientation in their nondiscrimination policy. Second, they need to provide support to students (assemblies, clubs, counseling). Third, schools need to provide professional training for all personnel and to revise curricula, not just the health curriculum to include sexual orientation but the English (gay and lesbian writers) and history (civil rights) curricula as well (Munoz-Plaza, Quinn, & Rounds, 2002).

In every content area, educators need to ask if all the students, including those of nonstereotype gender, feel welcome and have the same opportunities to learn.

■ Diversity of Special Needs

As defined by Public Law 101:476 in 1990, the Individuals with Disabilities Education Act (IDEA), special needs or disabilities include categories such as learning disabilities, speech or language impairments, visual impairments, and serious emotional disturbance. Although not listed in IDEA, the U.S. Department of Education allows students with attention deficit disorder (ADD) and attention deficit hyperactivity disorder (ADHD), which often occur in conjunction with learning disabilities or emotionally disturbed categories, to receive special education services.

learning disabilities (LD)
Difficulties that some students have with learning, especially learning literacy.

Because you will most likely meet students with *learning disabilities (LD)*, who account for 50.5 percent of the total disability population (U.S. Department of Education, 2001), and because this book is about literacy, we focus on students with these disabilities. Although there are various definitions of what constitutes a learning disability, most states use the IDEA definition that contains four major identifying characteristics (Lerner, 2003). First, the student has a disorder in one or more basic psychological processes, such as memory, auditory perception, or visual perception. Second, the student has learning difficulties in speaking, listening, reading, writing, and/or mathematics. Third, the learning problem is not caused by other disabilities, such as visual impairments or mental retardation. And fourth, the student is severely underachieving compared to his or her projected potential.

Middle and high school students with learning disabilities most likely bring many experiences with academic failure, poor self-concepts, and inept social skills in addition to the usual characteristics of adolescent development (Lerner, 2003). Furthermore, they may be at a disadvantage for content-area learning. In the elementary grades, they often were at the resource room during science or social studies periods. In their reading instruction, they frequently read stories, not content material, and they learned isolated reading skills, like sequencing, instead of strategies to understand content-area ideas (Bos & Anders, 1990).

Thus, LD students need additional instruction, especially in literacy. Some LD students may only need your support when you use the teaching tools in Part Two, although you may want to also consult with the special education teacher. Other LD students will need additional instructional and behavioral support from the special education teacher either within your classroom or in the resource room. Since these LD students need more support, you will want to collaborate closely with the special education teacher and share the planning, teaching, and resources with each other. Both of you need time within the school day to collaborate, although in most schools that is difficult to find (Lerner, 2003). You and the special education teacher can investigate strategy instruction programs (Harris & Pressley, 1991; Gaskins & Gaskins, 1991) that coordinate well with the strategies we will teach you in Part Two.

The gifts students have are many and diverse. As you accept their gifts, you will provide learning opportunities for students to enhance those gifts. Now let's discuss what learning experiences students bring to classrooms.

What Do Students Bring to Classrooms?

Although your students may appear similar to each other, each brings a unique constellation of learning experiences to class. Before you meet them, they have accumulated these characteristics:

- Content knowledge from past school experiences and from their everyday experiences

- Strategies for learning that may be conscious or intuitive

- Motivation, values, and beliefs about their own learning ability, your content area, and school in general

Cognitive psychologists theorize that people organize knowledge into what they call *schema* or *schemata* (plural of schema). A schema is an organized network of ideas, concepts, data, and experiences. You could picture the schemata in your brain as different web sites linked together on the Internet. People have different schemata for different areas of knowledge (such as mathematics) and different experiences (such as viewing the president on television) and make connections among schemata (such as using mathematics to interpret presidential polling data).

schema (plural schemata) A theoretical concept of the brain as an organized network of ideas, concepts, data, and experiences.

■ Content Knowledge in Schemata

Content knowledge schemata are what you know about the world (Anderson, 1994). What schema do you activate when you read the following passage? Who and where is Rocky?

> Rocky slowly got up from the mat, planning his escape. He hesitated a moment and thought. Things were not going well. What bothered him most was being held, especially since the charge against him had been weak. He considered his present situation. The lock that held him was strong but he thought he could break it. He knew, however, that his timing would have to be perfect. Rocky was aware that it was because of his early roughness that he had been penalized so severely—much too severely from his point of view. The situation was becoming frustrating; the pressure had been grinding on him for too long. He was being ridden unmercifully. Rocky was getting angry now. He felt he was ready to make his move. He knew that his success or failure would depend on what he did in the next few seconds. (Anderson, Reynolds, Schallert, & Goetz, 1977, p. 372)

Some students think Rocky is a convict planning an escape; others think he is a wrestler in a tough match; still others have different interpretations. Who you thought Rocky was depended on the content knowledge in your schema.

Throughout their lives, people build schemata from direct experiences with natural phenomena, from their social and cultural experiences within their communities, and from their learning experiences in school. When you have a new experience, for example, seeing a movie (perhaps the latest Matrix movie), you search for an appropriate, matching schema in your brain (the original Matrix movie). That schema allows you to recognize which details are important (the special effects) and to fill in details that may have been omitted from the movie. Later when you discuss the movie with friends, you will refer to your schema to recall the original Matrix movie. You may even include special effects that were not actually part of the new movie but from other movies (Anderson, 1994)!

Schemata can lead people astray when their schemata do not match the new information. Students may ignore a scientific explanation that seems to contradict their previous knowledge (Alvermann, Smith, & Readance, 1985). For example, most people read newspaper reports about the fragility of rain forests located in the tropics and think rain forests are only near the equator. They are surprised to learn that rain forests are also located in the Pacific Northwest of North America and in Alaska.

Cultural schemata can both help and hinder understanding of different texts. For example, Indian people comprehended a passage about a wedding in their home country better than a passage about an American wedding. In recalling what they read about the American wedding, they mistakenly included some Indian wedding customs that were not in the passage (Steffenson, Joag-Dev, & Anderson, 1979).

If your students have been in your school system or in U.S. schools, you have a general idea about what they may have been taught and probably learned. However, if your students are immigrants, they may have had little schooling (such as refugees from war torn countries), gaps in their schooling (such as migrant workers' children), or continuous schooling that organized the curriculum differently (Olsen, 1997; Suárez-Orozco & Suárez-Orozco, 2001). Compounding the amount of schooling, consider the ELL students who have conversational English (learned in two to three years) but have not yet acquired academic English that takes six to seven years to learn (Suárez-Orozco & Suárez-Orozco, 2001).

Naturally, as a content-area teacher, you will want to figure out what content knowledge students bring to your classroom so that you can build from their existing schemata. Learning is constructing knowledge by adding new schemata, recognizing gaps in and enhancing existing schemata, recognizing mismatches and revising schemata, and making new connections among schemata.

Furthermore, you will want to help students organize their content knowledge in their schemata. In deciding what content to teach, you will want to focus on significant ideas and understandings that relate to each other instead of fragmented, isolated facts. For example, if you state that arteries are elastic and veins are not, students will try to memorize those isolated facts. Suppose instead that you elaborated on the significance of elasticity: since arteries lead from the heart, they need to accommodate the pressure from a pumping heart; veins, going to the heart, do not. Then students could integrate the concept of elasticity with the operations of the circulation system. The result would be a more elaborate and organized schema (Bransford, 1994).

We will return to the topic of schemata and accessing and building on prior knowledge throughout Part Two. However, in your campaign to build schemata and dispel any misconceptions that students may have acquired, remember McDiarmid's dilemma with the Yup'ik Eskimo students. In our opinion, different worldviews, in that case a scientific worldview and a cultural-religious worldview, are contrasting schemata of the world, not misconceptions. Only students can resolve that dilemma of contrasting worldviews, and they may decide to live in two worlds.

■ Strategies for Learning

We think that all students bring ways of learning or strategies to classrooms from their learning experiences at home and in the community. In some cultures, children learn using a "watch–then do" strategy, while others are encouraged to learn by trial and error (Nelson-Barber & Estrin, 1995). In some cultures, students prefer to work in cooperative groups, while in other cultures students prefer to work independently. Students also bring strategies from past learning experiences in classrooms, such as the strategy of cueing into the teacher's questions to locate important information. Immigrant students may bring different classroom experiences and therefore not have strategies for participating in U.S. classrooms (August & Hakuta, 1998).

You recall from Chapter 1 that we define a *strategy* as a conscious plan of action for achieving an activity or goal. We predict that you use learning strategies that are effective in your content area. We want you to become aware of what strategies you use and when you use them so that you can teach them to your students.

In this book (especially in Part Two), we focus on literacy strategies that support students in learning and communicating content knowledge. We do not divorce strategies from content; instead, we select literacy strategies that will support learning content. We think some students have discovered literacy strategies on their own, perhaps from wide reading of texts. However, we think that most students—your average students and maybe even your above-average students—use only a few strategies repeatedly for most tasks. Moreover, we think that most students are not very metacognitively aware of how they learn and what literacy strategies they use or don't use. Thus, when we write about nonstrategic learners, we picture most of your students. These students need to be taught a variety of effective literacy strategies so that they will match their strategies to specific tasks. And all students need teachers' asking metacognitive questions such as, "How are you going to find that out?" or "What strategies will help you understand that article?"

We are concerned about the diverse students—especially LD students, students from an ethnic culture, and low SES students—who have not previously performed well in school. Both Delpit (1988), from the African-American perspective, and

TEACHER AS INQUIRING LEARNER

Like the think-aloud activity in Chapter 1, the purpose of this activity is to help you begin to explore a student's strategies. (Again, at this point, describe the student's strategies in your own words. Don't peek ahead!)

Find a middle school or high school student who is willing to help you learn. Ask the student to pick out an easy text and a hard text. Have the student first read the easy text aloud for about fifteen minutes. Instruct the student to stop and tell you what he or she is thinking. If the student doesn't think aloud periodically, stop the student and ask what he or she is thinking about or what connections he or she is

making to the text. Take notes on a copy of the text or perhaps tape-record the session.

Repeat with the hard text. If the student is clearly frustrated by the hard text, try to find a less difficult text to read or stop after eight to ten minutes.

After the session with the student, go over your notes or the tape. From ideas and comments the student stated, what reading strategies can you infer that he or she used? For example, if the student said he or she thought the book would be about how paleontologists searched for dinosaurs, you could infer that the student used prediction as a strategy.

Reyes (1992), from the Mexican-American perspective, argue for the explicit and direct teaching of literacy strategies and standard English within classrooms that are respectful and welcoming to the culture and language or dialect of the students. LD students, who struggle to learn from print, also need explicit and direct teaching of literacy strategies (Gaskins & Gaskins, 1991). If teachers and schools are to provide equal educational opportunity to learn, then teachers need to build on the strategies students bring by teaching strategies that support learning content.

■ Motivation for Learning

Your students enter ready to learn, wary of learning, or resigned toward learning. Their motivation is influenced by beliefs about themselves, by feedback from peers and adults, and by past and present experiences (Ames & Ames, 1991; Schunk & Zimmerman, 1997). However, you can influence their motivation through your teaching and the classroom atmosphere or culture you establish with them. Motivation is not a stable attribute but a characteristic that can change from class to class and from year to year.

When your students enter, they will have beliefs about their capabilities to learn and to perform school tasks. This belief, called self-efficacy, influences the tasks that students choose, the amount of effort they will exert, their persistence when difficulties arise, and their achievement. Students have learned about their abilities by evaluating their performances in past tasks, by comparing their performances with their peers', and by feedback from teachers and parents. When students have high efficacy, they will engage in challenging tasks; but when they don't, they will avoid trying. In addition to beliefs, students also need to have the strategies and knowledge required for the task (Schunk & Zimmerman, 1997). If you believe that your students can learn, that is a beginning but it is not sufficient. Your ELL students, your LD students, some of your ethnically diverse students, and even some of your female students will not believe you or will just pretend to believe you. Some students, particularly LD students, will not think they can complete tasks without help—a learned helplessness. You will need to convince your low self-efficacy students that they can improve by teaching strategies and supporting their learning with teaching tools. (We will teach you strategies and tools in Part Two.)

Even when students believe they have the ability, they choose to be motivated based on the perceived value of a task (Wigfield, 1997). Your students decide whether a task is useful, interesting, or important to engage in. The value they place on a task is related to their goals or the outcomes they expect. Some students study for the grade (an extrinsic reward), while others study just to learn or for curiosity (intrinsic rewards). When students' goals are grades, they concentrate on their performance, place value on their ability, compete with and compare themselves to other students, and become anxious about mistakes. In contrast, when students' goals are knowledge, they concentrate on the learning process, value effort and challenge, and consider mistakes part of the process (Ames & Ames, 1991). Influencing the value of a task is tricky. Students thinking about college attach value to grades but not all students do. Some ELL students attach value to grades and want to go to college but their dreams are not realistic (Olsen, 1997). For some racially and ethnically diverse students, grades represent acting White and so they resist placing value on school tasks.

Students are more likely to be engaged in their learning when they have a choice between tasks and see connections between the curriculum and their lives, their community, or society. Instead of listening to teachers talk, students are more likely to be engaged when they have opportunities to express their ideas, interpretations, or opinions, when they know that teachers are listening to their ideas, and when they can work and talk with peers. And finally, students are more likely to be engaged when teachers teach strategies and support learning with teaching tools (Oldfather & Dahl, 1994; Guthrie & Wigfield, 1997).

Our goal (and we hope yours) is that all students will build schemata that contain important concepts, acquire useful strategies for learning concepts, and have the motivation that will sustain their learning in school and beyond. Now let's turn to teaching suggestions for your classroom.

Teaching Diverse Students

Agreeing with Sleeter (1997), we do not set out a list of special methods for teaching diverse students. Instead, teaching all students, and especially diverse students, is accomplished by listening to and understanding students, building a dialogue with students, and sharing decision-making power with students. By incorporating the following general suggestions into your content-area teaching, you will communicate to your students that you have high expectations for them and that you will provide the opportunities to learn the content they will need. We offer suggestions for building your knowledge, creating your classroom, and adjusting your communication but we know that none of these suggestions can be accomplished in a day or a year. In addition, we discuss diversity students in subsequent chapters; look for the diversity icon.

DIVERSITY

■ Build Your Knowledge

One of the reasons you are going into teaching is that you enjoy students. Learning about your students—their cultures, their developing identities, their conflicts—is a career-long endeavor. You will also learn about yourself as well.

- **Build your cultural awareness.** First, recognize your own combination of cultural heritages, such as race, ethnicity, and religion; language; gender and sexual orientation; SES; and learning needs, as well as others we have not discussed. Acknowledge your cultural perspectives and become aware how your perspectives influence your attitudes, values, and behavior. Then learn about other cultures. You may begin with cultural festivals and music, but delve beyond those common cultural characteristics into more subtle characteristics, like conceptions of adolescence or gender roles and patterns of conversation.

- **Respectfully acknowledge students' identities.** First, for your culturally diverse students, learn not just their panethnicities but the specific cultures that are their heritages and identities. They may identify with the dominant culture, adopt an adversarial identity, create a new transcultural identity (Suárez-Orozco & Suárez-Orozco, 2001) or prefer a dual identity in which they maintain two languages because they travel between the two countries (Jiménez, 2003). Second, discover whether students with learning differences have adopted the hard-working student identity, an adversarial identity, or a learned helplessness identity. And third, learn how your boys and girls view themselves as students and as people with a sexual orientation. Knowing how students view themselves will help you understand them and build respect within your classroom, although that knowledge may not make teaching easier.

- **Build your awareness of possible student conflicts.** Your goal of equality and respect in the classroom may clash with students' prejudices. For example, Hindi students who believe in a caste system may not work with Indian students from a lower caste. Muslim girls do not associate with boys. Chicanos (American-born) may not respect Mexican-born students (Pappamihiel, 2002) and American-born students of immigrant parents may not respect foreign-born students also known as Fresh Off the Boat or FOBs (Olsen, 1997). Special education students may not be included when students choose study groups. One gender may dominate mixed gender groups. Finally as we stated earlier, gay, lesbian and questioning students are often harassed. Student prejudices are often not visible to teachers and so difficult to address. Yet, when teachers see prejudicial behavior, they need to discuss the prejudices and work toward a classroom and school policy of respect.

- **Learn different communication styles.** Different cultures have different styles of communicating with each other and different styles of communicating in classrooms. For example, a Vietnamese teacher would directly correct an ELL student's grammar, while an American teacher may not. Some cultures do not make direct eye contact with authority figures. Delpit (1995) maintains that African-American cultures explicitly direct students. Girls and boys may communicate differently. Some students may not recognize that a teacher's request is really a command—not a choice—and need an explicit, direct statement. Listen to yourself and your students—the tone, meaning, and words used—and discuss different communication styles with them.

■ Create Your Classroom

Your decisions about grouping, testing results, and curriculum can make your classroom inclusive of all students.

- **Form affinity groups.** Particularly in the beginning of the year, let students choose partners or form their own cooperative groups, after you've been explicit about guidelines for working together. After trust and a sense of community has been built, then diverse student groups may be formed. Recognize that the penalty for revealing information about oneself may be greater for some than for others. (Hynds, 1997)

- **Recognize the prior knowledge and vocabulary needed for standardized tests.** Historically, every immigrant group has performed poorly on standardized tests (Figueroa & García, 1994). Diverse students may not bring the same prior knowledge to the tests as dominant culture students (García & Pearson, 1994). Remember that immigrant students have had different amounts of schooling and so bring different amounts of knowledge to standardized tests. In addition, remember that LD students may have been pulled out of science and social studies classes and so have less content knowledge. Even math tests use vocabulary that students may not know. In addition, the directions may contain unfamiliar vocabulary (García, 1991). Treat test scores skeptically; ask students about their background knowledge; and teach vocabulary. Supplement the single test score with other assessment tools that evaluate their ongoing learning and their final understandings. (See Part Two.)

- **Find role models.** Search for racial/ethnic, gender, and special needs role models who have contributed to the knowledge in your content area. By enlisting the help of a librarian, you can find role models your students can read about in books, newspapers, and on-line. Contact a volunteer parent to enlist role models in the community that students can interview in class.

- **Publicly discuss and research cultural perspectives with your class.** Have students research the immigrant experiences or racial attitudes in the community. Research specific instances or events in which racial/ethnic/religious differences were a factor and consider also the historical roots of the differences (Fecho, 2001). Fecho's suggestion takes real nerve and perhaps you shouldn't embark on it until you've had teaching experience and cleared it with the administration. However, adversarial students may become engaged in learning when discussing controversial topics related to their lives.

■ Adjust Your Communication

Language and dialect are a part of personal and cultural identity. Teachers need to respect the language or dialect students bring and assist them in adding Standard English to their language or dialect repertoire. We recommend the following practices (adapted from Center for Applied Linguistics in Laturnau, 2003; Crawford, 1993; Delpit, 1995; E. García, 2002; and Olsen, 1997):

- **Speak distinctly.** ELL students need you to speak slowly, pause often, and paraphrase. Native speakers of any language naturally run words together—"Howyadoin'?" Listen to a native speaker of a language you don't speak. Can you distinguish the separate words? Probably not. Remember also that ELL students have difficulty understanding slang and idiomatic phrases and may not distinguish an aside from a main point.

- **Wait for answers.** When you ask a question or present a task, wait a long time for a response. Give ELL speakers enough time to formulate in English what they know.

- **Respond to the speaker's meaning.** Continue the dialogue by expanding on the content of the response instead of correcting the grammar.

- **Validate home language and add school language.** We accept home language and dialects in classroom discussions and expressive writing, like poetry. In addition, students need to learn the public situations where Standard English is expected.

- **Correct grammar in written text instead of oral language.** Because students' written texts are concretely displayed on paper, the students' written language can be more easily edited into Standard English than their oral language. Provide students with opportunities to write to students in other classrooms and schools and to people in the community so that they will have a purpose for editing into Standard English.

- **Don't force a reticent student to speak.** In second-language acquisition, like first-language acquisition, learners understand more than they can express. Think of ways other than speaking that students can show they understand, such as drawing. ELL students may talk to a partner or in an affinity group but not to the whole class.

- **Create opportunities to use language.** Instead of listening to the teacher talk or lecture, students can work in pairs or in cooperative learning groups. ELL students especially need English-speaking peers to talk with. However, to reduce anxiety and increase participation (Papamihiel, 2002), you may want to try affinity groups first as you work with the class on respect for each other.

- **Allow more time to complete tests.** ELL students may be using both languages to complete tests and so need more time (García, 1991; García & Pearson, 1994). You can arrange additional times for ELL students to complete your tests. Advocate for more time on standardized tests as well.

As you build your knowledge, create your classroom, and adjust your communication, you will accept the gifts each individual brings to your teaching.

SUMMARY

As a content-area teacher, you are at the confluence between your content area and your students. To teach your content effectively, you will need to learn about your students. Every school population has diverse students, even those populations that superficially appear to be homogeneous. You will want to delve beneath the surface to discover the diversity in your school population and also to discover each student's individuality.

In this chapter, we have first described who student populations are in terms of only five diversity characteristics:

- **Race, ethnicity, and religion**
- **Language**
- **Socioeconomic status**
- **Gender and sexual orientation**
- **Special needs**

In our discussion, we presented the major ideas or theories, new terms, and educational issues related to each diversity characteristic. Remember that as the U.S. population becomes more diverse, groups are not homogeneous and individuals are unique.

Second, we discussed students' diversity in terms of the content knowledge, strategies, and attitudes motivations they bring to classrooms:

- **Students' background knowledge in their schemata may be different depending on their everyday and school experiences.**
- **Students bring strategies for learning, although they may not be aware of the strategies they use.**
- **Most students need to be taught literacy strategies that will help them learn content more effectively.**
- **Students bring beliefs about themselves as learners and motivation for learning in your content area.**

As a content-area teacher, you will want to assess what your students bring to your content classroom and then provide instruction to further their learning. The literacy strategies and tools in Part Two and the Units in Part Three will help you.

Third, we offered guidelines and suggestions for teaching diverse students:

- **Building Your Knowledge**
- **Creating Your Classroom**
- **Adjusting Your Communication**

We recognize that our suggestions are general and that you cannot accomplish them in one year. Instead we expect you to work on learning about individual students for your entire career. If you are like most teachers, you decided to become a teacher because you liked students. Even though you are teaching content, you are really teaching students. We know you will enjoy learning about your students and learning with your students. We have, and we still do.

Inquiry into Your Learning

1. Choose a diversity characteristic and learn about it. Visit a community organization that serves that particular population, for example a special needs organization, an ethnic organization, or a local charitable agency. Interview the staff about the lives of the people in the community. What contributions are the people making to their community? What issues do they face? Try to find a member of the community who is willing to be interviewed about the story of her or his life.

2. Research the contributions of diverse people to your content area. What have people from a racial/ethnic minority culture, women, and people with disabilities accomplished? Look for biographies or news reports about their accomplishments. Identify organizations related to your content area for contacts that could inform you about the contributions of their members.

Inquiry into Your Students' Learning

1. Observe two classes—a low-track class and a high-track class—in your content area. If possible, observe the same teacher for both classes. Compare the content being taught and the instructional methods used. Compare the students' and the teachers' behavior. How do they affect each other? What does the teacher do differently in the two groups, and why? What are your conclusions about the teaching and learning in the two tracks?

2. Interview a teacher about his or her students. First, ask the teacher to describe the students in his or her different classes. Second, ask the teacher to describe a few students whom she or he finds interesting. Third, ask a series of questions about those students. What content knowledge do they bring to class? What strategies do they use to learn and study? What attitudes toward learning do they bring to class? How does the teacher learn about his or her students?

Resources

Books

Delpit, L. & Dowdy, J. K. (2002). *The skin that we speak.* New York: New Press. Essays on the intersection of dialect, identity, and culture from the perspectives of personal experiences, classroom experiences, and teachers' experiences.

Grant, C. A. & Sleeter, C. E. (1998). *Turning on learning: Five approaches for multicultural teaching plans for race, class, gender, and disability.* (2nd ed.). Columbus, OH: Merrill. For each approach, gives a rationale and specific lesson plans for K–12 classrooms.

Shulman, J., Lotan, R. A. & Whitcomb, J.A. (Eds.). (1998). *Groupwork in diverse classrooms: A casebook for educators.* New York: Teacher's College. Looks at the open-ended dilemmas faced when teachers use group work instead of traditional teaching. See also web site: **www.WestEd.org.**

Journals

Alexakos, K. & Antoine, W. (2003). The gender gap in science education. *The Science Teacher, 70* (3), 30–33. Discusses the research on the gap and closing the gap.

Conchas, G. Q. (2001). Structuring failure and success: Understanding the variability in Latino school engagement. *Harvard Educational Review, 71* (3), 475–504. Describes three high school programs: (1) the successful Medical Academy that supports students to build to success; (2) Advanced Placement & Graphic that has few diverse students; and (3) General Education that has failing students and poor teaching. The entire issue of the *Harvard Educational Review* contains articles on immigrant students.

Ernst-Slavit, G., Moore, M., & Maloney, C. (2003). Changing lives: Teaching English and literature to ESL students. *Journal of Adolescent & Adult Literacy, 46* (2), 116–128. Presents four stages of language learning from preproduction to early production to speech emergence to intermediate fluency. Also includes teaching suggestions, questioning techniques, and activities for each stage.

Mahoney, J. F. (2003). Benjamin Banneker's mathematical puzzles. *Mathematics Teacher, 96* (2), 86–91. Presents four puzzles devised by Banneker, an African-American mathematical wizard, scientist, astronomer, and scholar who was born a free man in 1731.

Moll, L. C., Amanti, C., Neff, D., & Gonzalez, N. (1992). Funds of knowledge for teaching: Using a qualitative approach to connect homes and classrooms. *Theory into Practice, 31* (2), 132–141. Describes the collaborative research to find funds of knowledge and an example of a classroom unit on candy that used funds of knowledge.

Web Sites

Office of Special Education: A Web Resource for Special Education, **www.curry.edschool.virginia. edu/go/specialed**. A comprehensive web site that organizes and updates information into five major areas related to special education. Particularly useful for K–12 and postsecondary educators.

Multicultural Pavilion: Resources and Dialogues for Equity in Education, **www.edchange.org/ multicultural**. A comprehensive, interactive educational Internet project useful for both K–12 and college educators, with links to other web sites. See the Teacher's Corner archive and database of multicultural activities, songs, historical documents, and literature.

Equity and Diversity, **www.iumd.edu/diversity**. A reference for research and policy information on diversity covering age, class, gender, ethnicity, and race.

Center for Research on Education, Diversity and Excellence (CREDE), **www.crede.ucsc.edu/tools/ research/standards/standards.html**. Researches 5 standards for effective pedagogy. Addresses issues of risk, diversity, and excellence involving the education of linguistic and cultural minority students and students at risk by factors of race, poverty, and geographic location. Offers publications.

Gay, Lesbian, and Straight Education Network (GLSEN), **www.glsen.org**. A national organization, GLSEN aims to create safe schools for gay, lesbian, bisexual, and transgender people. The web site offers information and resources for parents, students, and educators.

Choices and Decisions for Content Learning

PURPOSE-SETTING QUESTIONS

1 What different types of texts do you usually read in your content area? Are there some different types of texts you could incorporate into your content-area learning and teaching?

2 What makes a text readable, considerate or user-friendly, and fair or representative of diverse populations? How do you use this information to match texts to students?

3 Who governs communication patterns in classrooms: teachers or students? And what role can grouping patterns play in determining the learning and the communication in a classroom?

4 How can a teaching tool become an assessment tool?

5 What are the roles and importance of lesson plans for experienced teachers? What are the roles for you as a beginning teacher?

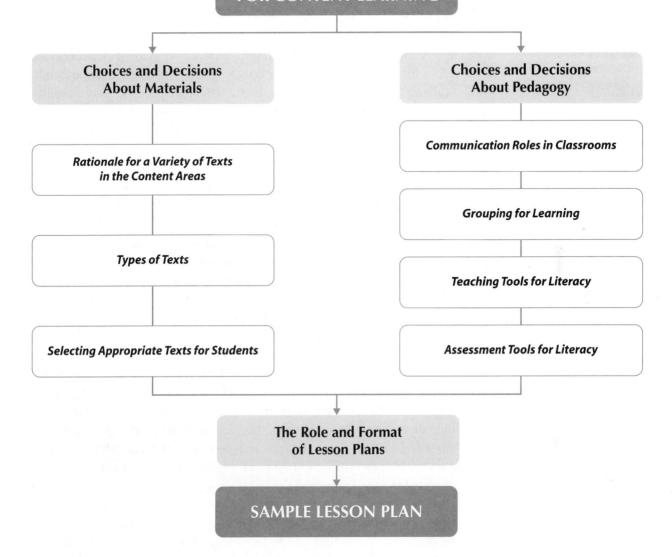

CHOICES AND DECISIONS
FOR CONTENT LEARNING

Choices and Decisions
About Materials

*Rationale for a Variety of Texts
in the Content Areas*

Types of Texts

Selecting Appropriate Texts for Students

Choices and Decisions
About Pedagogy

Communication Roles in Classrooms

Grouping for Learning

Teaching Tools for Literacy

Assessment Tools for Literacy

The Role and Format
of Lesson Plans

SAMPLE LESSON PLAN

As you will soon find out, if you haven't already, teaching is not a simple task. Experienced teachers can make teaching appear easy because they have a repertoire of teaching tools and a reservoir of knowledge. First, they have learned about their students, especially if they have been teaching in the same school and same grades for several years. Not only do they know what to expect from tenth-grade students and what will challenge them, they are attuned to their students' background, as we discussed in Chapter 2. Second, experienced teachers know the content required by state and local mandates. They have decided which areas to teach in depth and which to "cover." Third, experienced teachers have acquired materials, such as textbooks, magazines, and artifacts, that support the content they are teaching. Fourth, experienced teachers have refined their pedagogy and may even have preferred teaching tools, like small group discussions or whole class brainstorming, that work well for them and for their students. To you, experienced teachers may seem to have solved many of the day-to-day teaching questions in your discipline. Because most experienced teachers have learned to use a range of teaching tools and have collected an array of resources over time, their ability to make choices when planning or teaching may seem effortless.

Often spurred by questions from student teachers, their own professional reading, and new issues and trends in the field, teachers regularly reexamine their own practices and investigate new teaching practices, content, and materials. They make some choices and decisions before a lesson, some during the planning phase, and some after the action of teaching when they may revise their plans for instruction. And sometimes they make split-second decisions in the middle of teaching on the basis of their cumulative knowledge and experience. You will gain your own repertoire and reservoir just as they did with experience. In this chapter, we concentrate on the choices and decisions you will make as you plan your instruction.

In the chapter opening graphic we have shown the decision-making areas that a teacher is involved with when designing a lesson for a particular class or group of students. We remind you to keep your students as the focus of your planning because what you know about your students influences every decision you make.

First, we discuss the variety of literacy materials you can choose from to engage students with content and a rationale for using each material. We also discuss characteristics to consider when you evaluate and choose specific literacy materials. Having suitable materials for your students often affects your decisions about what content you teach and how you teach it.

Second, we discuss the variety of pedagogical decisions teachers make. In the confluence between students and content, teachers decide how best to teach and communicate with their students about content. Finally, we present grouping choices that range from whole class, to small group or cooperative learning, to individual learning.

In this chapter, we present a rationale and overview of materials, teaching tools, and assessment tools. In Part Two, we examine many of these materials and explain specific teaching and assessing tools you can use. You will make decisions about materials as well as the teaching and assessing tools to use based on the demands of your subject matter and the diverse needs of your specific students.

Choices and Decisions About Materials

When we use the terms *materials* or *resources* (in the unit plans in Part Three), we mean the objects you need to carry out your lesson. Materials could be beakers, spatulas, acrylic paints, tennis rackets, video cameras, as well as the more typical textbooks, pencils, and paper. Remembering to gather all necessary materials together and to have enough for every student makes a period go smoothly.

In this book, we use the term *text* to mean any material that is composed of words. A text could be a textbook, fiction or nonfiction books (often called trade books), a magazine, a newspaper, a primary source (a diary or document), student writing, or on-line text. We want you to think broadly about the types of texts your students could read and could write about.

■ Rationale for a Variety of Texts in the Content Areas

In encouraging you to think broadly about types of texts, we want you to begin that lifetime process of collecting a variety of materials suitable to your content and your students. We recognize that not every type of text is suitable for a specific content area, unit of study, or particular student in your class. We also recognize that you know of specific texts in your field, such as manuals or computer documentation, that we have not mentioned. We encourage you to begin your search for a variety of materials or resources that will complement your content area.

Your students will benefit from the incorporation of multiple resources in their classes in a number of ways:

- They will gain more in-depth knowledge because they have read more widely.
- They will remember concepts and important vocabulary because they have met them repeatedly in different contexts.
- They will have the opportunity to explore and practice a variety of literacy strategies as they learn from different types of texts.
- They will learn they can express their own ideas and knowledge through a variety of texts.

- They will recognize that authors write for different audiences and that they may too.

If students read only health textbooks, when will they learn how to evaluate the conflicting health advice that is often reported in news articles? Increasing the variety of texts will allow you and your students to explore different literacy strategies that support learning your content. In the next section, we briefly describe the variety of texts you might consider.

■ Types of Texts

Walk into most classrooms, and you will find textbooks (Goodlad, 1984). Often required by local or state boards or chosen to support districtwide curricula, textbooks are still the most prevalent curriculum material in every grade (Palmer & Stewart, 1997). In addition to textbooks, however, there are a number of other texts you might explore to enhance your content-area teaching.

Textbooks

In discipline-based courses and methods courses that you have taken, your professors may have expressed their views about the suitability of textbooks as a major source of content. Some may have criticized them and encouraged you to find a range of materials. They may also have encouraged you to create opportunities for hands-on experiences. We acknowledge the reality of getting to know the content in your courses and therefore think beginning teachers appreciate the organization and coverage that textbooks contain. As a preservice mathematics or science teacher, you probably have not studied every topic in your discipline in depth and will value the breadth of content that textbook writers provide. We also do not think you will be in a position as a beginning teacher to change state and district requirements for the courses you will teach. You may, in fact, be required to incorporate specific textbooks that have been adopted by the state or district in which you teach. Therefore, we encourage you to view the textbook as a resource for you and your students that you can supplement and adapt as you get to know your content and your students.

Remember that textbooks are designed to survey content and present a synthesis of agreed-on information. In this survey format, important understandings related to a topic may be glossed over or omitted entirely. Additionally, since it usually contains synthesized, agreed-on information, the textbook often presents a rather static view of your field. You will want to motivate students to be more active learners themselves by exploring the controversies, conflicting theories, and the tenuous facts about the content they are studying. This extension of content and opportunity to enhance understanding can be accomplished by using multiple sources.

This text focuses on enabling you to help the middle school and high school students you teach to meet the demands of their content-area classes by determining and building their background knowledge and their strategies for reading a variety of texts. In Part Two you will learn many strategies to guide your students' interaction with text. In this chapter we suggest that you consider choosing multiple formats of text that build on what students use for their everyday literacy tasks such as the Internet, various interactive communication technologies, and newspapers and magazines that are readily available both in print and electronically. We also suggest that you get to know and consider using the ever-expanding realm of trade books, both fiction and nonfiction, to complement your content area teaching. Table 3.1 provides a list of selected resources that will assist you in finding age-appropriate resources that will complement your content, as well as help you meet the range of literacy needs of your students.

Trade books

trade books All books published for sale to the general public.

The first category that is highlighted is *trade books*, comprised of fiction, nonfiction or informational books, and picture books. Imagine your high school students' reaction if you started an astronomy unit reading aloud from H. G. Wells' *War of the Worlds* or Ray Bradbury's *Martian Chronicles* each class period. Books like these science fiction works as well as fantasy, historical fiction, and realistic fiction can capture the mood of an event, not just the facts (Spiegel, 1987). Reading aloud an entire work or a selection from a particular work of fiction may lead the students in your content-area classes to recognize the human side of a given content-area topic or historical period. Furthermore, fiction writing is often more descriptive than nonfiction, so readers can obtain a clearer picture of an event that may then entice them to read more about the subject as well as help them learn the facts.

science fiction in science class

One advantage of nonfiction books, the second type of trade book, is that authors often treat a narrow subject in depth. This allows full discussion of topics rather than just a brief mention and it gives students multiple exposures to important content-related vocabulary linked to the key concepts throughout the book. Another advantage

When students read a variety of texts, they learn more content, increase their vocabulary, and practice a range of literacy strategies.
© Tom McCarthy/PHOTO EDIT

TABLE 3.1 Resources for Choosing Texts to Complement Content-Area Learning

I. Trade books	*Books*
Nonfiction	*Best Books for Young Teen Readers,* by J. T. Gillespie (2000).
	Beyond Words: Picture Books for Older Readers and Writers, by S. Benedict & R. Carlisle (1992).
informational	*Books for You: An Annotated Booklist for Senior High,* 14th ed. by K. Beers & T. Lesesne (Eds.) (2001).
	Children's Literature in Social Studies: Teaching to the Standards, by D. M. Krey (1998).
biography	*High Interest-Easy Reading,* by P. Phelan, (Ed.) (1996).
Fiction	*Kaleidoscope: Multicultural Booklist for K–8,* by J. Yokota (2001).
	Literature Connections to American History 7–12, by L. G. Adamson (1998).
realistic fiction	*Making Facts Come Alive,* by R. A. Branford & J. V. Kristo (1998).
	More Rip-Roaring Reads for Reluctant Teen Readers, by B. D. Ammon & J. W. Sherman (1999).
historical fiction	*Teaching with Picturebooks in Middle School*, by I. M. Tiedt (2000).
	Resources for Teaching Middle School Science, by the National Science Resource Center (1998).
science fiction	*Web Sites*
fantasy	Carol Hurst's Children's Literature Site, **www.carolhurst.com**
	Web English Teacher, **www.webenglishteacher.com**
Picturebooks	Eisenhower National Clearinghouse (for Math and Science), **www.enc.org**
II. Electronic Texts	*Books*
Internet	*Culturally Diverse Videos, Audios, and CD-ROMs for Children and Young Adults,* by I. Wood (1999).
	Teaching with the Internet: Lessons from the Classroom, by D. J. Leu Jr. and D. D. Leu (2000).
Electronic books	*Teen Resources on the Web: A Guide for Librarians, Parents, and Teachers,* by M. Mandel (2000).
(CD-ROMs)	*Web Sites*
Email	DiscoverySchool.com: Kathy Schrock's Guide for Educators, **school.discovery.com/ schrockguide/index.html**
III. Other Sources	*Books*
Magazines and Newspapers	*Magazines for Kids and Teens,* by D. R. Stoll (1997).
	Web Sites
	Humanities Text Initiative, **www.hti.umich.edu**
	The Internet Public Library—On-line Newspapers, **www.ipl.org**
	Kathy Schrock's Guide for Educators: News Sources, Journalism and Magazines, **school.discovery.com/schrockguide/index.html**
Primary Sources	Library of Congress, **www.loc.gov**
Student Text	New York Times Learning Network, **www.nytimes.com/learning/index.html**

of nonfiction books is that they have been written on different reading levels for different audiences. For this reason, using sources such as *Literature Connections to American History, 7–12* or *Resources for Teaching Middle School Science* included in Table 3.1, may help you identify books on related topics that meet the varied reading needs and background knowledge of the students in your class. For example, just by thumbing through *I Am an American: A True Story of the Japanese Internment* (1994) by Jerry Stanley and *Voices from the Camps: Internment of Japanese Americans During World War II* (1994) by L. D. Brenner, both informational books written about the Japanese internment in the United States during World War II, you can surmise that these books would enable students of differing abilities in an American history course to study the same topic and to contribute to whole-class or small-group work with their classmates.

Finally, both fiction and nonfiction picture books, which provide rich details and data by combining words and strong visual images of people and places, were originally written for very young readers. Today these books, many of which are written by individuals who are experts in their fields, can be used by older readers or adults to build background knowledge. For example, one can gain a great deal of knowledge about the environment from a picture book such as *A River Run Wild: An Environmental History* (1993) by Lynne Cherry, or learn about an historical figure such as Abraham Lincoln in a book such as Russell Freedman's *Lincoln: A Photobiography* (1993). Picture books can also make difficult or sensitive subjects more palatable, such as the image of the Vietnam War conveyed in *The Wall* (1990) by Eve Bunting. Picture books can also pique students' interest in a new topic or provide background knowledge for a new unit of study because of their attractive and varied formats. These books appear to be particularly appealing to a generation of students in our middle schools and high schools who have grown up with constant exposure to dramatic graphics and visuals in the media.

Electronic Texts

electronic texts A trade book or other text in a multimedia format.

The almost universal interest and motivation our students have with technology provides special opportunities to support the use of ***electronic texts*** in content-area classes today. Electronic environments foster real opportunities for students to engage in meaningful research and inquiry, they enhance communication by providing a myriad of resources and audiences for students, and they also provide environments that are interactive and captivating. The varied learning needs of your students can be met as never before from a single web site through the sound, graphics and video that are part of the hypermedia or multimedia environment a site provides. On many sites, understanding of concepts is aided by links to definitions and explanations, as well as through visuals and audio that accompany the content. Furthermore, students are able to effectively control their own learning pace and the format of the text in the electronic environment more effectively than they are able to with other texts (Wepner, Valmont, and Thurlow, 2000). In addition, many sites allow teachers to make adaptations based on their students' individual needs—background knowledge, language development, or reading level.

It should not be assumed that the use of electronic texts automatically makes learning in the content areas better, however. We know that students tend to go for extensive and often superficial use of the Internet rather than thoughtful, critical, and intensive use. If you have searched on the Internet, you have already discovered that quality varies greatly among sites. Second, you know that you can get lost among the links to other sites and that you can mistakenly or inadvertently travel to sites requiring parental consent. Therefore, we recommend that you identify a few productive sites before students begin their own searches in your particular content area. As a teacher you must supervise your students' use of technology, particularly the Internet, and carefully plan for its use as it relates to your content-area curriculum.

Technology can aid in improved teaching and more motivated learning, but it is necessary for teachers to evaluate materials for accuracy, quality of presentation, appropriateness for particular students, and the curriculum connections they wish to make. A web site selection guide, such as the one in Figure 3.1, can be used by teachers as well as by middle school and high school students to evaluate the materials they use.

Two other electronic resources that are particularly useful for extending and enhancing content-area learning are email and electronic texts. There are many uses for email, but the establishment of "key pals", email pen pals, is particularly useful. Students can extend their literacy as writers and their sense of audience by exchanging information with a university education class, such as yours, studying the same topic in biology or general science or reading the same trade book in English. Your students can also use email to communicate with students in regions around the world that they are studying in geography or social studies. Finally, your students can be connected to an expert zoologist or archeologist if you help them access a list serve of individuals in a given field related to what they are studying in your course (Wepner, Valmont, & Thurlow, 2000; Leu & Leu, 2002).

You may identify electronic books that complement your content-area study. Many text-centered electronic resources are superbly media enhanced. They provide students with powerful visuals as well as with audio enhancements that no content-area text alone can provide. Electronic reference sources such as *Grolier's Multimedia Encyclopedia* and Discovery Communications' *In the Company of Whales* provide students with depth and breadth on a variety of topics that match with the topics that correspond to many of the topics emphasized in the state and national standards of each discipline (Vacca & Vacca, 2002).

Other Sources

The third category of materials that enhance content-area learning includes magazines and newspapers, primary sources, and student texts. Each of these sources is found both in the school and the community of which the students are a part. These sources that are readily accessible to students add to the repertoire of texts that enable content-area teachers to meet the varied interests and learning needs of their students. We recommend incorporating magazines and newspapers into your content area for several reasons. First, for some students reading a short selection, like a magazine or newspaper article in a familiar format, is more appealing than focusing on an entire book. Second, magazines and newspapers usually contain current information that supports or serves to bring textbook information up-to-date. Third, magazine and newspaper articles

FIGURE 3.1 **Web Site Evaluation Form**

It is very important that students learn to evaluate the usefulness and accuracy of the Internet sites they visit.

Montgomery County Public Schools
Division of Technology Training
Electronic Literacy Pre K – 12

Web Site Evaluation Form
See also Web Site Evaluation Form: EXPLANATION OF CRITERIA

Student name _____

Research project title _____

General Infomation:
1. **URL** of the website _____
2. Name of the website _____

Authorship:
3. What organization and/or individual created this website?

_____

4. What does the domain represent? .com ___ .edu ___ .gov ___ .k12 ___ .mil ___ .net ___
.org ___ other ___

The author, editor, or institution is sponsored by:
(Write specific name in appropriate block. You'll probably only use one block.)

Domain	Name	Domain	Name	Domain	Name
.k12 – k12 school		.gov – government agency		.com – company (usually for profit)	
.edu – university		.org – organization (often non-profit)		other	

5. Is contact information provided? Check all that apply.
E-mail address: ___ Telephone number: ___ Mailing address: ___ Contact name: ___
6. Based on authorship, do you think you can rely on the information on this web site? yes ___ no ___
Why or why not? _____

Content:
7. What is the main purpose or point of view of the site? (check all that apply)

To inform		To persuade		To sell a product		Other	

8. Is there advertising? yes ___ no ___
9. If there is advertising, is it distracting? yes ___ no ___
10. Is the material: Primary/Original ___ Secondary/Derived ___?
11. Why is this web site helpful (or not helpful) for your project? _____
_____

Currency:
12. When was this page written or last updated? _____

Your Evaluation:
13. Rate this web page:

Use with caution		Good basic information		Excellent for assignment	

Electronic Literacy Pre K–12 http://www.mcps.k12.md.us/departments/isa/elit (February 2002)
This form created by: Linda French, Marjorie Geldon, Rebecca Olmstead and Myra Paul

From Montgomery County Public Schools, Rockville, MD, www.mcps.k12.md.us. Electronic Literacy K-12, Evaluating Web Sites, www.mcps.k12.md.us/departments/isa/elit/subtop/evalws.htm. Reprinted with permission.

focus on topics using photographs, graphics, and interviews that help students gain additional information related to the content topic. You can probably find a suitable magazine for every content area given the number of adult and adolescent magazines published today. For example, you can find a magazine such as *Ahora,* written in Spanish about a range of age-appropriate topics for teens, or a science-oriented magazine like *Wildlife Conservation,* whose major focus is to inspire young people to become active conservationists.

We also recommend that you consider using national and large city newspapers because they contain articles relating to every content area likely to be in a middle school or high school curriculum. Articles, and even entire sections of these newspapers, are devoted to science, technology and health-related discoveries, to stories about media and sports events, reviews of books and arts events, as well as many features and editorials focused on politics and current events. Today many newspapers, magazines, and 'zines are on-line. You might encourage your students to use these resources to complement their content-area study because they provide access to events around the world instantaneously.

Second, primary sources are recommended because they can make history, science, or mathematics come alive through their descriptions of real people's everyday actions and interactions. Public documents such as census records, town maps, death certificates, legislative laws or reports to government agencies, and personal records such as letters and journals, are primary sources that often lend support to study in a variety of content areas. Primary sources, both those found in one's community and those that are now available at Internet sites such as the one focused on historical documents at the Library of Congress (***www.loc.gov***), can supplement and extend the usual texts and print media found in most content-area classrooms.

Third, we recommend the use of student texts as an important source of materials because students are worthwhile audiences for each other whether their communication is on-line or in print. Students can share tentative writing in the form of notes, journals, records of observations, and interviews to receive support and challenge from other students as well as from you. Students can also create published writing and end products in various forms to be shared with appropriate audiences both in school and beyond the classroom setting. Such written documents produced by your students then may be included in their portfolios as summative assessment to demonstrate their understandings and their best work in a given content area.

■ Selecting Appropriate Texts for Students

The surest way to match a text to students is to ask the students to read the text and tell you what they understood. Sometimes school districts ask teachers to pilot a new textbook before they purchase it for all teachers. Then teachers can evaluate the match of the textbook to their particular students and their curricular goals. Unfortunately, when many teachers and textbook selection committees make decisions, teachers and students do not have the opportunity to try the books out. Instead, selection committees estimate the level of difficulty and the appropriateness of the textbooks.

When researchers first began to consider the importance of knowing the level of the texts their students were using, they measured textbooks for *readability*. More recently, researchers have examined textbooks for *considerateness* and *fairness*. We emphasize the importance of combining all three factors in order to obtain a good measure of a book's overall appropriateness for your students.

Readability

If you have used the grammar check on your computer, you may have seen a statistic that indicates the grade level of your text (you probably paid no attention to it). That statistic is a *readability* score. Textbooks from the beginning readers to high school physics textbooks can be evaluated to determine a readability level.

Readability formulas are designed to estimate what reading level a student would need to read a given text successfully. The most commonly used language variables are sentence length, number of syllables, and number of words.

The assumptions underlying *readability formulas* are not infallible. First, multisyllabic words, like *atmosphere* and *constitution*, are repeated often in a text, and explanations as well as supporting graphic aids may be provided. Second, because ideas are connected and explicated in longer sentences, sometimes readers find longer sentences easier to understand than short, choppy ones (Pearson & Johnson, 1978). Third, because language and dialect differences can change the number of syllables that individuals assign to a word, a particular text may be assigned different levels of difficulty by different individuals. Therefore, we examine the text's language and use the readability score in combination with considerateness and fairness.

The Fry Readability Formula is one of the most widely used to assess content-area materials, and you can easily calculate the readability of a text using the graphic provided in Figure 3.2. Remember that the score you find from most readability formulas represents a range of about plus or minus one grade for elementary texts and plus or minus two grades for high school texts—not the precise grade of the particular text throughout. Readability formulas are meant to be predictive devices to help you match materials and students; they are not meant to be exact (Conard, 1984) nor do they measure a student's motivation or background knowledge (Fry, 2002).

As a consumer of materials for your students, you need to understand how to figure readability so that you can make informed decisions when a sales representative tells you the textbook is on a ninth-grade reading level. Remember that readability formulas are used on a number of representative selections from a text to derive an overall estimate of the text's difficulty. They do not measure every variable that could affect students' comprehension of the text, such as the particular content or the chapter format (IRA, NCTE position statement on readability, 1984).

In addition to readability formula such as the Fry, the computer has made it possible to quickly analyze whole texts. However, many of these computer-based analysis such as Metametrics' Lexile Analysis (**www.lexile.com**) are available to publishing companies and to software developers, not to classroom teachers who need to make on-the-spot decisions about content related materials and their ability to match these with their students reading and instructional needs.

---

readability The reading level a student would need to read a given text successfully.

readability formula A procedure used to analyze a sample of text in a systematic manner in order to determine its difficulty level.

FIGURE 3.2 Fry Readability Formula and Graph

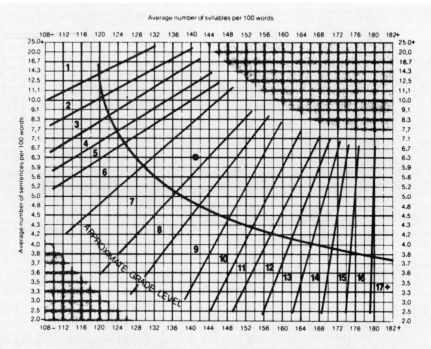

Expanded Directions for Working Readability Graph

1. Randomly select three (3) sample passages and count out exactly 100 words each, beginning with the beginning of a sentence. Do count proper nouns, initializations, and numerals.
2. Count the number of sentences in the hundred words, estimating length of the fraction of the last sentence to the nearest one-tenth.
3. Count the total number of syllables in the 100-word passage. If you don't have a hand counter available, an easy way is to simply put a mark above every syllable over one in each word, then when you get to the end of the passage, count the number of marks and add 100. Small calculators can also be used as counters by pushing numeral 1, then push the + sign for each word or syllable when counting.
4. Enter graph with *average* sentence length and *average* number of syllables; plot dot where the two lines intersect. Area where dot is plotted will give you the approximate grade level.
5. If a great deal of variability is found in syllable count or sentence count, putting more samples into the average is desirable.
6. A word is defined as a group of symbols with a space on either side; thus, *Joe, IRA, 1945,* and *&* are each one word.
7. A syllable is defined as a phonetic syllable. Generally, there are as many syllables as vowel sounds. For example, *stopped* is one syllable and *wanted* is two syllables. When counting syllables for numerals and initializations, count one syllable for each symbol. For example, *1945* is four syllables, *IRA* is three syllables, and *&* is one syllable.

Note: This "extended graph" does not outmode or render the earlier (1968) version inoperative or inaccurate; it is an extension. (REPRODUCTION PERMITTED—NO COPYRIGHT)

Source: From "Fry's Readability Graph: Clarifications, Validity, and Extension to Level 17," *Journal of Reading, 21* (December 1977), 249.

considerateness The manner in which the clarity of organization, appropriate vocabulary, and supplemental explanatory features combine to make a text comprehensible for the reader.

fairness The manner in which a text or selection equitably and fairly treats diversity and avoids stereotypes.

We think a readability range is one measure of a level of a text, but only one measure. ***Considerateness*** and *fairness* are the two other criteria used to assess and match texts with your students' learning needs. Fairness refers to whether a student can see themselves in a given text. Considerateness, on the other hand, refers to how well the content and format work together to enable a student to comprehend and learn the material in a text. Figure 3.3, a sample checklist you might use in evaluating texts, shows that the interconnection among these variables determines a text's overall appropriateness for use with your students.

Considerateness

When you are deciding how considerate a text is, examine *format variables* and *content variables* to determine how well topics are explained (Armbruster, 1984). Remember that your students will bring various background knowledge to the text and often they have little familiarity with content-area topics and specialized graphics and visuals.

Let's begin with the *format variables* of considerate textbooks and informational books (see Figure 3.3). First, the whole book should have aids for the reader. The table of contents should inform readers what content is covered and in what order. A glossary, index, and bibliography or references should aid readers in finding or extending specific ideas.

Second, within each chapter, an introduction should alert the reader to what information will be covered and how the information is organized. Purpose-setting questions might be included to guide the reader to significant information on the topic. Subdivisions or subheads should also indicate the organization of the chapter and alert readers to significant content. Illustrative material, such as pictures, tables, and graphs, should be explained in the text and in the caption as well. Finally, a chapter summary should remind readers of the major points.

TEACHER AS INQUIRING LEARNER

Using the Fry Readability Formula and Graph, calculate the readability range for a textbook in your content area.

- Does the score include the grade the textbook is intended for?

Look at the multisyllabic words in the samples of text you chose.

- Would the words be familiar or unfamiliar to your students? Are the words so important that

you would teach them in a prereading activity, or would you expect students to read them independently and figure out their meaning from the context?

Look at the length of the sentences.

- Are the ideas in long sentences clear or confusing? Are ideas in the short sentences clear or choppy? Are the ideas in the sentences connected to each other?

FIGURE 3.3 **Selecting Literacy Materials: A Checklist**

Selecting Literacy Materials: A Checklist

Readability Range _____

Would you teach the multisyllabic words?
Would you expect students to read them independently?
Do the long sentences have too many ideas, or do they clearly connect ideas?
Do the short sentences seem choppy or clear?

Considerate Format

Does the Table of Contents show an orderly sequence?
Does the book contain reader aids, like an index, bibliography, and glossary?
Do the introduction and subheads clearly represent the chapter's organization?
Are the illustrative materials clear and connected to the text?

Considerate Context

How many ideas are presented? Is that number reasonable?
Are the ideas explained clearly and connected explicitly?
Do the examples and analogies match the students' background knowledge?
Is an overarching principle evident?

Fairness

Do the illustrations have a fair representation of race or ethnicity, gender, and class?
Do the illustrations have people in nonstereotypical roles?
Do the examples and problems in the text represent a fair and nonstereo-
   typical representation of race or ethnicity, gender, and class?
Does the text use nonsexist language?

Now let's discuss the *content variables* of considerate texts (see Figure 3.3). First, the manner in which specific facts, events, and concepts are connected to each other and to the overarching understanding should be explicitly explained. For example, a high school history text that describes the French, English, Russian, and American revolutions should explicitly point out their similarities and differences. A science text explaining the functions of arteries and veins should highlight and clarify their differences in function in the human body (Singer, 1992). In physics textbooks and we think math textbooks as well, the words in the text should be explicitly connected to the formulas presented (Alexander & Kulikowich, 1994).

Second, new concepts or ideas need to be spread out and elaborated rather than presented in rapid-fire succession. The number of details or concepts should be carefully considered based on the topic and the assumed background knowledge of the students for whom the book was written.

Finally, any examples and analogies used in the text need to fit with the students' background knowledge if they are to assist in clarifying a point. If the examples or analogies are too abstract or unfamiliar, students will not understand the concept they are supposed to explain (Alexander & Kulikowich, 1994).

Although textbooks are usually examined for considerateness, we advise you also to examine for considerateness other texts you plan to use with your students. We think informational books, newspapers and magazine articles can be more considerate than traditional content-area texts to your students because their content is often more focused and supported by helpful visual aides. Adapted primary sources, rather than actual primary sources, are more considerate because the language and spellings are modernized. Additionally, with the explosion of the availability of text on the Internet, considerate format and content such as design features, ease of use, content, and credibility should be used to assess text. A site selection guide, such as the one in Figure 3.1, provides a means for both teachers and students to determine considerate and credible web-based text.

Students should also learn how to create considerate text of their own by organizing their content, including a reasonable amount of detail and evidence, and making explicit connections for their readers. You might want to develop a list of user-friendly criteria with your students for the texts they write. They could base their checklist on criteria found in Figures 3.2 and 3.3 in this chapter.

Fairness

DIVERSITY

As our school population becomes more diverse (see Chapter 2), we certainly want texts that treat race or ethnicity, gender, disability, and class fairly. But what is *fairness*? How important is it for students to see themselves or others like them in the texts they use? Is there a specific list of books or set of facts every student in the United States should know (Bloom, 1987; Hirsh, 1988)? Should required book lists and sets of facts be expanded to include the contributions of groups that heretofore have been underrepresented, and should they be representative of the demographics of the country as a whole as we begin the twenty-first century (Sleeter & Grant, 1991)? Educators on both sides have weighed in on this debate. Students need texts that serve as mirrors of themselves and texts that serve as windows to others. Therefore, we define fairness in text as being able to see oneself in some texts and being able to learn about others in other texts.

Compared to textbooks decades ago, textbooks appear to be fairer today. Sleeter and Grant (1991) found that for the most part, the textbooks they analyzed used nonsexist, nonstereotypic language. Furthermore, the distribution of pictures by race and gender closely reflected their percentage in the general population, although white males still dominated. Nevertheless, the texts they analyzed still did not reflect the distribution of class and disability found in the overall population. The middle class dominated, and persons with disability were almost completely ignored.

Just like textbooks, other texts such as trade books, magazines, and on-line sites, should be evaluated for nonsexist language and fair representation of people (see Figure 3.3). You and your students could evaluate the different texts they read for fairness.

In summary, we encourage you to examine texts using all three factors—readability, considerateness, and fairness—when you are deciding on texts for your students. Remember that all students benefit from a variety of texts—different types of text as well as both challenging and easy texts. As a teacher and lifelong learner, you should read widely in your content area and constantly be on the lookout for suitable materials that match the diverse background and learning needs of your students. Many of the sources listed in Table 3.1 can assist you in this pursuit.

Choices and Decisions About Pedagogy

You know what content you want to teach and you have found materials to use. Now you are ready to think about how you will teach. Your choices and decisions about pedagogy will define you as a teacher, and they will reveal your expectations and views of your students. Clearly pedagogical decisions are important.

We suggest that you think about four interlocking teaching decisions when you plan for a class period or lesson:

- Communication roles for the teacher and for the students

- Grouping patterns for learning

- Teaching tools for literacy

- Assessment tools for literacy

Within a single period, you and the class may experience several communication roles, groupings, and teaching and assessment tools. In order to cover the content and give your students opportunities to apply strategies and understandings, few lessons should use a single mode of instruction for the entire period. In fact, we recommend that you plan on using a variety of roles, groupings, and tools in one period whenever possible.

■ Communication Roles in Classrooms

By *communication roles in the classroom,* we mean who decides who can talk and actively participate. As the teacher, you can decide whether communication will be (1) teacher directed, (2) teacher-student interchanges, or (3) student-to-student interchanges. Each has its purpose as well as advantages and disadvantages.

Teacher-Directed Communication

In this communication pattern, the teacher decides who talks and when; often the teacher does most, if not all, of the talking. No doubt you have experienced the formal lecture in your own education. A second form of teacher-directed communication you have probably experienced is recitation, or in-class response to teacher-directed questions.

We object to lectures or recitation for an entire period because most students are passive during these times. Therefore, if you choose to use either of these direct approaches, we recommend that you intersperse your lectures with questioning and that during the questioning or recitation, when you call on a student for a response, you then ask another student to confirm or refute the answer. This sort of alternate response keeps the students on their toes and encourages them to be active listeners and learners during teacher-led communication.

Short teacher-directed communication can be useful. We like the term *mini-lesson* because it implies that the activity takes place for part of a period. Students may need clarification of specific content, so you explain the content in a mini-lesson of ten to fifteen minutes. You may decide to demonstrate an experimental procedure in science, a safety procedure for the bandsaw in vocational education, or how to interview someone or revise writing in a mini-lesson in language arts. In a teacher-directed mini-lesson, the teacher dominates the communication to explain or demonstrate specific concepts or strategies. Science, vocational education, home economics, arts, and physical education teachers have been conducting such short demonstrations or mini-lessons for many years. They give direct instruction, and then students do similar activities in order to practice and apply their new knowledge and strategy.

To free yourself and your students from teacher-directed lessons, you need to believe that students learn from each other and not just from you. If you want to build a community of learners in your classroom, you need to see yourself and your students as important participants and contributors to the construction of meaning. We suggest that you try a variety of options when planning communication within your own classroom to maximize your students' acquisition of the strategies and skills, as well as ownership of the content knowledge being covered.

Teacher-Student Interchanges

In these interchanges, the teacher and students share the communication decisions about who talks, when, and for how long. Instead of the one-word response often expected in the recitation pattern, the students are encouraged to explain and give reasons or evidence for their thoughts and understandings. The teacher assumes different roles depending on the situation.

Suppose you want to be sure your students understand the geographical concept of region. You might lead a discussion by asking students to give characteristics of regions they are familiar with. Using their examples, you then probe for students to summarize the features that can be used to define a region. In that situation, you are the *guide;* you direct the discussion, but the students are talking most of the time, to either you or other students.

In another teacher-student interchange, you could be a *coach* or *facilitator*. Suppose the students are designing models of aerodynamic flight in their science or physics class. You would ask questions or make statements that would lead the students to consider their design carefully, such as, "Will that wing span provide the lift needed?" When coaching, a teacher speaks very little and focuses on listening to the students' discussions with their peers or may wait for the students to initiate an interchange when they need assistance to answer a question or solve a problem.

Student-to-Student Interchanges

We think teachers should provide for more opportunities for student-to-student interchanges in which the students govern who talks, when, and for how long in the classroom. In these instances the teacher is either an observer or a participant-observer. In the role of *observer*, the teacher does not interject comments into the students' interchanges. Instead the teacher operates like an anthropologist collecting data about a cultural event. When the teacher adopts the role of *participant-observer*, the teacher takes on no more decision-making power than any student participant. For example, in a discussion of an issue, such as, "Does a dress code violate student rights?" you can express your views as a participant-observer. However, you would choose an opportune time so that you do not extinguish student-to-student interchanges, especially because students rarely forget who's the teacher!

■ Grouping for Learning

Although educational reforms call for less tracking, we acknowledge that tracking will continue in some form in many junior high, middle schools, and high schools. And although you will probably not change school policy and how students are assigned to classes and courses, you can usually determine the grouping patterns within your own classroom. You need to decide whether whole class, small groups, pairs, or individual configurations will best serve your teaching-learning purposes and, most important, the learning needs of your students.

DIVERSITY

We think the purpose for instruction should determine the grouping pattern chosen for any specific lesson. At certain times, either high- or low-achieving students need direct instruction, so perhaps you will carry out a mini-lesson on specific content or a strategy in a homogeneous small group. At another time, high- and low-achieving students have information about a topic to contribute to each other in heterogeneous small groups. Especially in science or math classes, you may find that same-sex small groups may allow girls more opportunity to learn actively (Guzzetti & Williams, 1996; Jones & Wheatley, 1990). The grouping patterns you choose should vary during a lesson, a unit, or a course. You should always be flexible with your grouping decisions so that they best meet instructional and student needs, and be ready to revise your plan.

Whole Class

When everyone needs to learn or to share similar information, teachers keep the whole class together. Teachers conduct whole class mini-lessons and whole class teacher-led discussions when a new topic or strategy is being introduced, such as at the beginning of a new unit or theme study or when a new text is introduced. Teachers also hold class meetings when students need to plan research projects or divide up learning tasks in the classroom. Another use of whole class grouping is when the students participate in a culminating activity, such as a debate or discussion, which gives them a chance to use their understandings or new knowledge. Also, as a culminating activity for a unit, the whole class might share their finished products—art works, research projects, or written texts—with each other.

Small Groups

Teachers usually choose to divide the class into small groups to meet different instructional purposes and to meet different student needs. Teachers make these decisions because of the advantages for students' learning that are inherent in small group structure:

- Students learn by interacting with each other cooperatively.

- Students construct meaning more actively by interacting with the materials and each other.

- Students with different information and strengths (heterogeneous groups) can contribute to each other.

- More students find it easier and more comfortable to talk and listen in a smaller group than in a whole class setting.

- Student participation in homogeneous groupings enables them to accomplish content-area goals and objectives more effectively and efficiently.

Teacher-Led Small Groups

We think that the purpose for a small group governs the teacher's particular communication role with that group. We have already mentioned teacher-directed minilessons to a small group when students need specific instruction. When students are learning together in a group, a teacher can be a coach, helping the students accomplish their task. For example, a teacher could act as a coach with a small group by teaching the students a process, such as how to comment on a peer's writing or how to compare different problem-solving approaches in mathematics.

Student-Led Small Groups

Although we use the generic term *small groups,* you will encounter special terms that refer to particular types of small groups where students take on a variety of roles in support of learning with one another. Cooperative learning groups (Johnson, Johnson, & Holubec, 1990; Slavin, 1988) and peer-led discussion groups are two student-led groupings that we find particularly useful. Perhaps you have participated in one or more of these small group settings while taking your college or university courses.

Pairs and Partners

Sometimes even a small group is too large for the purpose; in this case, it may be advantageous to have students work with only one other person. When students share ideas with a partner, they can trigger each other's ideas. In other instances, a student might benefit from having a *tutorial partner*—a peer who can help with the content or the processes in a particular discipline or within a particular unit of study. Such peer-aged tutoring has been particularly successful at the middle school level because both students, the tutor and the tutee, demonstrate increased self-confidence and higher motivation (Alexander & George, 2003). Additionally, pairs of students can help each other understand difficult text, work on a science project, and research a topic, especially when they have the same or complementary interests.

Although we have emphasized the value of small groups, pairs, and partners, students do learn individually, and you want to know your students as individuals. We strongly suggest that you mix independent or individual work into your grouping designs. Furthermore, some students have unique interests that no other student shares. Those individuals benefit from pursuing their interests in depth. Content-area teachers also have the opportunity to foster those individuals whose unique interests relate to their own interests.

Practical Considerations for Grouping Decisions

The major purpose for any grouping decision is to allow the teacher to meet the instructional purposes dictated by the content being studied and the objectives given the needs and strengths of the students in their class. If you teach several sections of the same course, you may have to change the grouping arrangements you chose for a lesson, a series of lessons, or for the entire unit because the students are different and require different teaching and learning arrangements in order for them to meet the instructional goals.

First, the size of the group can make or break the success of small group work. The size of a group should be determined by the complexity of the learning task at hand, the materials that are being used, and the outcomes that you desire, as well as the needs and strengths of the students. Groups are not meant to be static or permanent. They may vary in size and composition during the course of a series of lessons, a unit, or a semester in order to meet instructional goals and student learning needs that often become apparent as the lesson or unit is in process.

DIVERSITY

Second, you may wish to assign students to groups that are balanced by gender, race, achievement, and other factors that make them representative of the class as a whole (see Chapter 2). At the beginning of the year, you might want to allow students to choose their own partners or groups because you don't yet know the students and their learning needs. After you have had time to observe the students as they participate in their self-selected groups, you may choose to reassign them to groups.

Third, we think one of the most useful ways to teach students about working cooperatively is to create a list with students of the behaviors that contribute to learning—for example, simple items like listening to each other, reading directions, and ensuring that everyone participates in all small group work. It is important that each student learns how to assess his or her own contributions as well as what the group or partnership has accomplished. Coming together as a class to share the positive instances as well as the instances that need improvement, the class can pick one or two behaviors to stress in their next session with their small group or with their partner. Finally, these same criteria can be incorporated into self-assessment checklists for students to use in evaluating their own performance.

Finally, you know from your own group work that it is not difficult to stray off task. Few students, yet alone adults, work solidly on a single topic for forty minutes! Every group or partnership does stray, and sometimes the tangents taken are very beneficial. However, when students govern the cooperative groups or the pairs they are in, the crucial criterion for the teacher to determine is whether the students are returning to the task and whether they are using the grouping interactions in a purposeful manner related to the topic and content being studied. Such observation and reflection allow the teacher to determine the benefit of the grouping patterns chosen in terms of meeting both the instructional goals and the learning needs of their students.

One of the decisions you will make over and over again during your teaching career is how best to group your own students to maximize their learning experiences. Later in this chapter, you will see how this consideration is incorporated in a sample lesson plan. For the next week keep track of the different ways students are grouped in your university classes and labs or in your field placement settings.

Create a checklist using the categories for grouping that have just been described, for example, whole class, small groups, pairs and partners. Leave room also for comments and reactions about how you think these decisions about grouping helped you or got in the way of your learning or that of your students. Share your findings with other students in your discipline, for example science, art or math, or with other students at your level, for example middle school or high school.

■ Teaching Tools for Literacy

Because your students will have a range of literacy needs, you will need a repertoire of teaching tools to support their reading and writing in your content area. In Part Two, we present many specific teaching tools from which you can select. Here we define the three categories of teaching tools you will meet in Part Two.

Modeling and Explaining

modeling and explaining A teaching tool that demonstrates a strategy and explains why, when, and how to use it.

Because we emphasize the process of learning content, we consider the *modeling and explaining* teaching tool to be a primary teaching tool. The objective of this tool is to make literacy strategies visible and explicit so that students are aware of strategies they should or do use.

In modeling and explaining strategies, you both show your process of literacy learning and hold a running commentary on your process. Using the text your students read, you express out loud how you are learning (your strategies) and what you are learning (the content). As we stated in Chapter 1, you explicitly name each particular strategy and what it does (*declarative knowledge*), tell why and when to use the strategy (*conditional knowledge*), and show how you use the strategy (*procedural knowledge*). If you use your strategies without explicit explanations, your students may not recognize the strategies or learn why, when, and even how to use them.

You will want to model and explain the use of strategies with the different texts your students read throughout the year. To build your students' metacognitive awareness of strategies at the beginning of the year, you will model and explain your own strategies in a teacher-directed mini-lesson. Throughout Part Two, we include scripts in order to model and explain to you specific literacy strategies useful with different content-area texts.

As your students become more metacognitively aware, you may choose to hold a teacher-guided discussion in which you and the students identify the strategies to use, tell what the rationale is for their use, and decide when to use them. Perhaps at this stage a student could demonstrate how to use the strategy with the material and content at hand. You may even initiate student-to-student interchanges in which students model and explain their strategies in small groups and pairs for one another. Whenever your students face a difficult text, you may decide to model and explain your strategies in order to teach them useful strategies for that text. Remember also that your students will need guided practice or coaching in using strategies before they can use them independently (Pearson & Gallagher, 1983).

Direct Teaching Tools

direct teaching tool
A teaching tool in which the teacher tells students specific information.

Like a teacher-directed lesson, a teacher uses a *direct teaching tool* selectively to impart information to students. For instance, you may directly teach word parts—root words, prefixes, and suffixes—so that your students can decipher unknown multisyllabic words when they meet them in the content-area texts. Because students receive information only when a direct teaching tool is used, you will want to follow up with an activity in which students use the information or content in a meaningful situation. In the word parts example, you would have your students collect and define additional words with similar word parts when they read their own texts.

Teaching/Assessing Tools

teaching/assessing tool
A teaching tool that supports a student's learning and through which a teacher can assess the student's progress.

We like *teaching/assessing tools* because they serve two functions in instruction. First, they are teaching tools that support students' learning of content and use of strategies. Second, while the students use the tools to understand text or content, the teacher can assess the students' learning, turning a teaching tool into an assessing tool. From that assessment, the teacher can make decisions about what and how to teach next.

For example, to support your students in finding and interpreting important information in a new text or selection, you may decide to use the teaching/assessing tool of teacher-guided discussion or a directed reading activity (explained in Chapter 5). As your students read the text, you periodically ask questions about the text and discuss with your students how purpose-setting questions support their learning. As a teaching tool, your questions help students identify the important details and interpretations. The discussion among students helps them to comprehend the content. As the students discuss, you notice who comprehends the text, what ideas are understood, and where there is confusion, thus turning the teaching tool into an assessment tool.

In addition to informing you and your students about the direction of instruction, teaching/assessing tools are effective because the students operate on the content. Instead of just passively receiving the content through lecture or other direct instruction, students are being engaged in a process in which they construct their own version of the content. For example, in the teacher-guided discussion, the students explain their understanding of the content and how they interpret the information. Because the students are transacting with their ideas, they can also assess what strategies and content they know and what they need to learn. Specific teaching/assessing tools are included in every chapter in Part Two because they inform teachers and students how learning and instruction are progressing.

■ Assessment Tools for Literacy

If you think of assessments like standardized tests, weekly quizzes, and end-of-unit tests, then our use of assessment with pedagogy may seem unusual to you. However, we prefer

assessment tools
Tools that inform students and teachers about ongoing learning of content and/or strategies.

different *assessment tools*: ones that inform students and teachers about ongoing learning and that exhibit the content students have learned. When students and teachers use assessment tools in this manner, then assessment is interactive with instruction.

Assessment tools chosen to measure both literacy and content-area learning, during individual lessons or a series of lessons (Part Two) or at the culmination of a unit (Part Three), should be based on four guidelines.

The assessment tools and end products that are chosen should exhibit that the goals and objectives of a lesson or unit were accomplished

Students should be required to demonstrate their use of knowledge, not just their acquisition of facts

The degree of choice or how an assessment tool is chosen, and who—the teacher, the student, or the teacher and student in collaboration—decides how students' understandings will be demonstrated should vary according to student needs and teacher objectives

Students should have the opportunity to share their new understandings and knowledge with appropriate audiences

The tools we have chosen to emphasize throughout this text are all *performance assessment measures*—they exhibit student learning. In the lessons described in Part Two and the units designed for different curriculum approaches in Part Three, students are required to demonstrate their knowledge by showing ongoing learning (a journal entry, graphic, model) or creating a product (video, diorama, essay, poem). We prefer such performance assessments because they inform students about their own learning and inform teachers about what and how to instruct students. In Part Two of this book, we present primarily teaching/assessment tools that you and your students can use to inform each other about literacy and content-area learning and conclude with a focus on end products in Chapter 9. In Part Three, we incorporate both teaching/assessment tools and end products or culminating activities into different content-area units.

Formative Assessment Tools for Ongoing Learning

formative assessment
Assessment that occurs while a task or project is in process.

Assessment that occurs while a task or project is still progressing is called formative (McMillan, 1997). *Formative assessment*, detailed more fully in Chapter 10, allows the teacher to modify goals, directions, and assignments before a task or project or unit of study is completed. In both Parts Two and Three, we present four types of formative assessment tools: teaching/assessing tools, assessment-only tools, monitoring and self-monitoring questions, and working or collection portfolios.

Teaching/Assessing Tools

We have already discussed how you can use these tools to teach your students as you keep an eye on assessment. We repeat these tools here to stress that assessment angle: good teaching concentrates on students' responses. You have a wonderful opportunity to observe students' active learning when they are working or by using a teaching/assessing tool. Most beginning teachers concentrate on their own teaching, their role during the lesson, and what they are doing in the lesson. However, we want you to learn to attend to what your students do—their ongoing learning—which you can determine as you observe your students working alone or in small groups, as well as in whole class settings. Using teaching/assessing tools such as the ones described in detail in Part Two will allow you to be informed about your students' learning of both strategies and content throughout a given lesson or unit.

Assessment-Only Tools

As the name denotes, assessment-only tools indicate how or what a student is learning or has learned; they do not teach. Although you probably think of end-of-unit tests, assessment-only tools can be used during learning too. For example, in Chapter 4, we present an assessment tool in which the students rate how well they understand the important vocabulary you have selected from a particular unit or chapter. If a student doesn't know a specific word, this type of rating sheet or assessment tool doesn't teach the word. But you can examine the rating sheets to assess what words you need to teach for the student's future study.

Monitoring and Self-Monitoring

During every task, strategic learners are metacognitively aware, and they are able to monitor their own progress toward learning. These students stay with successful strategies, abandon unsuccessful ones, and change strategies as they work on different parts of the task. In the modeling and explaining scripts in Part Two, you will find statements that monitor what strategies are useful. Also, at the end of each chapter, you will find a monitoring checklist that lists questions to ask to help students monitor their ongoing use of strategies.

Collection Portfolios and Ongoing Performance Evaluation

collection (or working) portfolio Assemblage of artifacts that students produce as they learn in any content area.

Documentation portfolios, also called *collection or working portfolios*, contain the artifacts students produce as they learn in any content area—for example, a word map (see Chapter 4), a study guide with their responses (see Chapter 6), or a summary (see Chapter 7) that students have completed in whole class, small group, partner, and individual work during their study. Students and teachers can review their working portfolios to assess progress in learning, such as their understanding of the issues surrounding the Vietnam War, their competency in expository writing in both language arts and across the content areas, and their application of mathematical calculations during their science investigations. Periodically as the year progresses, students will need to weed their working portfolios to discard insignificant artifacts and save clear examples of significant learning. We discuss the collection portfolio more fully in conjunction with the integrated curriculum approach in Part Three.

Summative Assessment Tools for Evaluating Learning

summative assessment Assessment that occurs primarily as a concluding or culminating synthesis activity.

When assessment occurs primarily as a concluding or culminating activity for a series of lessons or a unit, it is called *summative assessment* (McMillan, 1997). Summative assessment is usually based on students' ability to synthesize knowledge and demonstrate their understanding in some concrete product that can be shared with others—teachers, peers, parents, and administrators. In Parts Two and Three, we present three forms of summative assessment tools: end products such as research papers and projects, as well as performances, classroom- and teacher-made tests, and showcase portfolios.

End Products and Performances That Actively Demonstrate Learning

Students can demonstrate what they have learned to audiences other than the teacher. Students can apply what they have learned in projects that inform other students in class, in other classes, and in other schools. Their projects could inform the local citizens, a historical group, or an ecology society.

In Chapters 8, on refining ideas, and 9, on learning through research projects, and throughout the chapters in Part Three, we present a variety of products and projects that are used as assessment tools. For example, debates, newspaper articles, and an ad campaign are end products suggested in Chapters 11 and 12. The term paper (both the traditional and several alternative forms), summaries and abstracts, reviews, and annotations are the focus in Chapter 9. Finally, dramatic as well as art and musical opportunities to communicate learning are presented in Chapter 8. Each of the products enables the learners to communicate their unique understanding of content to different audiences, one of whom is always the teacher. Although the unit has ended, the teacher can use the information to inform future units and to design new learning opportunities for individual students or groups within the class.

Classroom and Teacher-Made Tests

Lessons, units, and semesters do end, and students need to demonstrate what they have learned. We always prefer assessments that match with learning goals and actively engage students. However, paper-and-pencil assessment of a task may be useful in certain instances. Essay tests in particular, which prompt students to think critically and creatively as they synthesize information from their study of multiple sources, can be very useful and appropriate in all of the content areas (see Chapter 8 and all of the chapters in Part Three). Short-answer tests that demonstrate students' knowledge of facts and details related to a particular time period or event in history, science formulas, chemistry notations, and math theorems may assess a student's repertoire in a given content area.

Showcase Portfolios

showcase portfolio
"Best work" portfolios that display the synthesis or culmination of a student's work in a course, semester or year.

"Best-work" or *showcase portfolios* are summative assessment tools because their purpose is to display the culmination or synthesis of a student's work in a course, a semester, or an academic year. Often the showcase portfolios are referred to as display portfolios because other individuals—teachers, parents, administrators—will see and respond to them. In addition to the products themselves in the showcase portfolio, students are expected to provide written commentary to explain why they have chosen the particular pieces of work in their portfolio and to include some comments about their own growth and development as a reader and writer, a mathematician, a scientist, or an artist as displayed in the products they have chosen for display. In this way, the summative portfolios demonstrate not only a student's competency in a content area or several content areas, but also their ownership of their own work and their reflective and evaluative competencies.

The Role and Format of Lesson Plans

Student teachers and interns often ask us, "If experienced teachers don't write lesson plans, why do we?" Our answer is that experienced teachers do create lessons, based on their repertoire of teaching tools and their reservoir of knowledge about their content and their students. Teachers today, no matter what discipline or grade level, must consider various standards, especially the curriculum frameworks of their state, when planning a lesson or unit. In addition, they think about the purpose or objective of every lesson, the materials they need to have prepared, the groupings that will occur, and the teaching/assessing tools they will use. Often these experienced teachers write notes for themselves as they think through these components of a lesson. The only difference from you is that these experienced teachers are usually not required to write the plans for an outside audience, such as their supervisor or cooperating teacher or even their peers. Although their plans may seem invisible, they most assuredly are there.

In this section, we outline a generic lesson plan format and accompany it with a sample lesson plan. We do not expect you to understand many of the teaching tools and assessing tools in the lesson plan; we will explain those tools in Part Two. For now, we give you the lesson plan format so that you will have the structure in which to place the teaching and assessing tools described in detail in Part Two.

Lesson plans are not written in narrative paragraphs; they are organized lists or directions that you can refer to quickly. Everyone develops his or her own style of lesson plan; however, you may be required to use a preferred department or district format when you are a teacher in a particular middle school or high school. Most lesson plans have four basic parts: (1) goals and objectives, (2) materials, (3) pedagogy or teaching procedures, and (4) assessment or evaluation. In addition, most lesson plans today include the state standards that will be met. When you write lesson plans, you preplan the content and strategies you expect to accomplish. Although we estimate one period for each lesson, we know that some plans will take more than one period to complete because of either the nature of the activities or the students' performance and responses during the lesson.

In the sample lesson plan that follows, we emphasize using a strategy to support the learning of content. The pedagogical decisions a teacher makes, including procedures and grouping patterns, are also highlighted. This particular lesson proceeds from a teacher-directed mini-lesson with the teacher modeling and explaining for the students to the students working with each other in small groups and pairs. We also emphasize the choices a teacher makes related to materials—visual, graphic and electronic—which present the content in interesting ways and meet varying learning needs and reading levels of the students.

TEACHER AS INQUIRING LEARNER

Since the focus of this text is on the role literacy plays in helping students acquire and use content-area knowledge, we suggest you examine this sample content-area lesson and notice the many opportunities for students to engage in "real" literacy practices.

Make a list of the reading, writing, speaking, and listening activities that students are required to use as they proceed from the whole class preview activity to the culminating assessment activity included in this health lesson.

 SAMPLE LESSON PLAN

Goals and Objectives

We think this is the most important section of a lesson plan: Why are you and your students learning the content and the strategy? If you don't have an important reason, then you are wasting both your students' and your time. We think lessons begin with a teacher goal or goals and student learning objectives:

- A *goal* is your overall purpose for the lesson: what you want to accomplish and in a broad sense what you expect your students to learn.

You may state the goal in general terms, like *understand* or *know*. As you will see in Chapter 10, lesson goals are derived from even larger unit goals.

- *Objectives* are more detailed statements of what students are to learn about content and strategies. For objectives, you use more specific verbs, like *predict* or *diagram*. Objectives are derived from lesson goals and can help you focus your instruction.

For example, in a science/health lesson for high school students, the teacher's lesson plan includes the following goals and objectives:

Goal (major understandings; overall purpose of lesson): To change students' eating habits by building their understanding of the new nutritional guidelines.

Standards (learning standard from the Massachusetts' health curriculum frameworks [Massachusetts Department of Education, 1996]): Students will be able to evaluate health, safety, and nutritional advice and information.

Objectives (specific student learning and/or performances expected to be gained from the lesson): Students will examine and discuss their own ideas about nutrition and consider changes based on the article read by the class.

Content objective (a statement of what students will learn about a specific topic of the lesson): Students will compare the old nutritional guidelines to the new ones.

Strategy objective (a statement of the literacy strategy students will use to help them learn the content objective): Students will interpret the designs of the two graphs for how they portray information about nutritional value.

Materials

The materials or resource section is a list of what you and the students need that period. The sole purpose is to ensure that you gather all the necessary materials for the lesson and that allow you to meet the varying learning needs of your students. For example, in the sample lesson the teacher would need the following items:

- Transparency of circle or pie graph and pyramid graph of nutritional diets

- Newspaper articles such as, "The Power of the Pyramid: The Government's Symbol of Healthful Eating Still Reigns Supreme, but Should It?", the *Washington Post*, January 15, 2003 and "Take the Pyramid, Please", the *Washington Post*, January 28, 2003.

- Internet sources such as Nutrition Spotlight, Growing Nutrition Needs: the Adolescent Years (**www.nalusda.gov/fnic/consumersite/olderkids.htm**), and Are all food guide pyramids created equal? (**www.nalusda.gov/fnic/Fpyr/pyramid.html**).

Pedagogy or Teaching Procedures

This section is a step-by-step outline of the activities that will happen during the period, assuming that you and the class don't get off on a tangent or don't decide to change the activity on the spot. Both of these do happen.

Teaching Procedures

Preview: Whole class

Previewing is chosen to bridge the students' prior knowledge with what they will learn in this lesson. Students will write a list of what they ate yesterday and estimate the nutritional value of each food. As a class, discuss why their diets are or are not nutritional.

Mini-lesson on reading graphs: Whole class

Teacher displays transparency of circle or pie graph. Elicits from students what facts are portrayed on the graph. Asks what nutritional message is portrayed on the graph and what about the graph's design gives that message.

Teacher displays pyramid graph transparency. Asks how the message has changed. Asks students to think about why the government didn't just change the proportion on the circle graph.

Teacher discusses how the manner in which graphs illustrate information affects the way we interpret facts.

Guided practice: Pairs

Students read at least two different sources about the food pyramid. Students are guided by purpose-setting questions such as: What points about a healthful diet does the government think is portrayed well by the graph? What evidence supports the government's healthful diet? Is the pyramid persuasive?

Peer-led Discussions: Small groups engage in considering the following:

1. The pros and cons of the pyramid graph.

2. Why they think the meat and dairy products industry originally opposed changing from the circle pie chart to the pyramid.

3. How their diets yesterday fit with the pyramid. Put items on a pyramid.

Reporting out of small group discussions: Whole class

Assessment and Evaluation

We divide this category into student assessment and lesson evaluation. First, student assessment should answer the question, "How will my students demonstrate they have accomplished the student objectives?" How effectively did students participate in the different activities that made up the lesson? You can add information you have gained from your own observations, anecdotal records, and field notes.

Second, you want to evaluate the lesson as a whole. What helped the students understand? How long did the students need? Did the sequence fit the students' learning needs? You also want to evaluate the student assessment data carefully. Based on your assessment of the students' learning, you determine what the next teaching-learning experiences should be and what should be included in future lessons.

Tools and criteria to evaluate students:

1. Students' list of items in yesterday's diet, and placement of items on a pyramid.

2. Individual student comments about the message of the graphs during mini-lesson.

3. Individual student comments during discussions and reporting out of main points of their discussions—identify pros and cons; speculate on industry objections; evaluate diets.

Lesson evaluation—questions to ask yourself as a teacher:

1. Did the students practice the strategy of interpreting graphs during the reading of the articles?

2. Were the articles and web sites appropriately matched to the students' interest and reading ability?

3. Did the mix of groupings and activities support the students' learning of content and strategies?

Finally, remember that teaching is learning. You can make choices about pedagogy, materials, and assessment tools during a lesson. Try to focus on your students and the information they are giving you about their learning rather than what you are doing. By focusing on students' learning in process as well as the outcomes or products, you will increase your reservoir of knowledge and be better able to select from your repertoire of teaching tools for the next lesson you plan and carry out.

Summary

In this chapter about choices and decisions, we are advocating for variety and against the traditional educational routine: read the textbook at home, lecture next day, and test soon thereafter. Using a variety of texts will give your students the opportunity to:

- **Meet the content in different contexts.**
- **Meet different points of view.**
- **Recognize that the field still entertains questions to be asked and answered.**

Using a variety of communication roles and groupings will support different purposes for learning:

- **Teacher-directed, whole class, or small group mini-lesson learning purposes.**
- **Teacher guided or coached, small groups, pairs, or independent learning purposes.**
- **Student centered, small groups, pairs, or independent learning purposes.**

As you begin your teaching career, we recommend preplanning your choices and decisions using the lesson plan format. As you build a repertoire of teaching tools and a reservoir of knowledge, you will adopt an abbreviated form. To assist you, in Part Two we concentrate on teaching and assessment tools that support literacy strategies. As you read Part Two, think about your content area, and select the literacy strategies and tools that support learning in that area. Once again, you will need to make choices and decisions that support your students and meet their diversity needs.

Inquiry into Your Learning

1. Choose a topic in your content area that you enjoy but haven't had the chance to study in depth. How many different types of texts can you find on that topic? What different information does each text provide? How fair and considerate are the different texts? Would some match well to your students?

2. In one of your college classes or even in a social situation, observe who governs the talk. Does the teacher or the individual respond differently to men than women? Do the men in class act differently than the women do? Interview a talkative man and a talkative woman. How do they view the communication in the classroom? In a social situation, who governs the topic of conversation? Does anyone interrupt?

Inquiry into Your Students' Learning

1. Observe a science or math class and a social studies or English/language arts class. Tally whom the teacher calls on, who receives reprimands, who speaks out. Tally which gender talks more to the whole class or in small group work, or goes unnoticed by the teacher. Did you find gender differences? Did you find gender differences in science or math compared to social studies or English, or did the genders talk the same regardless of the class? Do you think the teacher's gender made a difference?

2. Select a text in your content area. Determine its readability, considerateness, and fairness using the questions for selecting literacy materials in Figure 3.3. Then interview two students about the text: a successful student and a student who is struggling a little. Have each one read the text aloud. Ask each one questions about whether the text was hard or easy to read, about their understanding of the content, and about their opinions of the fairness of the text. Do their views correspond to yours? Why or why not?

Resources

Books

Beers, K., & Lesesne, T. (Eds.). (2001). *Books for you: An annotated booklist for senior high* (14th ed.). Urbana, IL: National Council of Teachers of English. Provides annotated bibliographies for over a thousand texts thematically organized. Lists of award-winning books and web sites with additional book lists are provided in the appendices.

Shulman, J., Lotan, R. A., & Whitcomb, J. A. (Eds.). (1998). *Groupwork in diverse classrooms: A casebook for educators.* New York: Teachers College. Looks at the open-ended dilemmas faced when teachers use group work instead of traditional teaching. Invites readers to submit their reactions to the authors' web site, **www.WestEd.org.**

Tiedt, I. M. (2000). *Teaching with picture books in the middle school.* Newark, DE: International Reading Association. Discusses the benefits of using picture books, including wordless picture books. Suggestions are made for cooperative planning, adaptations for gifted and struggling readers, and text selection. Lesson plans are provided for a wide variety of student objectives.

Wepner, S. B., Valmont, W. J., & Thurlow, R. (Eds.). (2000). *Linking literacy and technology: A guide for K–8 classrooms.* Newark, DE: International Reading Association. Suggests various ways of incorporating technology in the classroom with regard to reading, writing, and the content areas. Recommends specific technological tools for instruction and lesson plans across all grade levels. Addresses for software resources are provided.

Journals

Allington, R. L. (2002). You can't learn much from books you can't read. *Educational Leadership, 60* (3), 16–19. Describes the pitfalls of a single-source curriculum and offers suggestions of how to avoid these problems, such as multilevel resources, student choice and individualized instruction.

Anderson-Inman, L., & Horney, M. (1997). Electronic books for secondary students. *Journal of Adolescent and Adult Literacy, 40* (6), 486–490. Discusses the advantages and disadvantages, the embedded resources, and evaluation criteria for electronic books.

Burke, J. (2002). The internet reader. *Educational Leadership, 60* (3), 38–42. Identifies the skills students need to navigate and interpret text on the Internet. These skills include asking effective questions, setting search goals, anticipating keywords, and scanning and evaluating web sites. Describes two "digital text books" that are used with great success in the classroom.

Fry, E. (2002). Readability versus leveling. *The Reading Teacher, 56* (3), 286–291. Compares and contrasts readability and leveling procedures, noting the benefits and limitations of each. Contains a brief history and an explanation of the process for both procedures.

Ivey, G., & Broaddus, K. (2000). Tailoring the fit: Reading instruction and middle school readers. *The Reading Teacher, 54* (1), 68–78. Proposes ways to address the challenges of reluctant readers, limited and/or mismatched materials, and teachers who feel ill-prepared to teach reading at the middle school level. Also provides a list of texts ranging from picture books to challenging fiction and nonfiction that are appropriate for middle school students.

Lord, T. (1998). Cooperative learning that really works in biology teaching: Using constructivist-based activities to challenge student teams. *American Biology Teacher, 60* (8), 580–588. Discusses the rationale for, problems of, and solutions to group work. Suggestions given on types of questions and activities, like concept maps, charts, and diagrams.

Web Sites

American Memories: Historical Collections for the National Digital Library. **www.memory.loc.gov/ammem/ammemhome.html.** A national digital library of its photos, prints, documents, maps, motion pictures, and sound recordings continually updated by the Library of Congress. The Learning Page has specific classroom ideas and search help for using the collection.

Kathy Schrock's Guide for Educators. **www.school. discovery.com/schrockguide/index.html.** Comprehensive collection of informative web sites and lesson plans for educators (K–12). Also provides links to exemplary web sites for the content areas.

Education Development Center. **www2.edc.org/ literacymatters.** Designed for middle and secondary school educators, this web site provides criteria for text selection, teaching methods for comprehension and response strategies, and guidelines for assessment. Includes links to web sites with booklists for adolescent readers and lesson plans that meet ELA Standards.

PART TWO

Teaching Tools for Strategic Learning

© Michael Zide

CHAPTER 4

Building on Students' Prior Knowledge

KEY CONCEPTS

- **purpose setting, p. 83**
- **activating prior knowledge, p. 84**
- **modeling and explaining, p. 84**
- **content objective, p. 86**
- **strategy objective, p. 86**
- **teaching/assessing tool, p. 89**
- **graphic organizer, p. 89**
- **previewing and predicting, p. 93**
- **monitoring, p. 100**

PURPOSE-SETTING QUESTIONS

1 How do you activate prior knowledge when you begin to read a new book or textbook, write a poem or nonfiction article, observe a science phenomenon, research a historical event or person, solve a mechanical or mathematical problem, create an art object or a special meal?

2 Think about a text you have read in your content area. What prior experiences and prior knowledge did you bring to reading that text? Did you consciously think about your background before you read the text?

3 When you approach a new text, do you preview or skim the text, and predict the content of the text? If you do, how does that help you? If you do not use these strategies, think about why you find no such need.

4 For your assignments, how do you devise your own purpose, within your professors' guidelines, and how do you monitor whether your work is proceeding well?

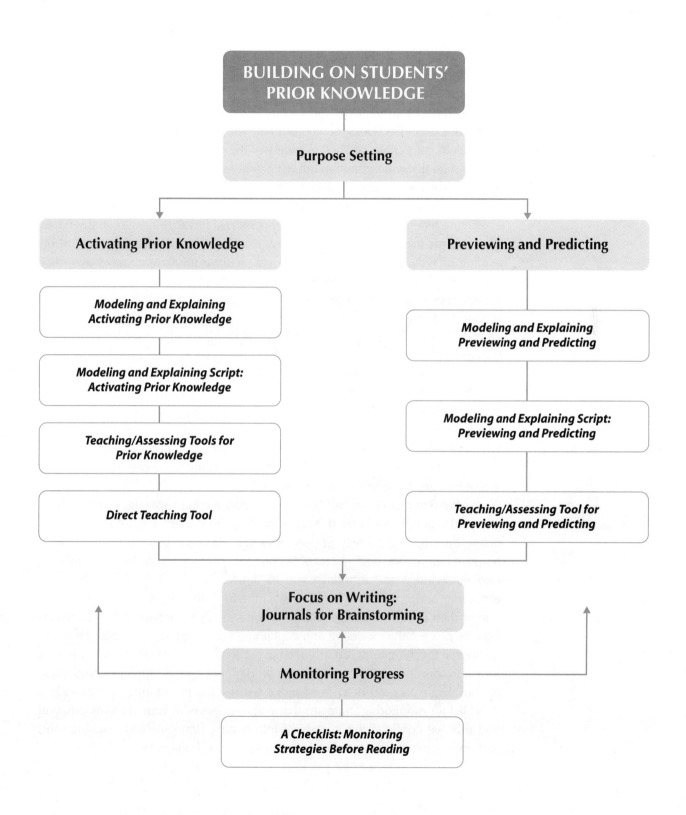

BUILDING ON STUDENTS'
PRIOR KNOWLEDGE

Purpose Setting

Activating Prior Knowledge

Modeling and Explaining
Activating Prior Knowledge

Modeling and Explaining Script:
Activating Prior Knowledge

Teaching/Assessing Tools for
Prior Knowledge

Direct Teaching Tool

Previewing and Predicting

Modeling and Explaining
Previewing and Predicting

Modeling and Explaining Script:
Previewing and Predicting

Teaching/Assessing Tool for
Previewing and Predicting

Focus on Writing:
Journals for Brainstorming

Monitoring Progress

A Checklist: Monitoring
Strategies Before Reading

W hat do you do to prepare yourself for taking a new course? When you reg-
ister for the course, do you read over the course description to learn what
will be covered? Do you think about how this course will build on your previous
courses and fit into your college program or your career plans? After groaning
about the cost of the books, do you skim the Table of Contents or leaf through the
textbook to get a more detailed overview of the course? On the first day of class,
do you skim the syllabus to find out what topics are covered and what the assignments are? If you do any of these things to prepare yourself, you are using strategies to generate ideas or building on your background knowledge.

Before reading, strategic readers call upon two literacy strategies that serve as
springboards from which to launch new learning. First, before they embark on
reading or writing a text, strategic learners *activate prior experiences and prior
knowledge.* They search their schemata for one that will match, or come close to,
the text they're about to begin. Second, strategic readers *preview and predict or
survey the text* and think about what they are likely to learn. Although we have
separated these two strategies in order to analyze and discuss what a strategic
learner can choose to do, you will find that they overlap and intertwine. Strategic
learners flexibly skip from one strategy to another, or use them in combination.

Underlying the literacy strategies are two ongoing strategies, *purpose setting*
and *monitoring*, which begin before starting a task and continue throughout it.
At the beginning of a task, strategic learners set their purpose, which guides their
selection of effective strategies. They also begin to monitor their progress
(or are metacognitively aware, a key term in Chapter 1) to determine whether
they have selected effective strategies.

As the first chapter in Part Two, we introduce you to specific literacy strategies and teaching tools used before reading. (See chapter graphic.) First, we
define the ongoing strategy of purpose setting because usually people have a
purpose before they begin to read. Second, we present the strategy of activating
prior knowledge and introduce you to the teaching tool of a modeling and
explaining script, followed by other teaching tools that support students' activation of their prior knowledge. Third, for the strategy of previewing and predicting, we present the modeling and explaining teaching tool in a script and then
additional teaching tools. Fourth, we have a section, Focus on Writing: Journals
for Brainstorming, that introduces several different entries students could make
as they begin to read or write. Finally, we discuss monitoring and provide a
checklist for monitoring strategies that you may use with your students. You will
find that we continue this pattern of introducing strategies and teaching tools
and ending with writing and monitoring in all the chapters in Part Two.

Purpose Setting

Do you use the purpose-setting questions at the beginning of each chapter in this book? You know that if you have a purpose for a task, such as reading a text, you will be more motivated to attend to the task. When people set purposes before reading, they keep those purposes in mind to guide their reading. Sometimes, they change their purposes, discover a new purpose, or find the text doesn't fit their purposes. When strategic readers tackle unfamiliar topics, they often refine their purposes as they read more. For example, when researching new topics, students often begin with general purposes and then refine to more specific purposes when they narrow their research topics.

Purpose setting is important to model first because strategic learners determine what schemata to activate, what knowledge to seek, and what information to remember based on their purposes. When learners have a purpose, they construct meaning and build the schemata purposefully rather than aimlessly memorize facts. Second, strategic learners use purpose setting to determine which strategies to use. For example, since reading for entertainment and reading to analyze an argument have two different purposes, strategic readers select different literacy strategies. And finally, strategic learners know when their tasks are completed because they know they have accomplished their purposes.

Before every modeling and explaining script, we state a purpose for reading the text. You will notice that in the editorial script in this chapter, the reader's purpose is very general in the beginning and changes to a specific purpose.

> **purpose setting**
> Establishing a reason or goal for reading a text.

[handwritten marginalia: motivates attention to text]

Activating Prior Knowledge

You probably *activate prior knowledge* and experience every day of your life when you face new experiences. For example, when you order from a restaurant menu, do you choose the steak, which you know, or the ostrich, which is unfamiliar? In school, you also activate your past knowledge, as you do when you think about last semester's foreign language course to make this semester's course easier. When strategic learners begin a new course for which they have little prior knowledge, they search their memory for any ideas that might be related to the course. When they activate their prior knowledge and experiences, they search their schemata for a match. When they find a schema that matches, then they have *hooks* on which to attach new learning.

We discuss strategies for activating prior experiences and prior knowledge because as a content-area teacher, you want to figure out what schemata your diverse students bring to your content area. Remember from Chapter 1 that we think general strategies are specifically applied in content areas. In Figure 4.1, we show how the strategy of activating prior knowledge can be specifically applied to literacy texts. (In each graphic for a strategy, we will suggest how it can be specifically applied to texts.) Figure 4.1 also shows the variety of teaching tools that you can select to use in your classroom. Because in this book we focus on literacy strategies that support content learning, first we present the teaching tool, modeling and

> **activating prior knowledge** Recalling what one learned or experienced.

[handwritten marginalia: also can clear up misconceptions]

Students activating their prior knowledge before reading the newspaper.
© Michael Zide

explaining, to demonstrate how a strategic reader activates prior experiences and prior knowledge.

■ Modeling and Explaining Activating Prior Knowledge

Throughout this chapter, and all the other chapters in Part Two, you will find modeling and explaining scripts that illustrate literacy strategies in action. Before we present the first one to you, we need to clarify three points.

modeling and explaining
A teaching tool in which you show how to use strategy and tell why and when you use the strategy.

First, you recall from Chapters 1 and 3 that *modeling and explaining* is a teaching tool that seeks to make literacy strategies visible. Using material that the students might read in different content areas, we select specific literacy strategies, explicitly identify the strategies, and tell why, when, and how to use them (Paris, Lipson, & Wixson, 1994). Remember that nonstrategic learners, who may not be metacognitively aware, need clear, direct statements. Because we are communicating to you in print, we present primarily teacher-directed mini-lessons in our modeling and explaining scripts because they are the clearest to demonstrate in a textbook. However, we also recommend teacher-guided mini-lessons in which you and your students discuss the strategies to use, as well as why, when, and how to use them. Students could also model and explain strategies to each other. Depending on how strategic your students are and how difficult the text and the content are, you will decide whether to model and explain through teacher-directed, teacher-guided, or student-to-student mini-lessons.

Second, you will notice that we use the "I" pronoun in the modeling and explaining scripts because on the printed page only one person's use of strategies can be visible. For example, although we both would activate prior experiences and knowledge, the specific knowledge would vary depending on which of us modeled because each of us has different schemata.

Third, in order to model and explain to you, the reading process needs to be slowed down. The newspaper editorial in the first script is not difficult to read, so we use our strategies automatically. For example, we know that an editorial tries to persuade, so we would not explicitly explain that to ourselves. But to model and explain to you, or any other student, we need to be explicit so that our automatic strategies are visible.

FIGURE 4.1 Prior Knowledge

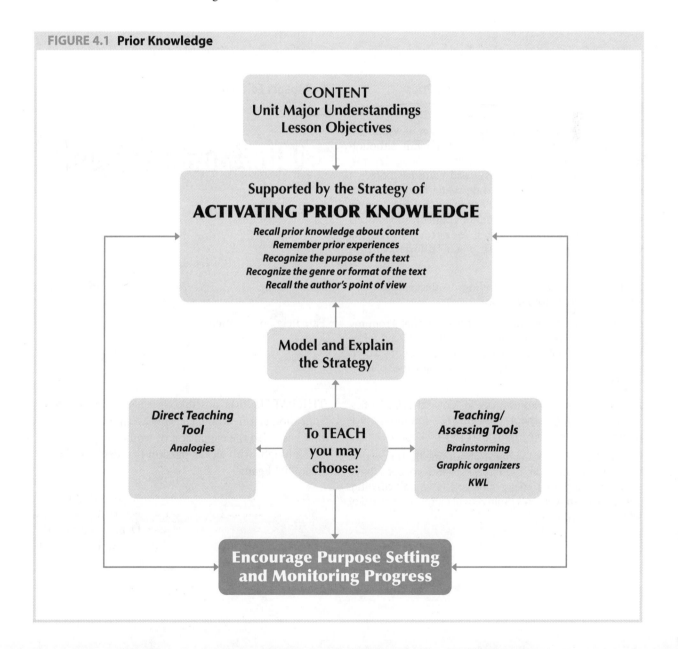

content objective A statement of what students will learn about the specific topic of the lesson.

strategy objective A statement of the literacy strategy students will use to help them learn the content objective.

For this modeling and explaining script, pretend that your class is studying the Constitution and the Bill of Rights. Your major understanding or goal is for students to recognize that these are living documents that continue to affect our lives today. For this lesson, your *content objective* is for the students to take a position on equal rights. You also have a *strategy objective*: for the students to recognize how to activate prior knowledge before reading.

As you read this script, notice that one of the authors is activating her prior knowledge about the topic, the source or author, and the purpose of the text:

 ## Modeling and Explaining Script: Activating Prior Knowledge

Modeling and Explaining How I Use My Prior Knowledge

Because the *Boston Globe* is my hometown newspaper, I read it regularly. I often agree with its opinions, although not always. My first strategy is that I recognize the source or author. Since I have read editorials before, I know an editor's purpose is to persuade readers to support the opinion or take an action in the community. When I read, I will look for the editor's opinion and reasons and then decide whether I agree. My second strategy is that I recognize the purpose of an editorial: to persuade.

So, I set my purpose for reading: to decide whether I agree with the editor's opinion.

I read the title to find the topic of the editorial. From my prior knowledge of vocabulary, I think "Fair Play" refers both to equal rights and to sports. I conclude it's about equal rights for women in sports. I also enjoy the "play on words."

I recall my prior experiences in high school athletics. When I was in high school—before 1972—few girls participated in sports and few sports were offered to girls.

I activate my prior knowledge about Title IX. I know that women's athletics in high schools and colleges have expanded and that many girls are now participating. There are even women's professional teams— unheard of when I went to school.

Newspaper Editorial

The Boston Globe

Fair Play For Women

THE BATTLE over possible changes in the 1972 equal education statute known simply as Title IX—a law that has aided the expansion of women's sports—is being fought with all the passion that explodes in a really tight game.

Continued

I also **activate my prior knowledge** about the two sides of the issue. I've read articles quoting men's wrestling coaches who think their sport has been cut because money is going to Title IX. I've also read news articles quoting women's coaches' responses, such as the huge budgets for football.

From my **prior knowledge about editorials**, I recognize that the words, "Paige should blow the whistle" and "consider the recent recommendations" is the opinion of *The Globe.*

I decide to read what those recommendations are and whether I agree with them because I also don't want Title IX weakened. Thus, I have **set my purpose** of continuing to read.

"Fair Play for Women," *The Boston Globe,* February 8, 2002, p. A14.

Both sides think they deserve to win and the other team isn't playing fair.

US Secretary of Education Rod Paige should blow the whistle on the rhetoric—and politics—and consider the recent recommendations for changes in the implementation of the law with a cool, fair eye that seeks compromise in some details but does not weaken the foundation of what both sides agree has justifiably blown open the locker room doors and initiated an electrifying boom in women's sports.

To summarize, at the beginning of reading the editorial, I explicitly modeled and explained my strategies for activating my prior knowledge and for setting a purpose. When I read the editorial:

1. I activated my prior knowledge about the source, The Boston Globe. (I often read and agree with my hometown newspaper.)

2. I activated my prior knowledge about the purpose of an editorial (to persuade readers).

3. I set my own purpose for reading (to decide if I agree with the editor) and later refined my purpose (consider whether I agree with the recommendations).

4. I used my prior knowledge about vocabulary (recognized the topic from the title and enjoyed the play on words).

5. I recalled my prior experiences (in high school athletics before Title IX).

6. I activated my prior knowledge (about Title IX and about the two sides of the issue).

In every content area, you can model and explain activating prior knowledge about the content, the source, and the intent or purpose of a text.

■ Teaching/Assessing Tools for Prior Knowledge

You want to know what knowledge your students are bringing to your content area so that you can plan instruction to match what the students need. Frequently when teachers assess students' prior knowledge, they are confronted with three different scenarios—little prior knowledge, misconceptions or mismatches in prior knowledge, and elaborate prior knowledge (Graves & Slater, 1996). As a content-area teacher, you will meet these scenarios many times, especially with your diverse students; so let's discuss each scenario.

DIVERSITY

First, some diverse students may bring little prior knowledge to the content area. LD students, who shun reading, will not have gained the background knowledge that comes from independent reading of a variety of texts. LD students may also have missed content-area lessons because they were in the resource room. ELL students may not know the content in their first language, much less in English. Immigrant students or migrant worker students may not have had much schooling and so had little chance for learning in content areas. Without wide reading and previous schooling, diversity students will have meager prior knowledge.

However, diverse students may have out-of-school experiences you can draw on. Many ELL and immigrant students serve as translators for parents, as a result they read a wide range of everyday texts—labels, forms, manuals, letters. Immigrant students and parents often pool their prior knowledge to understand texts, such as a jury summons (Orellana, Reynolds, Dorner, & Meza, 2003). As a social studies teacher, you can build on the prior knowledge they do have about the jury summons text in your study of the judicial system. For this scenario, you will search for any related knowledge that might serve as a bridge between what the students are to learn and what is familiar to them.

Second, students may have misconceptions or mismatches in their prior knowledge garnered from their everyday experiences or from their cultural background. Many people mistakenly think that stars twinkle, that heavy objects fall faster, and that Pluto is always farthest from the sun; you might hold one of those everyday misconceptions! In Chapter 2, we discussed the mismatch when Indian readers read about an American wedding. Diverse students, especially ELL students, may experience a mismatch between their own language and culture and an author's. If you have read Shakespeare or Zora Neale Hurston, you may have had a mismatch between your language and Shakespeare's Elizabethan English or Hurston's dialect. When you recognize that a student may have a mismatch or misconception, your instruction should aim to point that out and clarify it.

Third, students, especially those who read widely or are interested in the topic, may bring elaborate prior knowledge to your content area. LD students, who often have particular topics of interest, will persistently struggle through texts to learn more information (Fink, 1995–1996). Some diverse students may have studied the content because curriculum topics were sequenced differently in their home country. Affluent SES students will probably have read widely in their first language and have many print texts in both languages at home. Diverse students may attend community organizations or churches that support not only learning about their heritage but also school learning. They may be able to augment your curriculum with their cultural knowledge. Whenever students bring elaborate knowledge to any content area, they need opportunities to investigate topics in-depth through problem-solving situations and investigations in the community, and through contact with outside experts on the topic.

Assessing a student's or a class's prior knowledge is not a simple task. Sometimes, teachers discover students' misconceptions and mismatches during instruction rather than before. Nevertheless, teachers still try to assess prior knowledge in order to plan instruction better.

teaching/assessing tool
A teaching tool that supports a student's learning and through which a teacher can assess the student's progress.

Since we present this tool for the first time in Part Two, remember how we defined ***teaching/assessing tools*** in Chapter 3. You recall that you can assess and teach simultaneously, depending on your purpose or point of view in a particular situation. For example, using brainstorming, you teach your students to activate their prior knowledge so that they can use their schemata to learn the information in the text. At the same time, you use brainstorming to evaluate what background knowledge your students bring to a new unit—using the tool for assessment.

Remember too that your goal is to foster independent, strategic learners. You want to encourage learners to use these tools to activate their own prior knowledge, first under your guidance and then independently. Thus, as you use these teaching/assessing tools, you can also model and explain to your students why and how to use them independently.

Brainstorming

Brainstorming, or compiling a list of all the words associated with or related to a topic, is a common activity for exploring what students already know. You will want to notice what type of words the students are listing: everyday words or specialized words. For example, a teacher asked students to list all the words they associated with Native Americans, the topic of the new unit, because he wanted to know what factual information and what misconceptions the students had. The teacher found that the students' prior knowledge came from westward expansion texts and movies and that they had little cultural knowledge about the different nations.

English and language arts teachers often use brainstorming when students use dreary words in their writings. Students can be encouraged to rehabilitate tired words, such as *said* and *went,* by brainstorming lists of more descriptive, precise, and livelier alternatives. (A mini-lesson on the thesaurus could be combined with this brainstorming.)

Graphic Organizers

graphic organizers
Drawings that represent categorization systems visually and can have a variety of designs.

You will find that educators use many terms for schemata representations. Science educators refer to *models* or *concept models;* for example, they will ask students to draw a model of what the inside of the earth looks like. English and language arts educators often refer to semantic maps; they place the topic in a center circle, with categories radiating out (Figure 4.2 is an example). Math and science educators often refer to a *hierarchical representation;* they subdivide categories in a tree branching form. We will use the term ***graphic organizer*** to refer to all categorization systems, whatever the particular shape—whether webs, radiating suns, hierarchical trees, or a unique design. We have included graphic organizers as a teaching/assessing tool in many chapters (and in different sections in this chapter) because we have found them to be useful representations of students' schemata at various points in the learning process. You may also have noticed that we use graphic organizers at the beginning of every chapter, as well as inside the Part Two chapters, to help you organize your schema for the upcoming information in the chapter.

In many content areas, if the students categorize the words in a brainstorming session, you could consider the categorization as a representation of their schema. In

FIGURE 4.2 Seventh Graders' Graphic Organizer of Their Prior Knowledge

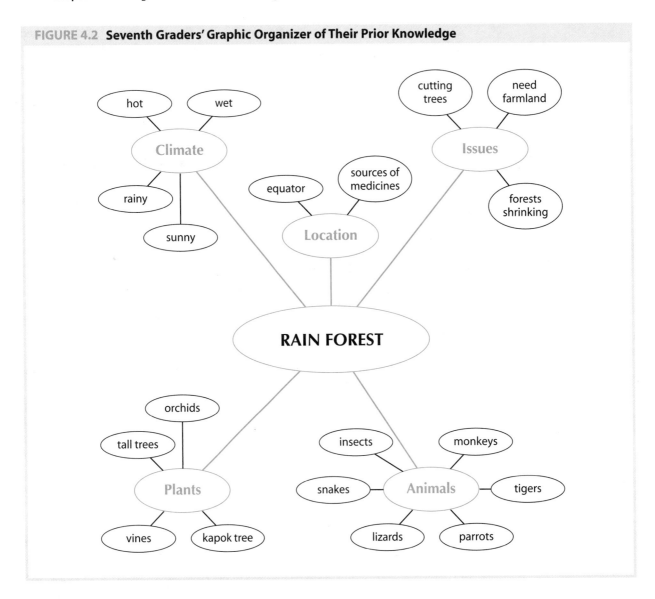

assessing graphic organizers, you are interested in discovering what categories of information the students have and what information is in each category without any hints from you. When a seventh-grade teacher used a graphic organizer in a lesson on the rain forest (see Figure 4.2), she noticed the students had no categories for different layers of the rain forest and had only superficial knowledge of the plants and animals.

When we teach, we ask students to categorize their ideas in any design that shows how the categories might be related. As the students develop their graphic organizers, they talk about the categories and the items in specific categories. That discussion of their prior knowledge is often a more important learning experience than creating the actual graphic organizer. As the students learn, they often revise these graphic organizers, both during the study and at the end.

KWL (Know—Want to Know—Learned)

KWL was designed to elicit students' prior knowledge and to arouse their curiosity about a text through exploring three separate topics: What We Know, What We Want to Find Out, and What We Learned and Still Need to Know (Ogle, 1986). First, the class brainstorms. What We Know about a topic—children's jobs in Figure 4.3—as you record their ideas. After students have generated their prior knowledge, they organize their ideas into categories of information and add categories they predict will be subtopics in texts they'll read. Using their categories and any confusing or conflicting ideas that have emerged, you help the class formulate questions for What We Want to Find Out. From the whole class discussion, the students individually could record their prior knowledge, questions, and categories on their own KWL sheets. After reading a text or different texts, they record What We Learned and Still Need to Learn or notes and new questions on their sheets. Finally, you and the class would discuss the information gained, any questions not answered, and new questions that arose. Thus, KWL begins with students' activating their prior knowledge and continues to support their learning during reading (examined in Chapters 6 and 7) and after reading (in Chapter 8).

FIGURE 4.3 KWL Chart About Children's Jobs

What We Know	What We Want to Find Out About Past Jobs	What We Learned and Still Need to Learn
paper route	1. Where did children work?	
baby-sitting	2. How many hours?	
raking leaves	3. How old were they?	
mowing lawn	4. How did they go to school?	
walking dogs		
getting good grades	5. How hard were their jobs?	
washing dishes	6. How much did they get paid?	
cleaning my room		
farm chores	7. Did they have to work?	
delivering things	8. What kinds of work did they do?	
house chores		
sewing		

Categories

1. Jobs we do

2. Jobs in the past

3. Conditions of work

4. Schooling

Variations have been suggested for the original KWL. In KWL Plus (Carr & Ogle, 1987), the students organize What They Have Learned in a graphic organizer and then write a summary about the topic. We encourage students to summarize both the information learned and the new questions they now have. When students write summaries, they have the opportunity to integrate their prior knowledge and newly learned information into their schemata, which helps them remember the information (see Chapter 8). Laverick (2002) suggests a B-D-A for vocational high school students—Before (what you know), During (notes about new information read), After (summary and three questions to ask other students).

TEACHER AS INQUIRING LEARNER

Assess the prior knowledge a middle school or high school student has about a topic in your content area. Ask the student to complete one of the teaching/assessing tools, like a brainstorming list or a graphic organizer. Let him or her work independently for a while. When you think the student has no more ideas, then ask him or her to tell you about what is written. New ideas may occur to the student during the telling. When you think the student really has no more ideas, you could ask a few questions about the topic to probe for any remaining knowledge. You may also want to ask the student where or how he or she gained this knowledge—in school or from the Internet, for example. When you have finished, analyze the student's knowledge.

- What did the student know well, and what not at all? Did the student have any misconceptions? In what aspects of the topic would you instruct the student?

■ Direct Teaching Tool

You recall from Chapter 3 that we define direct teaching tools as when the teacher imparts specific information to students. When you use this tool, you dominate the communication more than you do with the interactive teaching/assessing tools.

Analogies

Teachers use familiar topics and experiences from their students' prior knowledge and cultural backgrounds to create analogies. The purpose of an analogy is to use a familiar topic as a bridge to the unfamiliar, new topic. Obviously analogies must make sense to your students (Brown, 1992). Does the following example make sense to you?

> If you know how to skateboard, then you will find snowboarding simple to master. In both skateboarding and snowboarding, you place your feet and balance your weight similarly on a board. In both, jumps and stunts use the contour of the terrain as the basis for the stunt. However, in skateboarding, your feet are not attached to the board, while in snowboarding your feet are fixed to the board with a binding system. As a result, you will be able to do different types of stunts in snowboarding than skateboarding and won't land without your board.

You may understand the target topic, snowboarding, if you are familiar with skateboarding. If you are not familiar with skateboarding, the analogy will not be helpful to you. Notice in the example that we pointed out the similarities as well as the differences. No analogy is a perfect match, so students need to distinguish how the target topic is different from the familiar one. The familiar topic is only a bridge, not a replica.

Science teachers use analogies to explain phenomena that students cannot observe. They also use models as analogies for phenomena. For example, when thinking about carbon atoms, scientists pictured Buckminster Fuller's geodesic dome and named the model "Bucky Ball." That model served as an analogy while they tried to find evidence for the structure of carbon atoms.

These tools for activating prior knowledge and prior experiences will tell you what your students bring to your content area. When you teach your students to activate their prior knowledge and experiences, you will decide whether to model and explain strategies in action, use a teaching/assessing tool, or use a direct teaching tool, depending on your students' strategy use and content-learning needs.

Now let's turn to the previewing and predicting strategy.

Previewing and Predicting

Strategic learners try to figure out what is ahead. For example, strategic learners read through a mathematics problem to get a general sense of what information is given in the problem and what is unknown, as well as to predict or estimate an answer. In addition, they might paraphrase the problem in their own words to check their own understanding of the problem.

previewing and predicting Surveying and guessing the topics in the text.

Figure 4.4 shows how the strategy of *previewing and predicting* may be specifically applied to texts and also the ways you may choose to teach those strategies. Because most students rarely preview textbook chapters (except perhaps to count the number of pages), we first present a modeling and explaining script that takes advantage of the format or chapter aids. Before you read the script, think about whether you use the chapter aids that we have included in this book: the chapter graphics, the purpose-setting questions, and the subheads that divide the chapter into sections. Strategic learners quickly skim chapters to preview and predict what they will learn; they will read carefully later.

■ Modeling and Explaining Previewing and Predicting

Before we presented the first script in this chapter, we stated that most of our modeling and explaining scripts would be teacher directed because we are communicating to you in print. However, since we recommend that you use teacher-guided modeling and explaining mini-lessons, we present a teacher-guided one in this second script. When you want to involve students in an interactive discussion of strategies some of them might be using, then you would choose a teacher-guided modeling and explaining mini-lesson. Because the students are directly involved here in a back-and-forth exchange, this think-aloud script reads a bit differently from the previous script. In this script, the students and one of the authors (the "we" in the script) worked on the strategies together. This is an excerpt of the chapter because you don't need every example of a strategy to understand its use. When you model and explain with your students, you would include as many instances of the strategies as your students need and maybe every instance.

Pretend for this script that the unit's major understanding is how different cultures influence each other: Egypt and Nubia in ancient times as well as the United States and other countries today. The students will begin by reading the textbook and then read additional resources. For this chapter, the *content objective* is a comparison of the cultures of Egypt and Nubia, and the *strategy objective* is for students to recognize how to preview and predict using chapter aids. For this modeling and explaining script, assume the students have little prior knowledge about ancient Egypt and none about Nubia. As you read the script, notice the chapter aids incorporated into previewing:

FIGURE 4.4 Strategies and Tools for Previewing and Predicting

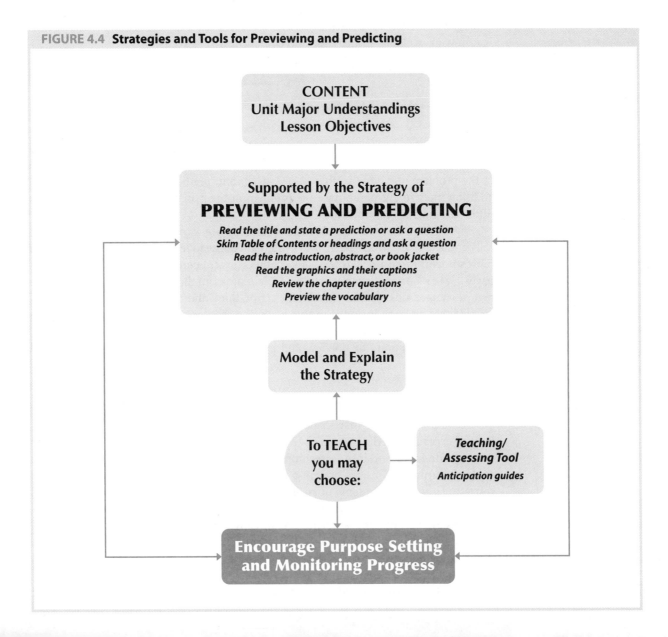

Modeling and Explaining Script: Previewing and Predicting

Modeling and Explaining with Students

Textbook chapters have several aids that help readers understand their content. When we read or **preview** those aids first, we prepare ourselves to read the whole chapter more easily. So let's discuss how we can use the **strategy of previewing** with each chapter aid.

The first aid to **preview** is the chapter title to learn the major topics of the chapter and then to use the strategy of **activating our background knowledge**. Who knows what and where the Nile is? What else do we know about the Nile River? What kingdoms are located on the Nile? Okay, Egypt is obviously one; do we know any others? No? Okay; so we have a question to answer when we read.

That's another strategy: **asking questions** to **predict** what we might learn.

The second aid to **preview** is the Thinking Focus box. The authors are **setting a purpose** for our reading. When we have a purpose, we stay focused our task.

The third aid to **preview** is a list of key vocabulary. Let's see if we can define the words . . ..

Let's read page 84, where *dynasty* is defined. Who can state the definition in his or her own words?

Where have you heard *dynasty* used? Why did basketball fans refer to the Chicago Bulls as a dynasty?

Social Studies Textbook

LESSON 1

Kingdoms on the Nile

THINKING FOCUS

Describe differences in the way kingdoms developed in ancient Egypt and ancient Nubia

Key terms
- delta
- cataract
- dynasty
- pharaoh

If you stood on the green banks of Egypt's Nile River and began walking west, the green under your feet would vanish within a few miles…

Prehistoric rock paintings show that the Sahara once supported human and animal life. Colorful paintings have been found throughout the desert.

Thinking Focus: Describe differences in the way kingdoms developed in ancient Egypt and ancient Nubia

Key terms: *delta, cataract, dynasty, pharaoh*

UNDERSTANDING DYNASTY

What Is a Dynasty?

A dynasty is not the same as a king. A dynasty is a series of rulers who descended from the same person. Egypt s First Dynasty had eight rulers. The Thirteenth Dynasty had about 70 rulers.

Continued

The fourth aid to preview is the headings and subheadings that divide the chapter into sub-topics. We should skim them to figure out how the chapter is organized and to see if we have any prior knowledge. Remember the purpose? What do you predict the topics of two sections will be?

Let's find the headings on pages 84 and 85.

What predictions can we make about what will be covered?

"Who are the kings of Egypt?"

Look at the time line on page 85.

Previewing a graphic can help us predict or ask questions about what we want to learn. Does anyone have a question about the time line?

"Why did Egypt rule Nubia and then Nubia rule Egypt?"

Where have you heard dynasty used? Why did basketball fans refer to the Chicago Bulls as a dynasty?

Egypt, Land of the Pharaohs

Trapping and storing the floodwaters of the Nile was a mighty job. Leaders emerged to organize such big projects. Between 4000 and 3000 B.C., some of these leaders grew very powerful.

No one knows exactly how kingdoms developed along the Nile. Some experts now believe that a group of people in Lower Nubia had the first government with kings of great power. These scholars also say that Egypt's first kings may have descended

The Beginning of History

A clearer picture of the history of kings emerges after about 3000 B.C. That is when the first written records appear. Historians are now debating whether the first writing is Egyptian, as is generally thought, or whether it is actually Nubian.

Kings and Kingdoms

Thirty dynasties ruled Egypt for nearly 3,000 years. Historians divide Egypt's ancient past into three periods, called kingdoms. On the timeline below, trace Egypt's Old, Middle, and New kingdoms.

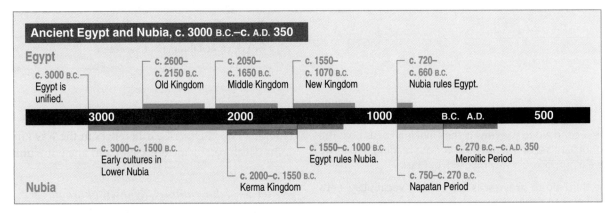

From *To See a World: World Cultures and Geography* in HOUGHTON MIFFLIN SOCIAL STUDIES by Armento, et al. Copyright © 1994 by Houghton Mifflin Company. Reprinted by permission of Houghton Mifflin Company. All rights reserved.

In this modeling and explaining script, I previewed the chapter aids, eliciting student contributions as I guided them through the following strategies:

1. After introducing them to the usefulness of chapter aids, the class and I previewed the chapter title to activate prior knowledge: Egypt. We also asked questions to predict what we might learn (the second kingdom).

2. We previewed the Thinking Focus box to clarify the purpose for reading the chapter (comparing the kingdoms of Egypt and Nubia).

3. We **previewed** the **key vocabulary words** to define them (*dynasty*, for example).

4. We **previewed** the **major headings to predict** the chapter organization (a section on Egypt and another on Nubia).

5. From the **subheadings**, we made **predictions** or **asked questions** about what we might learn (the kings of Egypt).

6. And finally, we **previewed the graphics** (the time line) and **predicted or asked questions** about what we wanted to learn (Why did Egypt rule Nubia and then Nubia rule Egypt?).

Thus, by skimming the chapter aids, we gained an overview of the information and set a purpose. In addition, we activated what prior knowledge we had, made predictions, and asked questions.

By modeling and explaining interactively with your students, you can assess how they use the chapter aids, whether they understand how the sidebars or graphics relate to the text (Afflerbach & VanSledright, 2001), and what prior knowledge they bring to the text. You may decide they are ready to read the chapter or you may decide to build more background knowledge first.

Now let's discuss teaching/assessing tools that you may select to support your students' prediction about texts.

■ Teaching/Assessing Tool for Previewing and Predicting

Because students tend to plunge right into their reading without previewing or predicting, you may decide to introduce a teaching/assessing tool, such as anticipation guides. When you introduce the tool, you will explain to the students that previewing and predicting will alert them to the content of the text.

Anticipation Guides

Sometimes students need hints to access their prior knowledge. To get thoughts and opinions flowing, students could complete an *anticipation guide* in pairs or independently.

The following steps for creating an effective anticipation guide (Duffelmeyer, 1994) are based on Herber's (1978) ideas about using prediction to arouse students' interest:

1. Determine the most important ideas to be learned.

2. Write five to seven statements about the important ideas that:

   a. activate the students' prior knowledge.

   b. invite students' opinions.

   c. challenge students' beliefs and misconceptions.

3. Reproduce the statements on a worksheet and add "agree" or "disagree" columns, which students will check. (See Figure 4.5.) Individually or in small groups, students indicate whether they agree or disagree with the statements. In addition, they must defend their responses to their peers.

FIGURE 4.5   Anticipation Guide for a Study of Gandhi

Agree	Disagree	Statements
_____	_____	1. Gandhi came from a prosperous and influential family.
_____	_____	2. While in law school, Gandhi dressed and behaved like a British gentleman.
_____	_____	3. In South Africa, Gandhi did not suffer the discrimination that blacks did.
_____	_____	4. In South Africa, Gandhi found his voice and acted against prejudice.
_____	_____	5. After witnessing the brutal treatment of Zulus, Gandhi agreed that violence should be met with violence.
_____	_____	6. Gandhi was never taken seriously by the British government.
_____	_____	7. Hindus and Muslims learned to coexist in India.

You can assess your students' predictions right away by observing how they respond and defend their responses in pairs, small groups, or whole class discussions. You might infer how their prior knowledge and diverse backgrounds might have influenced their predictions.

TEACHER AS INQUIRING LEARNER

Construct an anticipation guide. Find an informational book, a magazine article, or a newspaper article about a topic, issue, or problem related to your content area. Think about what prior knowledge, opinions, beliefs, and misconceptions students might have. Using your best estimate of their prior knowledge and opinions, write five to eight statements that invite students to think about the topic and even to take a position. Add "before" and "after" columns for students to check. You could construct an anticipation guide for a problem and possible solutions or an issue and various perspectives if you wish.

If you have the opportunity, use your anticipation guide with a small group of students. Have them discuss and complete the "before" column in pairs. After reading the text, the pairs complete the "after" column and discuss their answers. When everyone has finished, the whole group would compare their answers and discuss their reasons.

Think about what the group predicted and what they learned.

- How would you change the guide the next time?

Anticipation guides can be extended to after reading (the topic of Chapter 8). By changing the guide to include a "before reading" column to be checked first and then an "after reading" column to be checked later, students can record whether they changed their predictions. A further extension would have students write why they did or did not change their predictions and what information supported their stance (Duffelmeyer, Baum, & Merkley, 1987). You and your students can evaluate how their ideas changed, turning a teaching tool into an assessing tool.

In summary, the strategy of previewing and predicting is often used in concert with activating prior knowledge because strategic learners preview in order to learn what schemata to search for. Now let's turn to using these strategies in writing.

Focus on Writing: Journals for Brainstorming

Journals (also called learning logs) are places for students to record the evolution of their thinking and to express their personal reactions to both the content and the process of their learning. Thus, journals are a hybrid between diaries, which contain only subjective, personal reactions to events, and class notebooks that contain only objective, subject matter notes (Fulwiler, 1987). Journal entries may include drawings, diagrams, models, math problems, lists, phrases, sentences, or even paragraphs. The form of this writing is unconstrained and free-wheeling because the purpose is to understand one's thinking. We suggest several forms of brainstorming here.

As a part of your instructional plans, you may assign prompts, or questions, to direct students' entries. An ELL teacher asks his students to write their ideas in their native language on the left page and then in English on the facing page, providing a tool for the students to use their native language to support their growing English vocabulary. Teachers often ask students to record their brainstorming, graphic organizers, or KWLs in journals because the students can reread and revise them later as they learn.

Journals can also contain entries called freewriting. As originally designed (Elbow, 1973), students were asked to write on any topic for about fifteen minutes without interruption to increase their writing fluency. Teachers have since adapted freewriting for other purposes, such as to set a purpose for the class, cue prior knowledge, and make predictions about upcoming content. For example, before beginning a new novel, Robin McKinley's *The Hero and the Crown*, an English/language arts teacher asked the students to write about "What makes a hero a hero?" After writing, the students shared their characteristics that define a hero and their examples of heroes. Based on the characteristics of known heroes, the students predicted what the characteristics of Aerin, the heroine, would be. After observing scientific phenomena, students could complete a freewriting about their observations and predictions regarding subsequent observations or investigations. For example, after working with parallel electrical circuits, students could diagram and write their predictions for serial circuits.

Journals can also be a source for writing ideas when students compose their own entries. Students often brainstorm topics for writing and their knowledge about a topic in journals. Sometimes composing a graphic organizer helps students find a specific focus within a broad topic. A specific graphic organizer could be a positive and negative

FIGURE 4.6 **Significant Positives and Negatives Time Line**

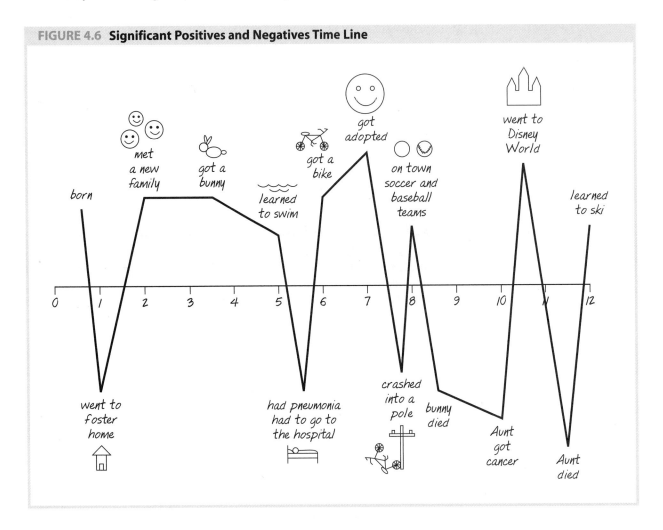

time line (Rief, 1992). For example, Tom used the time line graph shown in Figure 4.6 to record the high of being adopted and the low of his aunt's death.

Now that we've presented literacy strategies to you, let's discuss monitoring.

Monitoring Progress

During a learning task, like reading this book, do you monitor how your learning is progressing? Throughout learning and literacy tasks, strategic learners keep their purpose in mind and monitor their use of specific strategies until they decide they have accomplished their purpose and the task.

You recognize that *monitoring* is really being metacognitively aware of both content and strategies. First, you want your students to be aware of the content they know and what they don't know. Then they can construct meaning and build their schemata. When

monitoring Being metacognitively aware of content and strategies.

students can identify their misunderstandings or errors, then you will have clear direction for your instruction.

Second, strategic learners are aware of their strategies and monitor how well their strategies match the specific task. If their progress is smooth, then strategic learners may let their strategies work automatically. However, when their progress is stymied, strategic learners try to figure out why their strategies are not working and often do change strategies.

In most of the modeling and explaining scripts, our monitoring statements indicate successful learning of content and highlight successful use of different strategies. However, since students benefit from seeing what strategic learners do when they are confused or not comprehending, don't hesitate to model how to remediate confusion.

In Chapters 4 through 9, you will find a monitoring checklist at the end of each chapter. Each monitoring checklist contains generic statements related to the strategies discussed in the chapter as well as purpose setting. We present a checklist for you to use with your students because we have found a monitoring checklist useful in building metacognitive awareness, especially among less strategic learners.

A Checklist: Monitoring Strategies Before Reading

Purpose Setting
❑ Have you set a purpose for reading (or writing)?

Activating Prior Knowledge
❑ Do you have any background knowledge you can activate?
❑ Do you recognize the purpose, genre, or format of the text?
❑ Have you read this author before and so know the author's likely point of view?

Previewing and Predicting
❑ Have you previewed the text to help you activate your background knowledge?
❑ Did you find the title, subheads, graphics, or other chapter aids helpful in predicting what the text would contain?
❑ Did you skim the table of contents and ask questions to guide your reading?

SUMMARY

In this chapter, we have concentrated on the beginning of a literacy task: building on prior knowledge. We have emphasized four categories of strategies:

- **Purpose setting**
- **Activating prior knowledge**
- **Previewing and predicting**
- **Monitoring progress**

Strategic learners select specific strategies and use them in concert to build their background knowledge when they are beginning a literacy task. To teach these strategies, we have described specific teaching tools:

- **Modeling and explaining the strategies with texts the students read in your content area to make the strategies visible to students**
- **Teaching/assessing tools to support students' learning of strategies and content, such as brainstorming, graphic organizers, KWL, and anticipation guides**
- **Direct teaching tool to impart information to students, such as analogies**
- **Focus on writing by incorporating journals**

You will choose what strategies to model and what teaching tools to use based on the content objectives you have, the texts you use, and your particular students' needs. Remember that we have artificially separated the strategies so that we could explain them to you. Strategic learners move naturally between strategies guided by their purposes and monitor their progress as they tackle learning tasks, read nonfiction books, write research reports, or evaluate web pages.

Inquiry into Your Learning

1. Research a new area, issue, or topic in your content area. To choose, think about what you might need to teach that you have not studied in depth in your college program. Or what interests you personally that you haven't researched yet but might like to teach in the future? Keep a journal to track the generating strategies you use. How do you activate your prior knowledge and preview and predict? What specific strategies do you select in each category (remember that you need not use every one). Write your reflections about how you used the strategies, and assess their effectiveness. Review the teaching/assessing tools sections, and try using a few tools yourself. Write your reflections about the tools too. Having personal experience with strategies and tools will help you make your process visible when you model and explain with your students.

2. Begin a journal, learning log, or field notebook. We suggested in Chapter 1 that you might want to begin a field notebook or journal as you learn about your teaching. You could begin your teaching journal by writing about your prior knowledge of teaching in your content area. Complete a freewrite about your past experiences in classrooms. Do you think you have any misconceptions about what teaching was like then and what it is like now? Record how and what you learn about your teaching.

   Or you could begin a learning log about this course or a new topic you are researching. What prior knowledge do you have? Do you think you have any misconceptions? As you learn, record both how and what you learn.

Inquiry into Your Students' Learning

1. Interview a middle school or high school student about the strategies he or she uses when beginning to read or write in your content area. You might want to provide a specific scenario—perhaps a topic the student will be studying in your

content area or a particular reading or writing task. Begin with open-ended questions, such as, "What do you do to prepare to read or write?" Then ask about whether the student activates prior knowledge, previews or predicts, sets a purpose, or monitors his or her progress. For example, you could ask, "Did you think about what you knew before beginning?" Depending on the answer, you could ask more specific questions, for example, "Did you read the book jacket to see if you knew anything about the content or knew the author?"

Summarize what strategies the student uses. Based on what you have learned, what strategies would you model and explain to the student?

2. Think about a topic in your content area and find a text—a web site, a newspaper article, a book. Choose a teaching/assessing tool described in this chapter, for example, graphic organizers, KWL, analogies, or freewriting. Create a lesson plan with a content objective, and incorporate one of the teaching/assessing tools.

If you have the opportunity, use your lesson plan with students. Afterward assess what the students learned and your plan. Reflect on the changes you would make next time. Remember that teachers often revise their lesson plans, both during teaching and afterward, for the next time they teach the material—either next period or next year.

Resources

Books

Fulwiler, T. (1987). *The journal book.* Portsmouth, NH: Boyton/Cook. Defines the benefits of journals and discusses journals in different content areas.

Journals

Afflerbach, P. & VanSledright, B. (2001). Hath! Doth! What? Middle graders reading innovative history text. *Journal of Adolescent & Adult Literacy, 44* (8), 696–707. Describes how middle graders read and misread the inserted texts, such as primary sources, in their history textbooks. Recommends modeling and explaining how to read textbooks.

Bulgren, J., & Scanlon, D. (1998). Instructional routines and learning strategies that promote understanding of content area concepts. *Journal of Adolescent and Adult Literacy, 41* (4), 292–302. Describes how graphic organizers can support students' learning of strategies in social studies.

Cuicchi, P. M. & Hutchison, P. S. (2003). Using a simple optical rangefinder to teach similar triangles. *Mathematics Teacher, 96* (3), 166–168. Describes providing direct experiences with rangefinder to build prior knowledge for the study of triangles.

Laverick, C. (2002). B-D-A strategy: Reinventing the wheel can be a good thing. *Journal of Adolescent and Adult Literacy, 46* (2), 144–147. Gives an example of how she adapted KWL into Before, During, After reading strategy for vocational high school students and for teachers' lesson planning.

Manz. S. L. (2002). A strategy for previewing textbooks: Teaching readers to become thieves. *The Reading Teacher, 55* (5), 434–436. Describes how to introduce previewing to students.

Web Sites

The Graphic Organizer: References and Hotlinks. **www.graphic.org/links/html.** A source for graphic organizers submitted by content area teachers.

Inspiration Software, Inc. **www.inspiration.com.** K–12 and Professional software that has graphic organizer templates and five hundred symbols to make your own. Has the capacity to convert the graphic organizer to an outline.

CHAPTER 5

Building Students' Vocabulary

KEY CONCEPTS

- schema (schemata), p. 107
- concept, p. 108
- assessment tools, p. 111
- morphemic analysis (structural analysis), p. 117
- cognates, p. 117

PURPOSE-SETTING QUESTIONS

1 We have given you several new words in Part One, such as *strategies*, *teaching tools*, and *considerateness*. Do you remember what those words mean? Which word is easier to define? Why do you think you can recall that definition?

2 How were you taught new vocabulary in high school content-area classes? What assignments were you given? Did you learn words only for the Friday test or did you really add the words to your vocabulary?

3 Do you use word parts—roots, prefixes, and suffixes—to figure out new words? Have you found knowing word parts useful in figuring out unknown words?

4 Is learning new words an interesting task for you? Do you try to incorporate new words into your speech or writing? Do you notice new words wherever you encounter them?

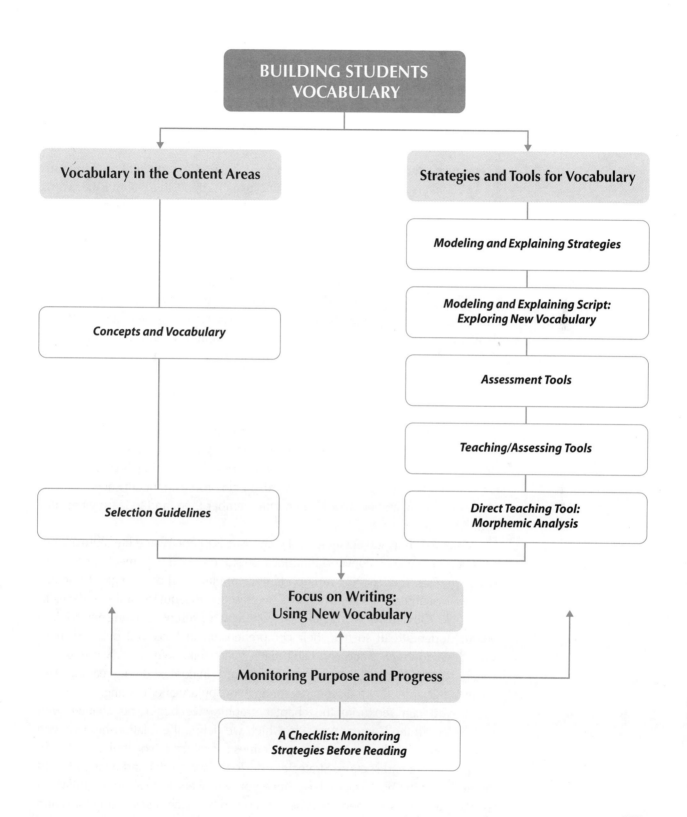

BUILDING STUDENTS
VOCABULARY

Vocabulary in the Content Areas

Strategies and Tools for Vocabulary

Modeling and Explaining Strategies

*Modeling and Explaining Script:
Exploring New Vocabulary*

Assessment Tools

Teaching/Assessing Tools

*Direct Teaching Tool:
Morphemic Analysis*

Concepts and Vocabulary

Selection Guidelines

Focus on Writing:
Using New Vocabulary

Monitoring Purpose and Progress

*A Checklist: Monitoring
Strategies Before Reading*

> *The difference between the almost right word*
> *and the right word is the difference between*
> *lightning bug and lightning.*
>
> Mark Twain

Have you thought about the words you use in different situations? In casual conversation with friends, people usually don't think about the words they choose unless they are avoiding an embarrassing situation. At other times, in a job interview, on a test, or giving a speech, people select their words very carefully because they want to express precisely what they know to their audience. In content-area classrooms, students' words tell teachers what they know. Students may enter with everyday words for ideas ("the top of the water is grabby; it holds on to objects"), but teachers want them to leave knowing content-area vocabulary ("the water has surface tension"). Teachers want students to learn the words that the discipline community uses to discuss ideas. Thus, teachers aim to build upon students' prior knowledge by teaching them content-area words for important ideas.

How do you learn new words? Think about the slang words or expressions you and your friends are now saying. Can you remember when you first heard the expression? Undoubtedly, after you heard the expression or read it on-line in a chat room or instant message several times, you began to say it in several similar situations until the expression was out of style. Learning the current slang is not much different than learning words in classrooms. Students need to hear, read, say, and write new words often to remember them and to learn what situations the words are used in.

Many words in subject areas and many words in poetry and literature are not common in everyday conversation. Because students will only meet uncommon words in texts, the teaching of important vocabulary and of strategies for learning new vocabulary is vital. Therefore, we discuss vocabulary in three places in this book. Obviously, we begin here where we present teaching vocabulary before students read so that their comprehension of texts will proceed more smoothly. However, since you can't teach every unknown word, we return to vocabulary in Chapter 7 to discuss defining words in context during reading. And finally, in Chapter 8, we discuss reinforcing vocabulary after reading.

As you can see from the chapter graphic, we begin the chapter with Vocabulary in the Content Areas, in which we define the relationship between concepts and vocabulary and give guidelines for selecting vocabulary to teach. Then in the second section, Strategies and Tools, we model and explain teaching and learning new vocabulary. Since you will want to teach only unknown words, we offer assessment tools next, followed by teaching/assessing tools and a direct teaching tool. Finally, we close the chapter with a Focus on Writing section and a Checklist for monitoring vocabulary strategies before reading.

However, we think the most important vocabulary teaching you can do with your students is to use uncommon words frequently when you speak and write, and to explore new words in many different sources found in school and outside of school. Long before digital cameras and personal computers, one of us remembers a biology teacher teasing two students for "interdigitaling." Why have I remembered that and forgotten the parts of the cow's eye? Perhaps because the teacher used vocabulary playfully or because I now use the word *digital* in many social situations. If you help your students playfully explore how words are used and encourage them to use new words frequently, they may continue to discover new words on their own.

Vocabulary in the Content Areas

schema (schemata) A theoretical concept of the brain as an organized network of ideas, concepts, data, and experiences.

Your goal is to increase your students' knowledge in their *schemata* by teaching the important words needed to understand ideas in your content area. However, only one or two exposures to a word will increase the likelihood that students will forget it. That's why you forgot all those words tested on Fridays! People learn words incrementally; they learn them in one context and then subsequently in another context. They learn one meaning and then at another time add another meaning. They learn different shades of meaning like when to say "thrifty" and when to say "cheap." (Nagy & Scott, 2000)

DIVERSITY

When you investigate your students' prior knowledge, you will pay particular attention to the words they use. Working class socioeconomic status (SES) students enter school with smaller vocabularies than middle class SES students (White, Graves & Slater, 1990). Although many working class students successfully read in the primary grades, between the fourth and sixth grades their achievement declines—called the fourth grade slump (Chall, Jacobs, & Baldwin, 1990). What changes? In the primary grades, students read common everyday words expressed in simple sentences. Beginning in the fourth grade, they read low frequency words, abstract words, and specialized content-area words expressed in complex sentences. In general, the vocabulary gap between working class students SES and middle class SES students remains through the higher grades.

ELL students also present vocabulary challenges for teachers. ELL students who have been to school might know the ideas in their first language but not know the English word. Other ELL students may not have the prior knowledge and vocabulary in either language and may not read English well enough to learn words on their own (Blachowicz & Fisher, 2000). In addition, the particular language the ELL student speaks makes a difference. Hispanic-American ELL students may notice that some English words resemble Spanish words, making translating easier. However, speakers of Asian and Middle Eastern languages will not notice similarities. Those languages are not like English in how they are written or how they sound (Bernhardt, 2003; Grant & Wong, 2003). Learning English vocabulary may be more difficult when languages are so different. Remember also that ELL students need six to seven years to learn academic language as opposed to two to three years for conversational language.

In general, students who read widely will have encountered a greater variety and number of words than students who do not. All students need to read not only in school but independently outside of school as well. Furthermore, they need to read challenging texts that contain low frequency words and complex sentences—words and sentences not heard in conversations.

You want to teach words that contribute to their understanding of content, words that occur in many texts, and words that connect to other content (Beck, McKeown & Kucan, 2002). English/language arts teachers teach words that occur in many different texts, while science, history, and other content-area teachers often teach words rarely encountered outside of their content areas. However, students need those infrequent words to understand and communicate ideas in that content area. So, in this section we define concepts and vocabulary and then discuss guidelines for selecting vocabulary.

■ Concepts and Vocabulary

concept A category of experiences or vicarious experiences that have the same essential attributes.

We define ***concepts*** as categories of real and vicarious experiences that have the same essential attributes or characteristics. One experience does not form a concept: it's just an instance or an example. For example, to form a concept for "dog," people need repeated experiences (with spaniels and boxers and other breeds) to deduce the common or essential attributes (domesticated, mammal) from the variable and idiosyncratic attributes (large, short haired) that pertain to only particular instances. Concepts can be concrete and simple, like *pencil*, or abstract and complex, like *freedom*.

Concepts, and the words used to represent them, have features or characteristics that people in a particular culture or community have agreed upon. When enough people use a word to express the same concept, the meaning becomes standardized, and lexicographers will add the word to dictionaries. These defining features or essential attributes constitute dictionary definitions and textbook explanations of concepts. For example, in the first exhibition of thirty-nine renegade artists in France in 1874, Claude Monet included a painting entitled *Impression: Sunrise.* Using the term *impressionists*, a critic derogatorily reviewed the works by these painters who strove to catch their immediate impressions of light and color interactions as they painted outside. Now, *impressionists* refers not only to that group of painters but to that style of painting.

In math, "infinity" and "pi" are agreed-upon concepts, and their symbols (∞ and π, respectively) function just like words. Mathematical notations function like sentences and paragraphs containing mathematical concepts or mathematical descriptions of scientific phenomena. Mathematicians compose the community of people who define and redefine the concepts and words in their domain. Thus, one part of content-area teaching is inducting students into that community by building and enriching their schemata with concepts and vocabulary important to your content area.

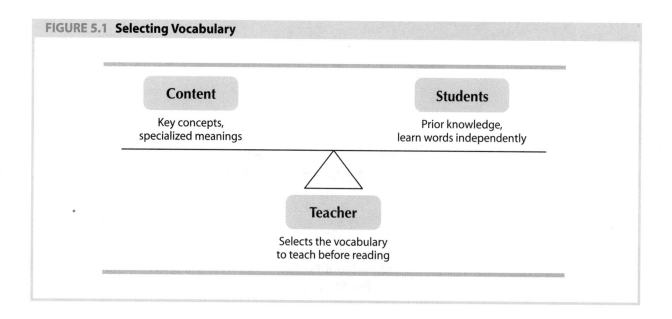

FIGURE 5.1 Selecting Vocabulary

■ Selection Guidelines

Most likely somewhere in your schooling, you had a teacher who passed out a list of twenty words for you to define, use in sentences, and be tested on. Instruction in definitions and one or two exposures to the words, however, will never solidify vocabulary meaning or integrate words (concepts) into anyone's schemata (Stahl & Fairbanks, 1986).

The first guideline for vocabulary building is to ask, "What concepts are crucial to students' learning?" Then teach the most important words (concepts), words that relate to one another, so that students build or extend their schemata (Nagy & Herman, 1987). Since you and your students will frequently use those most important words when talking and writing about the topic, the definitions will become well known or established. All students, and especially LD students (Bos & Anders, 1990) and ELL students with little prior knowledge, benefit from schemata-building vocabulary instruction.

Second, determine what related words extend and elaborate concepts and schemata. You need to decide whether to teach some related words or whether students can learn them independently. You may decide not to teach the related words because students could understand them within the context of a discussion or the text.

Third, because it is impossible for you to teach every word, ask yourself what words are less important to the text. Some students will learn these words through their reading (Nagy & Herman, 1987). We return to using context to learn words during reading in Chapter 7.

Thus, in selecting vocabulary to teach, you are balancing the concepts important to the unit of study and your students' prior knowledge (Herber, 1978), as depicted in

FIGURE 5.2 **Strategies and Tools for Exploring New Vocabulary**

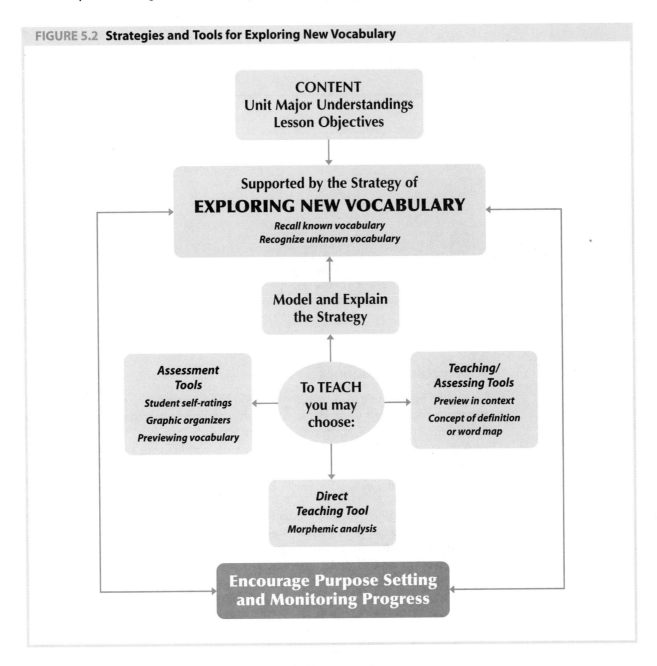

Figure 5.1. For example, English teachers may select vocabulary describing the characters of the novel; science teachers select words related to mitosis; health teachers choose words related to socially transmitted diseases.

Now let's look at strategies and tools for teaching and learning new vocabulary.

Strategies and Tools for Vocabulary

If students do not know the meaning of a word, they do need the definition but they also need to know when or how to use the word (Nagy & Scott, 2000). Otherwise, students write sentences like, "My hair protruded this morning," or "In my bright yellow shirt, I protruded in the crowd." These sentences were written based on the definition of protruded as "sticks out." In this section, we first present a modeling and explaining lesson in which the teacher defines new words and explains their uses. Next we present several *assessment tools* because you want to know which words are unknown to your students. And finally, we discuss teaching/assessing and direct teaching tools. All of these tools support the strategies of exploring new vocabulary, recalling known vocabulary, and recognizing unknown vocabulary (see Figure 5.2).

assessment tools Tools that inform students and teachers about ongoing learning of content and/or strategies.

■ Modeling and Explaining Strategies

You recall in the modeling and explaining script for Kingdoms on the Nile (in Chapter 4) that the key term *dynasty* was defined using background knowledge and the context of the chapter before reading. The purpose of exploring new vocabulary is to have definitions in place so that students' comprehension flows more smoothly during reading. Let's look at another modeling and explaining script; in this one, we use an analogy to explain the new math vocabulary. (Remember the direct teaching tool of analogies in the activating prior knowledge strategy?)

Suppose you are starting a math unit on the use of variables in algebra. The first chapter in the textbook unit discusses the order of operations, beginning with a vocabulary section. To assist your students with the vocabulary, you have decided to model and explain with them, defining the important vocabulary introduced in the first section.

 Modeling and Explaining Script: Exploring New Vocabulary

Introduction: Using an Analogy to Activate Prior Knowledge

Teacher: Everyone has several names; for example what name do your friends call you?

Student: *Beth.*

Teacher: What name did your family call you when you were little?

Student: *Bethie.*

Teacher: That was a nickname or a sign of endearment used by your family. What did your mother call you when she was mad or serious?

Student: *Elizabeth Laura Holmes.*

Teacher: Beth, Bethie, and Elizabeth Laura Holmes are three names that refer to you. When a particular name was used in a specific situation, you knew exactly what feeling was implied by that name! Particular names are used in specific situations. With that example in mind, let's discuss the new vocabulary on page 176 of our new chapter, "Order of Operations."

Continued

My Modeling and Explaining

This section of the chapter introduces the new vocabulary.

Thinking about my introduction to the lesson, how would you define *numerical expression?*

Yes, it is a name for a number.

A number could have different names or have different expressions. [paraphrasing definitions into own words]

Again thinking back to our name analogy, what is *value* similar to?

Yes, the person all the different names refer to. [connecting definition to analogy]

Evaluating the expression is like figuring out the situation: why did your mother use that name? Just like your names, each expression is used in a specific situation.

Let's discuss a few examples and the different "names" or expressions that stand for "2."

1. The first name, 2, represents the whole number.

2. 5 – 3 is a subtraction expression (or situation) for "2."

3. 20/10 is a division or ratio expression. A situation might be that you have 20 cookies and 10 friends and so 2 cookies per friend.

4. Let's go to 347.8 – 345.8, a decimal expression that could describe a 2-degree difference in temperature.

5. 5 x 2 – 8 is an algebraic expression. To ensure that all of the expressions mean the same for everyone across the world, mathematicians have agreed on rules for the order of operations. So, to get 2 in this expression, what operation would we do first? [define examples of the concept]

Mathematics Textbook

Numerical Expressions

A **numerical expression** is a combination of symbols for numbers and operations that stands for a number. The **value** of a numerical expression is found by performing the operations. Performing the operations is called **evaluating the expression**. For example, the seven expressions here all have the same value, 2.

2	5 – 3	20/10	5 x 2 – 8
21	347.8 – 345.8	$10° + 10°$	

The **value** of a numerical expression is found by performing the operations.

Performing the operations is called **evaluating the expression.**

For example, the expressions here all have the same value, 2.

2

5 – 3

20/10

347.8 – 345.8

5 x 2 – 8

Source: A. Usiskin et al., *Transition Mathematics* (2nd ed.) (Glenview, IL: Scott Foresman, 1995), p. 176

Let's review the strategies and tools used in the modeling and explaining script for exploring new vocabulary:

1. I **activated prior knowledge** by using an **analogy** (a student's nickname).

2. The class and I **paraphrased the definitions** by stating them in our own words ("A numerical expression is a name for a number").

3. I **connected the definitions to the analogy** (different numerical expressions to different names).

4. I defined the different examples of the numerical expressions (concept) for the number 2 (5–3 is a subtraction expression for 2).

During that modeling and explaining, I defined words with the students. Before you teach words, you might want to assess what words they need to learn.

■ Assessment Tools

You recall we discussed assessing the words students used to determine the prior knowledge in their schemata. Before you teach vocabulary words, you want to assess whether the students know the specific words for important concepts or if they use everyday words for the concepts. For example, do they use the everyday words *crackling noise* instead of the specialized word *static?*

Since some everyday words also have a specialized meaning in a particular content area, you want to assess whether students, especially diverse students, know that specialized meaning. Students may know the everyday meaning or the primary meaning of *line,* for example, but may not know the specialized meanings for *line* in math, geography, or music. Students may not understand words or phrases, like *Cold War* and *common market,* that have specialized meanings but use everyday words in a figurative rather than a literal sense.

Depending on the grade you teach, you might not expect students to know the specialized words in your content area. On the other hand, if students have attended school in the United States, you know students should have learned the words *longitude, latitude, equilateral triangle,* and *parallelogram* before high school.

Student Self-Ratings

Most students can rate their own knowledge of words accurately (Beck, McKeown, McCaslin, & Burkes, 1979). Thus, one way to begin assessing specific vocabulary knowledge is to ask the class as a whole or the students individually to estimate whether they know well the important conceptual words for a unit or text (they can give a definition), are somewhat familiar with the words (they are acquainted with them and may recognize them in context), or have no idea of what the words mean. For an upcoming science unit, a teacher made the rating chart in Figure 5.3.

After the students rate their knowledge of the important conceptual words, you and your students know which words to concentrate on learning. Some students may just need to refine their definitions, while others may need instruction in the concepts represented by the words. All students will need many opportunities to read and write those important words so that their meanings become established.

Students' Graphic Organizers

Once you have decided on the most important words for the concepts and schemata in the unit of study, you could ask the students to construct their own graphic organizers using the vocabulary you've selected. Your purpose is to assess the representations of their schemata when you have given them clues—the important conceptual vocabulary.

We recommend using the following steps:

1. Write each important word on an index card and make a packet of vocabulary words for each small group of students.

2. Give each group a packet, and instruct the students to create their own graphic organizer that illustrates the relationships among the words. The group members may add new words on cards or delete a word card.

3. As a group, the students arrange the cards and come to a consensus about the design of their graphic organizer, a task that usually involves them in much discussion. The students' discussion of their concepts and vocabulary allows them to explore their prior knowledge (Stahl & Vancil, 1986).

4. After drawing their graphic organizer on chart paper or an overhead, the students must explain the relationships that their design sets out to the whole class.

5. As each group explains its graphic organizer, the students in the full class compare the different graphic organizers and explanations composed by the other groups. The different designs indicate the different interpretations that students have made. At this point, you are not looking for a correct design; you are assessing their prior knowledge of the words.

■ Teaching/Assessing Tools

We stated earlier in this chapter that you will decide whether to teach important new vocabulary before reading or whether students could independently learn vocabulary during their reading. When students are learning new concepts, new words, or new meanings, teachers decide to preteach the most important conceptual words.

FIGURE 5.3 Student Self-Rating Chart

Word	Well Known: Please Define	Familiar: Take a Guess	Unknown
Ecology			
Photosynthesis			
Population			
Community			
Biome			
Biosphere			
Ecosystem			
Biotic			
Abiotic			
Respiration			

Students rate their knowledge of vocabulary words.
© Susie Fitzhugh

You may decide to use a teaching/assessing tool—either *preview in context* or *concept of definition.*

Preview in Context

In the Kingdoms of the Nile script (Chapter 4) when *dynasty* was defined, the script modeled the preview in context tool for teaching new vocabulary (Readence, Bean, & Baldwin, 1989). Drawing on the students' prior knowledge and the immediate context in the reading selection, the teacher and the students compose probable meanings for new vocabulary. Readence et al. outline the following steps, which are repeated for each new word:

1. **Preparation.** The teacher selects important vocabulary from the reading text.

2. **Establishing context.** Pointing out the first word in the text, the teacher and students read aloud or silently the surrounding sentences or context.

3. **Specifying word meaning.** The teacher questions the students to help them compose a probable definition for the word based on their interpretation of the text and their prior knowledge.

4. **Expanding word meanings.** After the students have arrived at a definition for the word in that context, they can extend their understanding by discussing synonyms, antonyms, or other contexts in which the word could occur.

During the previewing, you assess the students' prior knowledge, use of context, and resulting definitions. If your students have difficulty composing a definition, one student

FIGURE 5.4 Concept of Definition for Igneous Rocks

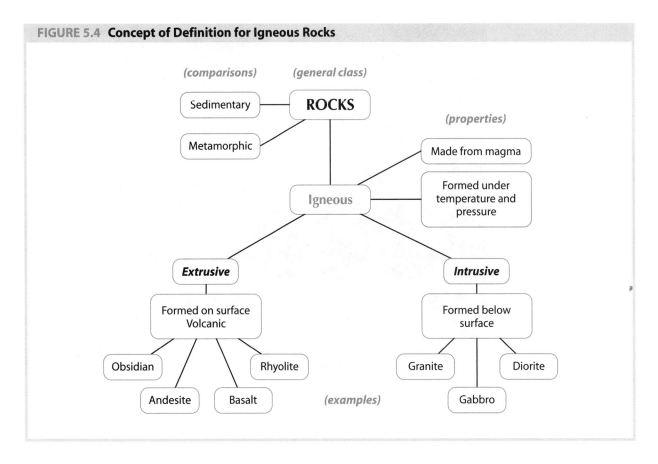

could consult the dictionary, and then you and your students could discuss how to select the appropriate definition for the specific context. If the definition is too vague or too concise, you can clarify and explain the definition (Beck, McKeown, & Kucan, 2002). We like this tool because you and your students discuss both the definition and the context for the word. Once you have modeled and explained previewing in context with your students, you remind them to use the tool in paired reading and independent reading.

Concept of Definition or Word Map

Replicating a concept learning model (Frayer, Frederick, & Klausmeier, 1969), the *concept of definition* (also called a *word map*) can be used to teach concepts as well as to teach what constitutes a complete definition (Schwartz, 1988). Essentially the teacher (and the students if they have prior knowledge) build a specific type of graphic organizer for the concept (see Figure 5.4) while previewing the chapter:

1. The teacher identifies the target concept and places it in the center of the graphic organizer. (*igneous*)

2. The teacher writes the general class to which the concept belongs—the superordinate category. (*rocks*)

3. The teacher (and possibly the students) explains the target concept by identifying its essential attributes or properties. (*made from magma*)

4. The teacher (and possibly the students) cites examples of the target concept. (*granite*)

5. The teacher (and possibly the students) compares the target concept to related yet different concepts in the same superordinate category. (*sedimentary*)

In the initial teaching of concepts and words, as in our earth science example on rocks, you would model and explain how to complete the graphic organizer. As the unit progresses, students may encounter additional properties as well as more examples, including comparative examples, which they can add to the graphic organizer. They should have opportunities to present and explain their additions. In our example, when they read, students could complete a word map for sedimentary rocks, and you would assess the properties and examples. Naturally, if particular students, like LD and ELL students, need support, you would build the word map or graphic organizer interactively with them. You may even show them a completed word map as a preview to the text and have them follow it as you read with them.

After students understand the format of the concept of definition, Schwartz (1988) recommends that students use the word map structure to evaluate definitions presented in textbooks. Does a definition identify the superordinate class and describe the essential attributes of the concept? Does the definition give examples and related concepts? If definitions are incomplete, students can decide where to search for the needed information.

■ Direct Teaching Tool: Morphemic Analysis

morphemic analysis (structural analysis) The examination of a word for its meaningful parts—root, prefix, and suffix.

cognates Words in different languages that come from the same original language and so are similar in form and meaning.

If you had to memorize the meanings of Greek and Latin roots, prefixes, and suffixes in high school, you've had experience with *morphemic analysis* or *structural analysis*. Morphemic analysis means breaking words into their meaningful parts. A *morpheme* is the smallest unit of meaning; it could be a whole word, like *atom,* or the parts of a word. *Hydrocarbon* has two morphemes—*hydro and carbon*—and atoms has two also—*atom* and *-s.* In content areas, morphemic analysis can allow readers to understand the meanings of new words. For example, very few students in our classes know the word *gynecocracy,* yet many figure it out from *gyne-* and *-ocracy.*

A special case of morphemic analysis is the recognition of *cognates,* or words from two languages that descend from the same language and so are similar in form and meaning. Because English and European languages, such as French and Spanish, have words of Greco-Latin origin, those languages have cognates. Having no common origin, cognates do not exist between English and Asian languages. Cognate examples from English and Spanish are species/especies, civilization/civilización, and fraction/fracción. Although you can see the similarities between the cognates, and successful ELL readers do also, intermediate ELL students and older low-literacy ELL students do not easily recognize cognates (Jiménez, García, & Pearson, 1996; García & Nagy, 1993).

Your direct teaching of morphemic (and cognate) analysis will help students when they read independently because they can recognize familiar parts of words and deduce the meaning, as you did for *gynecocracy*. Sixty percent of new words can be analyzed into parts that help access meaning (Nagy & Scott, 2000). Using the criteria of frequency and usefulness to choose words, you would model and explain how to analyze a word. Beginning with clear examples, you would model and explain how to detach the prefix from the root word, how to detach the suffix if necessary, how to recall the meanings for the different word parts, and how to infer the new meaning for the whole word. For cognates, you would highlight the similarities and differences between the two languages.

Root Words

In the content areas, you want to model and explain common root words or morphemes that occur in your content area—for example, *chromo-, anthro-, helio-, cardio-,* and *magni-.* Your goal is for students to be able to generate new meanings based on the familiar morpheme. For example, once the students know the math word *centimeter,* you can teach them to determine the meanings of several related words (see Figure 5.5).

Prefixes

You want to teach that common prefixes have more than one meaning and more than one spelling (*in-, im-, ir-, il-*). Sometimes when a prefix is removed, the root word is unknown (*-trigue* in *intrigue*) or the meaning of the root word is unrelated to the whole word (*-vented* in *invented*) (White, Sowell, & Yangihara, 1989).

FIGURE 5.5 Words Related to Centimeter

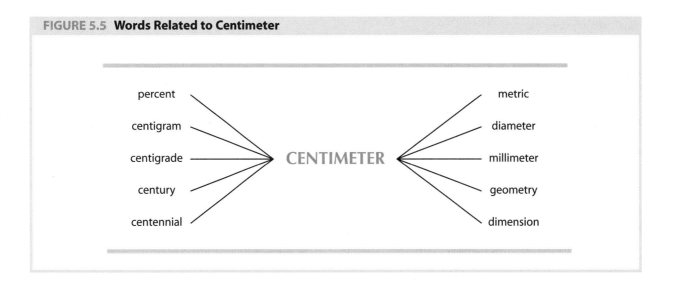

percent
centigram
centigrade
century
centennial

CENTIMETER

metric
diameter
millimeter
geometry
dimension

Suffixes

You may need to teach some students that there are two types of suffixes. *Inflectional suffixes,* the first type, occur most often and are different forms of the same word indicating verb tense (conversed) or number (pencils). ELL students may need mini-lessons in recognizing inflectional endings in text and in writing them in their own texts. *Derivational suffixes,* the second type, change the part of speech (*converse* to *conversation*) and may change the pronunciation and spelling (*sane* and *sanity*), and the meaning relationship may not be predictable (*vital* and *vitality*) (White, Sowell, & Yanagihara, 1989).

After mini-lessons in how to use morphemic and cognate analysis, students would apply the strategy independently during their reading. You could make a class chart of the important or frequent morphemes, and add words to the list as you and your students encounter them throughout the year. Most important, as you and your students explore morphemes, remember that the importance of morphemic analysis is not knowing a list of affixes and root words but *applying* known prefixes, suffixes, and roots to learn new words.

TEACHER AS INQUIRING LEARNER

Think about how many words you know that use the prefix *-trans* or the suffix *-ology*. You could compose quite a list. Think about your content area. You might want to survey the glossary of a textbook in your content area.

- What are the common prefixes, suffixes, and roots?

Begin a list or maybe a graphic like the one for *centimeter* (see Figure 5.5). If you are keeping a journal, you could devote a few pages to your collection. Clearly you will continue to build your collection throughout your teaching career.

Focus on Writing: Using New Vocabulary

In the Focus on Writing sections in Chapter 4, we discussed different types of entries students could make in their journals—brainstorming, graphic organizers, KWL and its variations, and freewriting. For any of those tools, you could note the vocabulary that students use. In addition, students could keep a vocabulary section in their journals. They could rate their knowledge of vocabulary, record their probable definitions (preview in context) and refine their definitions, or collect common morphemes they discover.

For example, at the beginning of a math unit, students were asked to define *decimal* and compare it to *fraction.* The fifth- and sixth-grade students exhibited a range of definitions for the term:

> c. I think decimals are little dots that can mean so much. I really don't no [sic] what decimals are. I think they are like fractions because they both make shapes. I think decimals and fractions are not alike because a decimal is small and a fraction can be any size.

d. A decimal is a fraction. We use decimals to show part of a number.
Decimals are like fractions except the lines separate the numbers and the
dots separate the decimals. (Gordon & Macinnis, 1993, p. 39)

Students could note when they found the unit's new words in out-of-school texts
(Beck, McKeown, & Kucan, 2002) and then record where they found the new vocabulary and the meaning used in that instance. Was the meaning similar to the class's definition or was a different meaning used? Of course, they could record new words
uniquely interesting to them as well (Chapter 7).

Most important, you want your students to use the key vocabulary words in several entries as they continue to write during the unit. By incorporating new concept
words in speaking and writing, the students will retain the words in their schemata and
learn the appropriate contexts to use the words.

You want students to explore their vocabulary before they read so that their comprehension will proceed more smoothly. However, they may meet unknown words as
they read and so we will return to teaching vocabulary in Chapters 7 and 8. Now, to
help your students monitor their vocabulary learning before reading, you and your
students could use the following checklist.

Monitoring Purpose and Progress

Strategic learners monitor their strategies before reading because they want their reading to proceed smoothly. While they activate their prior knowledge and preview and
predict, they are attuned to the vocabulary in the text that they know and don't know.
By monitoring vocabulary before they read, they decide whether the text will suit their
purposes. You may decide to use the following checklist with your students.

A Checklist: Monitoring Strategies Before Reading

Monitoring Purpose
❑ Did you use your purpose to guide you to important words to learn?

Exploring New Vocabulary
❑ Did you preview the vocabulary to see if the text was comfortable or too difficult for
you to read?
❑ Did you recall words you know related to this text?
❑ Did you recognize some unknown words you should define before you read?

 Summary

In this chapter, we have focused on building student's vocabulary because your goal
is to build the knowledge in their schemata. Therefore, we began the chapter by discussing Vocabulary in the Content Areas:

- Concepts and Vocabulary

- Selection Guidelines

Knowing their purpose for learning, strategic learners recall the vocabulary they know and recognize unknown vocabulary. To teach Strategies and Tools for Vocabulary we described:

- **Modeling and explaining new vocabulary in a math textbook**

- **Assessment tools such as student self-rating and student graphic organizers**

- **Teaching/assessing tools of preview in context and word map**

- **Direct teaching tool of morphemic analysis or word parts**

We concluded with the Focus on Writing section where we discussed incorporating new vocabulary in journals and finding the new words in out-of-school texts and a Monitoring Strategies section with a checklist for vocabulary learning before reading.

You will carefully choose which words to teach before students read. You will include the most important conceptual words that will contribute to your students understanding of the text and that will build their schemata. You and your students will meet those important words in reading different texts, in writing different texts, and in speaking about and listening to each other discuss the content. Vocabulary is so vital to understanding that we will return to learning vocabulary during reading in Chapter 7 and reinforcing vocabulary after reading in Chapter 8.

Inquiry into Your Learning

1. Choose a trade book (fiction or nonfiction) or a magazine article appropriate for your content area. Identify the most important information in a nonfiction text or the most important element (imagery, character) in a fiction text (that becomes your content objective). Select the ten most important content words for the vocabulary words you might preteach. If you selected a chapter book, you might decide to choose words from a few chapters. Do not select ten words for each chapter; remember the guidelines!

   Design a graphic organizer that depicts the relationships among the important content vocabulary. Do you need to add a superordinate term not in the text to show the relationships?

2. Examine the teacher's manual for a textbook or anthology in your content area. What new vocabulary does the manual list for you to teach before the students read? Read the chapter or story and think about the important concepts. Do you agree with the selection of vocabulary listed in the manual? What words would you select?

Inquiry into Your Students' Learning

1. Use an assessment tool, such as student self-rating, with a group of students. Select vocabulary words you think are important for the content they will be learning. Make a self-rating chart for the students to fill out. After they have completed the

chart, discuss their definitions for words they know, and their approximate definitions for words that are familiar. Can they talk about when and where they have heard or read the words? For unknown words, give them a sentence and let them guess the meaning. One student could consult a dictionary and everyone could discuss the appropriate definition to choose.

2. In a previous activity in this chapter we suggested that you make a word map. Now, complete a word map for the vocabulary in a text with a small group of students. Select a target concept and the general class to which it belongs (for example, totalitarianism, types of governments). With students, explore the likely attributes or properties of the target concept and possible examples. As the students read the text, you and the students can revise the attributes and examples on the map and add comparative concepts or complete comparative maps.

Resources

Books

Allen, J. (1999). *Words, words, words: Teaching vocabulary in grades 4–12.* York, ME: Stenhouse. Good discussion about selecting words to teach and levels of understanding plus examples of her version of teaching tools like the word map and word parts graphic organizer.

Beck, I. L., McKeown, M. G., & Kucan, L. (2002). *Bringing words to life: Robust vocabulary instruction.* New York: Guildford. Good discussion of how to categorize words by their usefulness and of dictionary definitions plus examples of words and instruction, primarily for English/language arts.

Michaels, J. R. (2001). *Dancing with words: Helping students love language through authentic vocabulary instruction.* Urbana, IL: National Council of Teachers of English. Describes vocabulary instruction that fuels writing, especially poetry.

Journals

Mountain, L. (2002). Flip-a-chip to build vocabulary. *Journal of Adolescent & Adult Literacy, 46* (1), 62–68. Putting word parts on chips, students flip the chips to form words, use words in paragraphs, and compete with each other.

Rosenbaum, C. (2001). A word map for middle school: A tool for effective vocabulary instruction. *Journal of Adolescent & Adult Literacy, 45,* 44–49. Describes using word maps with middle-school students.

Web Site

Collins Dictionaries. **www.cobuild.collins.co.uk.** Has word banks in English, French, and Spanish for vocabulary, grammar, and usage. Includes word-watch and idiom of the day features.

One Look: Dictionary Search. **www.onelook.com.** Searches for words in up to 949 dictionaries. Includes a quick definition and encyclopedia article.

Columnist Richard Lederer's Verbivores **.pw1.netcom. com/~rlederer.** On-line version of Lederer's newspaper column on language. Links to etymology, vocabulary development, puns, and word games.

Comprehending and Constructing Knowledge

PURPOSE-SETTING QUESTIONS

1. When you read a text in your content area, do you concentrate on the author's ideas (text-based information)?

2. When you read a text in your content area, do you converse with the author's ideas by agreeing or disagreeing based on your schema knowledge?

3. Think back to your high school classes or even your college classes. How did teachers use questions? Were their questions really tests of your knowledge? Did they ask real questions—questions for which they did not have one right answer?

4. In your past schooling, did teachers assign texts to be read independently or did they incorporate teaching tools, like discussions or study guides, to help you find and interpret the content?

5. When you discuss a topic among your friends, how does the discussion proceed? How does your discussion with your friends compare to discussions in class with a teacher?

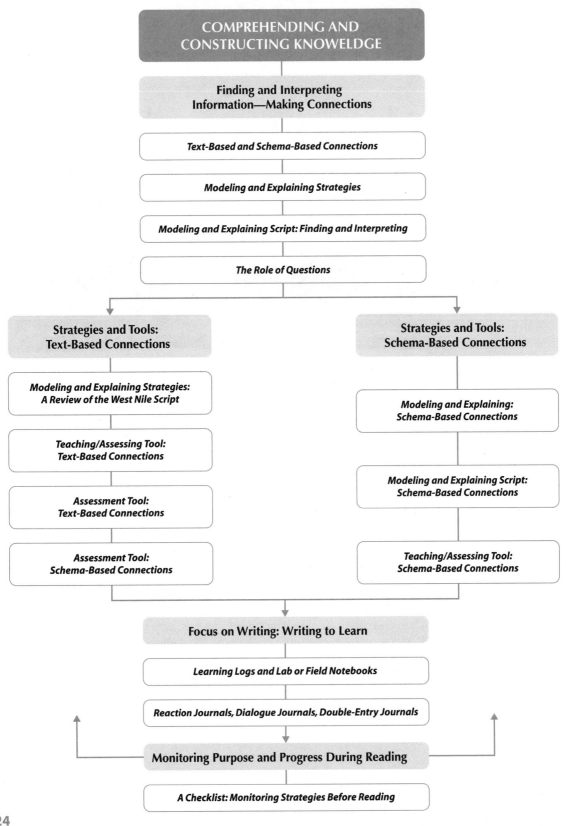

COMPREHENDING AND CONSTRUCTING KNOWELDGE

Finding and Interpreting Information—Making Connections

Text-Based and Schema-Based Connections

Modeling and Explaining Strategies

Modeling and Explaining Script: Finding and Interpreting

The Role of Questions

Strategies and Tools: Text-Based Connections

Modeling and Explaining Strategies: A Review of the West Nile Script

Teaching/Assessing Tool: Text-Based Connections

Assessment Tool: Text-Based Connections

Assessment Tool: Schema-Based Connections

Strategies and Tools: Schema-Based Connections

Modeling and Explaining: Schema-Based Connections

Modeling and Explaining Script: Schema-Based Connections

Teaching/Assessing Tool: Schema-Based Connections

Focus on Writing: Writing to Learn

Learning Logs and Lab or Field Notebooks

Reaction Journals, Dialogue Journals, Double-Entry Journals

Monitoring Purpose and Progress During Reading

A Checklist: Monitoring Strategies Before Reading

//"The facts, ma'am. Just the facts," stated the detective dryly. "Now what was the man wearing?" In the old television show of *Dragnet*, the detective continually admonished witnesses to tell only the facts. But telling just the facts is harder than it seems. People interpret facts, which results in differing accounts of everything from car accidents to history. People find and interpret facts when observing scientific phenomena, viewing an art object, or solving a mathematics problem. They relate one fact to another, attach significance to particular facts, and incorporate facts into arguments, solutions, or beliefs. In other words, they construct knowledge; they don't just list facts. In some classrooms, teachers require students to list facts and so students have an unrelated set of facts. But in real life, people rarely just list facts; they seek to understand or comprehend information, and with their comprehension of information they construct knowledge.

Can you remember when you learned a subject or a sport for the first time? Perhaps in your first encounter with physics, Spanish, or jazz, you felt adrift in a sea of information. Inundated with information, you may have had difficulty figuring out what information was important, what was supporting or related information, and what was nonessential information. The first time middle and secondary students study a content area, they often decide they must remember everything because they do not know which information is the most important. As a content-area teacher, you will want to use teaching/assessing tools that help your students find and interpret important information or comprehend and construct knowledge.

Comprehending and constructing knowledge is the heart of the reading process—making connections between the text and one's schema during reading. To prepare themselves for those connections, strategic readers have activated their prior knowledge, previewed and predicted, and explored the text for unknown vocabulary before reading (Chapters 4 and 5). Now during reading, strategic readers focus on understanding the ideas, concepts, and information in the text and also connect that text information with the ideas in their schemata. The background knowledge in the reader's schema influences how the reader comprehends the text, and the information in the text influences how the reader constructs, adds to, and redesigns his or her schema. This transactional view of the reading process (Rosenblatt, 1994, see Chapter 1) holds that meaning doesn't reside in just one place—on the page, for instance. Instead, meaning is constructed by the reader after thinking about schema-based ideas and interpreting text-based ideas. In this chapter, we concentrate on comprehending text and thus constructing knowledge about the subject while reading text.

In the first section of this chapter (see chapter graphic), Finding and Interpreting Information—Making Connections, we define text-based and schema-based connections, followed by a script modeling and explaining those connections and then by the role of questions in classrooms. In the second section called Strategies and Tools: Text-Based Connections, we discuss modeling and explaining, teaching/assessing tools, and assessment tools. Third, in a parallel section called Strategies and Tools: Schema-Based Connections, we present a modeling and explaining script, a teaching/assessing tool, and an assessment tool. Fourth, in the Focus on Writing section, we concentrate on writing to learn by describing different types of journals that help students comprehend. And finally, we remind you about purpose setting and monitoring which are ongoing strategies.

Finding and Interpreting Information— Making Connections

During a learning and literacy task, strategic readers negotiate their understanding of the text and of their schemata. Guided by their purposes and monitoring their progress, strategic readers concentrate on finding and interpreting information, thereby making meaningful connections in both the text and their schemata (see Figure 6.1). In the interplay between the text and their schemata connections, strategic readers comprehend and construct their knowledge.

Text-Based and Schema-Based Connections

text-based connections A literacy strategy that concentrates on information in the text and makes links among information located in different places in the text.

schema-based connections A literacy strategy that concentrates on what one knows or one's interpretations related to the text.

Every student needs both text-based connections and schema-based connections to construct meaning. For students to learn, *text-based connections* must be sorted—to distinguish what's important and what's not, what's understood and what's not, what's conflicting or what's not—and integrated from different places—the graphic and text, the beginning and end of text. However, text-based information is important only if it can be used to solve problems or issues, understand another human being, appreciate a universal theme, clarify a perspective, substantiate a theory, or provide a reason for action. To accomplish any of those purposes, *schema-based connections* need to be engaged. Inferences, elaborations, alternatives, themes, or issues need to be considered; comparisons to other sources of information need to be weighed; and applications to real situations need to be pursued.

What is interesting is when and how strategic readers make connections between the text and their schemata. Analyzing the think-alouds of only eight capable high school readers, Hartman (1995) found three continuously made both connections, four made text-based first with some schema-based connections, and one concentrated on schema-based connections. Even though we hesitate to generalize from Hartman's small study, we think strategic readers do choose how and when to make both text-based and schema-based connections.

1 Continuously Making Both Text-Based and Schema-Based Connections Scenario

Having activated their background knowledge before reading, strategic readers concentrate on negotiating both *text-based and schema-based connections* for meaning during the entire text. As they read, they sift through the ideas in the text and weigh the relevance of information as they make text-based connections. They are doing more than absorbing the text information; they are making connections to their schemata. Referring to their prior knowledge, they consider different interpretations from other sources and their own experiences and begin to alter their schemata.

We think strategic readers continuously make text-based and schemata-based connections when they have sufficient background knowledge about the content and when the difficulty level of the text is comfortably matched to their reading strategies. Although we'd like to think this scenario represents capable reading, we recognize that the two other scenarios are equally legitimate.

2 Concentrating on Text-Based Connections with Some Schema-Based Connections Scenario

Strategic readers decide to concentrate on the text because their purpose is to gain information or to understand the author's meaning. They make connections among the text information using their schemata primarily to verify whether they understand what the author has stated. During reading, strategic readers decide to hold other schemata connections, like connections to other sources or to their life, in abeyance until after they have finished reading.

We think one instance when strategic readers decide to concentrate more on the text-based connections is when they discover they have meager prior knowledge. Clearly they know they need to add information to their schemata. Another instance is when they read nonfiction text, such as, a scientific report, a set of directions, or an editorial about a community issue. Although they could continuously make text-based and schemata-based connections, they decide to concentrate primarily on text-based connections to make sure they understand the author.

3 Concentrating on Schemata-Based Connections Scenario

In this scenario, strategic readers focus on interpreting and reacting to the author's meaning using their background knowledge of other sources and their experiences. They are involved primarily in using their schemata as a guide to particular information or in rethinking their schemata-based information while grazing over text-based information.

We think this scenario can have positive and negative instances. When strategic readers have substantial prior knowledge, they use their schemata-based connections to react to new, contradictory, or even incorrect information. When the text contains information, issues, or themes that resonate with the reader, strategic readers may concentrate more on their schema-based connections. Both editorials and novels are texts that strategic readers may react strongly to and so focus on their schema-based connections. On the negative side, when readers ignore contrary reasons or uninteresting information, we could not call that concentration on schema-based connections strategic.

text-based and schema-based connections A literacy strategy in which one either negotiates the meaning in the text with what one knows or one has a dialogue with the text, based on schema knowledge.

good reader

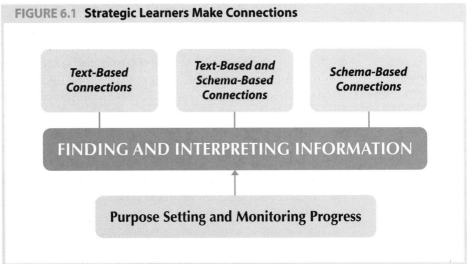

FIGURE 6.1 **Strategic Learners Make Connections**

Text-Based Connections

Text-Based and Schema-Based Connections

Schema-Based Connections

FINDING AND INTERPRETING INFORMATION

Purpose Setting and Monitoring Progress

Thus, in these three scenarios, strategic learners make both text-based connections and schema-based connections as they find and interpret information. Although the balance may differ in three scenarios, connections between text and schema are made in a symbiotic process of finding and interpreting information.

When you teach your students, you want to use teaching/assessing tools that engage both text-based and schema-based connections and help students decide how to balance those connections. Since many of those tools use questions, either asked by teachers in teacher-led discussions or posed by students in peer-led discussions, we discuss the role of questions first. Then we present tools that emphasize text-based connections and use teacher-led discussions and follow with tools that emphasize schema-based connections and use peer-led discussions.

TEACHER AS INQUIRING LEARNER

Draw a continuum and label one end "text-based" and the other end "schema-based," like in Figure 6.1. Label the middle of the line "text-based" and "schema-based." Think about different types of texts you have read over your lifetime. Where on the continuum would you place them? For example, if you read income tax directions paying close attention to the text, you'd place tax forms near that end of the continuum. Where would you place novels, sports page box scores, movie reviews, and recipes?

Compare your continuum with a peer's. How are they alike? How are they different? Why do the differences occur?

Every student needs both types of discussion: teacher-led and peer-led. At times, with difficult text (a primary source, for example), students may benefit from a teacher-led discussion to make connections. At other times, students need to take responsibility for their thinking about text. If given the opportunity, they will challenge each other by offering their constructions of meaning. In both types of discussion, teachers and students concentrate on finding and interpreting information by making text-based and schema-based connections. Discussions are not the only tools students need to make connections about meaning. We discuss additional strategies and tools in Chapter 7. However, before we discuss the role of questions and teaching/assessing tools for text-based and schema-based connections, we present a modeling and explaining script in order to make specific strategies visible to you.

■ Modeling and Explaining Strategies

Prereading Activity
- activate prior knowledge
- generate questions

Suppose that the health teacher and the science teacher are teaching an integrated unit on individual and public health that focuses on the question, "What is a person's responsibility when an individual's and the public's health is compromised?" The students will research to find information on various diseases that seem to put many people's health in jeopardy, such as, SARS (severe acute respiratory syndrome), AIDS/HIV, and the West Nile virus. To get them started, the teachers have gathered a list of useful web sites, and plan to model and explain how to find and interpret important information using an article from one web site, *The Why Files* (**whyfiles.org**), that posts science articles for secondary students.

To begin, the teachers review prereading strategies. First, the class has tapped into their prior knowledge of childhood diseases. Then, the class made a list of diseases that a large number of people are contracting and questions that students had about the diseases. The teachers use one of the questions, "How does the transmission of the disease differ across the diseases?" for the modeling and explaining lesson. Therefore, the **purpose** for reading the article, "Picture of an Epidemic," is to evaluate the evidence for how the West Nile virus is transmitted.

Modeling and Explaining Script: Finding and Interpreting Information

Strategies I Chose to Use

I make schema-based connections when the article mentions the SARS epidemic. I remember when the epidemic in China began in 2003. However, I'm interested in the West Nile virus now: so I'm going to ignore this irrelevant connection.

I think the text is trying to be cute when it mentions a July heat wave and KFC. I decide to skip that text-based information as irrelevant.

I finally find important, text-based information about West Nile virus. Slota says migratory birds carry the disease. I recognize it as the main thesis of the article. But he says "some evidence" and "belief." I will have to evaluate the text-based information in the article.

Excerpted Article from a Web Site

Picture of an epidemic
How far? How fast? What's next? Who's next? Even with a human epidemic like SARS, answering these questions can be gnarly.

When the subject is, er, birds, research money dries up faster than a prairie pothole in a July heat wave. But even if your avian interests tend more toward KFC and turkey dinner than American crows and great horned owls, you might want to consider the wild birds.

They are, after all the most likely mechanism for West Nile's geographic spread. "There is some evidence, and a fair amount of belief, that it's being carried around in migratory birds," says Paul Slota, who's in charge of public information at the national Wildlife Health Center in Madison, Wis. "We think it's pretty clear that is happening," Slota says.

Continued

Strategies I Chose to Use

From a schema-based connection, I decide that "host" means where the virus lives. But doesn't a host die from the virus? I am confused and so ask that question. From my schema, I recall vector from math, but this is a different meaning. From the text-based information, I understand that mosquitoes carry many diseases between animals.

This statement fits my purpose for reading—I want to know the evidence for the spread of West Nile. I skim down the article and see subheads like "Lab Studies" and "Field Studies." From my schema-based connections, I think the text organization will be categories of different types of studies. I decide to take notes about the results so that I can compare the different categories.

Here is the first category—lab studies—and text-based information about the results. I will make notes about these specific details on my chart. (See Table 6.1).

This is the second category—field studies. But it says "Dusek plans" and that means he has no results yet. Thus, I made a text-based and schema-based connection. I am going to add a column of no results to my chart.

The third category—population studies. Caffrey found 40 percent decrease in crows (text-based information). I write that result down.

Excerpted Article from a Web Site

Birds, like people and alligators, are a "host" of West Nile. A mosquito is the "vector" that carries the virus between animals. Mosquitoes carry innumerable pathogens, including viruses that cause other kind of encephalitis, and the malaria parasite. Oddly, at least 37 mosquito species can carry the virus.

As birds both spread West Nile and die of it, a multi-pronged effort to study the disease in wildlife is starting to yield results:

Lab studies of West Nile at the Centers for Disease Control in Fort Collins, Colo., pinpointed blue jays, common grackles, house finches, American crows and house sparrows as the birds that were most "competent" (able to infect new mosquitoes). Four species, again including American crows and blue jays, could also pass the disease to other animals by contact. And five species got infected by eating food containing pathogens. Overall, the studies showed that mosquitoes are one of several possible pathways to infection.

Field studies by scientists from the National Wildlife Health Center are looking at viruses and antibodies in the blood of migratory birds. Robert Dusek, a field biologist with the center, plans to recapture birds banded in previous years, "to see what species are recovering, which were exposed but survived.". . .

Population studies track groups of animals year after year, and are the best way to pin down the ecological effects of a disease when animal numbers naturally fluctuate. Last year, Caffrey of the Audubon Society noticed a population crash among American crows she's studied in Oklahoma for six years. Within two months after West Nile reached the area in September 2002, she says, "40 percent of 120 marked individuals disappeared." Three of the six corpses she found had evidence of West Nile, she says.

Continued

Strategies I Chose to Use

The fourth category—anecdotal observations. I evaluate this text-based information with my schema-based information. Redig thinks many owls died but didn't count how many. I think I need more specific evidence but I will note what he says on my chart in the no results column.

The fifth category—annual surveys. I make schema-based connections by recalling the summer when dead crows were found and were tested for West Nile all over the Northeast. I remember towns spraying against mosquitoes.

Sauer says not enough information to draw conclusions yet. This is his evaluation. I agree with that text-based connection. I'll write his observations and evaluation on my chart.

I also have a new specific source to look for more information—the 2003 annual survey. And new questions: "Have populations declined and can it be attributed to West Nile?"

I think about my purpose (transmission of West Nile) and review my chart: only two studies had results. This article states that birds and mosquitoes spread the disease but I think I need more specific information about transmission. So, I will look at the bibliography on the web site. Maybe I can also contact some of the people they interviewed.

Excerpted Article from a Web Site

Anecdotal observations by experts at wildlife rehabilitation centers indicate that certain birds of prey may be suffering from West Nile. Patrick Redig, director of the Raptor Center at the University of Minnesota, says that rehab centers across the upper Midwest reported that "a lot of great horned owls died" in 2002 . . .

Annual surveys give a broader and hopefully more scientific picture of bird populations nationwide. The biggest, the breeding bird survey, and the Audubon Christmas Bird Count, use . . . a rigorous approach to document long-term population changes. Still the West Nile epidemic may be too recent to appear in the results. "There are certainly some places around New York City that showed declines in crows in conjunction with the first occurrence of West Nile virus," says John Sauer, an ornithologist who specializes in survey data at the Patuxent Wildlife Research Center. "There are sites with big declines, but . . . from 2000 to 2002, there are not really any strong, slip in the face type of conclusions . . ." Nonetheless, the 2003 results should be "interesting," he adds.

Source: Excerpted from "Picture of an Epidemic," *The Why Files* (http://whyfiles.org/175west_nile/2.html)

Let's review and summarize the example of modeling and explaining. Don't forget that before reading strategies were reviewed: the purpose for reading the article and prior knowledge and previewing questions about diseases. As you read the strategies used to find and interpret the important information, think about the interplay between text-based and schema-based connections:

1. I had a purpose for reading (evaluate evidence for transmission of West Nile) and I recognized when the article fit that purpose.

2. I ignored irrelevant schema-based connections (SARS epidemic) and irrelevant text-based connections (KFC).

3. I found important text-based information and the main thesis of the article (migratory birds carry disease).

TABLE 6.1　**Notes on a Comparison Chart**

Type of Study	Results	No Results
Lab studies	1. blue jays, grackles, finches, crows, and sparrows able to infect mosquitoes. 2. Four species could pass virus to animals by contact. 3. Five species infected by eating food.	
Field studies		Plans to study—no data yet.
Population studies	40 percent of 120 marked crows disappeared. Three of six found corpses infected with West Nile.	
Anecdotal observations		"A lot" of owls died—not specific data.
Annual surveys		NYC decline in crows. Other sites big declines 2000–2002. But can't draw conclusion about West Nile yet.

4. I found and evaluated text-based information and specific details (the results of studies).

5. I recognized that I was confused by text-based information and asked a question (Doesn't a host die from the virus?).

6. I recalled schema connections related to one study (a summer of dying crows and mosquito spraying).

7. I decided I needed more text-based information (checked articles sources) and so the article did not satisfy my purpose completely.

To help me make text-based and schema-based connections, I also used three additional strategies (See Chapter 7):

1. I used schema connections to figure out new vocabulary from context (host, vector).

2. I capitalized on text organization by recognizing that the article was divided into categories (types of studies).

3. I also took notes on a comparison chart so that I could compare the results of the studies.

role-play have to be VERY metacognitively aware

In using these strategies, I was comprehending and constructing knowledge. Because my purpose was "to evaluate evidence about West Nile transmission," I judged the importance of the facts and how they would fit that purpose. Thus, I reached the conclusion that

I needed more information and that I had not achieved my purpose. I did not just accept and memorize facts. To construct meaning, learners need a challenging purpose or thoughtful question to address. Let's examine the types of questions teachers ask and the types of answers students give, keeping in mind a goal of critical thinking during reading.

■ The Role of Questions

Questions have been a part of a teacher's repertoire since Socrates used them as a teaching tool to help students think. Many teachers use questions as an assessment tool: they initiate with a question, a student responds, and the teacher evaluates (this is known as the *I-R-E pattern*). (You recall our discussion of communication roles in Chapter 3.) In I-R-E, or recitation, classrooms, questions are assessment tools used to determine whether the students have retained the information from the text (Alvermann, O'Brien, & Dillon, 1990; Nystrand & Gamoran, 1991). Students clearly recognize that the teacher knows the right answer and will keep asking the question until a student gives that answer.

In contrast to the I-R-E classroom, people in their everyday life ask questions because they don't have the answer. They seek unknown information, want to compare their understanding to another person's, or want another person's opinion or interpretation. Real questions instigate conversations, discussions, or even arguments. In everyday life, people ask questions to find and interpret unknown information.

Look back at the West Nile script and find where and why questions were posed. In finding and interpreting information, real questions were asked for these reasons:

- Guide comprehension or set a purpose—"How does the transmission of disease differ across diseases?"

- Highlight a confusion—"Doesn't a host die from the virus?"

- Highlight new questions—"Have populations declined and can it be attributed to West Nile?"

When you model and explain comprehending ideas, you will want to ask real questions so that students understand that posing questions helps negotiate between schema-based meaning and text-based meaning. Furthermore, because nonstrategic students tend to assume they understand the text, you will want to pose real questions that will assist them in making text-based and schema-based connections.

real questions Questions for which the asker does not know the answer.

In this introduction to questioning, we have used the term *real questions* to contrast with the test situation or the I-R-E pattern of classroom talk. Let's now look at questions more closely and define different types of questions. Our purpose is for you to recognize that different types of questions help students to negotiate text-based and schema-based information. After we have discussed types of questions, we will discuss using questions in teaching.

Types of Questions and Answers

We acknowledge that students need to retain factual information in order to interpret. However, we think teachers can ask critical thinking questions that will require students to exhibit their factual knowledge while they interpret the information. The West

[handwritten margin note: Kids are always surprised if I don't have the answer]

Nile question, "How does the transmission of disease differ across diseases?" requires both factual information and critical thinking. Thus, we think you should be aware of different types of questions and answers so that you can adjust your questioning pattern when you use questions to teach and to assess. You will also want to teach your students about different questions so that they pose questions that activate their thinking while they are reading.

In content-area materials, you may find types of questions labeled with different terms. You need to know those terms and the critical thinking that they imply. In addition, we will outline how the levels correspond to text-based and schema-based connections.

Question-Answer Relationship (QAR) Framework. The QAR framework corresponds to the different scenarios of reading in which strategic readers negotiate text-based information and schema-based information. Raphael (1986) suggests that teachers and students discuss where answers to different questions are located using the QAR classification scheme:

- **Right There**—Students can underline in the text the words in the question and for the answer. Both are explicitly in the text or text-based. Using the West Nile text, the question, "What birds infect new mosquitoes?" and its answer, "jays, grackles, finches, crows, and sparrows," are in the text.

- **Think and Search**—Students must find the answer by integrating information from different places in the text so the answer is text-based. We have found that readers encounter two situations in content-area texts. First, in some texts, the *author has explicitly linked the information across the text* so that the reader's task is to recognize those text-based connections, like Right There. For the West Nile text, the question, "What do the annual surveys report?" can be answered by locating information in separate places in the text where the author refers to survey sites. In the second case, the author has not explicitly linked the information and so the *reader must infer the connections or use his or her schema-based information,* as in Author and Me (the next point). In the West Nile text, to answer the main question "How is West Nile transmitted?" the reader must assess the results from different studies and then evaluate the evidence. Thus, we can align Think and Search with either Right There or with Author and Me, depending on whether the author or the reader makes the connection across the text-based information.

- **Author and Me**—Students must have read the text to understand the question but use their schemata knowledge to answer it. For the West Nile text, the question, "What is your evaluation of the results from the different studies?" would require the students to think about the text information but answer from their schemata knowledge about scientific evidence.

- **On My Own**—Students can answer the question using their schemata without having read the text. For the West Nile text, the question, "Has my community been effected by West Nile?" cannot be answered from this text but might be answered from the students' schemata.

We have found that QAR is a useful framework for making the process of negotiating text-based meaning and schema-based meaning visible to students when we model and explain. We also use the QAR framework to teach students to recognize where their answers to our questions come from and to pose a variety of questions that use both the text and their schemata.

Three Levels of Comprehension. We include Herber's comprehension levels (1978) because he applies the levels to a useful teaching tool: the levels of comprehension study guide for content materials. However, before we introduce his guide in the teaching tools section, we need to explain his three levels so that you can compare his levels to other classifications of questions.

Consolidating past reading research on levels of comprehension, Herber applied three levels to content-area reading. As you read the definitions for Herber's three-level classification, think about how the terms correspond to the QAR framework:

- **Literal.** The reader determines the essential information presented in the text. This is also referred to as "reading the lines" (text-based connections).

- **Interpretive.** Because of background knowledge, the reader recognizes the author's implied meanings by integrating information from sections of the text—also known as "reading between the lines." Although the author hasn't stated the relationship, the reader can infer the meaning (text-based connections and schema-based connections).

- **Applied.** The reader synthesizes new text information with background knowledge to extend existing schema knowledge and generalizes that knowledge to new situations or abstract principles—"reading beyond the lines." The reader thinks about the significance of text-based and schema-based connections to contemplate broader concepts, such as justice, or to understand community or global issues and problems (schema-based connections).

You might want to look back at the examples of questions about the West Nile text that we gave with the QAR framework. Where would you place those questions in Herber's classification?

In summary, although people use different terms, they are referring to similar concepts, which we have outlined in Table 6.2. These categorizations are not exact in practice. Remember that the importance of questions is not to categorize them but to use them to assist students in making connections as they find and interpret information. We encourage you to try out different taxonomies to determine which one you find most useful.

When teachers ask questions, they are pointing to what they consider to be important information. Unfortunately, teachers ask primarily literal, text-based questions (Alexander, Jetton, Kulikowich, & Woehler, 1994). However, those facts are only important if they are incorporated into solutions, themes, generalizations, applications, or arguments. Thus, teachers need to ask related questions requiring connections among text and schema information. In addition, when teachers ask connection questions, they need to give students time to think (called "wait time" by Rowe, 1974), especially ELL students who may be negotiating ideas in two languages.

TABLE 6.2 A Comparison of Terms for Types of Questions

Our Terms	QAR Terms	Three-Level Terms
Text-Based connections	Right There	Literal
Integrate across text-based connections	(author's text connections) Think and Search (reader's inferred connections)	
Text- and schema-based connections	Author and Me	Interpretive
Schema-based connections	On My Own	Applied

Strategies and Tools: Text-Based Connections

Although we discuss text-based connections in this section, we emphasize that schema-based connections should also occur. In Figure 6.2, we show how text-based connections can be specifically applied to texts.

In your content-area teaching, you will meet many students who would benefit from support in finding and interpreting text-based information. When your students bring little prior knowledge to your content area or to specific topics within your content area, you will assist them in learning by using teaching/assessing tools that point to the important information and to interpretations among text-based information. You want them to add information to their schemata in a well-organized manner that will serve them well the next time they study the topic.

 DIVERSITY

You already know that diverse students may bring different prior knowledge or meager prior knowledge to your content-area topics (Chapter 4). You also know that diverse students, especially ELL students, may not have the vocabulary needed for your content area (Chapter 5). So, you can predict that diverse students may have difficulty

 TEACHER AS INQUIRING LEARNER

Observe a teacher while he or she is questioning students. Using one of the taxonomies, keep track of the types of questions the teacher asks.

- How many text-based or literal questions are asked? What connection questions are asked?

Try to determine whether the answers are text-based, schema-based, or integrate text and schema.

- How long does the teacher wait after asking a question? Which students answer questions: boys or girls, diverse students and learning disabled students, "smart" students? Can you determine if the teacher is using questions to assess the students (an I-R-E pattern) or to teach the students how to find and interpret information?

FIGURE 6.2 Finding and Interpreting Information: Text-Based Connections

CONTENT
Unit Major Understandings
Lesson Objectives

Supported by the Strategy of
TEXT-BASED CONNECTIONS
Paraphrase what you understand
Ask questions about what you don't understand
Distinguish between important information and supporting details, and unimportant or irrelevant information
Connect graphic information to written text information
Make inferences among text information
Compare text information to prior knowledge
Identify conflicting text information

Model and Explain
the Processes

Assessment Tools
Retelling the text
Admit and exit slips

To TEACH you may choose:

Teaching/ Assessing Tools
Teacher-directed reading activity
Questioning the author
Reciprocal teaching
Comprehension study guides

Encourage Monitoring of Purpose and Progress

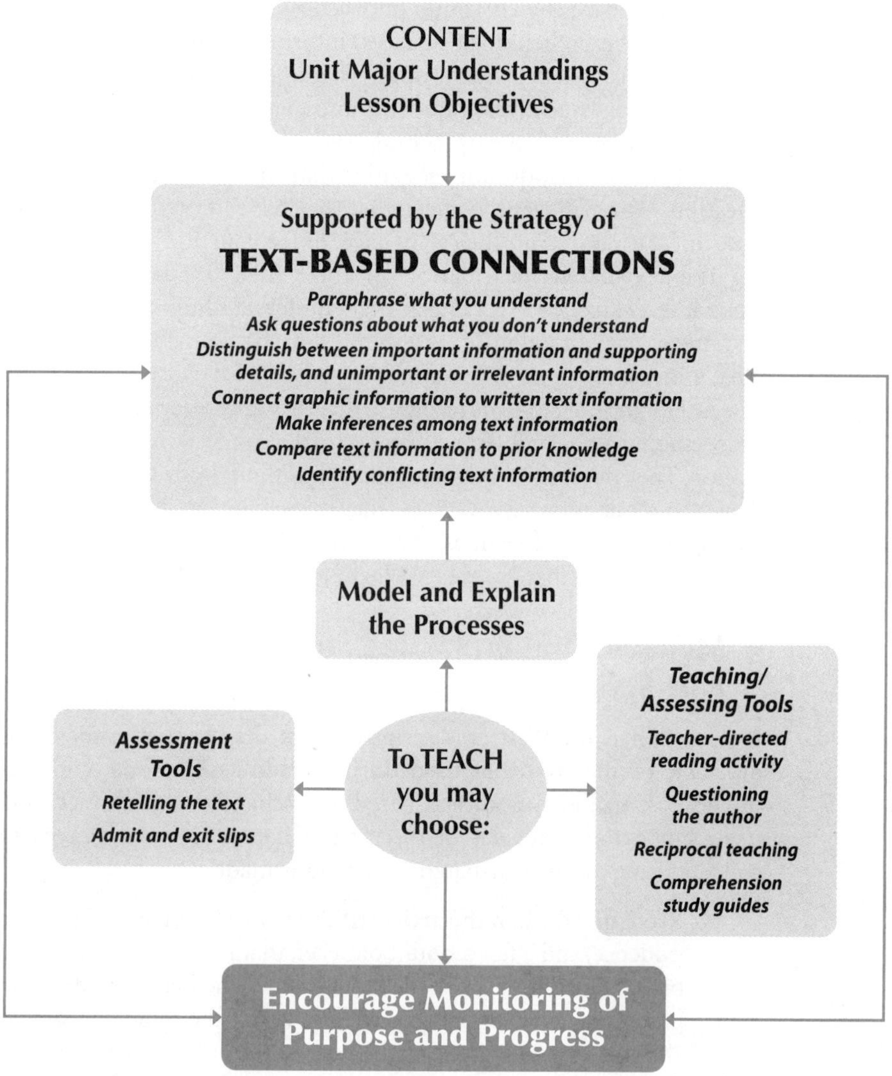

finding and interpreting important information. Diverse students who have not had much schooling may not have the background to understand the concepts you plan to teach. Diverse students, especially LD students but also others who do not read often, will also not have the enriching knowledge and vocabulary that can only be gained from texts. Comprehending text-based information and recognizing what is important information is very dependent upon what one already knows.

Therefore, your diverse students and many of your other students will need you to support them with the upcoming teaching/assessing tools. Some students, in particular LD students, do not recognize that they don't understand and so don't ask questions. You will want to check that they have located text-based information and seek out any confusion they may have. Since your ELL students may be paraphrasing the text-based information in their first language (García, 1998; Jiménez, García, & Pearson, 1996), check their understanding. Make sure that they haven't just memorized literal information but that they can connect those details to a main idea, a thesis or a generalization.

Although your students recognize that they are to learn information from nonfiction texts, especially textbooks, they may not make connections among the text-based information. They may proceed through the task without really thinking and then wonder why they can't recall information or why they missed the significance of the United States' not joining the League of Nations, for example. Many students would benefit from teaching/assessing tools that encouraged them to respond to the text as they read.

■ Modeling and Explaining Strategies: A Review of the West Nile Script

We positioned the West Nile script early in the chapter so that you would gain an overview of the strategies used during reading. To model and explain the whole process, we included both text-based and schema-based connections, as well as the three supporting strategies we discuss in Chapter 7. Now let's reexamine that script, concentrating on the text-based connections made.

- **Recognized when the article fit the reader's purpose.** The clue: "There is some evidence, and a fair amount of belief, that it's being carried around in migratory birds." Since strategic readers determine whether the text will match their purpose, they look for text-based clues about the topic, the source or author, and about the type or genre of the text. At the end of the first paragraph, the reader found important information confirming the article fit the reader's purpose.

- **Skipped irrelevant text-based information.** The clues: "July heat" and "KFC." Strategic readers sift through information, and when the author includes interesting or "seductive" details (Garner, Gillingham, & White, 1989), determine the relevance of that information. In this case, KFC has no connection to West Nile virus. Strategic readers skip irrelevant information.

- **Recognized when text-based information was understood.** The clue: "A mosquito is the vector that carries the virus between animals." Strategic readers check that they understand new information. They may paraphrase or restate the information in their own words to reinforce their understanding.

- **Evaluated and categorized text-based information.** The clues: "some evidence and a fair amount of belief" and "a multipronged effort to study the disease in wildlife is starting to yield results." Strategic readers search for text-based information on which to base their interpretations. Furthermore, strategic readers don't just memorize facts. Instead they organize the details so that they can draw inferences and analyze or synthesize the information. In this case, the reader categorized the studies as providing results or no results.

- **Decided on the need to look for more specific information.** The clue: "results and no results from the studies." Strategic readers draw conclusions and recognize when they need more information. For the West Nile, the reader reviewed the comparison chart and determined that only two studies gave results. The reader also recognized that the article listed new sources to look for additional information.

Although we have highlighted text-based connections, remember that schema-based connections were present, if to a lesser degree, in the script. Prior knowledge about vectors, SARS, dead crows, and spraying against mosquitoes supported the reader's focus on text-based connections. As the reading proceeded, the reader checked into schema-based information to understand and evaluate the results of studies. And finally, when all of the learned information was added to her schema, the reader decided more information was needed.

■ Teaching/Assessing Tools: Text-Based Connections

Before reading, remember that you and your students would have generated ideas by activating prior knowledge, previewing and predicting, and preteaching unknown vocabulary. From those prereading tools, you might have discovered that your students had meager prior knowledge and that the vocabulary and concepts in the text were difficult for them. When you make those discoveries, you will decide to emphasize text-based connections.

To guide their students in text-based connections for finding and interpreting information (see Figure 6.2), teachers choose to model and explain the strategies so that the connections are visible to students. Teachers also choose to use teaching/assessing tools, when students need more guidance. With some teaching/assessing tools—directed reading activity and questioning the author—the teacher asks questions to guide the students' comprehension as they read. With the teaching/assessing tool of reciprocal teaching, the teacher begins to guide, and then the students take over the guidance. With comprehension study guides, the teacher structures the students' independent reading.

Since these four tools—directed reading activity, questioning the author, reciprocal teaching, and comprehension study guides—are *teacher directed or guided discussions*, you need to plan your instruction before class. Here is a process you can follow:

teacher-directed or guided discussion A teacher-planned and teacher-led discussion in which the teacher's questions are addressed.

1. *Decide the main content objective or understanding for the entire text.* What major idea or theme do you want students to learn or focus on?

2. *Compose one or two connection questions* using one of the taxonomies to help you frame the question. Connection-level questions would be at least at the interpretive

level and integrate text-based and schema-based connections and set the purpose for reading the entire text. (See Table 6.2.)

3. *Formulate the supporting questions* to help students answer your connection question(s). Supporting questions could be literal questions or across text-based connections. Remember that all questions should relate to one another so that your students will build their schemata. (See Table 6.2.)

4. *Decide what vocabulary is important* for your main content objective and the questions you'll be asking. Then you need to decide whether to teach some words before the students read. (Refer back to Chapter 5.)

5. *Decide how to link students' prior knowledge to the information in the text.* (Refer back to Chapter 4.)

6. *Decide whether the students will read the text in its entirety or in sections.* If you divide it into sections, mark the appropriate places to stop and discuss the text.

As we describe using each of the five tools with students and give examples, remember the planning that needs to be done first. We also assume that you and your students will have completed prereading activities before using any of these tools.

Directed Reading Activity (DRA)

Most likely you experienced the DRA in elementary school when you met with the teacher in reading groups. If you read teachers' manuals for your content area textbooks, you will no doubt realize that their lesson plans are just like the DRA. The manual directs you how to introduce the textbook chapter (prereading), what to emphasize and ask in sections of the chapter (during reading), and, finally, what to review and extend through questions or activities (after reading).

If the text is difficult to read—perhaps it is a primary source document, a scientific report, or even a textbook—then you may decide to guide your students' reading through a whole class DRA. If you have ELL students, LD students, or perhaps students who ignore their homework, you may decide to provide direct support in a small group DRA. While you work with this small group, other students may support each other with a comprehension guide (an upcoming guide), for example, or be able to work independently.

Because you guide the students, you also assess how they are learning. If the students are unclear, you would need to stop and explain or provide further information. You also may need to rephrase your questions or ask new questions to help students comprehend the information. Use your content objective to keep yourself focused on what the students are to learn as you assess their progress. When teaching students to find and interpret important information with the DRA, you would use the following steps:

1. *Begin with prereading tools, which may be done in any order:*

   a. Introduce the text by activating the students' prior knowledge that relates to the text.

   b. Preteach important, unknown vocabulary words.

   c. Set the purpose for reading the text by stating your connection question(s) that will guide the students' comprehension of the entire text.

2. *Use the teaching tool of asking questions.*

   a. Ask a supporting question to guide the students as they read a section of text silently.

   b. Repeat the supporting question and ask additional supporting questions as needed based on your assessment of the students' answers. Use your questions to give students feedback on their understanding. Ask them to clarify their answers, explain their reasons, explain the source of their answer (QAR), and/or read aloud supporting sections of text. Ask the students to respond to each other's answers, even though in this teacher-centered DRA, students will probably direct their comments to you.

   c. Repeat a and b until the text is completed.

   d. Return to the connection question(s) and discuss the whole text.

3. *Assign after-reading activities*—for example, summarize the text, write a poem, or draw a map. (See Chapter 8.)

TEACHER AS INQUIRING LEARNER

Select any text appropriate for your content area: a magazine, newspaper, or on-line article; a chapter from a book or textbook; a primary source. As you read the text, think about what is most important for students to learn from the text. Compose your content objective(s).

- What is a text- and schema-based connection question you could ask? What related supporting questions, text-based, or across text-based questions will help students answer the connection question?

If possible, do a directed reading activity with a small group of students and a text they need to read.

- Do your questions help students find and interpret the important information? Would you change any questions for the next time?

Questioning the Author

Designed to help students make text-based connections, we think questioning the author (QtA) (Beck, McKeown, Hamilton, & Kucan, 1997) is a useful tool because students typically do not challenge authors, especially textbook authors (Wineburg, 1991). Usually when they read textbooks, students assume that all information is thoroughly explained. However, you know that not all textbooks explain concepts completely, and they make assumptions about students' prior knowledge that may or may not be accurate.

Like the DRA, you decide what the important information is and where to segment the text. In deciding the sections, you would note places where you think students should express their understanding of the text, might need more information than the text offers, could be confused by the author's information, or might miss text-based connections across different sections of the text.

At those points in the text, you ask generic queries, instead of content questions, to probe students' understanding of the text. Beck et al. (1997, pp. 34, 45) suggest two types of generic queries: initiating queries and follow-up queries. Here are some *initiating queries:*

- What is the author trying to say here?
- What is the author's message?
- What is the author talking about?

For *follow-up queries,* they propose one set for nonfiction text and a different set for fiction text:

Queries for Nonfiction Text

- What does the author mean here?
- Did the author explain this clearly?
- Does this make sense with what the author told us before?
- Does the author tell us why?
- Why do you think the author tells us this now?

Queries for Fiction Text

- How do things look for this character now?
- How has the author let you know that something has changed?
- How has the author settled this for us?
- Given what the author has already told us about this character, what do you think the character is up to?

We think QtA is particularly useful when the textbook authors have inserted poems, diaries, and several sidebars into the regular text exposition. Some students are confused by the different types of texts and do not understand why they are inserted (Afflerbach & VanSledright, 2001). Therefore, nonstrategic readers would benefit from queries and discussion about why the different types of text were inserted.

As with the DRA, you need to be ready to respond to students' specific answers with a query tailored to their thinking. You can also ask them to clarify their answers, explain their reasons, or find support in the text. This can be challenging but exciting because you need to assess their thinking in the midst of teaching.

When you decide to use the directed reading activity or questioning the author tools, you have decided that your students need direct teacher support in order to comprehend the text. In the next tool, the teacher models and explains the support and then turns the responsibility over to the students to provide support for each other.

Reciprocal Teaching

The teaching/assessing tool of reciprocal teaching (Palinscar & Brown, 1984) uses questioning and adds predicting, clarifying, and summarizing. Palinscar and Brown recommend that first the teacher model and explain the comprehension strategies in the following order:

1. Using the title, graphics, subheads, you **predict** the content of the text selection and explain what clues give you information. (Recall previewing and predicting in Chapter 4.)

2. You and the students read a section of text.

3. You ask the students **questions** about the section of text. You can explain to the students that the questions point to important text-based and schema-based connections and teach them QAR.

4. You pick a vocabulary word or a section of text to exhibit confusion or misunderstanding. You ask the students to clarify the point for you or search the section of text for information to **clarify** the point. You would also ask the students if they need clarification about any information. Needless to say, if the point is not sufficiently clarified, then you and the students have a question for the next section of text.

5. You **summarize** the section of text by stating what you learned or what text-based information was important to remember. You would also explain why the information is important and what text clues you used to summarize. (We discuss more on summaries in Chapter 8.)

6. Having completed one cycle with a section of text, your students now participate in the role of the teacher.

We would begin the second cycle by asking the students as a group to contribute their predictions, questions, points needing clarification, and summaries. This collaborative reciprocal teaching could easily continue for a number of lessons with different content-area texts.

As the students gain ease with the four comprehension strategies, different students can assume the role of teacher and lead the group through a section of text. You would participate and offer support or feedback as needed, gradually fading out until the students have complete responsibility for conducting the session with each other. You and the students can also gradually lengthen the sections of text covered in each cycle as students become more adept with the process.

Although we have described reciprocal teaching in a small group situation, we know teachers who have used reciprocal teaching successfully in whole class, partner, and tutorial situations too. Furthermore, teachers have used it successfully with a wide variety of students in many grades: students who are poor comprehenders, LD students, and ELL students. A well-researched tool (Rosenshine & Meister, 1994), reciprocal teaching encapsulates the comprehension process and directly teaches those strategies. You know we like tools that make the mystery of reading visible!

So far, we have suggested teaching/assessing tools in which you guide students' reading in class. However, you know that most content-area teachers assign reading to be completed as homework. You also know that some students don't complete that homework, and other students need more support to complete the reading successfully. Completed either in or out of class, study guides provide students with written support during their reading. Study guides can take many different forms. We present two comprehension study guides next, and in Chapter 7 we present text organization study guides. In essence, a comprehension study guide is a directed reading activity on paper.

Levels of Comprehension Guide

You recall that in the Types of Questions and Answers section, we set out the three levels of comprehension—literal, interpretive, and applied—because Herber 1978 uses those three levels to create his Levels of Comprehension study guides. Although questions can be used for each level, Herber's unique contribution is his recommendation to use statements instead of questions (see Figure 6.3). He maintains that students who have trouble answering questions need to be shown what answers are and how answers for each level differ.

Before reading the text, students read the statements on the study guide. Then students read the text to find supporting information for the statement. After reading the text, students check the statements they can support with text- and schema-based information. In addition, Herber recommends that students discuss whether and how they support or don't support the statements. We think this discussion is important because students must defend their answers. Inferential statements can initiate interesting discussions as students defend what they think the author implied. As the students defend their answers, you would observe and assess the ideas they support and the reasons they present. You want to know if they can locate appropriate text-based ideas and connect their schema-based ideas to the text.

We have found that creating a three-level guide with statements is an interesting task for teachers because teachers usually ask questions rather than find answers. You create the study guide in the same way you plan for a DRA. Herber recommends these guidelines:

1. Begin with the inferential level and write statements that connect text-based information and connect the text with the students' schemata.

FIGURE 6.3 **Excerpts from a Levels of Comprehension Guide**

Literal Level
_____ 1. Many of the 800,000 children working in agriculture are doing so legally.
_____ 2. Workers are protected from pesticides.

Interpretive Level
_____ 1. One of the reasons Americans can buy inexpensive vegetables is that farmers can hire children to work for them very cheaply.
_____ 2. The large farm owners are more concerned with the welfare of children than with economic competition.

Applied
_____ 1. Sometimes it's okay to break the law if it's the only way you can help your family.
_____ 2. We are all responsible for what happened to Rosa Rubio's son.

FIGURE 6.4 **Learning-from-Text Guide**

Following the Stock Market

In the stock table in the business section of the newspaper, locate one of your stocks, and answer the following questions with your partner. When you finish, find your partner's stock and again answer the questions.

Literal Level
1. What is the name of the stock you're checking?
2. What stock market is the stock traded through?
3. What was the highest price paid for the stock during the past year?
4. What was the closing price of the stock yesterday?

Inferential Level
1. Will you buy or sell the stock? Why or why not?
2. Should you have bought more stock last year?
3. How does your stock compare to a stock in a similar company—for example, Apple or Intel?

Generalization or Evaluative Level
1. Do you think this is a bull or bear market? Support your opinion.

---

2. Think about the essential literal information needed for those inferences, and write statements containing that text-based information.

3. Think about how the information could be applied or generalized to broad concepts, abstract principles, or other situations in the community or world.

Although the statement guide is to show students the correct answers, most teachers slip in a statement that cannot be supported by the text. They want to keep the students thinking rather than automatically checking every statement.

Learning-from-Text Guide

Like Herber's study guide, the learning-from-text guide proceeds from the literal level, to the interpretive level, to the applied or evaluative level (Singer & Donlan, 1992). The difference is that this guide uses questions instead of statements (see Figure 6.4).

■ Assessment Tools: Text-Based Connections

We predict that you have regularly experienced questions as an assessment tool during your schooling. We know that many teachers give a "Friday quiz" or an end-of-unit test. But in this chapter, we are looking at questions as part of the teaching/learning experience. We advocate that you use questions to help students find and interpret information by giving them feedback. Questions that produce discussion about the information help students comprehend text-based connections and help them make schema-based connections. When you are curious about how an individual or a class is comprehending text-based information, you could use the assessment tools of retelling or admit and exit slips.

Retelling

We use retelling when we want students to recall what they have read without any clues from our questions. Because a retelling is usually an individual assessment, we use it when we are puzzled about how well a student comprehends a text independently. Our purpose is to learn what the student thinks is important to remember—that is, the student's text-based connections.

In our experience, students often give very short answers when asked to retell. They state the topic of a nonfiction text without any details or elaboration. For a fiction text, they identify the main character and mention an event. Unlike a summary, a retelling of nonfiction should contain not only the topic but the main ideas and the details that explain that important information. A retelling of a fictional text should include main characters and the details of the setting, plot, and problem the plot turns on.

Students may give short answers because they have not been asked to retell before. To cue the student that you want an elaborate retelling, you may want to phrase your request like:

- "Tell me everything you remember about . . . "
- "Start from the beginning and tell me everything that has happened so far."

You may also ask the student to tell you more about a concept or a character he or she mentioned. Until the student clearly can recall no more, you can continue to ask:

- "What else do you remember about the topic?"
- "What did the character do next?"

Then you can ask the student questions about important information he or she neglected to mention. The student may be able to recall more information after you have prompted with your questions.

Since students usually retell only literal information, you may want to ask questions beyond that literal level—questions about text-based and schema-based connections and questions about schema-based connections. You will want to know if the students can offer an opinion about the action or a character or relate actions or characters to their own lives. With nonfiction text, you will want to know if students can connect information across text or relate the information to their observations, experiences, or other texts.

Admit and Exit Slips

Teachers often want a quick gauge on their students' understanding of the concepts, readings, and assignments. *Admit* and *exit slips* are quick comments written on index cards at the beginning or end of class, respectively. Anonymously students tell the teacher their confusions, their reactions, their frustrations, and even their celebrations.

For example, math teacher Don Schmidt uses admit slips as an avenue for students to communicate anonymously with him and as a tool to build a sense of community among the students (see Figure 6.5). At the beginning of class, every student writes a quick note anonymously, but it can't contain nasty language or hurtful comments about another person. After shuffling the notes, Schmidt reads a random selection aloud to the class (Schmidt, 1985). Schmidt thus learns about his students' feelings about math, their understandings of concepts, and their reactions to tests, activities, and assignments. The students learn that others are either struggling or celebrating too. The opportunity to write allows students to reflect on events and reconsider their opinions.

Exit slips are the reverse of admit slips. Students write a quick note at the end of class. You may want immediate feedback before you plan the next day's lesson. What did they understand, have problems with, need help on, or complete easily? You could read the exit slips aloud at the beginning of the next class and use them to lead into the day's agenda.

Although we have emphasized text-based connections in this section of the chapter, we hope you recognize that schema-based connections should be made too. You want your students to negotiate between text and schema whenever they read and at any point during their reading. So although we have emphasized text-based connections, we welcome schema-based connections whenever they foster a more complete understanding of content information. At times, we emphasize schema-based connections, the next topic.

 ## Strategies and Tools: Schema-Based Connections

You recall that we discussed schema-based connections in Chapter 4 when we looked at activating prior knowledge. As we return to a discussion of schema, we assume that students' schemata have been activated before reading.

Earlier in this chapter in the West Nile script, you found that schema-based connections were made even though text-based connections were more prevalent:

FIGURE 6.5 Admit Slip Example

> *Page 227 was hard.*
> *Mr. Schmidt,*
> *Can you explain 227 to me today?*
> *Thanks.*

Source: From *Roots in Sawdust: Writing across the Disciplines* by A. R. Gere. Copyright © 1985 by the National Council of Teachers of English. Reprinted with permission.

- **Made schema-based connections** about SARS but knew it was an irrelevant connection.

- From a **schema-based connection, determined the meaning** of "host," **recognized confusion,** and so **asked a question,** "Why doesn't the host die?"

- From a **schema-based connection, recognized how article was organized**—into categories.

- Used **text-based and schema-based connections to evaluate** the results of studies.

- Made **schema-based connections** by recalling prior knowledge about dying crows—information also mentioned in the text.

Just as schemata were not ignored when text-based connections dominated, text-based connections cannot be ignored when schema-based connections are made.

When comprehending, strategic readers make inferences, visualize concepts or characters and elaborate on ideas by connecting their schema-based knowledge to the text-based information (see Figure 6.6). From their schema-based ideas, they think about implied ideas like the theme, issue, or thesis that the author does not explicitly state. Based on their schemata, they make connections to other sources of information, their own life, or an actual situation in their community, the nation, or the world.

DIVERSITY

Now, think about your diversity students. (By now, you can probably write this paragraph!) You know that they may have different schemata. As you read the upcoming script, think about what schema-based connections a diversity student might make. When the reader visualizes a small-town drugstore, diversity students may not visualize a white wooden building with a plate glass window on either side of the center door located on the main street through town. When the reader makes inferences about cultural differences and thinks about the theme of a cultural clash, what inferences and themes might a diversity student think about? Especially when you ask students to make schema-based connections, such as applying ideas to their own life or applying ideas to a real situation, students will have divergent responses based on their differing schemata. In a receptive and respectful classroom climate, these differences can generate interesting discussions as students learn from each other.

To demonstrate how schema-based connections may be applied, we present a modeling and explaining script with an excerpt from a first novel, *Parrot in the Oven mi vida,* by Victor Martinez. A Mexican American, Martinez portrayed a year in Manuel Hernandez's life through scenarios with his out-of-work father, his trailer-cleaning mother, his older sister and brother, his toddling sister, as well as friends and gang members in and out of school.

■ Modeling and Explaining: Schema-Based Connections

If you are an English teacher, you might select this book because Martinez depicts adolescent experiences that your students could compare and contrast to their own. Your content objective would be the understanding that fiction portrays the human condition. Your strategy objective would be for students to make schema-based connections to their own lives.

FIGURE 6.6   Finding and Interpreting Information: Schema-Based Connections

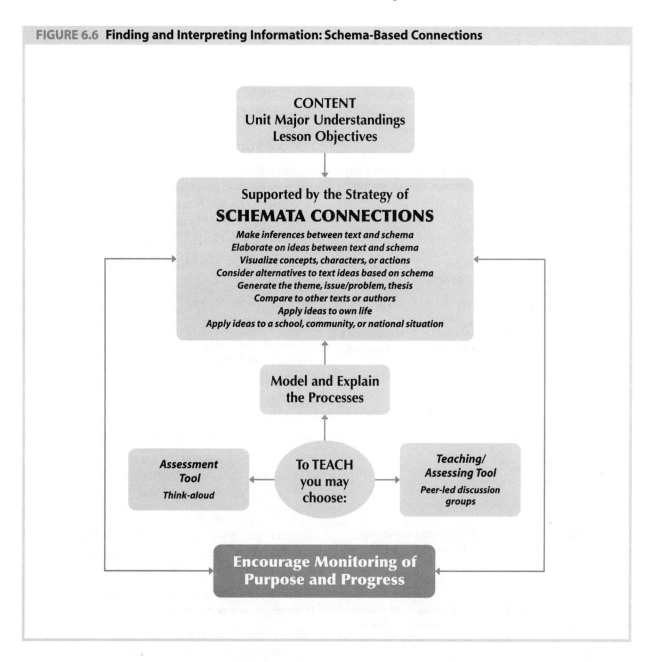

For this script, we have skipped prereading strategies because we want to focus on schema-based connections within finding and interpreting information. You know that in an actual situation, we would use before reading tools with students first. As you read this script, notice where the reader begins to think about the theme:

Modeling and Explaining Script: Schema-Based Connections

Strategies I Chose to Use	Fiction Text

Fiction Text

Parrot in the Oven
mi vida
by Victor Martinez

Remembering when I was a teenager, I worked Saturdays and summers as did my friends. [connecting to my life]

> To Mom's surprise, Dad actually found a job doing office work for the Awoni Building Company. To everyone's surprise, Nardo got a job delivering medicine for Giddens's Pharmacy. I helped him with his route on Saturdays. (p. 159)

I **visualize** a small-town drugstore with a mousy Mr. Giddens in the back filling prescriptions.

> . . . [A]gainst the nagging in my head, I stepped inside [the drugstore]. . . .

I have an ominous feeling reading this text—"against the nagging in my head" and "sizing me up." I sense a conflict between Manuel and Mr. Giddens that's based on cultural differences. [making inferences between text and schema]

> From the corner of my eye, I saw Mr. Giddens sizing me up. (p. 161) . . .

> [Then] I saw Dorothy, Mr. Giddens's daughter, although I didn't know her name or who she was at the time . . . (p. 163)

> When she saw me, she smiled, like she recognized me, then turned back around to Mr. Giddens who looked at me like suddenly an idea had popped into his head.

> "Oh, Manuel! Could you come over here a minute," he said, sending his arm around in a little corral. "I want to introduce you to my daughter."

Here is confirmation of my feeling: trouble is coming. Why does Mr. Giddens want to introduce Manuel to his daughter?

> He kept circling his hand for me to come over, but I couldn't get my shoes to budge. Something was screwed on wrong. Mr. Giddens inviting me over to introduce me to his daughter wasn't natural. . . .

Not knowing Manuel's last name is a signal of class and cultural differences. I think an underlying prejudice is operating here. [inferring alternatives to text ideas based on schema]

> "Dorothy, this is one of my delivery boys, Manuel, uh, Hernandez—or is it Herrera?" . . .

> "Hi, Dorothy!" I said, anxious to meet her, yet stiffening a little against Mr. Giddens's push.

> "Hi," she said smiling.

> She wanted to talk more with her father, but he didn't want to. (pp. 164–165)

Continued

Strategies I Chose to Use

Fiction Text

Why is Mr. Giddens inviting Manuel? This is a cultural clash. Dorothy doesn't want to bridge their differences. Manuel can only get hurt. Can't he see the danger? [thinking about the theme or issue]

"Would you like to come to Dorothy's party? Lots of food and punch?"

He said this enthusiastically, wiping his face with a handkerchief, but while he did, Dorothy was tightening her shoulders and her smile collapsed a little. "Dad!!" she said, stressing her voice. (p. 166) . . .

"Well," I said. I didn't know what to say, really; didn't know what was going on. Whatever was going on, though, I knew words wouldn't help.

"But he won't *know* anybody," Dorothy pleaded.

I remember the feelings of being outside the popular group. At times, I wanted to be inside, like Manuel, while at other times, I was content to have fun with my own friends. [connecting ideas to own life]

"That's what you'll be there for, honey," Mr. Giddens said with assurance, "to introduce him around, make him feel welcome. I'm positive he'll have a good time."

"Okay . . . okay. I give up!" Dorothy said, gritting her teeth and dropping her arms, exasperated. She handed me an invitation card. "Here, you're invited," she said halfheartedly. (p. 167)

. . .

From my vantage point, I want Manuel to resist, but I know I probably would not have when I was a teenager. The desire to be accepted is too strong for teenagers to resist.

He vaguely recognizes the prejudice of the Giddenses now. Later when he's hurt, he has directly experienced prejudice. [applying ideas to a real situation and issue]

Before walking out of the door, Dorothy turned and smiled. It was a smile that would tumble around inside my brain for days. I wanted to believe that it meant that somehow she'd changed her mind about me, and that I'd be welcome at her party, but deep down I knew it didn't. In any case I didn't care, and only later, when I realized that I should have cared, did it really hurt. (pp. 168–169)

Source: From *Parrot in the Oven* by Victor Martinez. Text copyright © 1996 by Victor Martinez. Used by permission of HarperCollins Publishers.

In summary, when I read *Parrot in the Oven* I made schema-based connections and linked them to text-based connections in order to find and interpret the information:

- I **applied ideas to my own life** (recalled my high school experiences).
- I **elaborated on ideas** from the text (remembered teen jobs).
- I **visualized** the setting and characters (the drugstore and Mr. Giddens).
- I **made inferences** between my text and schema (ominous feeling about an impending clash of cultures).

- I generated a theme or issue for the chapter (encountering cultural clash).

- I applied ideas to real situations (realistically knew Manuel couldn't resist, although I wished he would).

Earlier in this chapter, we emphasized teaching/assessing tools in which the teacher directs the focus of the discussion through questions. Now we focus on connections that students initiate. When you teach, you will decide when to be directive, because your students need to understand particular concepts and when to be open-ended, because you want to follow your students' selection of concepts and their reactions or their thinking about those ideas.

■ Teaching/Assessing Tool: Schema-Based Connections

Although this tool, peer-led discussions, is student-centered, emphasizing their schema-based connections, you would be wise to prepare backup questions or prompts in case a group is floundering. The students pose the questions, govern the course of the discussion, and challenge each other's understanding of the text. You may be a participant or provide support if necessary, but the students have the major responsibility for learning. For these discussions, you may decide to have the students read the same text or read a variety of texts on a theme.

In the teaching/assessing tools for text-based connections, we presented the DRA, QtA, reciprocal teaching, and discussion webs; in all of these, the teacher governs the discussions. Although we labeled those events as discussions, they are definitely school discussions designed to accomplish the teacher's objective. Outside of school, real discussions are governed by the participants who often have differing views about the topic.

peer-led discussion
Students determine the topics and question addressed and speak directly to each other during the discussion.

prepare back up questions

We use the general term *peer-led discussion*: students determine the topics and question addressed and speak directly to each other during the discussion because we want to refer to every content area. English and language arts teachers may encounter other similar terms, such as *book clubs* (McMahon & Raphael, 1997), *literature circles* (Daniels, 2002), and *grand conversations* (Eeds & Wells, 1989). Most other content areas use the term *small group discussion*, although *idea circles* has been coined for discussions of science texts (Guthrie & McCann, 1996).

In discussions, equal participants address a common issue—for example, math proofs, scientific evidence, or poetry reactions—in which the exchange of different views will augment the participants' understanding, appreciation, or actions (Dillon, 1994). We classify discussions as peer-led when the following characteristics are present (Dillon, 1994):

- Students talk directly to each other.

- Students ask questions of each other.

- Students' statements are longer than two or three words.

- Teachers ask questions for which they honestly don't know the answer (real questions!).

- Teachers are mostly silent and do not direct the speaking turns.

- Teachers occasionally reflect or rephrase a student's thought, connect two students' statements, or state their own genuine thoughts or interests.

As you see, we don't eliminate the teacher as a participant; however, the teacher is only a facilitator or coach (Maloch, 2002). In essence, by offering statements and evidence to support their statements, students discover what they think and are challenged by what other students think. Remember though that this is a social-cultural event and some students, especially diverse students, may consider expressing their ideas too risky.

Holding Discussions

We think that genuine discussion can occur when a teacher initiates the discussion by asking a real question, stating a problem or issue, or simply asking for student reactions. Although teachers may initiate peer-led discussions with a prompt, experienced discussants may find their own reactions or issues more engaging and ignore the prompt (Alvermann et al., 1996). When that happens, teachers must remember that the objective is for students to react thoughtfully, not necessarily to address the prompt.

Genuine discussion occurs when students initiate the questions, although low-track students rarely ask questions (Nystrand, Gamoran, Zeiser, & Long, 2001). In peer-led discussions, students sustain topics, recycle back to topics, clarify words or events, discuss literary devices and themes, ask more questions, offer alternative interpretations, and participate with longer and more complex responses (Almasi, 1995; Almasi, Oflahavan & Arya, 2001; Paterson, 2000; Seidenstricker, 2000). When students held their literature and science discussions on-line, more students participated but some students found the discussion harder to follow (Albright, Purohit & Walsh, 2002). Students can also manage their discussions by encouraging everyone's participation and organizing topics to discuss (Almasi et al., 2001).

Students discuss
their understandings,
reactions, and questions
regarding the book
they're reading.
© Susie Fitzhugh

Students know that they need to come to discussions prepared (Evans, 2002). Sometimes students respond first in their journals as they read (see the Focus on Writing section at the end of this chapter) or students may complete a freewriting or drawing before the discussion. Teacher Eric Paulsen has students mark important passages with small sticky notes on which students write a key word to remind them of the idea they want to discuss (Daniels, 2002). Another teacher has the motto, "If anything is odd, inappropriate, confusing, or boring, it's probably important" and students are to find those places in texts that are probably important (Rex, 2001, p. 294).

Guidelines for Holding Peer-Led Discussions

Forming the group is the first task. We prefer small groups of about five students—large enough to produce different views yet small enough so that each student has a reasonable chance to speak. Depending on the class or the particular unit, we sometimes assign students to groups and at other times allow students to form friendship groups. Experienced discussants prefer to work with peers who contribute to the discussion, whether they are friends or not (Alvermann et al., 1996; Evans, 2002).

When you compose groups, consider your diverse students. In the beginning of the year, you may form affinity groups until your classroom climate is respectful of diversity. Single-gender groups may give girls a chance to talk in science and boys a chance to discuss the plot in literature circles (Guzzetti, 2001; Lewis, 2001). ELL and LD students are reluctant to speak out even in small groups; however, as they gain experience with small groups, they will participate and maybe even lead them (Goatley, Brock, & Raphael, 1995). Once the groups have been formed keep the following guidelines in mind as students conduct peer-led discussions.

1. All students should be able to talk without fear of put-down or ridicule. Only then will diverse views be expressed. Students need to listen to understand the meaning, not just the words, of every student's contribution.

2. Students decide and agree upon the task before the group. Whether the task is to explore diverse reactions or to focus on the teacher's prompt, the students learn to monitor their productivity. Students also learn that they have complementary responsibilities—to talk and to listen, as well as to focus on the topic and explore different perspectives. In an exploratory mode (Short, 1992), students wander off topics, meander around various topics, and appear not to complete topics they begin to explore. Nevertheless, engaged students return to important connections, keep each other centered on important questions or positions, and reintroduce burning issues. When students know that the expectation is a mutual exploration of ideas and the topic is interesting or debatable, they will keep each other reasonably on task (Alvermann et al., 1996).

3. At the beginning of the year, teachers should explicitly model preparing for and participating in genuine discussions (Almasi et al., 2001; Rex, 2001). You and the class would read a short selection and respond on sticky notes or find important passages. You and your students would share the responses made while reading. You may decide to pursue one of the students' responses to initiate a discussion.

Or you would ask a real question or seek divergent interpretations to initiate a discussion. Afterwards, you would develop discussion guidelines with the class.

4. Throughout the year, to support peer-led discussions, teachers hold a debriefing session in which each group evaluates how the discussion proceeded compared to a list of criteria for the whole class. When a particular criterion is hard to achieve, such as valuing everyone's point of view, then the teachers make that an objective to focus on during the next discussion. The *fishbowl technique* can be a useful evaluation tool. A small group sits in the center and holds their discussion. In a circle around the center group, the rest of the students sit and take notes on how the discussion is proceeding. After the discussion, the class debriefs, citing the criteria met and the criteria needing improvement. At no time should an individual be singled out by name; instead students describe behaviors that did or did not contribute to the discussion.

Although we really like peer-led discussions because students challenge each other, both teachers and students take risks in participating (Christoph & Nystrand, 2001). Teachers risk not covering required topics, but if teachers keep track of the topics students discuss, they may find that the students have discussed the required topics (Paterson, 2000). Teachers also risk not being in "control" and heated discussions may occur. Students, especially diverse students, may need the teacher's support in reading, interpreting, and discussing the text (Boyd & Rubin, 2002; Christoph & Nystrand, 2001; Rex, 2001). Students risk their status with peers and ELL students risk speaking English. The classroom climate must respect differences but even then the classroom can be a risky place. However, in spite of the risks, we think the benefits outweigh the risks and encourage you to learn to guide peer-led discussions.

■ Assessment Tool: Schema-Based Connections

The purpose of the think-aloud tool is to determine the reader's strategies and the schema-based and text-based connections he or she makes. Thus, we could have placed the think-aloud with text-based connections just as easily.

For inquiry activities, we suggested in Chapter 1 that you complete a think-aloud and in Chapter 2 that a student complete a think-aloud. You might want to have another student complete a think-aloud now that you have been reading about strategies.

When teachers are puzzled about a student's learning process, they may ask that student to think aloud as he or she works on a task. Then the teacher can figure out the strategies and the information that the puzzling student is using during the task. A teacher we know asks her whole class to think aloud quietly with text. The students write their thoughts, questions, and reactions on sticky notes, which they stick on the pages. Later she carefully examines the comments written by the one or two students who were puzzling her and only quickly surveys the comments from other students.

When you use a think-aloud to assess whether students find and interpret important information, you are noticing examples of both text-based and schema-based connections as outlined in Table 6.3. After the think-aloud, you would discuss the student's specific comments with him or her. You want the student to be aware of the strategies that he or she used well. You might also ask questions about strategies that could be used.

TABLE 6.3 Connections to Assess During a Think-Aloud

Text-Based Connections	Schema-Based Connections
Comments on the important information	Comments by inferring or elaborating on ideas
Translates information into their own words	Speculates on the theme or thesis of the text
Comments on what they don't understand	Suggests alternative actions or solutions from own experiences or knowledge
Comments how later text relates to previous text	Comments on ideas from past sources read
Comments how the graphics clarify or augment the words	Comments on real situations from own life or own community

Focus on Writing: Writing to Learn

We introduced journals to you in Chapter 4 as a before-reading activity and in Chapter 5 as a place to use and extend new vocabulary learning. Now we continue that discussion by describing different types of journals: learning logs, lab or field notebooks, reaction journals, dialogue journals, and double-entry journals. Regardless of what the journals are called, students use them to discover how they are comprehending and constructing their knowledge.

Since the management of many journals from different classes becomes a juggling act, you will want to devise a reasonable schedule for assessing students' journals. Some teachers respond during class, ask students to label certain entries to which they respond, or respond to five journals per class each night. We know that finding time to respond can be irksome; however, students will use their journals more thoughtfully if you carve out time to respond.

You will want to model and explain how to use the journals. Your responses to students' journals will continue to support their journal writing.

■ Learning Logs and Lab or Field Notebooks

Teachers sometimes ask students to record their information, explain their understanding, and examine their learning processes in journals. You want students to express in their own words how they understand the text and how they understood class discussions and activities.

In science classes, students can record their procedures and their observations in a lab or field notebook. As the science teacher, you would review these notebooks for students' understanding of the concepts and their learning processes. Have they entered predictions or hypotheses? Are they appropriately reconsidering their previous ideas? Notice the questions or hypotheses the high school student records in this entry:

In lab, we are making models of molecules with different bonds, and have just made a butane molecule that has free bond rotation. Even though they have the capability of doing so, why would they? Also what makes them move? Kinetic energy? I wonder what the world would be like if there was not free-bound rotation—really cold? (Lozauskas & Barell, 1992 p. 44)

■ Reaction Journals, Dialogue Journals, Double-Entry Journals

We have already suggested that students prepare for discussions by writing in journals. Students can respond in three versions of journals:

- **Reaction journal** (the generic version). The student records questions, ideas, thoughts, drawings, comments, predictions, or any other connections to the text.

- **Dialogue journal.** A reaction journal that has a respondent. Usually the teacher responds, but peer-respondents work too. The student and the respondent hold a written conversation about the text. In conversing with the students, teachers build on the students' connections, offer connections to their own lives, probe for more information, and question the students' thoughts.

- **Double-entry journal.** The page in the journal is divided in half vertically. In Chapter 1, we suggested that you keep an inquiry field notebook in double-entry form. As a reaction journal, the student uses one side of the page to write a summary of the text or notes about the text. On the opposite half, the student records his or her reactions triggered by that text.

When Whitin (1996) used reaction journals in her seventh-grade class, the students responded to literature with both writing and drawing. Using the sketch-to-stretch technique (Harste, Short, & Burke, 1988), the students drew their interpretations of themes, characters, conflicts, and feelings using symbols, colors, shapes, lines, and textures. Whenever they drew, the students explained how their drawings represented their ideas to Whitin, the class, or their collaborative group. Heidi, one of the students, chose to sketch a pie chart to represent the feelings of Perry in *Fallen Angels* by Walter Dean Myers. She explained the chart also in her journal (see Figure 6.7).

From reading students' journals, you would assess what connections the students make independently. Then you would emphasize text-based and schema-based connections they don't make in a mini-lesson and encourage those connections in your responses in their journals.

TEACHER AS INQUIRING LEARNER

Trade dialogue journals with a middle school or high school diversity student (Bean & Rigoni, 2001). As you both read a text the student needs to read, both of you keep response journals. You respond to the student's journal and the student responds to yours. Investigate whether you and the student could do this on-line. How does the student respond? Do you have similar interpretations? Does the student need encouragement to make text-based and schema-based responses? Which of your responses encourage the student to read and respond more thoughtfully?

FIGURE 6.7 **Pie Chart and Journal Response for** *Fallen Angels*

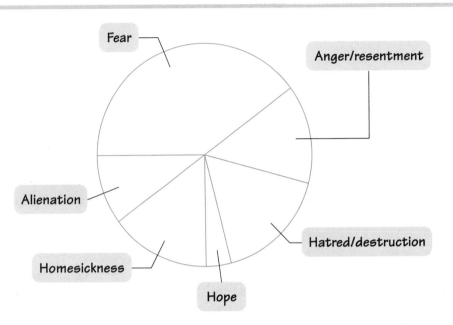

Portfolio comment: I was looking out for a chance to use the pie graph idea, and here it came! I was able to depict the feelings of the characters in the book. In doing this sketch-to-stretch, I was forced to look at the people in the book more closely, to imagine what they'd be feeling. It was an exercise in putting myself in their place.

Source: From *Research in the Teaching of English, 30* (1), p. 124. Copyright © 1996 by the National Council of Teachers of English.

 ## Monitoring Purpose and Progress During Reading

You know that we consider purpose setting and monitoring to be ongoing, underlying strategies throughout learning. You know that strategic readers set their purposes before reading. Now, during reading, they monitor those purposes, checking to see if they can accomplish their purposes. If not, then strategic readers decide whether to find a different text or to change their purposes. In addition, their strategies of activating prior knowledge, previewing and predicting, and exploring new vocabulary provide the initial ideas that they will continue to monitor during reading.

Throughout reading, strategic readers monitor their progress in constructing meaning. As they negotiate text-based and schema-based meaning, they determine how well they understand the connections among the ideas. Strategic readers concentrate on finding and interpreting text information to add to their schemata and on searching their schemata for information that helps them understand the text. When comprehension is proceeding smoothly, strategic readers focus on understanding the information. When they discover puzzling information, in either the text or their schemata, then strategic readers focus on their strategies and decide how best to change strategies.

People usually think reading means to proceed from page 1 straight through the text in order. However, when their purposes are served better, strategic readers move around in text. During reading, strategic readers regulate their pace through the text by rereading, reading on, reading aloud, skimming, skipping parts, jumping back to parts, reading ahead and around, or pausing to think. For example, strategic readers often read the conclusion section of a research report first, especially when no abstract is available. Some mystery readers read the ending first, although many others wouldn't want to spoil the plot by reading the ending first. When readers adjust how they are comprehending, they are monitoring their progress.

Thus, once again, monitoring progress is pervasive when strategic learners tackle texts.

A Checklist: Monitoring Strategies During Reading

Monitoring Purpose

❑ Can you accomplish your original purpose with this text?
❑ Should you change texts or modify your purpose?

Monitoring Text-Based Connections for Finding and Interpreting Information

❑ Can you paraphrase the information in the text in your own words?
❑ Are you asking questions about information you don't understand?
❑ Can you distinguish the important information and supporting information from the unimportant or irrelevant information?
❑ Does the graphic information help you understand the text?
❑ Can you elaborate or make inferences on the ideas in the text?
❑ Do you find conflicting information in the text?

Monitoring Schema-Based Connections for Finding and Interpreting Information

❑ Can you elaborate or make inferences between text ideas and your schema ideas?
❑ Can you visualize the concepts or characters?
❑ Do you know of alternative ideas that the text doesn't consider?
❑ Can you state the theme, thesis, or issue or problem that the text centers on?
❑ Can you describe how other sources of information or authors are similar to or different from this source?
❑ Can you describe how the text could apply to your own life, your community, or the world?

 SUMMARY

In this chapter, we have focused on the middle of a literacy task, when strategic readers are constructing their knowledge by making connections between text-based and schema-based information. First, we emphasized the interplay between text-based and schema-based connections with the strategy:

■ **Finding and interpreting information.**

We also discussed the role of questions and types of questions and answers so that you could guide your students in finding and interpreting important information.

You know that readers choose particular strategies to match the specific text they are reading because they continually:

■ **Monitor their purpose and their progress.**

To teach these strategies, we described tools that support text-based and schema-based connections:

■ **Modeling and explaining several strategies to make the entire process visible, like with the West Nile script.**

■ **Modeling and explaining specific strategies to concentrate on making particular strategies visible—like the Manuel script.**

■ **Teaching and assessing tools to assist students in finding and interpreting information, for example, the DRA, reciprocal teaching, comprehension guides, and peer-led discussions.**

■ **Assessment tools like admit slips to gauge the class's understanding or retellings and think-alouds to figure out a puzzling student's strategies.**

■ **Focusing on writing to learn in journals.**

You recognize that you must select when to model and explain, when to use a teaching/assessing tool, and when to focus on writing. Over the course of the year, you will use some teaching tools over and over again, and others you will use as your students need them with specific texts. You want students to be comfortable with classroom procedures, yet engaged by the variety of strategies and tools you infuse in your content instruction.

Finding and interpreting important information may be challenging if the content or the text format is unfamiliar. To help make text-based and schema-based connections, strategic readers call upon supporting strategies—capitalizing on text organization, making notes or drawings, and defining vocabulary in context. We turn to those strategies in the next chapter.

Inquiry into Your Learning

1. Find three to five peers to read the same text with you. Choose a controversial or issue-tackling text, such as the young adult novel *Witness* by Karen Hesse, an editorial, or a movie review. As you read, mark with sticky notes what strikes you and where you have an opinion or reaction. Meet as a peer-led discussion group and discuss the text. Notice what makes the discussion work well and what detracts from it. Compare when your group is on task and when it's off task. Did the off-task time contribute to or distract from the discussion? Did everyone feel like they had a fair chance to participate? Was there a leader of the discussion? Compare your peer-led discussion to a middle school or high school peer-led discussion.

2. Choose a fiction or nonfiction book about a subject in your content area, and write a reaction journal as you read it. Maybe two of you want to read the

same book or complementary books and exchange dialogue journals. What do you think about while you read certain sections? What do you question? What reactions, opinions, and feelings does the book arouse? How does the book relate to your own life or your community? What do you notice about the content or the author's writing? Would you use the book with students? How do you think students would react to the book? What would you discuss with students when they read the book?

Inquiry into Your Students' Learning

1. Create a comprehension study guide for a text in your content area. You could choose a textbook, a magazine or newspaper article, or a chapter from an informational book, if you want nonfiction text. If you choose a fiction book, you may decide to make a guide for one chapter, several chapters, or the entire book. Decide your content objective for the text or what is important to learn from the text. Devise the connection questions or statements first and then the supporting questions or statements. Have a small group of students read the text and complete your study guide. Evaluate your guide to determine whether to change it for another group.

2. Plan and hold a small group discussion about a text in your content area. Discuss with the teacher what text to have the students read, when they should read it, and whether to conduct a teacher-led discussion or to participate in a peer-led discussion. If you choose the teacher-led discussion, you need to plan questions that will initiate and facilitate discussion—real or connection question(s) and supporting questions. You also need to decide what teaching tool to use, for instance, the DRA. If you choose a peer-led discussion, you also need to plan a prompt to initiate the discussion and comments or real questions to facilitate discussion. You want to be prepared in case your students don't lead the discussion or finish the discussion too quickly.

Resources

Books

Alford, K. (1999). "Yes, Girl, You Understand": History logs and the building of multicultural empathy. In S. W. Freedman, E. R. Simons, J. S. Kalin, A. Casareno & the M-CLASS teams (Eds.), *Inside city schools: Investigating literacy in multicultural classrooms*, (pp. 126–141). New York: Teachers. Diverse students study slavery throughout history from different perspectives. A white girl understands she could not have written the Black girl's poem; hence, "Yes, Girl, You understand."

Daniels, H. (2002). *Literature circles: Voice and choice in book clubs and reading groups*, (2nd ed.). Portland, ME: Stenhouse. Explains how to incorporate peer-led discussions in a range of middle school and high school classrooms. Contains good examples of nonfiction discussion sheets.

Journals

Albright, J., Purohit, K., & Walsh, C. (2002). Louise Rosenblatt seeks QtAsnBoi@aol.com for LTR: Using chat rooms in interdisciplinary middle school classrooms. *Journal of Adolescent and Adult Literacy, 45* (8), 692–705. Discusses how students interacted online in literature class and science class.

Albright, L. K. (2002). Bring the Ice Maiden to life: Engaging adolescents in learning through picture book read-alouds in content areas. *Journal of Adolescent and Adult Literacy, 45* (5), 418–528. Presents questions used before, during, and after the teacher read-alouds in a middle school social studies class. Also discusses strategies questions evoked, although we would identify the strategies explicitly with students.

Connolly, B. & Smith, M. (2002). Teachers and students talk about talk: Class discussion and the way it should be. *Journal of Adolescent & Adult Literacy, 46* (1), 18–26. Describes a teacher implementing small group and whole class discussions and students reluctance to express themselves to the whole class.

Fourneir, D. N. E. & Graves, M. (2002). Scaffolding adolescents' comprehension of short stories. *Journal of Adolescent & Adult Literacy, 46* (1), 30–39. Describes activities that supported students' reading such as personal responses, questions, and character grid.

Rierson, S. & Duty, L. (2003). Conscientizacao: Latina women, American students, and empowerment in the social studies classroom. *Social Education, 67* (1), 33–37. Presents teacher-led discussion questions as well as mapping and journal prompts to use with testimonials by Latina women.

Sprague, M. M. & Cotturone, J. (2003). Motivating students to read physics content. *The Science Teacher, 70* (3), 24–29. Describes teacher-guided discussions, comprehension questions, and summary writing that students did with literature containing science, such as *The Science of Star Wars* (Cavelos, 2000).

Stephens, A. C. (2003). Another look at word problems. *Mathematics Teacher, 96* (1), 63–65. Has students describe linear equations in words—the reverse of the usual paraphrasing task (text-based connections).

Williams, K. M. (2003). Writing about problem-solving process to improve problem-solving performance. *Mathematics Teacher, 96* (3), 185–187. Describes a study of students' writing to learn (metacognitive awareness of their processes) and shows examples.

Web Sites

LiteratureCircles.com. **www.literaturecircles.com.** Contains book reviews, articles, and book excerpts and has a peer coaching section and a student's section. Students can submit their own book reviews.

CHAPTER 7

Supporting Strategies for Comprehension

KEY CONCEPTS

PURPOSE-SETTING QUESTIONS

1 Do you use a text's organization to help you locate important information to comprehend? Do you recognize various text organizations, such as a fable or newspaper article?

2 When you read a text with a confusing or difficult text organization, did a teacher help you with a teaching/assessing tool? Did your high school teachers discuss text organizations?

3 How did you learn to take notes? Do you use a system or have you just discovered techniques through practice?

4 What do you do when you meet an unknown word while reading—skip it, figure it out from context or word parts, or look it up in the dictionary? How do you decide what you're going to do with unknown words?

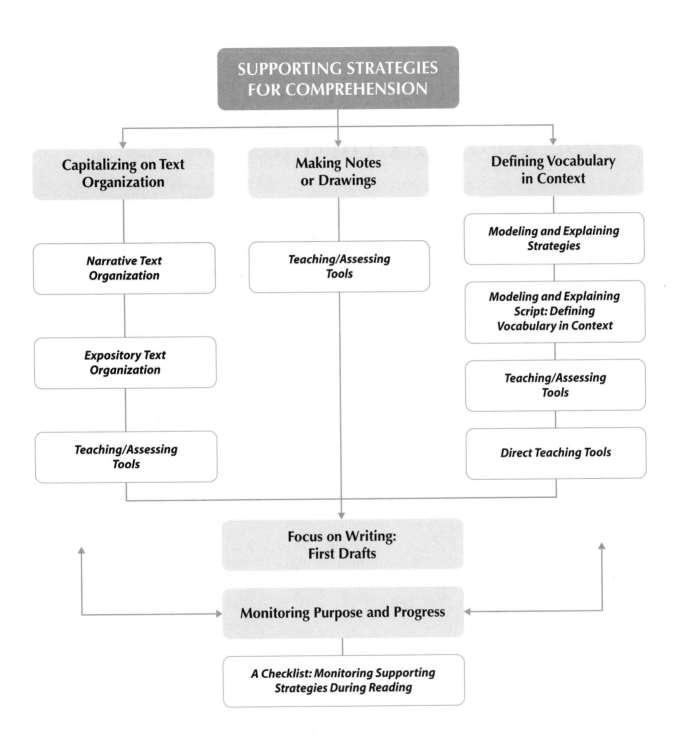

SUPPORTING STRATEGIES
FOR COMPREHENSION

Capitalizing on Text
Organization

Making Notes
or Drawings

Defining Vocabulary
in Context

Narrative Text
Organization

Teaching/Assessing
Tools

Modeling and Explaining
Strategies

Modeling and Explaining
Script: Defining
Vocabulary in Context

Expository Text
Organization

Teaching/Assessing
Tools

Teaching/Assessing
Tools

Direct Teaching Tools

Focus on Writing:
First Drafts

Monitoring Purpose and Progress

A Checklist: Monitoring Supporting
Strategies During Reading

Comprehending and constructing knowledge is the core of the reading process. Strategic readers negotiate schema-based knowledge and text-based knowledge to learn. In the last chapter, we emphasized that negotiation and the teaching tools you could use to support students' comprehension. You recognize that sometimes your students need to emphasize text-based connections, while at other times their schema-based connections may dominate. However, with every text, strategic readers balance how they use both text-based and schema-based connections because they are constructing their knowledge.

While strategic readers are making connections, they often use three supporting strategies, especially if the text is difficult for them. First, strategic readers use the strategy of capitalizing on text organization. From their schemata, they know how texts might be organized and look for clues in the text that fit one of those organizations. Recall in Chapter 4 that, from schema knowledge, the reader recognized the source and the persuasive genre of the editorial and used that knowledge to comprehend. Strategic readers search for the author's clues to the text's organization because those clues indicate where the most important information is. When strategic readers capitalize on text organization, they can more easily connect text-based information across different places in the text.

Second, knowing that remembering complex information can be cumbersome, if not difficult, strategic readers make notes or drawings to help them construct meaning. Strategic readers know that when they make notes during reading, they should pull out the most important information and details to remember. Sometimes, strategic readers draw a diagram or model to help them picture the information. They review their notes or drawings and may also add their schemata information.

Finally, strategic readers define new vocabulary or concepts they meet during reading. Strategic readers may decide they can get the gist of the meaning from the surrounding words or context. At other times, they decide the word is an important conceptual word for which they need a precise definition. When they need the word for understanding, readers define the word using the context, figure out the word parts (morphemic analysis), and consult the dictionary to make sure they comprehend the text.

As you read about these three supporting strategies—capitalizing on text organization, making notes or drawings, and defining vocabulary in context—think about when and how you learned to use those strategies. We find that many students have learned the strategies on their own without help from teachers. You cannot assume all of your students will acquire the strategies independently. Instead, you will teach them to use the strategies to support their comprehension.

Therefore, in this chapter we build on the text-based and schema-based strategies and teaching tools in the previous chapter because these three strategies help students comprehend and construct knowledge (see chapter organizer). First, we discuss capitalizing on text organization for narrative texts and expository texts by referring back to scripts in previous chapters, present teaching/assessing tools to help students use text organizations, and refer to previous assessment tools. Second, we discuss teaching tools for making notes or drawings. Third, we present a new script for defining vocabulary in context, teaching/assessing tools, and direct teaching tools. We conclude the chapter with a Focus on Writing section that discusses composing first drafts and with the section on Monitoring of Purpose and Progress.

Capitalizing on Text Organization

S ometimes readers have difficulty finding where important text-based information is located or separating important information from less important or irrelevant information. In this situation, strategic readers use their schema-based knowledge to *capitalize on text organization* to assist them in finding and interpreting important information and in recalling that information later (Myer, Brandt, & Bluth, 1980; Richgels, McGee, Lomax & Sheard, 1987; Taylor, 1980). Before we begin our discussion of tools, let's examine two basic categories of text organization: narrative text organization and expository text organization (see Figure 7.1).

capitalize on text organization A literacy strategy in which one uses how a text is constructed to find important information.

We usually divide text organization into narrative (fiction) organization or structure and expository (nonfiction) organizations or structures. However, authors are not so cleanly categorized. For example, journalists sometimes use the narrative organization to communicate factual information. Some authors decide to reorder the typical expository or narrative organizations. For example, scientists may state the conclusion and implications of their research first. Or a novelist may tell the final outcome in the first sentence, as Toni Morrison does in *Paradise.*

DIVERSITY

In every culture, generations tell oral stories to the next generation. Stories from different cultures may be organized differently. For example, Ball (1992) describes three types of text organizations that occur in African-American culture. First, African Americans tell stories that are a series of topics or anecdotes connected by an implicit theme (circumlocution organization). Ball uses the example of a letter telling about a trip, a job, and a driver's license linked by the unstated theme of summer. Second, when discussing a topic, African Americans embed a personal story to clarify or elaborate on a point (narrative interspersion organization). And third, African Americans, especially preachers, repeat a topic using different words or images to emphasize a point (recursion organization). For example, Martin Luther King, Jr. often used recursion in his speeches.

Children hear oral stories from adults and are prompted to tell their own stories unconsciously using the patterns they have heard. Young African-American children tell stories that link different topics (Michaels, 1981)—the circumlocution pattern. In

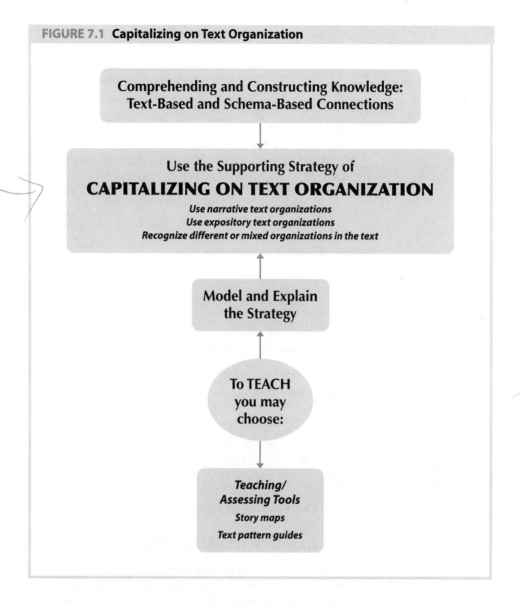

FIGURE 7.1 Capitalizing on Text Organization

**Comprehending and Constructing Knowledge:
Text-Based and Schema-Based Connections**

Use the Supporting Strategy of
CAPITALIZING ON TEXT ORGANIZATION
Use narrative text organizations
Use expository text organizations
Recognize different or mixed organizations in the text

**Model and Explain
the Strategy**

**To TEACH
you may
choose:**

*Teaching/
Assessing Tools*
Story maps
Text pattern guides

contrast, European-American children tell stories that focus on a single topic (Michaels, 1981). Arapaho children tell stories that have no ending because adult stories are continued night after night—a series pattern (Delpit, 1995).

Thus, every culture has story patterns that usually originate in oral texts and may also occur in written texts—what Gates has termed, "speakerly texts" (Gates cited in Lee, 1993).

We don't expect you to know how every culture tells stories or communicates information. Especially if you are going to be an English teacher, you will want to read authors of different cultures to find out if their styles differ. In your classroom, you can also ask students to write informal letters to a friend or relative to learn how they might use cultural patterns of writing. Then you can show your students how to recognize various cultural patterns, including patterns of the dominant culture. You can help your students choose the pattern appropriate for their specific audience. Now, let's examine the typical organizations found in school texts.

■ Narrative Text Organization

Many of the stories students read in middle school, the required literature high school students read in English classes, and even many of the movies they choose to see follow the European-American generic *story structure* or *story grammar* (Stein & Glenn, 1979; Mandler & Johnson, 1977). That generic story structure includes:

- Setting—time, place, main characters

- Problem and goal

- Plot or sequence of events

    Event 1—attempt and outcome

    Event 2—attempt and outcome

    Event 3—attempt and outcome

- Resolution of problem and attainment of goal

[handwritten note: Students always notice circle stories and fairy tale stories]

Not every narrative text includes these elements; for example, some books have an unresolved ending. Diverse authors may or may not follow a different pattern or may include culturally relevant elements. Recall the script about Manny in the drugstore in Chapter 6. We excerpted Martinez's book in which he depicted different episodes Manny experienced during one year. Do you think Martinez followed the generic story structure in which each episode is an event in the plot? Or did Martinez choose the circumlocution organization in which the episodes are united by an implied theme? Comparing how various stories and films are structured can be an interesting investigation for you and your students.

■ Expository Text Organization

Nonfiction writers use a wide variety of text organizations. Think about how differently front-page news reports and directions for a game are organized. Writers may use a single organization throughout the text, although often writers combine different text organizations. For example, authors writing history often combine chronological and cause-and-effect organizations when they explain the events leading to the American Revolution. Sometimes authors indicate the text's organization by signal words—but sometimes they don't. (See Table 7.1.) You might want to look back to the West Nile script and note how the comparison organization was signaled.

Whether the writer used a single organization and signal words or multiple organizations without signal words will determine how difficult the comprehension task will be for your students (Hare, Rabinowitz, & Schieble, 1989). You will want to examine the texts in your content area for the different text organizations that writers in your field commonly use. In addition, you will want to model and explain how to capitalize on text organization for finding and for recalling important information. (See the West Nile script in Chapter 6.)

Do in Class!

➡ TEACHER AS INQUIRING LEARNER

Explore different types of fiction, short stories, or movies to see how the types compare to the generic story structure.

- What elements do different authors include? What elements do different authors change?

Alternatively, you may want to compare fables and folktales from different cultures. For example, the librarian could help you find the cultural variations of the Cinderella story or creation myths.

- Do tales from different cultures exhibit similar elements?

teaching/assessing tool
A teaching tool that supports a student's learning and through which a teacher can assess a student's progress.

■ Teaching/Assessing Tools

From the questions you ask during a directed reading activity or from a student's retelling or think-aloud, you will be able to assess whether a student uses text organization as a supporting strategy. When students seem to be confused about what and where the important information is, we recommend introducing a guide to the text's organization. Although we have used the term *text organization*, you will find the terms *text pattern* and *story map* used to refer to specific guides that assist students with text organization.

Story Maps for Narrative Texts

From their past fiction reading, many of your students will have the common elements of a story in their schemata. However, LD students often do not recognize narrative

TABLE 7.1 Expository Text Organizations and Common Signal Words

Text Organization	Signal Words
Sequence, chronology, biography, life cycle, procedures	*a specific date, now, then, before, after, when, first, second, finally*
Cause and effect, causal chain of events	*because, consequently, as a result, thus, therefore, since, if … then*
Problem-solution, hypothesis-results	*because, consequently, as a result, thus, therefore, since, if … then*
Persuasion, argument	*therefore, thus, if … then, because, since*
Comparison and contrast, similarities and differences	*but, although, yet, however, while, either … or, neither … nor, on the other hand, more than, less than*
Main idea and supporting details, topic and attributes or examples	*for instance, for example, one … another*
Collection or topic and list of items in no particular order	*next, then, and, one … another*

organization and would benefit from instruction that uses story maps (Gersten, Fuchs, Williams, & Baker, 2001). You will want to use a *story map* to support students' reading in the following situations:

- The story pattern is from a culture unfamiliar to the student.

- Your students cannot recognize story elements in familiar books.

- Time switches like flashbacks or foreshadowing complicate the text's plot.

- Significant events, like a character's mental states, are difficult to follow.

Even high school students have difficulty following the mental states of Henry Fleming in *The Red Badge of Courage*.

A story map can take different forms. Some teachers outline the story elements, as we did earlier in the chapter. After each element, the students record the specific details as they read. When students read quest, survival, or adventure stories, a circle graphic organizer may capture the character's journey from "home," through trials, and back to "home." "Home" may be a physical place, or it could represent a mental state, with the events serving as episodes in the character's development or growth.

Text Pattern Guides: Single Organization

We think expository text organization is more difficult than narrative text organization because students have less experience with nonfiction texts. With practice reading expository texts, some students discover different text organizations. However, LD students are not aware of different expository text patterns (Gersten, et al., 2001). Since most students would benefit from guidance, we prefer to teach expository text organizations directly by modeling and explaining, discussing text organizations with students, and creating text pattern guides for students to use while they read (Armbruster, Anderson, & Ostertag, 1987; Taylor & Beach, 1984).

When you create a *text pattern guide* for students, your goal is to show students how text organization can lead to the important information and how to connect information across sections of the text or interpret information. You will want to begin with a text that has a single, clear organization. Here are the guidelines:

1. Examine the text to determine how the author organized the information: sequence, cause and effect, problem-solution, comparison and contrast, main idea and supporting details, persuasion or argument, listing or collection.

2. Determine whether the author used signal words explicitly to highlight the text organization.

3. Create a graphic organizer that depicts the text organization. You may decide to complete part of the graphic organizer to assist the students or have the students fill in all of the graphic organizer. The graphic organizer in Figure 7.2 is designed to guide students in describing the roles and hierarchy of ancient Egyptian society.

4. Have the students read the text and fill in the text pattern guide.

When they have completed the guide, you would have the students discuss the information in small groups or with the whole class.

FIGURE 7.2 Graphic Organizer for Text Pattern Guide

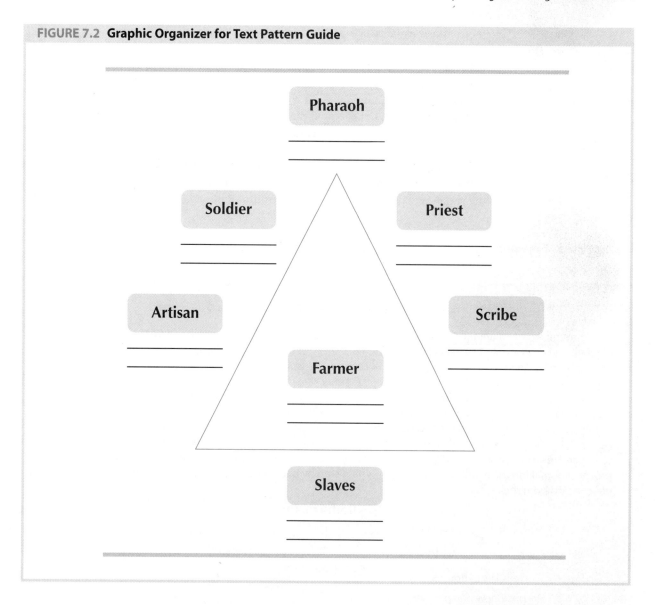

Text Pattern Guides: Mixed Organizations

In many texts, different sections of the text may use two or more organizations. For example, social studies textbooks often combine chronological and cause/effect organizations. Another example of a text with mixed organizations is web sites. Some are organized for easy navigation; others are not. Your students may become confused by mixed organizations and need help in locating the important information. For textbooks, web sites, or any text that has mixed organizations you could create a text pattern guide to direct students to the information you want them to concentrate on.

For example, in "Traveling the Long Road to Freedom, One Step at a Time," the author, Donovan Webster, relates historian Anthony Cohen's experiences in retracing the routes runaway slaves took on the Underground Railroad. From the title, we expected that the essay would be a chronology of Cohen's journey (*sequence pattern*). However, in addition, Webster contrasts Cohen's trip to the runaways' trips (*comparison pattern*) and periodically explains a specific topic (*main idea* and *supporting details pattern*)—resulting in three text organizations. Figure 7.3 shows an excerpt from the article in which the comparison pattern is in boldface and the sequence pattern is underlined.

Suppose your students will read this text in their study of the Civil War. You would choose one organization to emphasize and give them a text pattern guide to assist them in locating the factual information you want to emphasize. We would choose a comparison pattern guide to emphasize the similarities (and differences) of Cohen's trip to the runaway slaves' trips on the Underground Railroad (see Figure 7.3).

FIGURE 7.3 Excerpt from Text with Mixed Patterns and Text Pattern Guide

Traveling the Long Road to Freedom, One Step at a Time

Through a dark midnight drizzle, Anthony Cohen is on the run. **Like a slave escaped** from a plantation in the antebellum South—**only 150 years later**—Cohen is testing his fate on the Underground Railroad. He has **now** spent 700 miles and six weeks engaged in hook-or-crook transport, moving fast and light, **retracing a route once used by runaway slaves** as they sought refuge in Canada.

As it was for his predecessors, Cohen's trip has been difficult. "I'll go by foot, boat, train, horse, buggy, **any historically accurate way** I can hitch a ride," he's fond of telling listeners. . . .

Right now, though, Cohen is traveling by every escaped slave's most standard means: his feet. In tonight's case, he's hoofing a rainy towpath along the Erie Canal in western New York State. He's exhausted and behind schedule. He's a little discouraged, too, though he's trying not to show it. Earlier tonight, he'd been buoyed by the prospect of making the nearly 40-mile trip to his next stop by boat, but departure time came and went—and he never heard from the captain.

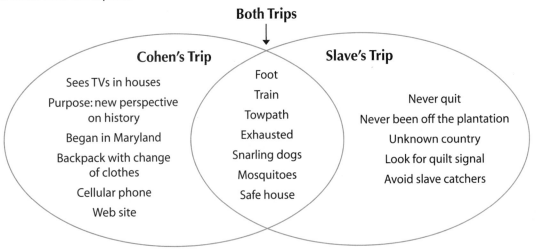

Source: D. Webster, "Traveling the Long Road to Freedom, One Step at a Time," *Smithsonian, 27* (1996): 48–49.

Thus, although the author of this text combined three text organizations, in our instruction we would guide students to the comparative information because it would be most useful to their study of the Civil War.

Making Notes or Drawings

make notes or drawings
A literacy strategy in which one records important information to support comprehension and memory of information.

We have already modeled and explained the supporting strategy of *making notes* in Chapter 6 with the West Nile script. Do you remember the results from the different studies? Knowing those details would be hard to recall, the reader took notes but didn't just jot them down in linear fashion on a page. Instead, the reader organized the notes into a comparative chart (or graphic organizer) in order to draw conclusions more easily. Taking notes is a common strategy, but people also draw pictures, make diagrams, construct models, visualize images, or think of examples and analogies to assist their memories and study ideas (see Figure 7.4). We recommend teaching note taking, graphic organizers, models, and diagrams rather than highlighting the text with a special marker because students who have little prior knowledge tend to highlight nearly everything and wind up with a text that is nearly solid yellow!

■ Teaching/Assessing Tools

How did you learn your system for taking notes? Most of our college students invented their own system, although a few were taught outlining or the note-taking system for learning. Many novice students have a disorganized array of notes. Because note taking is an individual process, we recommend modeling and explaining note taking interactively with students, comparing students' notes to yours and to each other's, and incorporating note-taking practice situations not only with texts but with videos, guest speakers, and observations. Two tools for making notes or drawings are the Note-Taking System for Learning and the use of graphic organizers.

Note-Taking System for Learning

Like the double-entry journal, the *Note-Taking System for Learning* (Palmatier, 1973) helps students organize lecture notes and textbook notes into a format useful for studying. This system is particularly helpful when students need to integrate two sources of information, like lecture and readings, but it can be easily used with one source too.

Using a notebook page with a wide 2-inch left margin, the Notetaking System for Learning involves four steps (see Figure 7.5):

1. Students record notes from their first source on the right-hand side of the notebook, using subordination, numbers, and other format clues. They leave space for additional notes from a second source if another is used. They leave the back of the paper blank and number the pages.

2. Students organize the information by labeling the major topics in the left-hand margin.

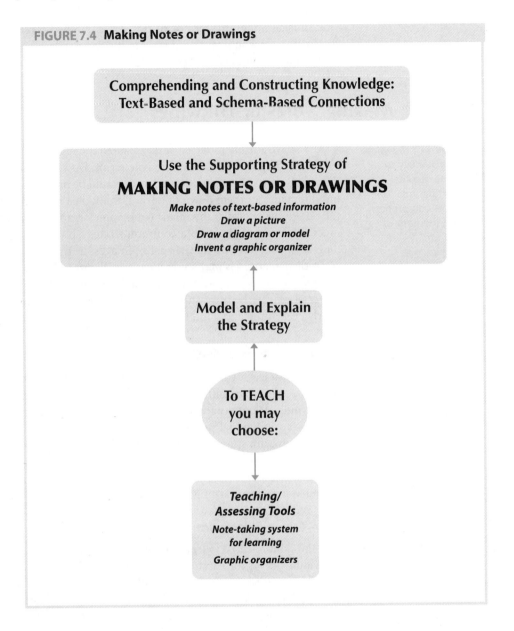

FIGURE 7.4 **Making Notes or Drawings**

3. In the spaces left in the notes from the first source, students add information from their second source. If they need more space, they write on the back of the page.

4. Students study the information by covering their notes on the right-hand side of the page, leaving only the labels on the left side visible. Turning the labels into questions, students recite the answers they recorded in their notes on the right side.

Assessing the quality of students' notes requires evaluating each individual student's notes. Therefore, we recommend that students work in pairs, and compare each other's notes or their notes to your model. You will want to discuss the criteria

---

FIGURE 7.5 **Note-Taking System for Learning**

1. **Record notes** from first source—
   lecture, video, textbook, reference book,
   informational book. For each major topic,
   leave space if another source is used.

2. **Label units**
   to organize
   information.

3. **Add information** from a second source.

4. **Study**
   Turn labels
   into questions
   and recite the
   notes that are
   covered up.

---

of useful notes—the format, the organization, and the content (Stahl, King, & Henk, 1991) and develop your own criteria.

Graphic Organizers, Diagrams, Models, or Pictures

You have no doubt figured out by now that we like graphic organizers. Often in content areas, drawing a diagram, model, or picture and labeling it is more useful than notes in only words. Notes on a graphic organizer are more likely to show connections among ideas than are linear notes. If you have introduced a graphic organizer before reading or as a text pattern guide, then your students could take notes directly on that graphic organizer. When students have many experiences with both graphic organizers and text organization, they can create their own graphic organizer for their notes.

Another use of graphic organizers for notes is to teach the formal outline. That formal outline, with its Roman numerals, capital letters, and numerals, is clear only when the student understands how the text (and content) is organized into subcategories. Many middle school students cannot visualize subcategories in a formal outline but can in a graphic organizer. Therefore, we recommend you first use a graphic organizer to illustrate the subcategories. Then, directly on the graphic organizer, you write Roman numerals on the major categories and capital letters on the first layer of subcategories. And finally, you convert the graphic organizer into the formal outline format.

When you are assessing students' notes on graphic organizers, you again are assessing how adequately they have recorded information—enough information, that is, but not too much. We have found that an advantage of graphic organizers is that students record primarily essential information instead of reams of details. If you have given your students a graphic organizer, then you are evaluating whether they recorded the major categories and the essential supporting details. If they have created their own graphic organizer, you will assess how they have shown the relationship of major ideas and details.

Defining Vocabulary in Context

We assume that you have already taught the most important conceptual words before your students began to read. Now, during reading you will return to vocabulary to help students with related words that elaborate the conceptual vocabulary. Furthermore, individual students may find different unknown words they should learn rather than just skipping them as they read.

define vocabulary in context A literacy strategy in which one uses the surrounding words to figure out the meaning during reading; sometimes used in conjunction with morphemic analysis and the dictionary.

We also have three pedagogical reasons for *defining vocabulary in context* during reading. First, you want to model and explain how readers use context to guess the meaning, try to decipher the meaning from word parts (root, prefix, and suffix) and consult the dictionary or glossary to find a specific definition for that context (see Figure 7.6). As you will see in the script that follows, we discuss what strategies readers use and how figuring out the meaning contributes to comprehension (Goerss, Beck, & McKeown, 1999). Second, you want students to practice using context, word parts, and the dictionary in conjunction rather than using only one strategy. Students also need to become metacognitively aware of how they are figuring out meanings (Baumann, Edwards, Font, Tereshinski, Kame'enui & Olejnik, 2002; Kuhn & Stahl, 1998). Pairs of students could practice figuring out and discussing meaning together, although struggling readers may need the teacher to facilitate (Harmon, 2002).

Third, for some words, like those that use figurative language or contain connotative meaning, readers need the context to understand the author's implied meaning. Take the sentence: "The course of modern events appears to have been good to the Sherpas, but a few storms loom on the horizon" (Reid, 2003). You know that "storms loom" is figurative language but a student, especially an ELL student, may need you to point out that the "problems" discussed in the subsequent text are the "storms." Your explanation will be clearer when you can refer directly to the context.

DIVERSITY

Like text organizations, how people use words, especially figurative language, is learned from their cultures. Read authors of diverse cultures and you will find some authors include very elaborate descriptive phrases in sentences, while others are more concise using simple declarative sentences. Think back to your high school English classes where you read American and British literature. Perhaps you remember learning about similes and metaphors in European-American culture. What you may not have learned is the ways other cultures use language figuratively and creatively.

African-American oral and written texts contain a category of figurative language called *signifying* (Lee, 1993). Signifying includes irony, double entendre, satire, and metaphorical language. The speaker must be quick and witty, show style and flair, and play off familiar knowledge of the listeners. One does not signify with strangers. An example of signifying is, "yo' mamma so old her wrinkles got wrinkles!" (Lee, p. 66). Most African-American adolescents are quite competent in signifying with each other because it's part of their culture. However, they do not recognize that it is a cultural,

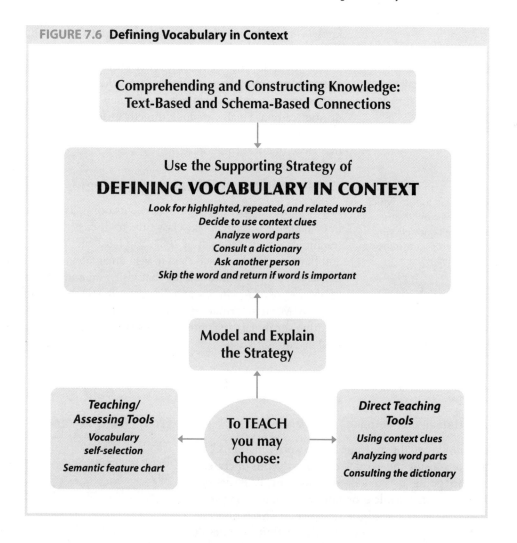

FIGURE 7.6 **Defining Vocabulary in Context**

Comprehending and Constructing Knowledge: Text-Based and Schema-Based Connections

Use the Supporting Strategy of
DEFINING VOCABULARY IN CONTEXT
Look for highlighted, repeated, and related words
Decide to use context clues
Analyze word parts
Consult a dictionary
Ask another person
Skip the word and return if word is important

Model and Explain the Strategy

To TEACH you may choose:

Teaching/ Assessing Tools
Vocabulary self-selection
Semantic feature chart

Direct Teaching Tools
Using context clues
Analyzing word parts
Consulting the dictionary

historical, and literary use of language. Lee taught urban African-American teens to use their interpretations of oral signifying when interpreting literature, such as Alice Walker's *The Color Purple,* that contains signifying.

Deciding that hip-hop was common to the variety of cultures of their high school students, Morrell and Duncan-Andrade (2002) incorporated hip-hop's imagery and metaphor to teach irony, tone, and point of view in the required traditional English poetry. As one of the many activities in the unit, the multicultural students chose a pairing of an English poem and a hip-hop song to interpret. For example, one group discussed the role of allegory in "The Canonization," a poem by Donne and in "Manifest," a song by Refugee Camp. Throughout the unit, both hip-hop and English poetry were critically examined for the language used and the issues addressed.

Thus, both Lee (1993) and Morrell and Duncan-Andrade (2002) began with urban adolescents' familiar figurative oral language to lead students to interpret the language of literary texts. But, you know we advocate connecting what every student knows—prior knowledge—to what they are to learn. That connection makes learning meaningful for all students.

In the following sections, we first present a modeling and explaining script that uses context, *morphemic analysis*, and the dictionary in conjunction to figure out words students probably do not know. Then we discuss teaching/assessing tools useful during reading. Finally, we look directly at teaching context clues, morphemic analysis, or the dictionary because either a small group of students or individual students may need that information.

morphemic analysis
The examination of a word for its meaningful parts—roots, prefix, and suffix.

■ Modeling and Explaining Strategies

modeling and explaining
A teaching tool in which you show how to use strategy(s) and tell why and when you use the strategy(s).

When important natural or human events occur, like Mars passing the closest to Earth in 60,000 years, teachers take class time to discuss those events. Pretend that you were teaching science in the fall of 2003. You have encouraged your students to view Mars and have arranged for each class to visit an amateur astronomer to view Mars through her telescope. In preparation for that visit, you and your students will read an article, "Mysteries of Mars" in *Sky and Telescope*, in which the author has selected pictures of different Martian formations to discuss. You decide to model and explain strategies for defining vocabulary in context because the article contains specialized vocabulary that students do not know.

 ## Modeling and Explaining Script: Defining Vocabulary in Context

My Strategies for Defining Vocabulary in Context

I do not know the meaning of the word *innocuous*. The author is using the word to describe the pits or craters; so I'm going to consult the dictionary. It defines *innocuous* as harmless or not producing strong feelings. I need to reread the sentence to check how the definition fits the context. The definition doesn't really fit well. I think the author is saying the seemingly ordinary craters are really important to the history of Mars.

Degradation and *erosional* are words that I can use morphemic analysis to define. I know the root *degrade* means to lower and *erode* meads to wear away. So the author is explaining that the craters have worn down to different levels.

I know the word *rampart* from reading fantasy literature: knights fight from the ramparts. But, I'd better consult the dictionary. It says a fortification having an embankment. Looking at the picture to check the context, I see the sides of the crater are like an embankment. So that's why they named it a *rampart crater*.

Excerpt from: "Mysteries of Mars"

[First]…are some beautiful images of Martian craters. These seemingly innocuous pits shed light on Martian history.

Their abundance within a given area is a sign of the surface's age, and their various levels of degradation hint at Martian erosional processes.

My first favorite image shows a type known as a rampart crater (see p. 179).

Continued

My Strategies for Defining Vocabulary in Context

I'm going to use the context to define the word *slurry*. Mars craters are not like moon craters that have fine dust and boulders. In contrast, Mars rampart craters have thick mud. Checking the dictionary, I find that *slurry* is a liquid, so the mud must be a little runny.

Look at the word *ejecta.* Using morphemic analysis, I recognize that the author has turned the verb *eject* into a noun. *Ejecta* is the muddy slurry thrown up to make the crater.

Excerpt from: "Mysteries of Mars"

Instead of creating a blanket of fine dust and boulders like those surrounding lunar craters, these impact events eject a thick, muddy slurry.

Most researches believe the rampart craters have penetrated into ice-rich soils, producing muddy ejecta.

Excerpt from: Hartmann, W. K. "Mysteries of Mars." *Sky & Telescope,* July, 2003, *106* (1), p. 37.

In summary, to define vocabulary in context, I used three strategies sometimes in conjunction with each other:

- I consulted the dictionary for a definition (innocuous, rampart, slurry).
- I checked the context to see how the definition fit in the sentences (the picture of a rampart crater) and sometimes had to revise the definition to fit the context (seemingly innocuous craters).

NASA/Jet Propulsion Laboratory/Malin Space Science/photo provided by *Sky and Telescope Magazine*

- I used morphemic analysis to recognize root words (degradation, erosional, ejecta).

- I used context clues to guess at the meaning and checked the dictionary to confirm the meaning (slurry).

Now, lets turn to teaching/assessing tools and direct teaching tools for defining vocabulary in context.

■ Teaching/Assessing Tools

To emphasize the importance of learning new vocabulary, teachers often have students record new words in a section of their journal or notebook. The two tools we present could easily be used in conjunction with journals.

Vocabulary Self-Selection Strategy

When you want students to locate the important words and yet have a common class list of words to study, you could use the *vocabulary self-selection* (Haggard, 1982, 1986). In the beginning, you would model and explain the strategy with your students:

1. You select a target word—the most important conceptual word.

2. You and the students, in pairs, read the text to identify related words important for learning the content, stopping when a student pair finds an important word.

3. When a student pair locates a word related to the target word, they nominate it for the class list. The teacher writes the word on the board. The class defines the words from their prior knowledge and the context.

4. The class proceeds through the text, nominating and defining words until the reading is complete.

5. Student pairs consult glossaries or dictionaries to refine the class's definitions.

6. The class and the teacher narrow the list to a reasonable number of words. We suggest around ten words.

7. The students record the final list in vocabulary journals and use the words in future study.

During the interactive modeling and explaining mini-lesson, you would notice who is able to locate important vocabulary related to the target concept you selected. You could also ask students why they selected their words and how they knew they were important. In this way, students would be teaching each other about locating words. Remember that you can nominate words too, especially when you think the students have skipped an important word.

To build student interest in the vocabulary they needed, Shearer did not limit her at-risk students' selections. The students found words in a wide variety of in-school and out-of-school sources and chose words for many different reasons, such as because they were interesting, useful, or unique (Ruddell & Shearer, 2002).

Semantic Feature Charts

When teachers focus on a specific category of concepts, like clouds or character traits, they want students to learn the names (examples) that identify different items and the descriptive words (attributes or features) that distinguish among the examples. Related to the word map (see Chapter 5), the *semantic feature chart* is a grid on which examples (cirrus, cumulus clouds) are listed vertically and features or attributes (wispy, rising towers) are listed horizontally. If an example has a particular attribute, students record a plus (+) in the square; if not, a minus (–). (Cirrus clouds would have a plus in the "wispy" and a minus in the "rising towers" columns.) By surveying the patterns of pluses and minuses, students can compare the variation in attributes and draw conclusions about similar examples (Johnson & Pearson, 1984).

In introducing the semantic feature chart, we recommend that you model and explain how to compose and complete this chart. Thereafter, students could use it as a study guide for a text. Depending on the text and your students, you may decide to list all of the attributes and require students to find the examples in the text and then mark the chart. Or you may decide that your students need more support: both the examples and the attributes on the grid. Then the students would mark the grid while they read the text. After your students have completed the semantic feature chart, the class should discuss and assess how they defined the concept and allocated the attributes. This discussion can be more important than marking the charts because students verbalize their understandings.

A semantic feature chart (see Figure 7.7) could also be used to depict the shades of meaning among words or connotative meanings (Baldwin, Ford, & Readence, 1981). *Denotation* is the general meaning of words, while *connotation* is the subtle meaning. For example, you know the difference between *scent* and *odor* and when to say and not to say each word. However, ELL students may need to be taught the subtle, culturally tied, connotative meaning of words.

FIGURE 7.7 Semantic Feature Chart for Connotations

				Feature			
Synonym	positive	negative	loud	meaningful	mindless	redundant	articulate
verbose	—	+	—	—	—	+	—
talkative	—	—	—	—	—	—	—
voluble	+	—	—	+	—	—	+
garrulous	—	+	+	—	+	—	—
loquacious	+	—	—	+	—	—	—

Source: From R. S. Baldwin, J. C. Ford, and J. E. Readence (1981), "Teaching word connotations; An alternative strategy," *Reading World, 21* (2), p. 107. Used by permission of the College Reading Association.

In this chapter, we recommend that students use semantic feature charts while they interact with text. However, we also recommend using semantic feature charts after students have read the text. At that time, students can review and refine their ideas.

direct teaching tool A teaching tool in which the teacher tells students specific information.

■ Direct Teaching Tools

As you model and explain strategies for learning unknown words while reading, you want to include information about context clues, word parts, and consulting the dictionary or glossary.

Using Context Clues

We think that using context clues is the preferred strategy for most experienced readers. For many new words or new definitions for familiar words, readers infer the meanings because they understand the topic and the surrounding text. From the context, readers learn the connotations of words and the figurative meaning of words and phrases. ELL students may interpret words, slang, and proverbs literally. They will need help understanding the implied or figurative meaning of words and phrases. Even when using other tools to learn the meaning of words, you will want your students to refer to the context in order to check that the meaning makes sense.

We think modeling and explaining the use of context clues is the most realistic way to encourage students to adopt the strategy (Buikema & Graves, 1993). When an author has clearly defined a word in context, point that out to students and discuss how the author is defining the word. Was a definition given? Was the concept described? Through a discussion with the students, identify the specific context clue and how it informed everyone of the unknown word's meaning.

Table 7.2 lists five types of context clues that we think are the most useful ones for your students to be taught to use (adapted from Vacca & Vacca, 2002). Teaching the list in isolation will not encourage your students to use context clues. However, like you, they can use the list to recognize and point out context clues when they meet them in a text. Your students could create their own lists and examples.

A note of caution is in order: using context clues alone will only acquaint students with the unknown word. Students will need to meet the word many times and may need to consult the dictionary for a precise definition if unknown words are to become established as a part of their vocabulary.

Morphemic Analysis

In Chapter 5, we discussed teaching word parts when you have selected vocabulary that contain useful word parts for students to know. Now you will model and explain using word parts to decipher unknown words. As your students meet new words, they can create a class list of common roots, prefixes, and suffixes useful in your content area.

You will also remind your Spanish-speaking ELL students to search for cognates as they read and to create a list of useful cognates. You and your students may want to explore how J. K. Rowling combines morphemes in her *Harry Potter* books to make new words, such as *bludgers, portkey,* and *omniculars* (Nilsen & Nilsen, 2002). Students could create their own new words from morphemes.

TABLE 7.2 Context Clues

Definition	Clue Defined	Example
Definition	The author tells the definition within the same sentence as the unknown word.	The longest side of a right triangle **is called** the *hypotenuse.*
Description	The author gives additional information of category, examples, or attributes.	Martha Graham was an influential *choreographer,* **inventing movement that united dance steps and emotions.**
Synonym	The author links the unknown word with a known synonym or restates the concept.	The *Emancipation* Proclamation did not give **freedom** to all the slaves on January 1, 1863.
Contrast	The author gives an antonym or opposite phrase.	Unlike the **extensor** muscle, the *flexor* does not extend the arm.
Cause-effect	The author implies the meaning by denoting a cause-effect relationship.	*Physical weathering* **produces soil by** breaking down rock and mineral matter into smaller pieces.

Source: From Richard T. Vacca and Jo Anne L. Vacca, *Content Area Reading: Literacy and Learning Across the Curriculum*, 7th edition, Copyright © 2002. Published by Allyn and Bacon, Boston, MA. Copyright © 1999 by Pearson Education. Reprinted by permission of the publisher.

Consulting the Dictionary or Glossary

In our opinion, most students view consulting the dictionary as drudgery because they have been required to look up twenty words for a Friday test. Therefore, we view the dictionary as a reference tool to consult—not use—for specific information.

Since your students should know basic word-finding skills, such as using guide words, we think the most important strategy for them is *selecting the meaning that fits the context.* If the text has a glossary, then the author has already selected the appropriate definition for that subject. When consulting a dictionary, students need to learn to consider all of the definitions and to read the complete entry carefully. Students can focus on a familiar fragment of a definition (Scott & Nagy, 1997). For example, a student wrote the sentence, "My family erodes a lot," from the dictionary definition of "eats out" or "eats away" (Miller & Gildea, 1987). Now, those usage mistakes are not entirely the student's fault. Dictionary definitions can be terse and vague (Beck, et al., 2002). Students, especially diverse students, need explanations about the word's meaning and part of speech, as well as when to use the word—that is, its usage and connotation.

Four characteristics of dictionary entries will assist students and are worth modeling and explaining:

1. The definitions are listed in a particular order depending on the specific dictionary—frequency of use, primary meaning first, or historical order.

2. The part of speech may determine the meaning.

3. Subject labels indicate the meaning for specific content areas.

4. Derivations can be a clue to meaning.

As we have stated, when you teach the important words you've selected, students need to use new words in many settings—reading, speaking, writing, and listening—if they are to incorporate them into their permanent vocabularies (Stahl & Fairbanks, 1986).

TEACHER AS INQUIRING LEARNER

Survey a text in your content area.

- What are the important vocabulary words you would preteach? What words do you think students should learn independently?

Select about ten words that you think students are unlikely to know.

- Does the text provide clues to the meaning of the unknown words?

Determine whether the unknown words have known word parts that the students could use to decipher the meanings. Consult the dictionary to find out how the dictionary defines the words.

- What order does the dictionary list meanings for its entries? Could a student find and understand the dictionary definition that fits the context?

Decide whether your students could learn words independently or whether you should teach additional words as they read the text.

Focus on Writing: First Drafts

Writing a first draft means figuring out what ideas are important to communicate. Some writers explore their major ideas, and even details, before they write. Writers who know their purpose, their audience, and their genre or format can generate most of the ideas they will include in their first draft before they write it. Nevertheless, turning notes into sentences is not always a simple task, and writing a first draft may or may not go smoothly.

Some writers need to compose a *discovery draft* to find ideas—that is, a free write in which the writer pours out any likely idea to discover what might be communicated. A discovery draft can be useful because the writer can actually see ideas in sentences. However, most discovery drafts are extensively revised.

We recommend using the supporting strategies of capitalizing on text organization and making notes or drawings to assist students in writing first drafts. When students learn how stories, recipes, or arguments can be organized from their reading, they can use those text patterns to plan, compose, and revise their written texts (Allan & Miller, 1995; Englert, Raphael, Anderson, Anthony, & Stevens, 1991). We recommend adapting generic graphic organizers to fit the particular format or genre that the students are writing. For example, we previously suggested the circle graph as a story map for fiction or quest stories. Students could also use the circle graph to represent a life cycle for a biography and an autobiography or a seasonal cycle to chronicle a specific species or habitat.

Students can make notes or drawings on the graphic organizers as they generate ideas for their writing or take notes from different sources. Thus, before they begin to write, they would have a concrete picture of the information they have and how they will organize it in their first draft. They may also refer back to the graphic organizer to evaluate whether they have included enough information and followed that organization in their draft.

Since first drafts are written to communicate students' ideas, students should include not only the important vocabulary you have selected, but also the new vocabulary they have learned independently. Students can review their graphic organizers to assess their use of new vocabulary. When they write, they will want to check that the new words are used in the appropriate context.

We discuss revising first drafts in Chapter 8.

Monitoring Purpose and Progress

During reading, strategic learners monitor their progress in finding and interpreting information by determining when and how to use three supporting strategies. When they capitalize on text organization to locate and recall important information, they monitor what the organization is and where the signal words or clues about the organization are. Depending on how complex the ideas are, strategic readers recognize when they need to make notes or drawings in order to understand and recall the information. Furthermore, when readers spot unknown words within text and decide what strategy to use to define them, they monitor the importance of the unknown vocabulary for their comprehension. Thus, strategic readers monitor their flexible use of strategies as they also monitor whether they can accomplish their purposes for reading the text.

A Checklist: Monitoring Supporting Strategies During Reading

Monitoring Purpose

❑ Can you accomplish your original purpose with this text?
❑ Should you change texts or modify your purpose?

Monitoring Capitalizing on Text Organization

❑ Can you recognize the overall organization of the text?
❑ Can you follow the different organizational patterns in the text?

Monitoring Making Notes or Drawings

❑ Do you need to take notes to study or recall the information?
❑ Do you need to draw a diagram, model, or graphic organizer?

Monitoring Defining Vocabulary in Context

❑ What words in the text are unknown to you?
❑ How do you determine if the unknown words are important?
❑ What strategy can you use to learn the words: context clues, word parts, dictionary, or glossary?

Summary

Building on Chapter 6, Comprehending and Constructing Knowledge, this chapter focused on three supporting strategies that strategic readers use to help them make text-based and schema-based connections.

- Capitalizing on text organization
- Making notes or drawings
- Defining vocabulary in context

In addition, they monitor if they need to use those strategies and when to use them to further their purpose and their comprehension.

To teach the supporting strategies, we described teaching tools.

- **Modeling and explaining strategies of text organization (reviewed the West Nile script in Chapter 6) and of defining vocabulary in context in the Mars script.**
- **Teaching/assessing tools, such as story maps, text pattern guides, graphic organizers, vocabulary self-selection, and semantic feature charts.**
- **Direct teaching about context clues, word parts, and the dictionary.**
- **Focus on writing first drafts.**

Just like a strategic reader makes choices about strategies to use to comprehend, as a teacher you will decide when your students need which teaching tool in order to support their comprehension and construction of knowledge. Some students will need to learn these supporting strategies and so you will use teaching tools to support their comprehension. Other students may use strategies more automatically and only need your teaching tools with difficult texts.

Both in Chapter 6 and here in Chapter 7, we have discussed strategies and tools used with students during reading. Many of those text-based and schema-based connections have been tentative. Strategic readers begin to make those connections to construct their understanding, but they hold those connections in abeyance. When strategic readers finish the text, they refine and consolidate those ideas. We turn to strategies and tools to help students remember ideas after they have read in the next chapter.

Inquiry into Your Learning

1. Plan a modeling and explaining mini-lesson with a text from your content area. Find a text that is interesting to you or that your students might read. Read the text and think about different strategies you are using either automatically or consciously to understand the text. (Do a think-aloud.) What strategies would be particularly useful for students to use with the text? Does the text lend itself to particular strategies, like vocabulary strategies in the Mars script? Or does the text lend itself to a variety of strategies, like text-based, schema-based and supporting strategies in the West Nile script? Choose which strategies to model and explain, and make notes on the text. Think about how you will explain the usefulness of the strategies and how it is helping you understand the content. With another college student in your class, model and explain your texts to each other, and offer each other advice on how to explain strategies to students.

2. Read a text by an author from another culture. If you know a peer of a culture different from yours, you could exchange two different texts and exchange your understandings. What do you notice about how the author uses language? What words are unknown to you? How do you figure out the meaning of the unknown words? Does the author use figurative language? How do you determine the implied meaning of the figurative language?

Inquiry into Your Students' Learning

1. Create a text pattern guide for a text in your content area. You could choose a textbook but we recommend choosing a magazine or newspaper article, a chapter from an informational book, or even a web site. If you choose a fiction book, you may decide to make a guide for the whole book, several chapters, or one chapter. Decide on your content objective. Create a graphic organizer that depicts how the text is organized. Have a small group of students read the text and complete your text pattern guide. Discuss with the students how the guide supported their comprehension. Evaluate your guide to determine whether to change it for another group.

2. Interview two or three struggling students about what they do when they meet unknown words during reading. Do they skip them or try to figure out the meaning? Do they use context, word parts, or the dictionary? Have them read a text silently or aloud and stop whenever someone comes to an unknown word. Ask them to help each other figure out the meaning of the word. You may also coach them on finding the meaning. Notice whether they improve their strategies for defining new words in context.

Resources

Books

Collins. (1987). *COBUILD English language dictionary.* London: Collins. Explains the definitions of words in language helpful to students, especially ELL students, better than other dictionaries.

Journals

Benson, R. (2003). Island watershed activity. *The Science Teacher, 70* (2), 26–29. Describes using models and maps (making notes or drawings) to understand the concept of watersheds.

Brinkmann, A. (2003). Mind mapping as a tool in mathematics education. *Mathematics Teacher, 96* (2), 96–101. Describes using mind maps (graphic organizers or concept maps) for making notes in math and includes examples.

Lee, J. K. & Robinson, K. (2003). The graphing calculator: helping students explore social studies topics. *Social Education, 67* (3), 151–153. Discusses how a teacher uses data on the calculator to help students understand monetary policy in the Populist Era (making notes).

Nilsen, A. P. & Nilsen D. L. F. (2002). Lessons in teaching of vocabulary from September 11, 2001 and *Harry Potter. Journal of Adolescent and Adult Literacy, 46* (3), 254–260. Explains why Arabic words are difficult for English speakers and why Rowling's words in *Harry Potter* are easily pronounced and understood. Includes more examples from *Harry Potter.*

Web Sites

Tom Snyder Productions: A Scholastic Company. **www.tomsnyder.com/index.asp.** Find information about Timeliner 5.0, software that enables students to construct time lines, include historical photographs, and clip art, and to add multimedia features.

Allyn & Bacon/Longman. **www.ablongman.com.** Once at the home page, search for Take Note! software, in which students create electronic note cards, reorganize the cards, and export to a word processor or use with a database program. Also creates a reference page and outline from the cards.

CHAPTER 8

Studying: Reviewing and Evaluating Knowledge

KEY CONCEPTS

- reviewing, p. 193
- summarizing, p. 193
- evaluating, p. 196

PURPOSE-SETTING QUESTIONS

1. How do you study information? Do you remember information after one reading? Do you use supporting strategies, like notes? What do you do when you finish reading to remember the information?

2. Do you write summaries of articles or chapters you have read? Have you written an annotated bibliography or written a review of a book, performance, or event that includes a summary? How do you decide what to include in a summary?

3. Did you have a high school teacher who used teaching tools to help you study? Did a teacher hold review sessions or use a postreading guide to help you review and evaluate information?

4. When you finish writing a first draft, what do you do to evaluate whether you expressed your ideas clearly? Have you ever asked a peer to read your draft and offer revision suggestions?

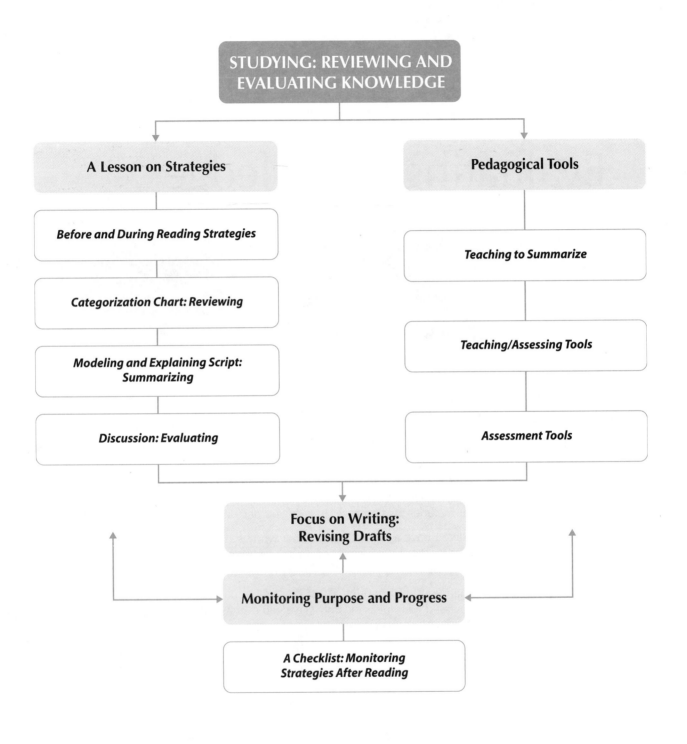

STUDYING: REVIEWING AND EVALUATING KNOWLEDGE

A Lesson on Strategies

Before and During Reading Strategies

Categorization Chart: Reviewing

Modeling and Explaining Script: Summarizing

Discussion: Evaluating

Pedagogical Tools

Teaching to Summarize

Teaching/Assessing Tools

Assessment Tools

Focus on Writing: Revising Drafts

Monitoring Purpose and Progress

A Checklist: Monitoring Strategies After Reading

Walk through any school and you will find students who slam books shut after reading a chapter and students who copy over a first draft without any revisions. Just having read a text once doesn't necessarily mean that you will remember the ideas, even if you have comprehended the ideas during reading. Just having put ideas on paper doesn't necessarily mean that you have expressed your ideas clearly enough for a reader to understand. Nonstrategic learners consider their tasks finished when they make the first, and sometimes only, pass. Strategic learners, on the other hand, know they don't just absorb ideas but must study the information if they want to learn it. If you want your students to build their schemata, you will want to plan opportunities for them to study, or to review and evaluate, both their prior knowledge and new knowledge, after reading.

Reading a text is an accumulating process. When strategic readers activate their prior knowledge before reading, they build a platform on which to erect new information. During reading, they begin to reconsider their prior knowledge in light of new information and begin to make decisions about revisions to their knowledge. They make tentative hypotheses, interpretations, or conclusions. Now, after reading, strategic learners have the advantage of viewing the text as a whole. They can take the time to review, reflect, or revisit without being immersed in the details of the text. They may decide that they missed some information and so reread to locate it. Or they may ask a new question and search for a new source. Thus, strategic learners build on the knowledge gained before and during reading to review their knowledge or even revise it.

If you have ever been in a heated discussion with friends who refused to change their opinions in spite of the evidence you presented, then you know how difficult revising ideas can be. The same process of weighing evidence that occurs in a discussion among friends also takes place in courts of law and at science conferences. In our courts, people on the jury hold their beliefs, opinions, and theories in abeyance while they consider which side has the preponderance of evidence. At scientific conferences, scientists want verification from more than one research study before they are convinced to alter their theory or to adopt a new theory. When new information jars or contradicts everyday experiences, then people have even more difficulty changing their prior knowledge. For example, although researchers have provided evidence that the *Heliobacter pylori* bacteria cause ulcers, some people still attribute their ulcers to stress and eating spicy foods. At other times, people hold on to their theory or belief in spite of everyday experiences to the contrary. In World War II, the U.S. government interred Japanese Americans based on the theory they would be more loyal to Japan than to the United States despite evidence of their business and community contributions. People hold on to their prior knowledge, theories, and beliefs tenaciously; nevertheless, *learning*

*Goal into
integrate into
reconstruct schemata*

some people often learn and change because they evaluate new information and revise their knowledge.

Thus, after reading, strategic readers not only review the information they have learned but, in addition, evaluate both the new information and their own knowledge. You don't want your students to simply memorize information. Instead you want your students to integrate information and reconstruct their schemata.

In this chapter, we emphasize strategies and tools that support students studying or reviewing and evaluating (see chapter graphic). First, we describe a lesson on strategies in which a teacher guides students before, during, and after reading, and models and explains summarizing with the class. Second, in the pedagogical tools section, we elaborate on teaching summarizing because we find writing summaries useful, but difficult to teach. Next, we present teaching/assessing tools—either revisiting previous tools or introducing new tools. At this point, after reading, you may choose to continue a tool that students began before reading, such as KWL, or during reading, such as a peer-led discussion. Revisiting tools to revise one's ideas is a good study practice. On the other hand, you may decide that a new tool, such as a postreading guide or new graphic organizer would benefit your students. Then, we consider assessment tools and their use. The third section, "Focus on Writing," discusses revising drafts. Finally, we close the chapter with the monitoring section and checklist.

A Lesson on Strategies

Pretend the class will study a unit on ancient civilizations of the world organized around the major understanding, "What is a civilized society?" To initiate the unit, the students will brainstorm their ideas about what constitutes a civilized society today. During the unit, the students will read a variety of sources about ancient peoples who lived on every continent. To culminate the unit, they will devise criteria to evaluate their definition of a civilized society.

■ Before and During Reading Strategies

To introduce the article and set a specific purpose for reading, the teacher calls the students' attention to the first paragraph, where the author informs readers of the old and new theories about Pueblo ruins. The students identify the three Pueblo centers mentioned—Chaco Canyon, Aztec Ruins, and Casas Grandes—in the paragraph and on a map. The teacher points out that the text is probably organized around the three centers. During reading, the students' task is to mark where the author states the old and new theories and cites the evidence for the theories. Table 8.1 shows an excerpt from the article with evidence in bold and notes marked.

TABLE 8.1 **Making Notes**	
My Notes	Excerpts from "Rewriting Southwestern Prehistory"
	New studies suggest an overarching political system dominated much of the Southwest from A.D. 850 to 1500.
Old theory	**The ancient Southwest has long been viewed as a patchwork of boom-and-bust cultures.** Pueblos were thought to have come and gone independently of one another and archaeologists rarely looked beyond the areas immediately surrounding their excavations.
New theory	But a new study of the Southwestern landscape has revealed that **three of the largest and most important ancient centers were linked by a 450-mile meridian line**—Chaco Canyon, in New Mexico; Aztec Ruins, 55 miles due north near the Colorado state line; and Casas Grandes, 390 miles due south in Chihuahua, Mexico.

Excerpted from "Rewriting Southwestern Prehistory" by Stephen H. Lekson, with permission of *Archaeology Magazine*, Volume 50, Number 1 (Copyright the Archaeological Institute of America, 1997), p. 52.

■ Categorization Chart: Reviewing

After the students have read the article, the teacher introduces a blank categorization chart by defining the labels on the columns and rows. (For a completed chart, see Table 8.2.) The purpose of the chart is to help students *review* the evidence in preparation for summarizing. In pairs, the students complete their charts using jigsaw groupings. First, the teacher assigns one center to each pair and has pairs reviewing the same center meet together (called expert groups). After the expert groups are finished, one pair from each center forms teaching groups and shares the evidence from their respective centers in order to complete their charts. While the students are working, the teacher circulates to observe their progress and offers assistance as needed. If necessary, the teacher will model and explain with struggling students how to complete their charts.

Upon completion of the charts by the teaching groups, the teacher models and explains summarizing ideas the next period.

■ Modeling and Explaining Script: Summarizing

Because the students have made notes during reading and reviewed the evidence by completing the categorization chart after reading, they are now ready to summarize. The teacher has decided to model and explain the strategy of *summarizing* interactively with the students. To introduce the strategy, she first explains the purpose of summarizing or why the strategy is useful and reminds them about the purpose for reading the article:

reviewing An after-reading literacy strategy that reflects on important information in order to study.

summarizing A literacy strategy that concisely and completely condenses the main ideas in the text.

TABLE 8.2 Categorization Chart of Evidence for the New Theory

Does the evidence support the new theory that an overarching political system linked three large regional centers?

	Archaeological Evidence	Geographical Evidence	Astronomical Evidence	Oral History Evidence
Chaco Canyon, 850–1125	1) Great Houses 2) Great Kivas 3) 150 communities with Great Houses and Kivas 4) Great North Road 5) Macaw skeletons	1) Located on meridian 2) Buildings on north-south axis 3) Great North Road on meridian	Southwestern sky: All three centers have a daily rotation of sky on north-south axis around the meridian.	Today's Acoma and Zuni live near the meridian. They have similar oral histories.
Aztec, 1110–1275	1) Black and white ceramics 2) Great Houses	1) Located on meridian 2) No geographical advantage to location		Some people went south from a great center to find macaws.
Casas Grandes, 1250–1500	1) Pueblo-style buildings 2) Macaw pens 3) Macaw skeletons	1) Located on meridian 2) Is there a Great South Road?		They returned with macaws.

Teacher's Introduction: Purpose Setting

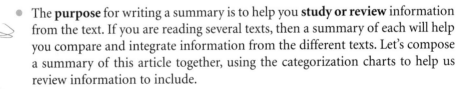

- The **purpose** for writing a summary is to help you **study or review** information from the text. If you are reading several texts, then a summary of each will help you compare and integrate information from the different texts. Let's compose a summary of this article together, using the categorization charts to help us review information to include.

- When summarizing, we want to remember our **purpose** for studying the information—how to define a civilized society. We read the article to learn about how the Pueblo society was viewed.

Interactive Modeling and Explaining Script: Summarizing Ideas

Teacher's Prompts to Students for Summarizing	Examples of Sentences in Class Summary
Often in writing summaries, we begin with a statement that synthesizes or integrates all of the information—a main idea, thesis or theme. I can either write a thesis now or I can wait until after I have summarized sections of the article. What does the author want us to think about Pueblo civilizations? Does anyone have a thesis statement to offer?	Archaeologists are revising their theory about ancient Pueblo civilizations.
Ok, the thesis is they are rethinking their theory. How can we state a comparison of the old and new theory?	Instead of isolated, separate, "boom and bust" cultures, they now think the three largest centers were linked by a great road and formed a political system.
Good. Now, let's examine our categorization charts for common evidence across the three centers. Who can compose a summary statement about one piece of evidence?	All three centers—Chaco Canyon, Aztec, and Casas Grandes—were located on the same meridian.
What else is mentioned in each? Yes, evidence about the buildings. Anyone want to try a summary statement?	Although Chaco Canyon may have had the most Great Houses and Great Kivas, all centers had Pueblo-style houses and kivas.
Any other common evidence? Yes, macaws. Who has a summary statement?	People tell stories about finding macaws from the south and evidence of macaw skeletons was found in the Chaco Canyon and Casas Grandes.
Ok. Do we want to say anything about the Great North Road? Yes, we could add that to the location statement.	All three centers—Chaco Canyon, Aztec, and Casas Grandes—were located on the same meridian and so was the Great North Road that linked them.
Let's review our summary and think about how we can draw a conclusion.	Archaeologists are revising their theory about ancient Pueblo civilizations. Instead of isolated, separate, "boom and bust" cultures, they now think the three largest centers were linked by a great road and formed a political system. All three centers—Chaco Canyon, Aztec, and Casas Grandes—were located on the same meridian and so was the Great North Road that linked them. Although Chaco Canyon may have had the most Great Houses and Great Kivas, all centers had Pueblo-style houses and kivas. People tell stories about finding macaws from the south and evidence of macaw skeletons was found in the Chaco Canyon and Casas Grandes.

Continued

Look at the end of the article. What are archaeologists still questioning? Anyone have a **conclusion statement**?

Archaeologists need evidence for a Great South Road and for why the centers were abandoned. If the centers formed a political system covering a large area, archaeologists will have to revise their history of the region.

■ Discussion: Evaluating

evaluating A literacy strategy that reconsiders evidence or information after reading.

After writing the summary, the teacher and the class discuss whether the evidence was sufficient to support a new theory (*evaluate* **evidence**). They also discuss the author's point of view of the Pueblo society:

- What does his use of the word, *prehistory* connote about his point of view? (**review author's point of view or bias**)

- How do you define Pueblo society? Is it civilized and by what criteria? (**devise and apply criteria to evidence**)

Upon completion of the discussion, the students will read about other ancient civilizations in pairs and summarize the different texts for each other.

Let's review all the strategies used in conjunction with this lesson.

Before Reading Strategies

- **Set a purpose** specifically for the article (to note the old and new theories and to find evidence for the new theory)

During Reading Strategies

- **Capitalized on text organization** (three Pueblo centers).

- **Found and interpreted important information** (old and new theories and evidence).

- **Made notes** (marked important information on copies of the article).

After Reading Strategies

- **Reviewed** the article by completing a **categorization chart**

- **Summarized** the article by:

    1. Composing a **thesis or theme** for the article.

    2. Writing **summary statements** for the common evidence.

    3. **Reviewing** our summary.

    4. **Drawing a conclusion** and writing concluding statements.

- **Evaluated** the ideas through a class discussion

    1. **Evaluated** evidence (sufficient to support new theory).

    2. **Reviewed** author's point of view or bias (use of word *prehistory*).

    3. **Devised and applied criteria** (define *civilized*).

This lesson could easily take two or three periods but the teacher choose to spend the additional time because the students will not only remember the information but will also learn how to study. In addition, notice that the teacher planned to have the students practice summarizing with other sources. Students need opportunities to apply the strategies you model and explain.

To conclude this section on strategies, let's look at Figure 8.1. You will find listed specific applications of the strategies of reviewing and evaluating—many of which were included in the lesson you just read. Additionally, you will find other specific applications of reviewing and evaluating that are useful after reading. For example, although strategic readers may react to the author's craft during reading, they will review and evaluate the author's craft considering the whole text after reading. After reading, they may decide information is missing, compare the text to others, or apply the information to their life, their community, or the global society. Thus, by reviewing and evaluating strategic learners strive to increase their knowledge or augment their schemata or even completely revise it.

Now, let's turn to pedagogical tools.

Pedagogical Tools

When we ask students to study information, we aim for them to integrate and interpret factual information. For example, in social studies, students may read the facts about the Lend-Lease Act but also need to understand the reasons for and the political controversies behind the act. They may learn about the artist, Andy Warhol, but they also could compare the critics' reactions to his Campbell soup can pictures to earlier critics' reactions to cubism or to impressionism. Thus, we want students not only to learn facts but also to evaluate the information and experiment with their own perspectives and conclusions about the facts. For that, you may choose to support them with tools.

In Figure 8.1 you will notice we suggest you can revisit tools because you and your students want to review and revise ideas expressed earlier. Students can revise a graphic organizer, or an anticipation guide begun before reading. They can discuss the comprehension guides or the text pattern guides completed during reading. And finally, they could finish their KWL or peer-led discussions by reviewing and evaluating what they learned. We have listed only a sampling of the tools from previous chapters to remind you that continuing to use a tool is perfectly legitimate.

In addition, you will notice in Figure 8.1 that we have listed other teaching/assessing tools useful after students have read a text. Sometimes you will introduce these tools in addition to previous tools. At other times, you will decide that students can read the text independently but need support when studying. Even strategic learners may benefit from the support of a summary or postreading guide, for example, when they need to critically examine information. You will also want to reinforce the new vocabulary and make sure the students use their new vocabulary to express their understanding.

DIVERSITY

Whether you choose to revisit a tool and revise the students' ideas or you introduce a new tool after reading, your diversity students, especially your LD students, will

FIGURE 8.1   Strategies and Tools: Reviewing and Evaluating

CONTENT
Unit Major Understandings
Lesson Objectives

Supported by the Strategies of
REVIEWING AND EVALUATING
Categorize ideas
Look back, reread, and recite ideas
Summarize ideas
Draw a conclusion
Infer a theme or thesis
Reconsider prior knowledge
Decide what information is missing
Devise and apply criteria for evidence
Review author's purpose or point of view
React to author's craft
Compare to other authors and sources
Apply to own life, own community, or society

**Model and Explain
the Process**

*Revisit Tools:
A Sampling*
KWL, Anticipation guide,
Reciprocal teaching,
Comprehension and text
pattern guides,
Peer-led discussions

To TEACH
you may
choose:

*Teaching/
Assessing Tools*
Teaching summaries
Graphic organizers
Postreading guides
PORPE
Reinforcing vocabulary

Assessment Tools
Tests and essays
Portfolios

**Monitoring Progress
and Purpose**

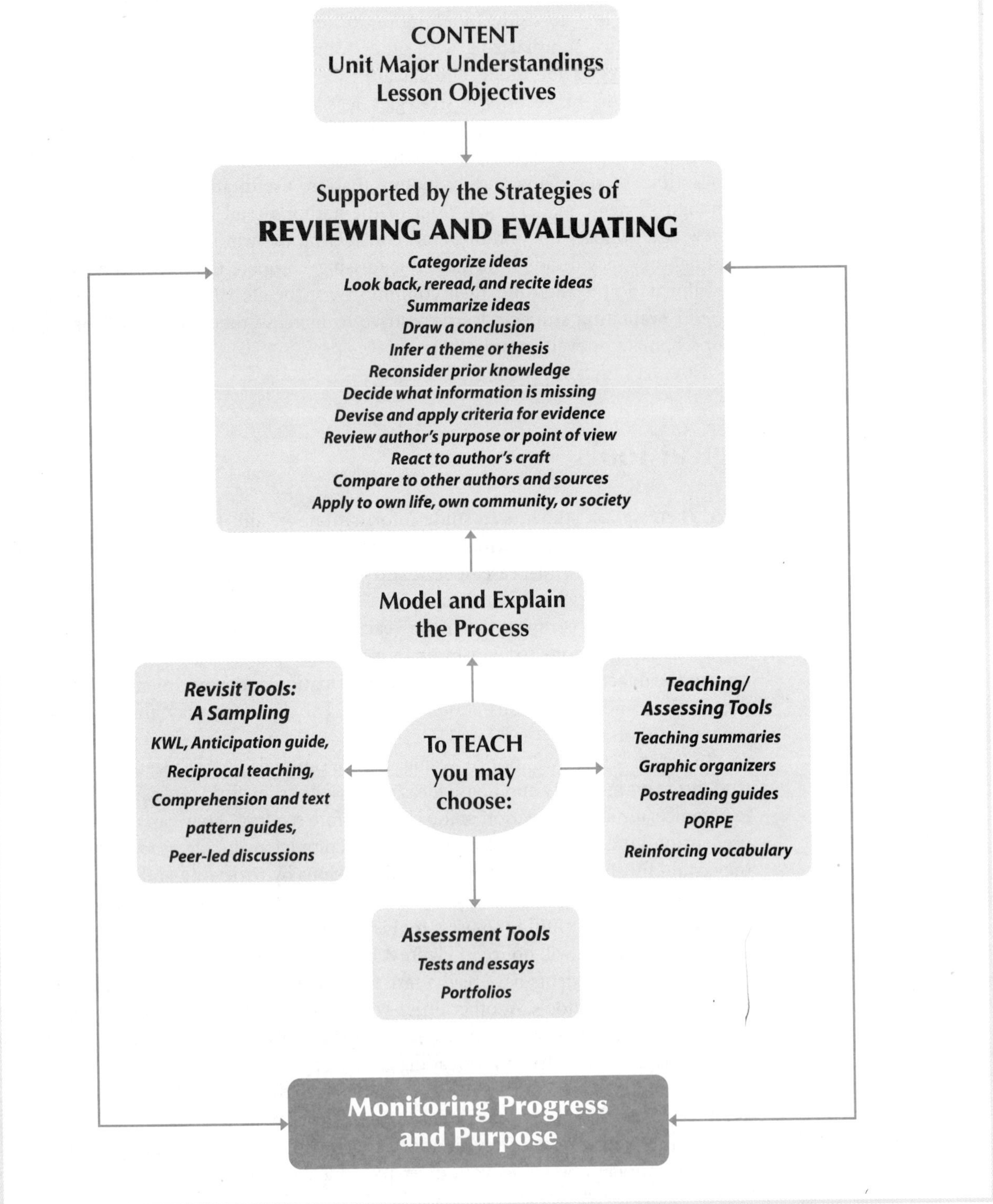

need support throughout their reading of a text (Gersten, et al. 2001). Because LD students have difficulty deciphering print, they will need continued coaching, prompting, and support to use strategies and to complete teaching/assessing tools. They need to learn to continuously use strategies—before, during, and after reading. Since LD students do not recognize that they do not understand the text, they also need to learn to continuously monitor the status of their comprehension. Thus, LD students need the support of teaching tools—the modeling and explaining tool as well as teaching/assessing tools—at every point of the reading process.

While teaching LD students strategies is productive, the problem is that they do not develop the habit of using them (Resnick, cited by Gersten, et al., 2001). Careful consideration of text difficulty (recall Chapter 3), use of small group discussion and teaching students to question (recall Chapter 6), as well as teaching literacy strategies are supported by research on LD students' comprehension but further research is needed (Gersten, et al., 2001). You could participate by conducting your own classroom inquiry in conjunction with a special education teacher (see Chapter 13)!

We now turn to tools to support students' studying. LD students, who have difficulty determining the main idea and summarizing (Gersten, et al., 2001), will need support in learning to summarize. Furthermore, they will need the support of the other tools included here: graphic organizers, postreading guides, and essay writing. You will decide when to use one of these tools with all your students.

We have separated the teaching to summarize section from the other teaching/assessing tools because sometimes you would model and explain as we presented in the lesson earlier and at other times support students in their summary writing. Because we think summarizing is so valuable for studying, we want to give you more information about teaching it. After that section, we will discuss other teaching/assessing tools, and then assessment tools.

■ Teaching to Summarize

Writing a summary is not an easy task because it needs to be both concise and complete at the same time. Students need to determine what information to include and exclude from their summaries and how to organize those ideas clearly and succinctly. A succinct summary could combine and synthesize information, but this is difficult even for high school and college students to do (Brown & Day, 1983). Inexperienced summary writers will probably follow the text organization— the sequence of the plot or the main topic and subtopics—when composing their summaries.

The audience who will read the summary also determines what information students include (Hidi & Anderson, 1986; Hill, 1991). If the students are writing to help themselves remember information they intend to use later, their summaries could contain the important ideas they need to study. A concise summary in this situation would not be as important as a complete one. In contrast, if they are writing a summary to inform a reader, as in a review, then the students need to be concise, and yet also give a complete picture of the text. Later we will discuss writing summaries for readers in the expanding summary writing section.

When teaching students to summarize, first you will have a preparation activity, then writing activities, and finally activities that expand their summary writing. We discuss each of these in the following sections.

Preparation: Graphic Organizers

For texts of any length, students need a preparation step to help them determine what to include in and what to exclude from the summary. Although graphic organizers can take many forms, we chose to use a categorization chart when we modeled and explained with the Pueblo article because it matched the text's organization. You already know that you would select the graphic organizer that best depicts how important information is organized. We will discuss graphic organizers again in a later section.

The graphic organizer serves as a tool on which students can reduce and organize the extensive information given in a text. By reviewing the text in order to complete the graphic organizer, students clarify what is important information to include in a summary and concurrently study the information as well. You recognize that nonstrategic students, especially LD students, will need a tool like a graphic organizer to revisit and study information.

Summary Writing

Your students' purpose for learning the information will determine what they include in their summary and how they organize the material. In the modeling and explaining script, we could have summarized each center separately following the text's organization if the purpose had been to catalogue information about each center. However, since the purpose was to evaluate the evidence for a new theory about Pueblo civilization, we summarized information across centers.

When you discuss the main idea or moral of a story with your students and when you ask them what a text is all about, you are beginning to teach summarization. When you and your students find and interpret important supporting information, once again you are beginning to teach summarization. Building on those strategies, you want to teach students to write a summary as a tool for studying independently.

When you teach writing a summary, you would begin by modeling and explaining with a short, well-organized text that your students can comprehend easily. For both the graphic organizer and the summary, you would emphasize four guidelines (adapted from Hidi & Anderson, 1986):

- Include only the most important ideas.

- Exclude unimportant and redundant information.

- Use the organization of the text to help organize the summary.

- Combine, integrate, generalize, or synthesize information.

You could write a whole class summary, as in the modeling and explaining script, or have individuals or pairs of students write summaries.

When individuals or pairs write summaries, then you and the class can compare several students' summaries anonymously, and discuss the similarities and differences. You and your students would review the following topics:

- What information (including concepts and vocabulary) did most students include? Did they include that information because it was a main idea? Did they think details were needed to support that main idea?

- What information did only some students include? Why did they think those details were important to include?

- What information did students exclude? Why did they think the information could be excluded?

- How did students combine information?

- Did students write a thesis or theme statement that synthesized the text?

Your nonstrategic readers will have more difficulty than strategic readers in both finding the important ideas and writing those ideas in their summaries (Winograd, 1984). A comparison of students' summaries for different texts over time can help the students learn the variety of ways that their peers compose summaries. They can experiment with different combinations of information and recognize that completeness and conciseness can be achieved in different ways.

Expanding Summary Writing

After your students have written summaries for clearly organized texts, you will want to model and explain writing summaries for texts that contain less familiar content and less clear or mixed organization patterns. With less clear texts, your students will have more difficulty deciding what information to include and exclude. So in addition to modeling, you will want your students to compare and evaluate their summaries to learn from each other.

You will also want to model and explain how to synthesize, generalize, and integrate information in summaries. You would model how to combine the information, reorder information, or invent a new version of the information. When you summarize text, you may find generalizing and synthesizing the information more difficult than condensing the author's information and organization, and your students will, too.

And finally, you can expand students' summary writing with *reviews*. Reviews contain a short summary or synopsis of a work, an analysis of its strengths and weaknesses, and opinions of it or advice to the reader about purchasing or attending the work (an art show or play, for example). You and your students could examine the reviews written by both students and critics that are published in newspapers, magazines, and on-line sites and decide how persuasive they are.

Students could write reviews of books, videos, movies, CDs, software, or events. In assessing either published reviews or other students' reviews, students would consider the following questions:

- In the synopsis or summary, does the reviewer provide a clear overview of the entire work?

- Does the reviewer discuss the strengths and weaknesses of the work?

- Does the reviewer offer convincing opinions about the work or advise you about attending or purchasing the work?

If the reviewer is experienced or knowledgeable in the field, then the review often compares the work to other similar works in the field. For example, a critic may compare the current movie to past movies in the same genre. Students who are well versed in a field could include comparisons in their reviews.

great idea! to evaluate reviews (summaries) effective

We encourage you to write summaries as a studying tool. Write a summary of a chapter or a text in your content area.

- What strategies do you use? Does a graphic organizer help you distill information before you write the summary? Why do you include or exclude particular information? Do you follow the organization in the text, or do you use a different organization? Do you integrate information from different sections of the text? Do you synthesize ideas in your statements?

When we assign our students a written review of the research on a topic of their choosing, we ask them to complete a categorization chart first. On the chart, the columns are labeled with the components of the research—question or hypothesis, method, results, conclusions—and the rows are the different studies. Using their categorization charts, our students write a summary or a review of the research. Instead of writing a summary of one text, you might choose to summarize several texts or write a review of the research.

We encourage you to incorporate summaries into your assignments so that students can practice summarizing for a useful purpose. Next we discuss teaching/assessing tools that you can use to support students' studying.

■ Teaching/Assessing Tools

We have included four tools in this section. First, the familiar graphic organizers put to the new purpose of reviewing information in order to study. Second, postreading guides, which are similar to the comprehension guides discussed in Chapter 6, are presented. Third, we include a completely new tool, PORPE, that supports students studying for essay tests. And fourth, we return to vocabulary because you need to reinforce students' learning of new words.

We remind you that sometimes students only need support in their studying after reading. Perhaps the text is not difficult but you want them to review the content; then you'd use a teaching/assessing tool to support their review of the ideas. At other times, students need support throughout their reading and so you would use one tool or different tools before, during, and after reading.

Graphic Organizers

By reviewing a graphic organizer completed before reading, students eliminate the misconceptions or incorrect information from their prior knowledge and add newly learned information. They elaborate on the earlier information to create a more complete representation of their current knowledge. Similarly, if during reading, students used a graphic organizer as a text pattern guide or for note taking, they could review their graphic organizers and the text to see that they recorded all the necessary information and to determine what they need to add or revise.

For some texts, you may decide to use graphic organizers only after reading because you want to help students study the information (Peresich, Meadows, & Sinatra, 1990). Because students are engaged in organizing the information into another form, they are more likely to remember it or enhance their schemata. You could ask the students to create their own graphic organizer that would represent how they've

Students make own organizer

added ideas to their schemata. Or you could provide the students with a blank graphic organizer, like a semantic map, a flowchart, a cause-and-effect chain for events, a story map, or a Venn diagram, which represents how the information is organized in your content area. For example, after studying the digestive system, a biology teacher presents a diagram of the digestive system on which students must describe the sequence of consuming an ice cream cone. First, students write what they recalled and then they review the text to add any missing information.

Whether your students are revising earlier graphic organizers or creating new ones, you will want to assess how they organize and represent information:

- Have they included the important information and added new information?

- Have they used the new vocabulary for the important concepts?

- Have they shown relationships among concepts by how they have placed them on the graphic organizer?

- Can they explain how their graphic organizer represents the concepts they've been learning?

From the vocabulary the students use for the newly learned information and their explanations of the relationships on their graphic organizers, you will be able to decide how clearly and completely they understand the concepts. You may decide that the graphic organizer is an end product representing the students' learning, or you may use it as a tool to prepare for other end products, as we did in summary writing.

Postreading Guides

You may choose to use study guides that are like comprehension guides except that students complete them after reading. By using guides and questions now, you provide your students support in organizing the information and their thoughts. If your students are reading several texts, then postreading guides and questions will help them integrate information across the different texts.

An example of a postreading guide is from a unit on the homeless. Each group of students read a text about a different homeless population. The questions on the postreading guide in Figure 8.2 helped the students organize the factual information and their interpretations about homeless people. After completing the guides, the class pooled their information and conclusions about homeless people.

Another example of a postreading guide is a *point-of-view* guide in which students take on the role of a person or character (Wood, 1988). Using their schema-based connections, they elaborate on, interpret, and speculate on text-based information. By creating the perspective of a particular role, they reconstruct and reconsider the ideas they have read about in their textbooks. For example, in Figure 8.3, students take the point of view of different workers in the United States during World War II (Wood, Lapp, & Flood, 1992).

English teachers can create a guide in which students take the role of a specific character in a novel and speculate about the character's actions and perspectives toward a new situation—one that is not in the book. Alternatively, the students could choose a minor character in the book and relate that character's point of view toward the main characters and the events. You could read your students *The True Story of the*

FIGURE 8.2 Postreading Guide for a Text on Homeless People

1. What homeless group is the focus of this report?

   _____

   _____

2. What percentage of the general population does this group make up?

   _____

   _____

3. What percentage of the homeless population does this group make up?

   _____

   _____

4. Where did members of this group live before they became homeless?

   _____

   _____

5. What are their family backgrounds?

   _____

   _____

6. List three reasons that members of this group became homeless.

   _____

   _____

   _____

7. List three facts that you think are important to share with other students.

   _____

   _____

   _____

8. List three things that members of this group have in common with you or someone you know.

   _____

   _____

   _____

9. If you could pick only one word to describe members of this group, what would it be?

   _____

FIGURE 8.3 Point-of-View Guide

America After 1941

America's Huge War Needs (pp. 617–618)

1. As a worker in a U.S. defense plant, tell what effect the War Production Board has had on you, your co-workers, and the soldiers overseas.

Americans Go Back to Work (p. 618)

2. As one of the leaders in a national labor union, what is your reaction to the need for war supplies?
3. As a farmer, tell how your life has changed from the Depression days to the present days of wartime.

Opportunities for Blacks (pp. 618–619)

As a black person from the South:

4. Tell why you and others moved to the Northeast and Midwest sections of the United States.
5. Describe the effect of Hitler's racist doctrine on your situation at home.
6. Tell why Executive Order 8802 was important to you.

Source: Wood, Karen D., Lapp, Dianne, & Flood, James (1992). *Guiding Readers Through Text: A Review of Study Guides* (p. 13). Newark, DE: International Reading Association and Karen D. Wood. All rights reserved.

Three Little Pigs, a picture book by Peter Scieszka, written from the wolf's point of view, as a fun, mood-setting example.

If you can accept a little anthropomorphism in science, you could create a guide on which students would take the perspective of an animal in an environment, a chemical in a solution, or an asteroid in space. Students would describe their surroundings and the events that might occur, as well as their reactions to those events and surroundings.

Both you and your students would assess the reasonableness of the point of view or new perspective. Did the students incorporate the important information that would support the particular perspective taken?

PORPE

Designed to assist students in studying for essay exams (Simpson, 1986), PORPE consists of five steps: **p**redict, **o**rganize, **r**ehearse, **p**ractice, and **e**valuate. You would need to model and explain each step with your students and allow for much collaborative or partner work for students to gain competence in writing essays:

1. **Predict** potential essay questions. Students can find predicting potential essay questions difficult. If you have asked both text-based and schema-based questions and

discussed different types of questions students may have less difficulty devising likely essay questions. As you model and explain potential essay questions with them, you would also explain the key words used in essay questions, such as *explain, compare* and *contrast, discuss,* and *critique.*

2. **Organize** information to answer the predicted questions. Just as we used the categorization chart earlier in the chapter, you would present a graphic organizer for students to use. If students have had experience in organizing information, they could create their own graphic organizers to depict the important information and supporting details or examples they will need in their essays.

3. **Rehearsal** of the organized information. The students study the information by reciting from memory the major ideas on their graphic organizers. Gradually over several days, they will recite more and more details. We recommend that students work in partners and quiz each other on the information.

4. **Practice** writing the essay. Having rehearsed the information, the students are ready to write their answers to the questions from memory. You would model and explain the sections of an essay: the opening statement that rephrases the question or takes a specific stand; the paragraphs, each containing a major point and supporting details; and the concluding or summarizing paragraph. Or you and the students could compose the opening statement together and perhaps the first paragraph. Then the students could compose the rest of the essay in pairs or independently. On subsequent essays, students could work in pairs or independently to practice writing the entire essay.

5. **Evaluate** the practice essay. Students compare their written essays with their graphic organizers to see if they included the important information. They also evaluate whether they answered the question, clearly supported their major points, used transitions between paragraphs, and presented their position clearly in the opening and concluding paragraphs. Model and explain how to evaluate an essay using examples of class work (anonymously, of course) or even a poorly written one you created specifically for this purpose. Subsequently, students could evaluate and give revision suggestions to each other.

 TEACHER AS INQUIRING LEARNER

Find a text in your content area that your students could read, and create a postreading study guide for it. You could think of an issue or problem in your content area and find one or two texts that address the issue. You could rephrase a topic like the Civil War into a contemporary issue. Or you could examine the theme or issue in a novel.

Consider different perspectives on the issue, problem, or theme, and create a study guide or a point-of-view guide on which students would organize the information.

● What questions could you ask so that students would evaluate, apply, or reconsider those perspectives and their own?

If you have the opportunity, try your postreading guide with your students, and discuss what they learned.

● How would you revise the guide?

As you recall from Chapter 7, diverse students may include features of oral stories in their essays. You and the students can decide if those features are appropriate for the essay or whether the essay is a formal test requiring a revision of the oral features.

Reinforcing Vocabulary

We have already discussed preteaching and previewing vocabulary in Chapter 5 and defining vocabulary in context in Chapter 7. If students are going to remember the new vocabulary for new concepts, they will need to study and use the words in a variety of ways.

One natural way to reinforce vocabulary and concepts is for you and your students to use the words in speaking and writing. ELL students benefit from using the new vocabulary in context, and LD students benefit from the repetition in different contexts. When students are recording in their journal entries, composing first drafts, and discussing their text-based and schema-based connections with text, you can encourage (or require) them to use the new vocabulary. You might ask them to compose freewriting using the vocabulary words, use new vocabulary in exit slips, include new vocabulary in the predictions and summaries of reciprocal teaching, or count every time a new vocabulary word entered the peer-led discussions. Semantic feature charts could be used now to reinforce vocabulary so that students could revisit and discuss how the features of the concepts or examples compared. LD students with learning disabilities learned more vocabulary with semantic feature charts than with definition activities (Bos, Anders, Filip, & Jaffee, 1989). All students could revise an earlier graphic organizer to include the new vocabulary and concepts. And when writing summaries of texts, students should use the new vocabulary.

Some students may need additional practice to learn the words. Familiar activities, like crossword puzzles or matching exercises, help students study words because students must link the words with definitions. We introduce a less familiar tool, the word continuum, because it can reinforce the connotations of words.

Word Continuum

A *word continuum* is like a number line in mathematics (see Figure 8.4). Students order the words from negative to neutral to positive meanings or from less to more of a characteristic. Thus, a word continuum visually depicts the shades of connotations or the nuances in the meanings of similar words for a concept. At the end of a unit on nutrition, students completed a word continuum from junk food to healthy food. In English, a word continuum of adjectives could depict the nuances of descriptive words.

■ Assessment Tools

You know that we have been discussing assessment tools (and teaching/assessing tools) in every chapter because we view assessment as informing both a teacher's instruction and a student's learning. However, at the end of a lesson, the end of a series of lessons, and the end of unit, both teachers and students expect an assessment of what was learned. We have already mentioned revisiting teaching/assessing tools, like KWL or graphic organizers, so that students can assess for themselves how they have enhanced their prior knowledge. Students working together can compare summaries and postreading guides to help each other assess what they have learned. In addition, teachers and students use tests, essays, and portfolios to evaluate learning.

FIGURE 8.4 Word Continua

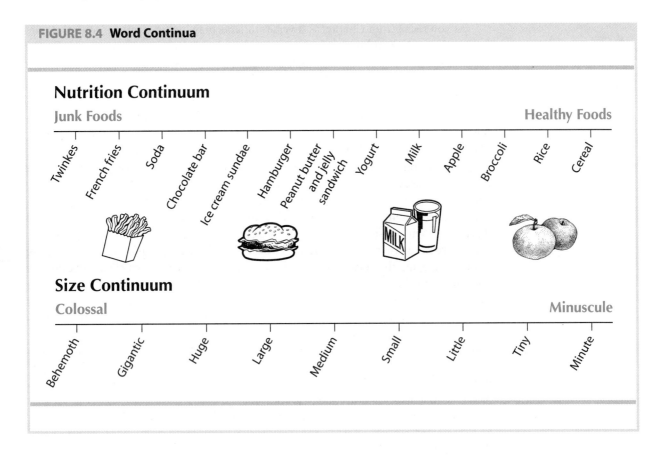

Nutrition Continuum

Junk Foods   Healthy Foods

Twinkes · French fries · Soda · Chocolate bar · Ice cream sundae · Hamburger · Peanut butter and jelly sandwich · Yogurt · Milk · Apple · Broccoli · Rice · Cereal

Size Continuum

Colossal   Minuscule

Behemoth · Gigantic · Huge · Large · Medium · Small · Little · Tiny · Minute

Tests and Essays

Tests are common in middle and secondary classrooms. Certainly students need practice in taking tests, but we remind you that some students do not perform well on tests or perform well on only certain types of tests, such as multiple-choice tests. You know how you perform on tests and you may know friends who say they test well or poorly. So we encourage you to create different testing formats—true-false, multiple choice, and essay—and to evaluate students through class work and portfolios.

Many teachers test vocabulary by asking students to write a definition or sentence for the words. Then, students dutifully memorize the definitions only to forget later. Other students write sentences that use the word in an inappropriate context. One student wrote the sentence, "In my yellow jacket, I protruded in the crowd," for the word *protrude*. Instead, we suggest that you ask students to explain meanings of words similar to the following examples excerpted from Beck, et al., (2002 pp. 97–99):

- Describe how someone shows they are *diligent*.

- What is alike or different between this word pair: *seize/embrace*.

- How much energy does it take to

    1. *meander* down the hall?

    2. *vault* over the car?

Least energy_____Most energy_____

- Mr. Robinson, the high school principal, was in a very good mood after his meeting with the *philanthropist*. Why do you think Mr. Robinson was happy?

Students' explanations will exhibit their understanding of both the definition and the context in which the word is used.

When you create tests, we recommend that you return to the "Types of Questions and Answers" section in Chapter 6. You will want to consider carefully whether to ask literal questions or connection questions. Think about your major understanding or objective and what type of question would allow students to exhibit their understanding of content. Questions that ask students to explain, interpret, compare, analyze, or describe will allow students to organize their ideas and show how they have increased their prior knowledge. We also recommend that you model and explain how to write an essay and use the teaching/assessing tool PORPE.

Portfolios

When you want students to evaluate their own progress, we recommend portfolios. A *collection portfolio* contains work that students have completed during the year. A student's portfolio could contain a brainstorming list, a study guide, journal entries, and notes from conferences or discussions, for example. At various points in the semester, you will want students to review the portfolio contents and weed out less significant items. Students should keep items that demonstrate how they have progressed and revised their knowledge over time. From the collection portfolio, students would select items for their *showcase portfolio*—exhibitions of learning progress. They also would write essays evaluating the items and telling how the items demonstrate their learning progress. In Part Three, we return to collection and showcase portfolios when we present units for different content areas.

Focus on Writing: Revising Drafts

Most writers, especially students, consider their first draft to be clear and complete. Some writers have learned to set aside a first draft for a few days so that they can reread the draft more critically or more like a reader would. Most writers need another reader to ask questions about specific information or to state where they experienced confusion while reading. From that reader's questions and comments, writers learn where to revise their drafts.

In schools, particularly in English classes, teachers confer with students about their drafts, and students confer with each other. These conferences could occur during prewriting, and during composing of the first draft, as easily as now, during revising, because the purpose is not merely to have students rewrite. Instead, the conferences are to assist the students in expressing their intended meaning clearly and completely.

We encourage you to model and explain revising conferences so that your students can conduct peer conferences. In revising conferences, you would concentrate on the ideas and information, and save editing comments (for example, spelling and punctuation) for after the ideas are clearly presented in the writing. Conferring with students both individually and in small groups, you would ask questions and point out confusions that you have. You would also model and explain several strategies and suggestions for them to use when they revise their drafts.

Whether students are writing nonfiction, fiction, or poetry, we recommend that you selectively model and explain revision categories focused on exploring the following questions (Allan & Miller, 1995; Atwell, 1998):

- What is the purpose and meaning or subject of the draft: to tell a story, to give directions, to explain a subject or topic, to persuade, to create poetry?

- Who is the audience: peers, a specific person, people in the community?

- How is the text organized: sequence, problem-solution, or some other way?

- Is the amount of information or detail enough, accurate, and specific but not too much, too general, or too redundant?

- Is the information focused and not tangential to the purpose?

- Is the beginning engaging and the ending fitting?

- Are the words and sentences clear, specific, precise, and flowing?

- Does the writing have voice—personality, uniqueness, character—instead of being dry, listless, and dull?

You would not explore all of these revision categories in one conference because that could overwhelm the student; rather, you would choose the ones that are most

These students are helping each other revise their ideas in written drafts.
© Susie Fitzhugh

important to the student's draft. Whether each student has chosen his or her own type of text (poem, fiction narrative, biography, personal memory) or you have assigned the same type of text (reporting information, eyewitness accounts, letters to the editor), you will confer on only the most important category. Over the course of a year, you would model and explain different categories for revision. As students gain experience, they may come to a conference with their peers knowing they need help on a specific category of problems.

Monitoring Progress and Purpose

After reading, strategic learners monitor whether they have accomplished their purposes. They may decide that they accomplished their purpose satisfactorily and their strategies were successful. They may decide that they have discovered a new purpose (question) worth exploring and begin thinking about strategies for their new purpose. They may decide that their purpose has not been accomplished satisfactorily, and they need to locate another source.

In deciding about whether they have accomplished their purposes, strategic learners monitor or assess what they know now compared to their earlier knowledge. They decide how to organize the information clearly so that they can study it. They monitor themselves as they review the information, checking to see if they can recall most of it. Strategic learners also think critically about the information by evaluating the ideas. They reconsider their own prior knowledge, the author's ideas and bias, and the ideas in other sources. Throughout reading, strategic learners monitor whether they have increased or revised their prior knowledge.

Thus, strategic learners are really engaged in self-evaluation and goal setting for future learning.

A Checklist: Monitoring Strategies After Reading

Monitoring Purpose

❑ Have you accomplished your original purpose?
❑ Have you accomplished the new purpose you changed to during reading?
❑ Have you discovered a new purpose to pursue after reading?

Monitoring Reviewing and Evaluating

❑ Can you organize the important ideas into categories that build your schema?
❑ Can you summarize the important information for your purposes?
❑ Can you draw a conclusion, infer a theme, or determine the thesis?
❑ Do you need to review important vocabulary?
❑ Do you need to reread, look back, review, or recite the information to study?
❑ Have you reconsidered your prior knowledge based on the new information?
❑ Have you decided information is missing?

❑ Have you applied criteria to evaluate the information?
❑ Do you recognize the author's point of view, bias, intent, or purpose?
❑ Can you compare these ideas to other authors or sources?
❑ Can you apply the ideas to your life, your community, or society in general?

 ## SUMMARY

In this chapter, we have focused on studying after reading a text. To study information, strategic learners:

■ **Review and evaluate information**

To explain the strategy of reviewing and evaluating, we first presented a lesson on strategies:

■ **Before and during reading—setting a purpose, making notes**

■ **Categorization chart—reviewing**

■ **Modeling and explaining—summarizing**

■ **Discussion—evaluating**

Second, we presented pedagogical tools to support students after reading:

■ **Teaching summaries—preparation with graphic organizers, writing summaries, and extending summary writing to more difficult texts and to different audiences**

■ **Teaching/assessing tools—graphic organizers, postreading guides, *PORPE*, and reinforcing vocabulary**

■ **Assessment tools—tests and essays, and portfolios**

We do not think that students regularly review texts or evaluate the information in texts after they have finished reading. You can engage them in reviewing and evaluating by using a teaching tool. You may model and explain the strategy or introduce a teaching/assessing tool. Don't forget that you could also revisit an earlier tool.

Third, we presented the section

■ **Focus on Writing: Revising Drafts**

When students revise their drafts, they critically review and evaluate whether they have written what they intended or not. They also evaluate whether they have clearly expressed their ideas for their intended audience.

And finally, we presented the section on

■ **Monitoring progress and purpose—checklist for monitoring after reading**

You know that if you and your students discuss strategies and how they are used, then your students will be metacognitively aware of how they learn. Your students will consciously plan to use the strategies that will accomplish their purpose and the task at hand.

So far in Part Two, we have separated before reading (Chapters 4 and 5), during reading (Chapters 6 and 7), and after reading (Chapter 8). We needed to separate those events in order to explain literacy strategies and teaching tools to you. However, you know that before, during, and after reading could flow one into the other during one period or may take more than one period, like the lesson in this chapter. In the next chapter, we will present a research project that discusses strategies before, during, and after researching a topic.

Inquiry into Your Learning

1. Write a review of a curriculum material in your content area: for example, a text, computer software, web sites, teacher's guides, or textbooks. Summarize the material concisely yet completely, so that your peers understand its contents. Identify the strengths and weaknesses in the material. If possible, compare it to other curriculum materials you know. Finally, offer suggestions on how and with whom to use (or not use) the curriculum material. You might want to compile your classmates' reviews into a curriculum resource booklet.

2. Survey curriculum materials, textbooks or anthologies in your content area. How do they assess vocabulary? Do they use the traditional methods of multiple-choice, write a sentence, or write a definition? Compare the assessments you found to the explanation assessments suggested by Beck, et al. (2002) in the Reinforcing Vocabulary section in this chapter. Using one vocabulary list, change the assessment into one of the explanation formats. Of course, you may need to add comparison words and to think about how the words are used. Ask a peer to take both the textbook assessment and your assessment. Which does your peer prefer and why?

Inquiry into Your Students' Learning

1. With a small group of students, write a summary for a text they need to study. Choose a text that is well organized and contains information they will understand easily. Devise a graphic organizer that will help them organize the information. You can decide whether they should complete the graphic organizer as they read or afterward. After they have organized the ideas, you might want to discuss the information before writing the summary. Depending on the students, you may decide to write a summary together, in pairs, or independently. Guide the students through sections of the summary: writing the opening overview sentence, summarizing sections of the text, and composing a concluding sentence. Have the students share their summaries and discuss the similarities and differences. Can you tell if they condensed information or synthesized information?

2. With a small group of struggling learners, who have difficulty writing essays, model and explain the PORPE tool. **Predict** likely essay questions with them. Pick one question and **organize** information on a graphic organizer. You may choose to skip the rehearsal step or keep it and add more details to the graphic organizer. You and the students may need to review texts to add sufficient information. When you think the graphic organizer has sufficient information, compose a **practice** essay either as a group, in pairs, or individually. Help them compose an opening sentence and first paragraph. Can they compose subsequent paragraphs or do they need help? When they have finished, **evaluate** the essay or essays together. Discuss what the essay did well and how to improve next time.

Resources

Books

Almasi, J. F. (2003). *Teaching strategic processes in reading.* New York: Guildford. Explains literacy strategy instruction that complements this textbook.

Beers, K. (2002). *When kids can't read, what teachers can do: A guide for teachers 6–12.* Portsmouth, NH: Heinemann. Describes teaching literacy strategies before, during, and after reading that complement this textbook.

Journals

Dickson, T. (2003). Comparative decades: Conservatism in the 1920s and 1980s. *Magazine of History, 17* (20), 37–39. Outlines a lesson plan that contains a comparative postreading guide.

Hardy, D. C. (2003). Lab Check, 1 . . . 2 . . . 3. *The Science Teacher, 70* (1), 31–33. Provides a checklist for students to use when drafting or revising lab reports.

Totten, S. (2002). What will students remember? Closing a lesson on the Holocaust. *Social Education, 66* (7), 436–440. Suggests several activities (tools) to use after learning such as writing letters, making a graphic organizer, and writing a summary in the form of an encyclopedia entry.

Web Sites

Our Documents. **www.ourdocuments.gov**. Has a Teacher Tool Box with lesson plans and a Sourcebook for using 100 Milestone documents in the classroom. Is also a regular column in *Social Education*, which reprints documents and suggests a variety of activities (tools) before, during, and after reading the documents.

Researching Multiple Sources

PURPOSE-SETTING QUESTIONS

1. What kinds of research projects have you done: researching known facts and interpretations from library and internet sources, or investigating a question or problem by collecting new data from experiments, observations, or interviews? What did you learn from each?

2. What sources have you used—print sources, electronic sources, experiments, observations or interviews? Did you use different strategies for different sources?

3. What strategies help you organize, synthesize, and evaluate your research? When do you discover a theme or thesis?

4. How did you learn to conduct research? How did your elementary and high school teachers support your research projects?

5. What types of end products have you completed? Who was the audience for your products? What did you learn from completing different products?

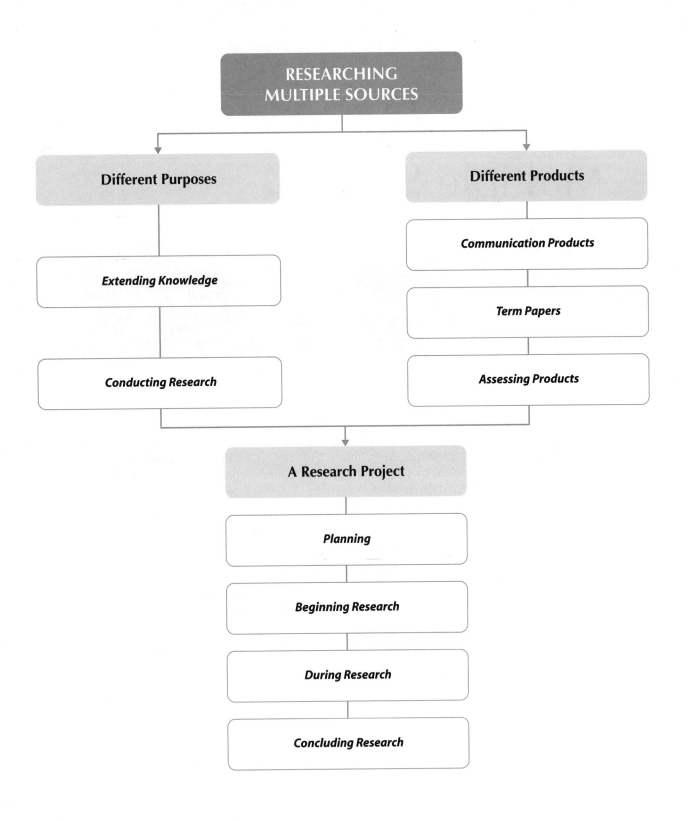

RESEARCHING MULTIPLE SOURCES

Different Purposes

Extending Knowledge

Conducting Research

Different Products

Communication Products

Term Papers

Assessing Products

A Research Project

Planning

Beginning Research

During Research

Concluding Research

In how many courses have you skimmed the syllabus to find a research paper required? Are you given a list of possible topics to choose from or can you devise your own topic? Do you think about your prior knowledge and interest in choosing a topic? Do you rush to the library for print sources; hop on-line for electronic sources; or collect your own data through observation or interviews? Is a written term paper required or can you devise other ways to communicate the information to different audiences? We predict that you have primarily written traditional term papers using print sources and electronic sources. We also predict that you may have learned to write those papers simply through practice by writing many papers without much instruction from teachers. Contrary to our predictions, our goal is for you to incorporate a variety of research projects into your content area and to support your students' research efforts with teaching tools.

In previous chapters, we have discussed reading single texts because we needed to explain literacy strategies and teaching tools useful before, during, and after reading. We emphasized the variety of readers' strategies and teachers' tools that might be selected to learn the information in a particular text. You now have a repertoire of literacy strategies and teaching tools that you can draw upon to teach students how to research using multiple texts.

In this chapter, we begin by first explaining the different purposes for research projects in content areas. You know your students need to learn more knowledge in your content area and to learn information independently or to research information from more than one source. In learning how to conduct research, we will discuss different sources of information that are available to students today—especially print versus electronic sources. Second, we describe different end products—communication projects for different audiences and the traditional term paper. When you launch a research project with your students, you will want to clearly explain both the purpose and the product of their research.

Finally, we present a scenario of a middle school research project. We use a middle school project because we want to show you how a teacher could instruct relatively inexperienced students how to research using multiple sources. In our fictionalized scenario for Women's History Month, the teacher models and explains how he is researching photographer Dorothea Lange, while his students are researching an outstanding woman of their choice. He also supports his students with teaching tools for researching a variety of sources—print, electronic, community—appropriate for each project. At the end of the research, students choose a communication project to exhibit their learning.

Although we have included a scenario for middle school, you know that some secondary students need support when conducting research or may need support in particular tasks. When teaching secondary students, you will need to monitor their progress and conduct mini-lessons when they need support.

Different Purposes

Y ou know from your own school experiences that many teachers initiate research projects in conjunction with their mandated curriculum, such as westward expansion or weather. At other times, teachers use research projects to supplement the curriculum with topics, such as Black History Month or the problem of homelessness. In both cases, the teachers have two goals for the research project. First, they want their students to gain in-depth learning about a particular topic related to their content area. Second, they want their students to gain expertise in conducting research using different sources—known data in print and on-line as well as their own original data. As a content-area teacher, you have both of those goals in mind and research projects serve to foster those goals.

■ Extending Knowledge

Your first purpose of research projects is to build your students' knowledge about specific topics in your content area. You may ask students to choose specific topics related to a curriculum area they have studied; for example a student may choose to research Louis Howe, political advisor to Franklin Roosevelt, during a study of U.S. history in the 1920s and 1930s. Offering choice, even within a limit like a historical era, will increase your students' motivation to enhance their knowledge about your content area.

Sometimes you may broaden the choice spectrum so that students may research any topic that interests them within your content area. When students choose their own topic, they can be very motivated to thoroughly research their topics. For example, a special education student, who had completed no reading or writing all year, avidly researched the Columbine shooting and gun violence. He presented his research to fourth and fifth graders in an assembly explaining to the audience how the Columbine shooting or other such violence does not have to happen (Bausch, 2003).

Whatever topic choices you offer, you and your students need to be clear about your aims and expectations for the content to be learned. You may expect students to extend their prior knowledge by assembling *known data* and interpretations. Learning more about a topic is a worthy goal in the content areas, especially when students have little in-depth knowledge before they begin the study. Furthermore, assembling a coherent review of known information is a useful goal in some of life's research projects. Suppose you want to buy a car; you would research consumer information to assemble known facts and interpretations that inform your decision. However, you would be unlikely to make a new or original discovery that would revolutionize other consumers' purchases.

You may aim for students to collect *new data* concerning an issue or question. Students can produce unique insights, make original discoveries, or establish their own positions by collecting their own data from observations, experiments, interviews, or surveys. For example, students may provide evidence for local options about a national problem, like homelessness. Or their local experimental evidence could provide support for influencing U.S. policy on global warming.

Students could assemble known information and collect their own new data. In fact, that is what researchers in every content area really do. Students could research what is known about monarch butterflies, collect their own data about the monarchs

known data Existing information reported in print or on-line sources.

new data Original data that students collect from sources such as interviews, experiments, primary documents.

in their community, and then report their data to the national research study. Students could assemble information about the Vietnam War and then interview former soldiers and older citizens for their perspectives and experiences during the war. In our middle school example, the teacher extends their research from assembling known data to using community sources for new data.

When you initiate a research project, you will discuss with your students whether they are to assemble known data, discover new data, or combine the two. Now let's turn to how you will teach your students to conduct research.

■ Conducting Research

goal: to create independent learners

Your second purpose is to teach students strategies and tools for conducting research so that they can learn content independently. Every research project begins with activating prior knowledge, asking questions to pursue, and deciding upon sources of information. Then the project continues with collecting, interpreting, and analyzing information, and ends with synthesizing information, drawing conclusions, and asking new questions. At every level, teachers need to model and explain strategies, to incorporate other teaching tools in support of their students' learning, and to assess or monitor their students' use of strategies and tools. Middle school teachers expect to instruct their students in how to research multiple sources; however, even high school teachers may need to instruct students at particular points in their research. We advocate using class time during research projects so that teachers can monitor and instruct as needed.

When researching known data, students learn what others have discovered by reading library and electronic sources—the starting place for most research. When researching new data, students have the opportunity to work with data like professional researchers in your content area do. Students need both opportunities.

Known data

Once upon a time not that long ago, when students faced a report, they went to the card catalogue and the encyclopedia. Today, 71 percent of teens with access to the Internet use it as their major source of information, while 24 percent use library sources (Lenhart, Simon, & Graziano cited in Bruce, 2002). Are you like those teens? You may be adept at surfing the web for worthwhile sites and evaluating those sites. However, your students probably are not as adept at finding credible sites, even though they use the Internet. You will need to teach your students how to find and use a range of sources including the Internet, and then how to compare and synthesize the information they have found. Let's discuss both of these teaching opportunities.

Finding and Evaluating Sources   First, you will want your students to become adept at finding and using a range of sources. Students need to become acquainted with print sources in the library—reference materials such as encyclopedias, atlases, almanacs, magazines, newspapers, informational books, biographies, and perhaps fiction, poetry, and picture books. In addition to print sources, they need guidance finding electronic sources—on-line newspapers and magazines, 'zines, web sites, CD-ROMs. Students need to use researching strategies and tools applicable to both print and electronic sources.

Just right ones

using search terms
A research strategy
that identifies the key
words useful in finding
information about
a topic.

To find sources, students need to *use search terms* or key words to locate information in a card catalogue, a book, and the Internet. You recognize that *weather* is too broad a search term *Hurricane Andrew* is too narrow but *hurricane* is just right. When students need help thinking of search terms, different sources offer different amounts of help (Eagleton & Guinne, 2002). For example, compare a book on weather and an Internet search on weather. The book's table of contents will outline the subtopics allowing the student to see several research paths. An Internet search on weather yields an unorganized list of sites (although each search engine has its own formula for ranking sites) that necessitates that students compose their own subtopics. Although middle school students with Internet access may have navigation skills (Luke, 2000), they may not have efficient searching skills and may hop randomly from site to site. Furthermore, if teachers always provide bookmarks for preselected sites, students will not learn to search efficiently on their own (Eagleton & Guinne, 2002). We recommend using the teaching tool of a word map (Chapter 5) to help your students outline subtopics and superordinate topics and think about search terms, especially when searching the Internet.

Teach to:
• search Internet
• evaluate sources

Upon finding sources, students need to evaluate them. Many students do not pay attention to the author of the book, the primary source, or the web site. Often they evaluate a source by the amount of information rather than judge the point of view of the source (Stahl, Hynd, Britton, McNish, & Bosquet, 1996; Van Sledright,

Students searching the
Internet for worthwhile
web sites for their
research project.
© Bob Daemmrich Photography

& Kelly, 1998). Students may skillfully navigate to Internet sites but they do not critically evaluate those sites (Luke, 2002). Students may not know to search for the most current source and for the author's qualifications. Conditioned to automatically accept the information in textbooks, students need to learn to be alert for the author's point of view or bias. Students need to recognize the point of view and examine the evidence supporting the viewpoint. Furthermore, they need help deciding whether to search for alternative or opposing points of view. Thus, students need instruction in how to *evaluate their research sources.*

evaluating sources
A research strategy that checks the date and credentials of the sources and that assesses the accuracy, point of view, and historical context of the sources.

First, students need to **check the date** of the source. Students need to check the copyright date of books and the date web sites were last updated to ensure that those sources have recent information. They can check the date of magazines and newspapers to determine when the information was current. You may decide to discuss how important the date of a source is for research in your content area. For example, science researchers value the most recent sources for the new data they contain. On the other hand, while historical researchers value sources produced at the time of the event, they also consider sources written later that provide more objective perspectives.

Second, students need to **check the credentials** of the source for the first clue about the quality of the information. Who are the author and publisher of the text? For books, students can check a blurb about the author's qualifications and the bibliography of the author's most important sources. For magazines and newspapers, the reporters' credentials are more difficult to find. Authors of web sites are not always identified unless an individual created their own site and then he or she should post credentials.

In place of authors, students may need to check on the organization that publishes the magazine, newspaper, and/or web site. They should learn that some organizations have strong credentials but also explicitly support certain positions on issues, such as the Sierra Club on the environment. Other organizations, for example newspaper publishers and news magazine publishers, aim for objectivity and express opinions only in editorials. For web sites, students can check the domain—government, education, organization, or commercial. Students need to recognize that educational, governmental, and some organizational sites, such as museums, rely on their institutions' status for their credentials. Of course, students probably recognize that most commercial sites provide favorable information about their products.

Third, students need to learn to **evaluate the accuracy** of the information in books, periodicals, and web sites. After checking credentials, students should determine which of their sources have been reviewed by experts in the field. In general, students can assume that books have been reviewed prior to publication. Magazine and newspaper articles are not typically reviewed by outside experts but editors usually check for accuracy. However, their checking is not foolproof. In 2003, *The New York Times*, considered a reputable newspaper, had to embarrassingly admit that a reporter had fabricated numerous facts in many articles and that the newspaper failed to check the accuracy. Therefore, although evaluating the accuracy of an article is not easy, students should attempt it.

Unlike print sources, no one checks the accuracy of the information on a web site; anyone can create a web site with accurate information, inaccurate information, and even unwanted information. That's the beauty and the curse of the Internet. Students also need to keep in mind that just because a web site has flashy multimedia doesn't mean the site is worthwhile. On the other hand, sometimes multimedia enhancements can be advantageous. For example, listening to Gwendolyn Brooks read her poem, "We Real Cool," can help a student interpret her poetry.

Fourth, students need to **evaluate the point of view** or position the author expresses. Recall that in Chapter 6 we discussed how people don't just find facts, they interpret facts. When researching their topics, since they can't include every fact, authors select which facts are most important to include in their explanations. As authors do extensive research, they form viewpoints on the topics. When they write, they don't just list facts; they explain and interpret those facts in order to present their positions or theses. Students need to recognize when authors of books and articles explicitly state their views and when others imply their positions by how they explain the facts. Daily readers of newspapers and magazines sometimes discern viewpoints in the news articles or viewpoints implied by the news events reported upon, although students may have difficulty discerning viewpoints. Web sites posted by individuals usually express a point of view but students need to be aware that institutional or organizational web sites may also present a position. Students can learn that governmental sites may express a policy position in addition to information. For example, the U. S. Labor Department implied a position about child labor when it posted information and its policy on its web site a few years ago. Students need to search for explicit statements of point of view and to be alert to implied points of view. Furthermore, they need to compare the points of view from multiple sources, if possible.

And finally when reading primary sources such as diaries, speeches, and news articles, students need to **recognize the historical context** in which the document was produced in addition the author's viewpoint or purpose (Stahl, et al., 1996; Van Sledright & Kelly, 1998). For example, when students read Patrick Henry's "give me liberty, or give me death!" speech, they would benefit from knowing that he spoke to the Virginia convention on March 23, 1775, one month before the British and colonials clashed at Lexington and Concord. They should also know that the patriot's intent was to persuade reluctant Virginians to align themselves with the Massachusetts patriots and establish a Virginia militia to defend themselves against the British. Having that historical context helps students comprehend the argument presented in Patrick Henry's speech. They should also find the opposing views expressed in that Virginian convention.

To evaluate sources, especially for accuracy, point of view, and historical context, students need to read multiple sources and, if possible, different types of sources. They should not rely solely on the Internet, but consult books as well. Then they need to compare the information and viewpoints in the various sources.

Synthesizing Multiple Sources   Next, you will teach students to compare and contrast the information from different sources. According to Many, Fyfe, Lewis & Mitchell (1996), twelve-year-olds have three methods of researching topics on their own: (1) some collect interesting information on random subtopics without an encompassing topic; (2) some copy or paraphrase information using one source for each subtopic of the overall topic; and (3) some synthesize and check information from a variety of sources for each subtopic related to their encompassing topic. Even the tenth grade students in Stahl et al. (1996) only reported the common or repeated information from the sources, ignoring the different information. Furthermore, when asked to take a position about the topic, the students wrote unsupported opinions and did not cite any evidence from the sources that they had read (Stahl, et al., 1996). Clearly, students needed instruction in *synthesizing multiple sources*.

synthesizing multiple sources A research strategy that compares the similarities and differences in the information and viewpoints of different sources.

Students need to find similar information in several sources to corroborate the accuracy of the information and the viewpoint of the authors. On the other hand, they also need to find sources that have different information or interpretations to further their knowledge; not all experts agree about topics. And finally they need to learn to draw conclusions from the similar and different information they have found. Synthesizing research from multiple sources is not easy and you will need to support your students with the teaching tools we have described in previous chapters.

In your instruction, you could select KWL teaching tool (refer to Chapter 4) so that students would search for answers to the questions they posed. You could decide to have students record the information found in the different sources on comparison charts so that they can see the similarities and differences in the information (see the project discussed in this chapter). You can model and explain how you check information found in different sources for consistencies or inconsistencies in the facts and interpretations. You can teach students to write summaries for their subtopics (refer to Chapter 8). Thus, many of the teaching tools we have described in previous chapters will support your students when they synthesize their sources.

And finally, you want to teach your students to avoid plagiarism—the appropriation of another person's ideas or words as one's own. When students directly copy sentences or paragraphs or fail to give credit for a quote or an idea, they are plagiarizing—probably innocently. You can teach how to credit authors in the text and in a bibliography. In addition, teaching students to ask their own questions, to paraphrase in short notes, and to compare multiple sources will help them assemble their own interpretations of the facts and avoid plagiarizing others.

New Data

Real investigations in your field necessitate asking questions or tackling problems for which new data are needed. By doing real investigations, you introduce your students to the research strategies and sources used in your field. Often these real investigations require students to seek sources beyond the school. The students may conduct experiments or observations locally, interview or survey people in the community, or locate primary documents from local historical societies and on-line sites. Since the sources may be unfamiliar to the students, you may need to model and explain strategies for finding and interpreting data from these sources.

Like any real investigation, students begin by asking questions or defining their problem and identifying data sources. During their investigation, they determine what data are relevant and analyze and interpret their data. Students' data has not been collected by anyone else, even when they may be corroborating what researchers elsewhere are collecting. Their data could be different; so they need to compare their data to data others have collected. Thus, since the students have new data, their synthesis and conclusions are unknown until they make them.

To give your students the opportunity to experience real investigations, we encourage you to locate questions, problems, or issues in your curriculum. Questions or issues may arise from your field: what is unsettled in your content area? Questions or issues could arise from the local community: what are officials and citizens discussing or writing to the newspaper about? Questions or issues may arise from the national or world news:

how are those events affecting local citizens? While you may decide not to tackle hot controversial questions your first year, those questions will engage your students and they may be already discussing those same topics among themselves.

Different Products

assessment ✗

Remember that one goal is to teach students to conduct research independently. Therefore, the entire research project—every step along the way, not just the end product—is worthy of assessment by both you and your students. You might ask students to keep working portfolios, which are useful vehicles for collecting the ongoing learning during a research project.

Throughout this book we have emphasized the process of learning by concentrating on strategies, yet we recognize that most people have a reason, a goal, or a product in mind when they embark on a project. For example, both the athlete and ordinary jogger have goals for their training: to be physically fit, to perform well, or to live a healthier life. Few run just to run without regard to a distance, time, or performance goal. Therefore, the product or goal can provide the motivation for the process, especially when you embark on an extensive project like a research project.

The end product also serves to give students a sense of accomplishment. Because they communicate what they have learned, the students have verification that their strategies resulted in increased knowledge. If students have the opportunity to communicate their learning in different end products, they exhibit different strengths and accomplishments. So, let's discuss communication products, term papers, and assessing products.

■ Communication Products

As you plan research projects for and with your students, you can explore the variety of opportunities through which students can communicate their learning to others. In Table 9.1, we have suggested a sampling of products; you can probably think of others. Although we discuss these *communication products* in conjunction with research projects, you could incorporate communication products with other units you are teaching—artistic responses to a novel or a role play of the Continental Congress.

communication products Products that exhibit student learning to audiences through speaking, drama, the arts, writing, or electronic vehicles.

We labeled the products communication products because we encourage you to think about different audiences for the students' products. When students engage in extensive research projects, they are prepared to inform their peers, younger students, and students in other schools. Students may have information to inform or persuade community citizens, local officials, or national representatives to take action on issues. Particularly when students choose their own topics and when they research new data, they should choose the product and the audience for their learning.

DIVERSITY

By expanding the range of products that students can create to communicate their learning, teachers discover strengths and talents in students, especially in diverse students, that may have not been evident before. Historically, the school culture has primarily sanctioned term papers and essays to the neglect of other communication products. Yet, out-of-school cultures sanction sermons, speeches, letters, plays, music, and art forms to name a few. By encouraging other cultural forms of communication, not only do teachers learn about their students but students may learn about themselves.

TABLE 9.1   Communication Products: A Sampling

Speaking	Drama	Arts	Writing	Electronic
Choral reading	Readers' theater	Collage	Biopoems	Computer graphics
Book talk	Role play	Drawings	Diamantes	Web page
Panel presentation	Informal or creative drama	Photographs	Feature or interview article	Digital Pen Storyspace™
Debate	Pantomime	Lyrics or raps	Character sketch	PowerPoint presentation
Speech or presentation	Video a reenactment	Select music recordings	Fictional journal	Hypermedia
Radio report or documentary	Script and play	Select art reproductions	Front-page news report	
Read Aloud	Dance	Picture book	Pamphlet	
Dialogue	Puppetry	Quilt squares	Eyewitness report	
		Diarama	Letter to the editor or officials	

For example, through his church, Anthony researched the history of African-Americans in his community and learned African communication forms of drumming and dance (Kelly, 2001). Anthony did not exhibit learning strengths in school until his English teacher assigned a persuasive writing task in which students chose their own topics and audience. Because Anthony felt many Black students did not have his opportunities to learn about African-American culture, issues, and scholarship options, he wrote a successful persuasive letter to the principal to establish a Black Student Union. Kelly concludes that through church and school experiences, Anthony developed a sense of self within both communities.

In another example, middle school students participated in a radio documentary project that digitally incorporated spoken narration, interviews, music, song lyrics, proverbs, and reflections (Callahan, 2002). In her documentary about the loss of her father, Naomi combined narration with music and song lyrics to communicate about her loss for the first time. Naomi reflected, "It invited me to open my heart. Not only did it touch people, but also I touched people." (p. 56) For another documentary, Max and Matt went to the airport to interview strangers. They wove the strangers' stories together with their reflections, proverbs, and music. After their documentary, "Airport Stories," Max stated he viewed strangers differently and would smile, wave, or say "hi" in a friendly manner. In presenting the documentaries to the school committee and interested parents, "Students saw the impact of carefully crafted language on an audience" (p. 62).

In these examples, the students used community resources—the African-American church, the local historical library, one's family, and the airport—for their sources of information. By incorporating community resources as sources, students had the opportunity to learn information not usually available in schools. In addition, they addressed audiences beyond their classrooms—the high school population, the school committee, and parents. By addressing community audiences, students had a real purpose for their product. By incorporating communication products and actual audiences, the teachers of those students learned about the different capabilities of their students and students learned about themselves.

■ Term Papers

In many classrooms, from elementary school through graduate school, students assemble known facts and interpretations in written reports or term papers. If only because of the prevalence of written products, students need to learn to write term papers in the standard format, consisting of title page, introduction, subtopics or categories of information, synthesis or conclusion, and bibliography.

You might assign the other traditional reports in your field that are based on the term paper, especially when your students research new data. Research reports in the sciences and social sciences published in professional journals are variations on the term paper. Journalistic articles published in specialized magazines for specific audiences, like *Smithsonian, Scientific American,* and *Canoe,* report and synthesize information, albeit more informally in some sources.

While students are researching, they need to begin thinking about composing their term papers. The strategies to review and evaluate ideas discussed in Chapter 8 are useful when writing term papers. You can support students by having them complete a graphic organizer of their information. The advantage of a graphic organizer is that it encapsulates or distills the reams of information in the students' notes. By viewing the whole report on one page, students can decide which subtopics (or questions) have more information, which need more information, and which should be eliminated. Based on the evaluation of the subtopics, students can decide how to sequence the subtopics before they begin to write.

The next challenge is turning their notes into sentences and paragraphs. You can review the Focus on Writing sections in previous chapters for tools, like freewriting (Chapter 4) and discovery drafts (Chapter 7), that support students' composing. When students write in the almost stream-of-consciousness style of freewriting and discovery drafts, they may jump-start their composing and find the important ideas, themes, or theses for their papers. In addition, your students may offer suggestions, like writing several titles or writing the most important part first, that help each other begin to compose.

And finally, you will want your students to share sections of their first drafts in peer conferences in order to help each other revise and edit their papers. A term paper is a published document and so needs to contain complete and well-organized information expressed in standard grammar, spelling, and punctuation.

■ Assessing Products

Naturally the criteria you and your students use to assess end products will depend on the types of end products they produce. Whether your students complete communication products or term papers, you should discuss with them the criteria both of you will use to assess the products.

For every end product, students should communicate the overall topic or issue, the most important information, and a synthesis or conclusion. We think a creative art project, a poem, and a term paper can communicate those three aspects, although each will communicate the same aspects very differently.

When your students complete communication products in speaking, drama, art, music, and writing, they should assess their products considering the following focused questions:

- Can the audience interpret a central idea, thesis, theme, and position in the product?

- How or where does the audience learn about the important aspects, characteristics, and information?

- What aspects of the product contribute to the audience being more informed or persuaded to the creator's position?

- How does the product accomplish the creator's goal and demonstrate the creator's new learnings?

When your students write term papers, they should assess their first and final drafts using the following focused questions:

- Is the overall topic (theme or thesis) clear to the reader?

- Can the reader tell when each subtopic is introduced?

- Does the order of the subtopics make sense to the reader?

- Does the reader have enough information about each subtopic? Where does the reader need more information? Where is there extraneous information?

- Are the introduction and conclusion satisfying to the reader?

In the rest of the chapter, we present an example of a middle school research project.

TEACHER AS INQUIRING LEARNER

Reflect on your research experiences in a freewrite.

- Were you taught strategies or guided through your first research report? Did you always write the traditional report, or did you sometimes present your information in a skit or a poem? Did your motivation change when you could choose your topic rather than being assigned a topic? How do you research topics now in college? Have you found a way to change an assigned topic into a personally meaningful topic? Do you think your professors are asking you to assemble known facts and interpretations? When have your professors asked you to research new data? How can you learn from your experiences to provide research opportunities for your students?

A Research Project

In this fictionalized sixth-grade classroom scenario, the social studies/English teacher introduces a research project on outstanding women during Women's History Month. His content major understanding for the unit is for students to answer this question: "Why are the women outstanding in their fields?" He also wants to emphasize strategies for researching multiple sources.

Choosing the particular woman they want to learn about, the students research known information from sources in their school library. The teacher emphasizes not only the common information in different sources but also the different information in specific sources. Because he wants students to interpret the life and times of the women they are studying, he will ask students to consider what the women would be doing today by interviewing a community person in the woman's field. The unit will end with a presentation of their communication products.

Planning

Once the teacher decides on the curriculum topic for the unit, he has three tasks: increasing his own knowledge of the topic, checking on available sources for students, and outlining the activities in the unit. Knowing he would teach this unit, he has been collecting information from newspapers and magazines throughout the year, continually learning about the topic. In addition to increasing his general knowledge, he chooses to research an outstanding woman photographer because of his interest in photography. He plans to use his own research as a model for his students.

Although the students will find their own sources of information, the teacher wants to be assured that the school library has enough different biographies on women to meet the wide range of reading levels in his classroom. The school librarian suggests displaying the biographies since she is going to feature Women's History Month too. In addition, she will contact the local library for books to supplement the school's collection. She also suggests biographical encyclopedias and *Faces* magazine as additional sources. Later that week, the teacher and librarian meet to make a list of the women that they have library sources for. They decide to divide the list to search the Internet for sites to supplement the library sources. Finally, the teacher also contacts the parent in charge of community resources to alert her that he would like his students to interview people in fields related to the women they are researching.

Satisfied that the students will have enough sources available to them, the teacher sketches a plan for the unit. Although these sixth graders have written research reports before, his experience tells him that they need guidance and instruction. During the research process, he decides to model and explain the specific strategies he uses to research photographer Dorothea Lange, as the students concurrently research the women they have chosen to study.

Since he wants the students to interpret the women's lives—not simply report events in their lives—the teacher plans several culminating activities. Students who are researching women in related fields will form cooperative groups for these activities.

First, to build their historical context and to compare the women they've chosen, the students will make a time line of major events in the women's lives and compare it to the classroom time line of major events in the nation and the world. Second, to think about what their women might be accomplishing today, the students will interview community people in fields related to the women they are researching. And finally, the groups will decide how to communicate their learnings about the women—perhaps a role play, an artistic display, a free verse poem, or a web page.

Having a general plan and being assured of sufficient sources, the teacher begins to plan specific lessons for the beginning, during, and concluding phases of the research project. Figure 9.1 outlines the research strategies in the project.

■ Beginning Research

The teacher first plans to introduce the research project to the students and to allow them time to think about their selections. After the students have chosen which women to research, he plans to model and explain his strategies as he begins to research the life of photographer Dorothea Lange. He will also support their beginning research process with teaching/assessing tools.

Finding a Topic

To open the unit, "Why are the women outstanding in their fields?" the teacher holds a **brainstorming discussion** with the whole class **to assess the students' prior knowledge**. On chart paper he draws a **semantic map** with the topic, outstanding women in different fields, in the middle and different fields radiating outward (see a sample map in Figure 9.2). He asks his students to contribute the names and accomplishments of the important women they know. He expects that some fields, like math or computers, will be empty, and many interesting women he knows, like Rear Admiral Grace Hopper (U.S. Navy, Retired) who invented the computer language COBOL and the term *bugs*, will not be mentioned.

TEACHER AS INQUIRING LEARNER

With your peers, you might see how many outstanding women you could contribute to the sample semantic map in Figure 9.2.

- What names can you add? What other fields can you add? Do you know of outstanding women in your own field?

Most people don't know many outstanding women unless they have researched the topic. You might want to take this opportunity to research famous women in your field. Start by skimming the biographical encyclopedias in the library. Make a list of the women in your field and their accomplishments. Perhaps you can find a full biography written about one woman to read. Save your list, because you might find it useful in the future.

After the students have contributed the names of the outstanding women they know to the class's semantic map, the teacher takes the students (and the semantic map) to the library. The librarian gives a **book talk to preview** the biographies: for some just

FIGURE 9.1 **Research Strategies**

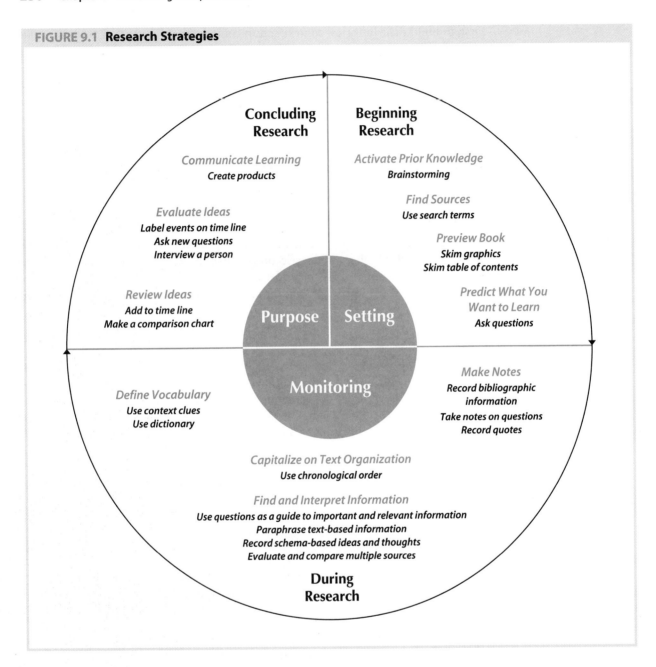

mentioning the woman's contribution; for others giving a brief biography. As the librarian mentions each biography, the teacher adds the name to the semantic map. After the book talk, the students begin thinking about which women they want to research and browse among the books.

In a few days, after the students have had time to mull over their choices, the teacher asks them to write three choices on a piece of paper (**choosing a topic**). After matching the students and their choices as best he can, he begins to model and explain his research process.

FIGURE 9.2 The Teacher's Brainstorming Map of Outstanding Women

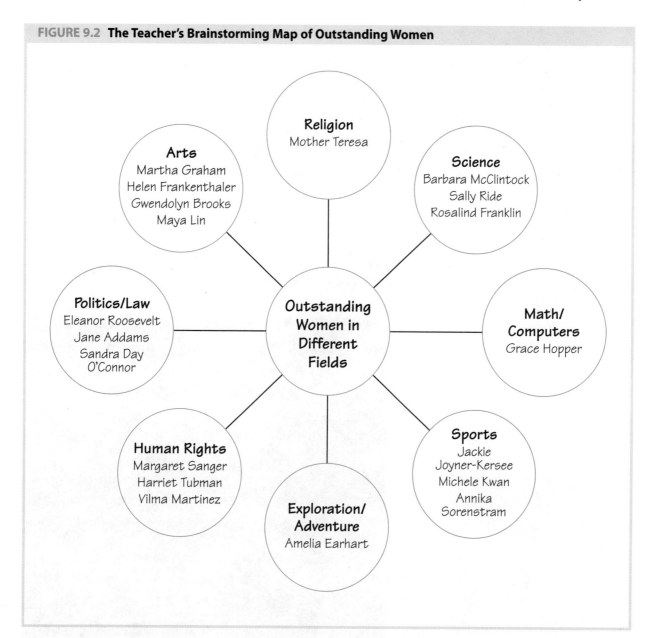

Modeling and Explaining Strategies

The previous weekend, the teacher planned the strategies he wanted to model and explain. Now, while he models and explains, he refers to those written plans to make sure he covers every strategy.

First, he relates to his students his **prior knowledge** about photographers and famous pictures. He knows Alfred Stieglitz's and Ansel Adams's photographs, remembers the name Margaret Bourke-White but not her photographs, and recalls seeing Dust Bowl photographs, especially one of a worried mother with her children, but not the photographer.

Second, he models and explains **previewing a book**. He **skims** through the book on Dorothea Lange, looking at the **pictures**, and finds the Dust Bowl photograph he recalled; he learns the title, *Migrant Mother*. He also **skims** the **Table of Contents** and finds a chapter about the photograph.

Third, after skimming the book and thinking aloud about the overall question for the research project ("Why are the women outstanding in their fields?"), he models and explains how to **predict** what he'll learn. In addition, he models turning those predictions into **questions that he will research**:

- How did Lange decide to become a photographer?

- What obstacles did Lange encounter as she practiced in the field?

- How did Lange happen to photograph the mother for the famous photograph, *Migrant Mother*?

When he finishes modeling and explaining, he initiates a similar process for his students using selected teaching/assessing tools.

"Migrant Mother" by
Dorothea Lange.
Copyright The Dorothea Lange
Collection, The Oakland Museum
of California, City of Oakland, Gift
of Paul S. Taylor

Teaching/Assessing Tools

The teacher outlines the activities the students will engage in to **activate their own prior knowledge** and **to preview and predict** what they will research:

- Tell your partner what you already know about the woman you will research.

- Skim through your book on the woman you will research, looking at the pictures and captions. Look at the book jacket too.

- Skim your Table of Contents to make predictions about what topics will be covered in the book.

- Write your questions to research, and share them with your partner.

During this time, the teacher circulates to help the sixth graders, especially when they compose their questions. Once they have shared their questions with their partner, the students begin their research.

■ During Research

Since most of the students have little prior knowledge about their women, the teacher wants them to begin their research with book or encyclopedia resources. Because the print sources have organized subtopics, the students will gain an overview of the women's lives. After the students have progressed in their research, he will introduce the Internet sources.

The teacher knows that some students will charge ahead in their research, while others will lag behind. He decides to make a **checklist as an assessing tool** to monitor where the students are in their research and what strategies they are using. On graph paper, he writes the strategies across the top and the students' names down the page. (We depicted the strategies he listed in Fig 9.1.) When he confers with individual students, they will check the strategies they discuss so that the checklist serves as an ongoing **monitoring tool** for both of them. He will also note what strategies to model and explain and what teaching/assessing tools the student might need.

Modeling and Explaining Strategies

The teacher decides to model and explain **finding and interpreting information, capitalizing on text organization**, and **note taking** using his research on Lange. He plans to spread out the modeling and explaining lessons over the many periods that the students are researching.

First, he models how to record the sources of information on a **bibliography page** as he writes his source on the overhead:

> Meltzer, Milton. *Dorothea Lange: Life Through the Camera.* New York: Viking, 1985.

He also explains why the students need to give credit to the authors they read.

Second, he models and explains how to begin **finding and interpreting important information** by writing each of his **questions** on a separate transparency. Beginning with his first question, How did Lange decide to become a photographer? he asks the

---

FIGURE 9.3 Taking Notes

---

1) How did Lange decide to become a photographer?

As a child:
      looked in people's windows and watched them
      studied photographs in the library
      cut out photos from newspapers and magazines; put on bedroom wall
      never owned a camera or took a picture
After graduation:
      announced to mother wanted to be a photographer
      mother made her go to teacher-training school but she quit
Took jobs in photographers' studios and camera shops to learn
Took a course with Clarence White, School of Photog.

[Amazing that she did not have a camera and never took pictures—how did she know she wanted to be a photographer? What fascinated her?]

---

students where in the book he is likely to find that information. Referring back to the table of contents, he and the students discuss **capitalizing on the text organization**. In biographies, the table of contents is usually in chronological order.

Third, the teacher models and explains **making text-based connections** and **schema-based connections** and **taking notes** about those important connections. Reading aloud to the students the first chapter in the Lange biography, the teacher stops periodically to have them suggest notes to write under the first question on the transparency. The teacher discusses the following points when writing his notes (see Figure 9.3):

- Was the **text-based information important and relevant** to answering the question

- What words to write in notes (how to **paraphrase text-based information**)

- How to record **schema-based connections** or your own ideas and questions in brackets to distinguish them from text-based information

Fourth, he models and explains how to **record quotations** using his third question: How did Lange happen to photograph *Migrant Mother*? He explains *when* to use quotations—for an especially unique or memorable statement—and *how often*—sparingly. (See Figure 9.4.)

Teaching/Assessing Tools

Using his assessment tool, the strategy checklist, the teacher determines which students to support with additional teaching/assessing tools. He recognizes that the students' research questions operate like **comprehension study guides** for finding and interpreting both text-based and schema-based connections. As he circulates through the classroom reading students' notes, he initiates a modified **reciprocal teaching** with specific students. He asks them to summarize what they've learned so far, to point out any confusing information, and to predict what they're likely to learn next. In addition, he discusses specific students' **note-taking processes** and suggests a note-taking system to some students.

During one period, the teacher asks the class to use the **vocabulary self-selection strategy** and record new words to learn. After collecting words from students, he reviews with them how to use context clues, word parts, and the dictionary to **define unknown words in context** independently.

Incorporating Internet Sources

When the teacher notices that a small group of students have progressed well, he introduces using Internet sources. He will repeat the mini-lesson with other small groups as students make progress.

FIGURE 9.4 Quotations in Notes

3) How did she come to photograph *Migrant Mother*?

1. Job for govt. agency to photo migrant life in Calif.
   Drove past sign "PEA PICKERS CAMP"
   20 mi. later turned back and drove into camp
   "'I was following instinct, not reason,' she recalled later. 'I drove into that wet and soggy camp and parked my car like a homing pigeon.'
   'I saw and approached the hungry and desperate mother, as if drawn by a magnet. I do not remember how I explained my presence or my camera to her, but I do remember she asked me no questions.'
   Dorothea made five exposures, working closer and closer to her subject. 'I did not ask her name or her history. She told me her age, that she was thirty-two. She said they had been living on frozen vegetables from the surrounding fields, and birds that the children had killed. She had just sold the tires from her car to buy food. There she sat in that lean-to tent with her children huddled around her, and seemed to know that my pictures might help her, and so she helped me. There was a sort of equality about it.'" (Meltzer, 1985, pp. 35, 37)
2. Pea picker story and photo reported in San Francisco paper.
   Fed. govt. sent food to feed migrants

Using the Google search engine (**www.google.com**), the teacher emphasizes **choosing search terms**. The students guess how many sites might be listed if they used the terms, *women, famous women, women photographers, Great Depression women photographers, Dorothea Lange*. Using the search term *Dorothea Lange*, the students examine the listings and discuss which seem the most useful. They also find Google's ranking strange since they consider the Oakland Museum the most useful site. The teacher informs them that Google ranks sites by the most popular, not by the most credible information. He prints out the first two pages of the search results for students to make notes on.

Next the students begin to **evaluate the web site addresses**, noting the location of the different sites. They decide to quickly click on the sites to evaluate which sites might be worth using. They discover one site is not alive; another has no author even though located at an educational institution; and the commercial site does have information, links, and a bibliography—not just items for sale.

Dividing the useful-looking web sites among the student pairs, they begin **to evaluate** and **make notes** about the information found at their sites. Their purpose is to advise the teacher where he could find new information to add to what he has learned from Meltzer's book. After the students have had a chance to peruse the sites, the teacher recalls them to summarize what each site has to offer.

Since all the students in the group want to see the "Migrant Mother" photographs, they visit that site together. Because the teacher wants to emphasize different information found in different sources, he has transferred his notes about "Migrant Mother" from Meltzer's book to a comparison chart (Table 9.2). The students recognize that Meltzer tells the events leading up to taking the photo, the quotes about the photo, and the effects of the photo's publication. Next they examine the web site and add that information to the chart. They disagree that the order Lange took the photos can't be determined since the quote said she moved closer and closer. They decide to ignore the numbers and rely on the quote. The teacher and students discuss their interpretations of different information communicated in the faraway shot of the tent and the close-up portrait.

The next day, the same small group meets with the librarian to search the Internet for sources about their women. The librarian has bookmarked specific sites but she wants the students to search on their own first. The students add Internet information to their questions and note when information is similar and when it's new or different.

The teacher and the librarian repeat the Internet mini-lessons with other groups. The teacher knows that the students need many class periods and homework time to complete their research. Yet to prevent the project from dragging on too long, he encourages, supports, and pushes the students toward concluding their research.

■ Concluding Research

Nearing the end of the research project, the teacher wants students to organize and to evaluate their ideas in order to enhance their prior knowledge and maybe even restructure it. Once again, he will model and explain his strategies and provide teaching/assessing tools to support the students' learning as they start the culminating activities.

TABLE 9.2 Comparison of Sources

Source	Information
Meltzer's book	Job for govt. agency.
	Drove past sign but 20 miles later turned back
	Quote about following instinct and seeing the mother.
	Meltzer states she made 5 exposures, moving closer and closer.
	Quote about woman and her life
	Story and photo in paper
	Fed. govt. sent food
"Migrant Mother" (FSA site)	Quote about seeing the mother.
	Quote says that she "made 5 exposures moving closer and closer from the same direction."
	Site states that the order of the photos taken can't be determined from the numbers on the photos.
	Site shows 6 photos from close-up of mother to faraway scene of the tent, children and mother.

Modeling and Explaining Strategies

The teacher plans to model and explain how he has enhanced and restructured his prior knowledge through his research on Lange.

During one period, he **organizes** his information about Lange on a **time line**, which serves as a **summary** of her life. (See Figure 9.5.) He **evaluates** the events in her life as either obstacles (below the line in Figure 9.5) or as opportunities (above the line in the figure). Then he discusses how he expected a woman photographer to confront more obstacles than Lange actually did and must restructure his prior knowledge because Lange's life was filled with opportunities.

During a second period, he and the students **study** his time line, compare it to the class's world events time line, and discuss two interesting **themes**. One theme is that Lange's career had two parts: a studio portrait career that was funded by paying customers and then portraits of ordinary people in the field career that government grants funded. Another interesting theme is how her career changed after she photographed *Migrant Mother*. The students speculate about the reason for the change. They discuss the different effects of her photographs, especially the "Migrant Mother" photo compared to the Japanese-American internment photos.

FIGURE 9.5   Partial Time Line of Lange's Professional Life

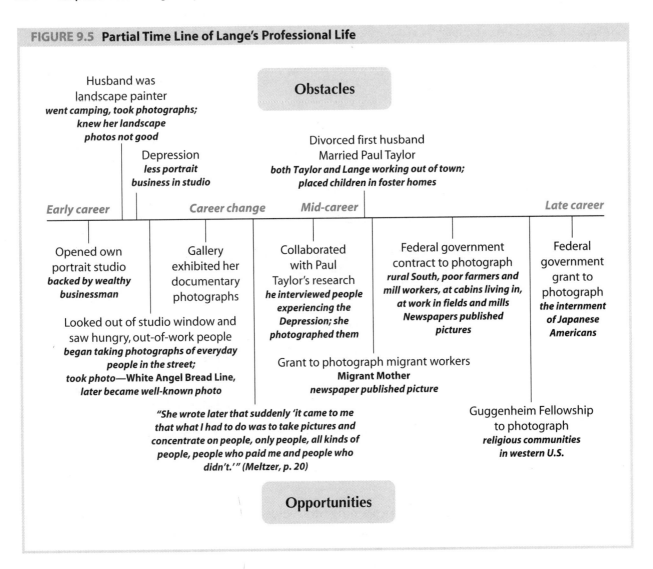

Teaching/Assessing Tools

To assist his students in organizing and summarizing, he asks the students to record major events in the lives of their outstanding women on time lines. He suggests either dividing their **time lines** into different periods, like childhood years and early career years, or recording specific years. When the students have completed their time lines, he introduces the culminating activities.

A Comparison Activity

The teacher's objective is for the students to compare the women's lives by searching for the commonalties and the differences in their experiences. To model comparing women's lives, he shows two time lines—his for Lange and another for photographer Bourke-White. Studying the two time lines for similar events, he and the students create a comparison chart.

Then, the students meet in their cooperative groups (those of students research-ing women in related fields) and spread out their time lines. Looking across the sev-eral time lines, the students search for similarities and differences in the lives of their outstanding women and record their interpretations on a comparison chart.

Interviewing Activity

The parent in charge of community resources has gathered a list of volunteers willing to be interviewed by the students. In their groups, the students compose questions to ask the volunteer about their job and their knowledge of the women the students researched. Some students meet with the person in school; while others visit the person at work or at home. After the interview, the students speculate about what their women would accom-plish in the field today. The teacher interviews a local photographer and together they take pictures of homeless people and shelters in their community.

Communication Project

Throughout the research project, the teacher shares his checklist with his students so that everyone can assess and monitor the use of strategies and their progress in the project. In his conversations with students and from their notes, time lines, and com-parison charts, he knows they have been increasing their knowledge about outstand-ing women. Although the students have assembled enough known information to write a traditional term paper, he offers the students the opportunity to interpret cre-atively what they have learned about the women.

The class brainstorms end product ideas, such as these:

- A skit of a real or fictional event at which the women in the same field meet

- A collage to show how the women changed their field

- Character sketches that highlight a comparison of the character traits of women in a particular field

- A visual depicting what the women would be accomplishing today

The teacher decides to create a collage of photographs that Lange and Bourke-White might take today to emphasize the differences between the two women. The cooperative groups meet to brainstorm how they will communicate the lives of the women they studied.

When the cooperative groups have decided on their end product, the teacher con-venes the whole class to discuss evaluation criteria. The teacher and the students devise the following criteria:

- Can the audience identify the women and what field they represent?

- Can the audience tell what contributions each woman makes to the field?

- Can the audience identify some similarities and differences among the women?

- Does the creation entice the audience to think more thoughtfully or more appreciatively about the group of outstanding women?

When the cooperative groups complete their end products, the class shares them with each other. The teacher videotapes their performances and projects, which are then displayed in the school library.

Summary

As a result of reading this chapter, you have learned and reflected upon students researching multiple sources to complete a research project in the content areas.

First, we examined the different purposes for research projects in content areas:

- **Extending knowledge**
- **Conducting research with known data and new data**

In discussing purposes, we emphasized the strategies that students need to learn when conducting research:

- **Use search terms to find sources**
- **Evaluate sources:**
  - **Check the date of the source**
  - **Check the credentials of the source**
  - **Evaluate accuracy of the source**
  - **Evaluate the point of view of the author or organization**
  - **Recognize the historical context**

Although students need to use the strategies with every source, they certainly need to check and evaluate sources on the Internet.

Second, we described different products that could culminate a research project:

- **Communication products for audiences**
- **Term papers—the traditional product**
- **Assessing both types of products**

We encourage you and your students to explore community resources as sources and as audiences for communication products.

Finally, we described a middle school research project for Women's History Month researching "Why are the women outstanding in their fields?" When the students begin their research, during their research, and when they conclude their research, we described how a teacher would:

- **Plan for the research project**
- **Model and explain research strategies**
- **Support students' research with teaching/assessing tools**
- **Monitor students' progress**

You know teachers choose research projects based on their curriculum goals, the available resources and time, and their students' learning needs. However, we think every student needs the opportunity to experience different research projects with known and new data.

You also know that teachers choose which strategies to model and explain and which teaching/assessing tools to use based on their assessment of their students' needs. They will assess what their students can accomplish independently and select a few strategies to teach now. If the students need more strategy instruction, teachers will schedule another research project later in the year to teach more strategies.

We enjoy completing research projects with students because we often learn new information. Students can also affect their peers, citizens in the community, and national figures when they communicate the results of their projects. We encourage you to include research projects with multiple sources in your content area curriculum.

Inquiry into Your Learning

1. Think about a hobby you pursue, an interest in your content area that you have, or a current issue that concerns you. Perhaps you want to research a new hobby, such as rock climbing. You might want to research the new information on volcanoes for your earth science class. Or you might research the issue of high school dropouts. Choose a topic new to you—one for which you have little prior knowledge.

   Gather information in three very different ways: read a book or article, interview a person, make an observation, or search the Internet. What different information do you learn from each source?

   Record in a journal how you investigated your new topic. During the beginning, middle, and conclusion, what strategies did you use to research? How would you describe your process to your students?

2. Investigate topics you might teach in your content area. Survey the topics in a textbook or a curriculum guide (see also Part Three). Look for topics that you could extend into research projects. Skim professional journals in your content area and think about what questions are being asked that you could convert into research projects for your students. Skim newspapers and magazines for current issues in your field that your students could investigate.

   Compile a list of curriculum topics and possible research projects that you and your students might pursue in the future.

Inquiry into Your Students' Learning

1. Interview a struggling student and a thriving student. What types of research projects do they complete in school? What types of end products do they complete? How much choice do they have in the topics they research? Do they receive guidance or instruction? Do they do most of the work at home or in school? What suggestions do they have for teachers who assign research projects?

2. Investigate a topic in your content area with a student. Record the strategies the student uses independently. What strategies would help the student? Choose one or two strategies to teach the student.

Resources

Books

Rief, L. (1999). *Vision and Voice*. Portsmouth, NH: Heinemann. Describes multimedia investigations or projects—rainforest, cartoons, musical. Appendices contain examples of student work and teacher's handouts. Multimedia CD available.

Romano, T. (2000). *Blending genre, altering style: Writing multigenre papers*. Portsmouth, NH: Boyton/Cook. Describes a communication product in which students create different genres to explain their research. See the picture book, Kurlansky, M. (2001). *The cod's tale*. New York: Putnam, as an example of a multigenre text that, although primarily an expository text, includes maps, time lines, recipes, diagrams, and poetry.

Journals

Bunton, M. (2003). Predicting population curves. *The Science Teacher*, *70* (4), 41–44. Describes a research unit on the wolf population in Wisconsin concluding in a class prediction statement that was posted in the high school.

Cushner, J. (2003). Sharing teaching ideas: Problem solving the problems of society. *Mathematics Teacher*, *96* (5), 320–323.

Munoz, J. S. (2003). Community resource mapping: An exciting tool for decision making in the social studies classroom. *The Social Studies*, *94* (1), 20–22. Suggests students map community resources from libraries to hang-outs and then describe their community and communicate with policymakers.

Munson, B. H., Huber, R., Axler, R., Host, G., Hagley, C., Moore, C., & Merrick, G. (2003). Field trips online: Investigating water quality through the Internet. *The Science Teacher*, *70* (1), 44–49. Describes Internet inquiry with two data sites, Water on the Web (Minnesota lakes **www.wow.nrri.umn.edu/wow**) and River Run (North Carolina rivers **www.uncwil.edu/riverrun**).

Web Sites

Journey North: A Global Study of Wildlife Migration. **www.Learner.org/jnorth**. Offers investigations into wildlife migration and seasonal changes in which students may contribute their local data.

Noctilucent Cloud: Observers' Homepage. **www.nlcnet.co.uk**. Research and information about night clouds called *noctilucent clouds* and collects observations from amateurs or interested persons.

Sky and Telescope. **www.skyandtelescope.com**. Information about professional and amateur astronomy projects, such as observations of supernovae.

AFRO-American Almanac. **www.toptags.com/aama/index.htm**. Documents about the history and experiences of African Americans from slavery to the present.

The Academy of American Poets. **www.poets.org**. Includes biography, bibliography, recorded readings by poets and a link to the Online Poetry Classroom (**www.onlinepoetryclassroom.org**).

American Memory: Historical Collection for the National Digital Library. **www.memory.loc.gov/ammem/ammemhome.html**. Primary documents and multimedia from the archives of the Library of Congress and Educator's Page.

WebQuest. **www.webquest.sdsu.edu**. Has examples of webquests (Internet searches) created by K–12 teachers.

PART 3

Enhancing Learning Through the Disciplines

© Michael Zide

CHAPTER 10

Designing Curriculum for Learning: Teaching for Major Understandings

KEY CONCEPTS

- curriculum, p. 246
- curriculum guide, p. 246
- standards documents (national), p. 249
- national standards, p. 249
- curriculum frameworks, p. 249

PURPOSE-SETTING QUESTIONS

1. How do I identify the major understandings in my discipline to which I want to expose my students?

2. What are the pervasive factors or new knowledge and content I should consider in shaping curriculum in my field?

3. Are there models that will help me design or modify curriculum in my discipline?

4. Is there a way to design or modify curriculum so that the emphasis includes the theory advocated in Part Two where literacy and learning act as underpinnings in every discipline?

DESIGNING CURRICULUM FOR LEARNING: TEACHING FOR MAJOR UNDERSTANDINGS

Defining Curriculum

The Standards Movement and Curriculum

The Current Movement

Standards for Selected Specific Disciplines

Concerns and Questions About the Standards

Models for Curriculum Development

Three Curriculum Models

The Unit Plan

When you hear the term *curriculum* in conversation or when you read about curriculum in journals or newspaper articles, what do you think of? What personal associations do you have with curriculum? Have you heard of curriculum referred to outside of a school, college or university setting? Is this term always used in conjunction with courses and programs of some sort? Perhaps when you did a field placement as part of your teacher education program, you were asked to implement either a middle school or high school curriculum in the content area you are specializing in. Perhaps you have been asked to survey a curriculum guide that goes along with the mathematics or biology textbook the students and the teacher were using as their major resource in a particular course.

Most experienced educators, no matter what their level or their setting, are likely to be able to share with you firsthand experiences they have had as both an implementer and a developer of curriculum in their discipline or area of expertise. As a beginning teacher, you will most likely study and implement curriculum that educators more experienced than you have developed. As you will learn in this chapter, some important factors currently are shaping curriculum in every discipline across the country.

Among them, national curriculum standards and individual state's curriculum frameworks are being used to shape instruction as well as assessment. You will also learn about some models for delivering curriculum as well as of developing curriculum that help teachers across disciplines and levels plan and carry out instruction with their own students. As you read this chapter, we suggest you ask yourself some questions related to curriculum that we believe you will continue to come back to no matter what your particular discipline, the grade level you teach, or your particular student population.

Defining Curriculum

curriculum The educational experiences that are planned for and provided by a school, usually focused on particular disciplines or domains such as English, history, reading/language arts.

We define *curriculum* in the broadest sense as a school's entire program of studies, comprising discrete disciplines and the individual courses that are available to students in those disciplines. The major discipline areas most prevalent in schools today are mathematics, science, social studies, English/language arts, foreign or world languages, health, physical education, and the arts. The curriculum and course offerings in the major disciplines determined by local school districts and guided by individual state mandates are fairly similar in middle schools and high schools across the United States.

Within each discipline, districts often devise district-level plans for curriculum across the grades. These plans are commonly organized into documents known as *curriculum guides*. Curriculum guides are usually written documents that focus on the major goals or understandings and the experiences that students are expected to have within a given discipline as a whole or in the particular courses comprising that discipline. For example,

TEACHER AS INQUIRING LEARNER

Think about your own definition of and experiences with curriculum.

- In high school and college, did the year-to-year progression of the science (general science to biology) or the social studies (world history to American history) program make sense to you? Were there connections made and opportunities to link your learning from one year to the next? Were the courses you took treated as discrete elements of your academic experience? How frequently did you have a course that made explicit links to another course of study?

Think about how these ideas about curriculum have been transmitted in the discipline in which you are now majoring as an educator.

---

curriculum guide
A written plan that is focused on the entire academic curriculum of a single school or system, or focused on a specific program of study or discipline.

a science curriculum guide may be an outline of major goals that all students K–12 will be expected to achieve. Students will realize these goals through participation in general science lessons and courses at the elementary and middle school levels and in their discipline-specific courses such as biology, chemistry, or physics at the high school level. Finally, curriculum guides may contain the major goals in a discipline for a single grade level or for all grades K–12.

We view curriculum guides as a means for teachers and curriculum specialists in a discipline to coordinate and sequence major understandings and goals for a discipline at a single grade level or across grade levels. These guides can be useful in providing continuity from grade to grade or from course to course in a discipline. Such guides should be flexible enough so that teachers can revise them based on student needs, as well as changes in the field and in the outside world. We believe the most important contribution that curriculum guides can make is to stimulate teachers to design creative teaching/learning opportunities for their own learners.

Another predominant source that teachers use to shape curriculum are the major content-area textbooks available in every field and at every level. The publishers know, as we do, that in designing curriculum guides, teachers and curriculum specialists review textbooks and related materials. District-level committees then choose materials to support the curriculum guides, and teachers design their curriculum based on the materials readily available for the discipline and the grade level in which they are teaching.

Knowing the wide appeal and use of content-area textbooks and anthologies, publishing companies move quickly to incorporate new trends in discipline-based content, as well as strategies or processes that appear in the professional literature and at conferences. Publishing companies often create particular texts and sets of materials that support these new concepts or strategies. They hope their materials designed for the school market will be used to implement the curriculum in schools across the country. For example, social studies educators recently placed an emphasis on economic education and global perspectives. Publishers of social studies materials responded by creating numerous texts and related resources on these topics. Another recent example is the focus on diversity that has affected every discipline. We see multicultural literature in the anthologies and collections of trade books that many companies are publishing to support the English/language arts curriculum as well as the other disciplines. In addition, there are numerous other resources available in the form of videos, software, and a variety of specialized publications to support the current emphasis on multiculturism and diversity.

DIVERSITY

TEACHER AS INQUIRING LEARNER

You may have found a middle school social studies guide in the classroom where you did a field placement recently. Examine a guide and ask yourself some questions.

- Who created this guide? Is the classroom teacher using the guide, or did he or she file it away in a drawer or on a shelf? Was it created by a committee of teachers in the school or by a districtwide committee? Or is the curriculum guide being used one that was developed by the publisher to go along with their materials?

Next, think about what you see teachers using to guide their teaching in the middle schools and high schools where you are working.

- Are the instructional focus and the lessons that make up the everyday life of the classroom drawn primarily from a content-area textbook in the subject area where you are working? Is the focus of the curriculum on major understandings, subject-based knowledge, and principles in a particular field of study? Are broad topics or themes—such as the effects of pollution and what we can do about it, or what is meant by a balance in nature and how the building of new highways and bridges near waterways can destroy or alter that balance—used as the organizing focus of the curriculum in the school where you are teaching? Finally, do you see any attempts to link the learners' academic competencies in the classroom to the real world?

The Standards Movement and Curriculum

You have heard throughout this text that there are many factors that impact a teacher's curriculum design and instructional planning. In this chapter, we will address the impact that the national standards movement is having on every discipline. You will learn about particular trends or issues faced by the individual disciplines. Finally, you will learn about some pervasive concerns and questions that have emerged as a result of the standards movement that, we believe, affect every discipline.

The Current Movement

Educators in many schools across the country are revising their curriculum guides because of the standards movement. Concerns raised in the 1983 report by the National Commission on Excellence in Education, *A Nation at Risk: The Imperative for Educational Reform*, put the nation's educators on notice. In 1989 President George Bush Sr. and the fifty state governors met, unified by their concern for the quality of American education. The major outcome of this meeting was the creation of six national goals that the president and the governors believed would serve as a framework for excellence in education in the United States. These goals were meant to set a tone for high expectations and equity in educational opportunities for all students in America's schools. Six broad national goals emerged as the substance of the Goals 2000: The Educate America Act (PL 103-227), enacted in 1994. Among the goals that have guided national and state curriculum reform for a decade are:

- All children in America will start school ready to learn.

- American students will leave grades 4, 8, and 12 having demonstrated competency in challenging subject matter, including English, mathematics, science, history and geography.

- Every adult American will be literate and will possess the knowledge and skill necessary to compete in a global economy and exercise the rights and responsibilities of citizenship.

The federal government realized that these goals were merely a first step to both recognizing and addressing the need for improved education in the United States. Subsequently, the U.S. Office of Education encouraged nongovernmental organizations in subject areas to create discipline-based standards documents that would focus these broad goals specifically on the individual disciplines. Although the various standards documents that have evolved with the standards movement differ greatly in approach and in format, each addresses what students need to succeed in their careers. The national goals and the development of discipline-based standards were meant to ensure that all schools, states, and districts work toward the same ends, although that does not mean a national curriculum.

The *standards documents* are designed to highlight the most important understandings in a discipline, and to provide exemplars that identify worthy tasks for students in which to engage. Of course, no matter how clear and reasonable they are, the standards cannot alter the quality of education in a state, a district, a school, or an individual classroom. In order to be successful, teams of teachers and administrators within individual districts and individual schools must have time for discussion, planning, and implementation of specific curriculum in the form of units and lessons for their students. The standards can provide coherence to a district's or a school's program. However, the changes indicated in the standards documents can come about only through improved instruction, classroom materials, teacher education, and assessments (Ravitch, 1995). The development of criteria that could be used to judge students' output and the quality of their performance relative to the standards was also considered an important component of the standards documents. Therefore, it is the responsibility of local curriculum development bodies and teachers within each discipline to use the standards and the specific objectives and criteria expressed in the standards documents, and to turn these into meaningful curriculum, lessons, and tasks.

From across the nation, school-based and university-based educators in various fields have come together motivated by concern for our schools and the students in them. Their intent is for the standards documents to serve as guides, not prescriptions, for improved curriculum and instruction across the disciplines and across the grades. The developers of the standards did not intend them to be final or static end points for the students or the schools that serve them. The standards are primarily statements of educational goals. These goals can be realized only if teachers choose to realign their curriculum and instruction, examine the textbooks and other resources that support instruction, and employ multidimensional, authentic assessment of their students' outcomes. Each group responsible for developing the standards hopes that they will foster high expectations for all students, as well as promote equitable educational opportunities for all students (Porter, 1994).

In addition to these *national standards*, teachers in many schools are being expected to implement state-level *curriculum frameworks* as well as district-level curriculum goals. For example, middle school math teachers in the Boston Public Schools are expected to be familiar with and to use the standards proposed by the National Council of Teachers of Mathematics (NCTM) to design curriculum and shape units and lessons. Second, they are expected to implement the Massachusetts

standards documents (national) The documents created by subject matter organizations and agencies to establish standards in their respective discipline area.

national standards Goals or expectations focused on essential knowledge in each discipline area included in the K–12 curriculum; these standards are designed to create excellent and equitable educational opportunities for *all* students.

curriculum frameworks Documents that address subject matter goals and assessment of knowledge in the disciplines for students K–12; developed by each state in response to the expectations set forth by Goals 2000.

State Curriculum Frameworks and to prepare their students for state-level assessment on measures directly related to these frameworks. And they are responsible for implementing goals within the discipline that have been presented in a citywide standards document, *Citywide Learning Standards and Curriculum Frameworks* (Boston Public Schools, 1996), that emphasizes literacy and communications skills across the disciplines. Most teachers today, and you will be among them, are expected to use this three-tiered set of expectations—national standards, state-level curriculum frameworks, and district-level plans—to design curriculum for all their students across grade levels, disciplines, and courses of study. Think about this recent occurrence. Is it feasible or appropriate for teachers to try to balance three sets of expectations in their discipline? What should be done so that these various documents complement one another and support the role they will play in enhancing teaching and learning?

As part of the educational reform movement, teachers at every grade level and in every discipline must understand and use the national standards and state curriculum frameworks to design their curriculum and instruction.

Photo © Michael Zide. Foreground, left: *Curriculum Standards for Social Studies: Expectations of Excellence* (1994) © National Council for the Social Studies. Reprinted by permission. Foreground, right: *Standards for the English Language Arts,* by the *International Reading Association and the National Council of Teachers of English,* Copyright 1996 by the International Reading Association and the National Council of Teachers of English. Reprinted with permission. Background, right: *Making Connections Through World Languages,* by the *Massachusetts World Languages Curriculum Frameworks,* published in 1996 by the Massachusetts Department of Education.

TEACHER AS INQUIRING LEARNER

Search the Internet for the state-level curriculum frameworks for your discipline, in either the state where you are doing your teacher training or where you think you might teach after you finish your degree. A state's core curriculum standards are often on a web page created by the State Department of Education; therefore, you might enter the following statement: *"State* [the one you are interested in at this time] Department of Education Core Curriculum Standards."

Survey your state web site that has the curriculum frameworks.

- How many different disciplines are covered by separate state documents?

- Which document would be used by teachers in your discipline?

- How is that document organized—how many levels are there within the document, how many standards or strands are there of the particular discipline, are there actual activities to help the teacher plan for instruction, and are there assessment suggestions to go along with the standards?

- Can you determine how students will be assessed on their competencies with these standards?

- How will teachers be held accountable for their implementation and the outcomes in terms of student learning? If this latter information is not available at the state department of education web site, what are some other ways you could pursue to discover how the outcomes and benefits of the curriculum frameworks in your state will be evaluated?

STANDARDS ■ **Standards for Selected Specific Disciplines**

The many educational commissions and professional organizations that have convened groups to develop discipline-based standards have produced a plethora of reports to guide the development of curriculum and the subsequent instruction in our schools. Kendall and Marzano (2000) have compiled a compendium covering twenty content areas built on 137 documents across the disciplines. Given that there are so many sources of the standards reports, we have chosen to focus on the standards put forth by either national teacher organizations or major commissions in six major disciplines. The standards we look at were developed by the National Council of Teachers of Mathematics, the National Council of Teachers of English and the International Reading Association, the National Council for the Social Studies, the National Science Association, the American Council on the Teaching of Foreign Languages, and the Joint Committee on National Health Education Standards (see Table 10.1).

We recognize the striking differences in both the depth and breadth of the understandings included within these six documents. We note as well the great differences among the documents in the specificity of the information they provide and the activities they detail to support teachers' development of actual instruction. In examining these standards documents, we also found marked differences in the specificity about student assessment provided. These differences may stem chiefly from differing beliefs by the standards' developers themselves about how the standards will and should be used.

Yet, regardless of the differences, the common goals and overall impetus for the various standards documents are that educators across the disciplines want to see curricula designed and learning opportunities created that will enable all students, elementary through high school, to do the following:

- Solve problems.

- Reason and think critically.

- Apply their knowledge and their strategies in a variety of settings.

- Communicate effectively with others in a variety of forms, both spoken and written.

There are many similarities in these documents as well. Each discipline-based document is designed to highlight the standards of the discipline stated in the form of goals statements or understandings. For example, in foreign language, there are five major areas for understanding that shape the standards. Two of the areas covered by the standards in foreign language are *communication* in languages other than English and *community participation,* focusing on multilingual communities at home and around the world. The standards are often supported by performance criteria or objectives for students. And finally, these objectives are delineated by levels of difficulty—primary, intermediate, junior high/middle school, and high school—that correspond to the grade levels found in most school districts.

As you begin your role as a teacher and as a curriculum adapter and developer, think about how you will use the standards within your own courses, units, and lessons. We especially would like you to think about how you will use the literacy strategies we described in Part Two to teach your students and to assess their grasp of the major understandings in your discipline, highlighted in the particular standards document or documents associated with your content area.

TEACHER AS INQUIRING LEARNER

We think you should be familiar with the national standards in your discipline. In the reference section of this chapter you can find the names and web sites of the six major national organizations associated with a discipline. As a preservice teacher, you should use the standards to examine the knowledge, strategies, and attitudes you have developed in your own discipline. Find some opportunities to discuss these standards with your peers. Talk about how you could use the standards to design curriculum and day-to-day lessons. Discuss the standards and their implementation with your professors or with the teachers and department chairs in a school where you are working.

- How can you teach or hold your students responsible for understandings and processes with which you are not personally familiar? Why is it important for you to implement the standards of your district as well as of your state as they relate to your content?

You will now have an opportunity to learn about some of the predominant features of the six standards documents listed in Table 10.1. We hope that you will be curious about your own discipline and that you will also read about other disciplines to learn what your colleagues are being asked to emphasize in their respective fields. You may also begin to see some similarities in the focus of the standards documents, which you will be able to use when working with teachers in other disciplines to create curriculum.

TABLE 10.1 **The National Standards Documents: A Summary**

Disciplines/ Organization(s)	Levels	Number of Standards/Strands	Information Within Standards	Special Features
Mathematics/ National Council of Teachers of Mathematics (2000)	PreK–2 3–5 6–8 9–12	10 standards for each of the 4 levels; 5 content and 5 process oriented	An appendix provides detailed standards and performance expectations for students at each of the 4 levels	Clear narrative explanation of both mathematical content and processes and their interrelationship from level to level; 6 themes stressed across the standards and levels—equity, curriculum, teaching, assessment, and technology
Social studies/National Council for the Social Studies (1994)	Early grades Middle grades High school	10 standards for each level	Performance expectations stated for each standard	At the early, middle, and high school levels there are 2 to 3 classroom examples for each standard
Science/National Academy of Science and National Science Association (1996)	K–4 5–8 9–12	7 key content standards and substandards as well as classroom examples for each of the three levels	Objectives provided for each standard at each of the 3 levels	In addition, detailed narrative focused on teaching, professional development, science education assessment, and program and system standards provided
English/language arts/National Council of English and International Reading Association (1996)	Elementary Middle High School	12 standards	Rationale statement and narrative discussion provided for each standard	5–7 vignettes provided for each standard covering situations at the elementary, middle, and high school levels
Foreign languages/ American Council on the Teaching of Foreign Languages (1999)	K–4 5–8 9–12	5 common goals for each of the 3 levels	Sample progress indicators for each goal at each of the 3 levels	33 learning scenarios that emphasize the use of foreign language in a range of domains; additional standards and scenarios for 9 different languages

TABLE 10.1 *(continued)*

Health/Joint Committee on National Health Education Standards (1995)	K–4 5–8 9–12	7 standards for each of the 3 levels	Performance indicators focused on concepts and skills students should know by the end of each of the 3 levels	Rationale statement for each standard; opportunity-to-learn standards focused on local, state, and national organizations, higher education, and community roles in order to ensure the standards are met

Mathematics

The National Council of Teachers of Mathematics (NCTM) was the first national discipline-based organization to address the need for a new approach to teaching and a new view of the goals of learning for the K–12 population. Once many classroom practitioners and teacher educators recognized the need for an overhaul of the existing math curriculum, they launched a grass-roots effort to shape a set of standards that convey understandings that are necessary for a math-literate population. They developed the following broad goals for all students, from the primary through the secondary years:

- Value math and its many uses.

- Be confident in their own ability to use math operations and computations.

- Become mathematical problem solvers.

- Learn to communicate mathematically using the language of math to clarify or refine a situation or problem.

- Learn to reason mathematically and to gather evidence or to build an argument using mathematical principles, processes and structures. (NCTM, 1989)

Mathematics educators advocating for these standards are convinced that such standards are necessary if students are to improve their academic performance. These advocates also believe that the standards highlight the mathematics understandings and practices necessary if students are to be prepared for a range of employment opportunities. Finally, these educators believe that in order for the average citizen to deal with the everyday demands of the information age and to participate as an informed member of society, they must understand the role that mathematics plays in areas such as defense spending, taxation, and health care.

Principles and Standards for School Mathematics (2000), the most recent document produced by the National Council of Teachers of Mathematics, builds on these goals and presents a vision statement for school mathematics for all students who comprise our school population PreK–12. The document makes explicit that mathematics education for the twenty-first century must meet the needs of students who ". . .exhibit different talents, abilities, achievements, needs and interests. . ." (p. 8). All students should be provided with curriculum that addresses the content standards—numbers and operations, algebra, geometry, measurement and data analysis, and probability—as well as process standards—problem solving, reasoning, communication, connections, and representation. The clearly outlined standards and expectations for each of the four levels, PreK–2, 3–5, 6–8, and 9–12, are designed to be a resource for teachers, education leaders, and policymakers in their respective roles, to guide development and assessment of curriculum frameworks, instruction and assessment tools, and instructional materials.

Social Studies

The standards document for the social studies, *Expectations of Excellence: Curriculum Standards for Social Studies* (National Council for the Social Studies, 1994), was designed to help curriculum specialists and teachers address four key questions in the field of social studies:

- Why should social studies be taught?

- What should be included in the curriculum?

- How will we teach what we decide is of value for all students?

- How will we assess whether students can apply what they have learned? (National Council for the Social Studies, 1994)

The developers of these standards believe that students will not benefit from curriculum that emphasizes only discipline-specific knowledge. Rather, the curriculum and the lessons should focus on helping students become adept with strategies and skills that will enable them to acquire information on their own by reading, studying, or searching for information. Like their math colleagues, these educators advocate for teaching and learning events in social studies that will help students learn how to deal with issues and resolve differences in the real world. Furthermore, they believe students need literacy strategies and communication skills infused into the social studies so that they will be able to demonstrate their personal understandings, as well as applications of various social studies principles. For example, after studying the First Amendment in a government or civics course, students might discuss current issues related to censorship on the Internet and decide whether their own rights or those of others in their community have been infringed on.

This standards document is organized into ten thematic *strands,* or areas of major understanding, to give a broad vision of social studies and to highlight areas of emphasis. These strands range from a historical focus on power, authority, and governance to an economic focus on production, distribution, and consumption, to a focus on global connections.

Performance expectations for students are the second component of the social studies standards. These expectations have been provided to assist teachers and curriculum specialists in designing activities for students that will lead to opportunities for students to demonstrate what they have learned. Using an example from Standard 1, Culture, students at the high school level might be asked to study a variety of resources and to compare the ways in which groups, societies, and cultures have addressed human needs and concerns in the past and today.

Each standard has specific activities for the three levels. These sample activities can be used to shape learning experiences within the different courses of study that make up a typical social studies department. For example, at the high school level, the following classroom-based problem provided as a sample vignette related to Culture might be used:

> "I don't see why we can't have prayer in the school," says 17-year-old Marcus to his teacher, Bill Tate, and the rest of the U.S. government class. "After all," continues Marcus, "every important document of this country makes reference to God. When a president or judge is sworn in, they place their hands on the Bible. You place your hand on the Bible before you testify in court. What is the big deal?"
>
> "What is the big deal?" Tate asks the class. "Marcus makes an interesting point."
>
> "Well for me the big deal is that I'm Buddhist," says Amy Wantanabe. "My concept of God and religion is probably different from what Marcus is talking about."
>
> [Additional student comments are included.]
>
> Tate records the students' comments on the board in columns that represent positions that are either for or against religion in the schools. As he writes, more students chime in their opinions. . . . As the period draws to an end, Tate presents the students with a case study about a city's decision to have a nativity scene on public property. For homework the students are to state which side of the argument they agree with and list all of the reasons with which they can support their opinions. In addition, they are to research analogous historical or contemporary situations.
>
> In the next class session, students present their homework in small groups. Each group is given a recording chart to list the points students make to support their opinions. The results are presented to the class and compared. Tate evaluates the individual assignments and group charts on the basis of the clarity of presentation and reasoning and the demonstrated understanding of the historical or contemporary comparisons used to support the argument. (National Council for the Social Studies, 1994, pp. 111–112)

The issue focused on and the questions asked concerning Culture found in this vignette could be applied to a history, a civics, or a government class within the social studies departments of most high schools.

We believe the social studies standards provide a framework for rich curriculum development beyond a single discipline or course. The standards can be enacted in a single discipline or course, they can be used in different courses within the same discipline, and they can act as a stimulus for coordinating disciplines.

Science

In science there has been an evolution of reports and standard-setting attempts in the past decade. The seminal work aimed at improving science education was *Science for All Americans: A Project 2061 Report on Goals in Science, Mathematics and Technology,* written in 1990. *The National Science Education Standards* (1996) introduced in Table 10.1 organize the content of science into seven major areas that are inclusive of the discipline and useful in developing curriculum for each of three levels, K–4, 5–8, and

9–12. The seven areas that the science standards focus on are: science as inquiry, physical science, life science, earth and space, science and technology, science in personal and social perspectives, and history and the nature of science. Specific objectives and explicit classroom examples appropriate for the different levels of sophistication are also provided in the standards document. For example, in the life science area, students at level K–4 focus on the basic characteristics of an organism, the life cycle of an organism and the relationship between an organism and its environment. However, later at the high school level, the more sophisticated expectation in the life sciences is that students will, "know that organisms are classified into a hierarchy of groups and subgroups based on their similarities and reflecting their evolutionary relationships; and that the similarity of organisms inferred from similarity of their molecular structure closely matches the classification based on anatomical similarities" (Grades 9–12 Life Science Content Standard of the National Science Education Standards, p. 185). Clearly a high school student studying biology, botany, or zoology would have difficulty dealing with the knowledge expressed in the objective for grades 9–12 without having prior experiences and knowledge related to the differentiation of plant and animal species focused on in grades K–4.

English/Language Arts

The English/language arts standards were created jointly by the National Council of Teachers of English and the International Reading Association, two national organizations focused on literacy education from early childhood through the college levels. The educators who wrote this document developed twelve broad standards as a framework for literacy education.

Unlike the mathematics and science standards documents, which include specific objectives for each standard or strand, each of the twelve English/language arts standards statements is followed by a narrative explanation applicable across grade levels. A separate section of the document contains sample vignettes that highlight actual classroom practice in varied elementary, middle, and high school settings. Following each vignette are questions appropriate for consideration by in-service as well as preservice teachers. In order to use the English/language arts standards to shape curriculum, teachers might begin by examining the genres and themes they are currently focusing on in their courses. They could then use the standards to make some changes or revisions in the existing curriculum rather than starting from scratch. For example, Standard 9 is focused on students' "developing an understanding of and respect for diversity in language use, patterns and dialects across cultures, ethnic groups, geographic regions and social roles" (National Council of Teachers of English and International Reading Association, 1996, p. 41). Teachers in a middle school using a folk tale unit might consider what changes they would make in their own classrooms to enable students with limited English proficiency to affirm their own primary language and culture while at the same time being encouraged to work toward proficiency in English while learning about folk tales from their own and from different cultures.

Foreign Languages

Standards for Foreign Language Learning: Teaching in the 21st Century (1999) was developed as a collaborative effort of the American Council on Teaching of Foreign Languages and a number of language-specific organizations for teachers. The educators who contributed to the national standards document created five broad standards designed to act as major goals for all students engaged in foreign language learning for the elementary (K–4), middle school (5–8), and high school levels (9–12).

Among the goals that the *Standards for Foreign Language Learning* emphasize are those that focus on the active role and everyday applications of a second language:

- Use the target language to engage in conversation expressing their personal feelings and thoughts.

- Comprehend and use written and spoken language on a variety of topics and from a variety of sources, individuals as well as media.

- Have knowledge and understanding relative to the target culture of the language being studied (its institutions, traditions, literary, and artistic expressions).

Each of the five standards includes specific progress indicators for students, and learning scenarios to assist teachers in the design of curriculum for their individual language-specific courses.

This document contains a strong recommendation that students have opportunities to reinforce their knowledge of foreign language in other disciplines, as well as opportunities to acquire information from authentic documents such as foreign language newspapers, which can be used in studying other school subjects.

Although it may not be simple to implement or to assess these real-world applications of a foreign or second language, this seems to be an important educational goal, which could be enhanced by coordinated or integrated curriculum described in Chapters 11 and 12 of this book. The *Massachusetts World Language Curriculum Framework* (1996) states, "In our society knowing another language is an essential part of every student's education, not just for the many benefits it brings the individual, but for the important lessons it provides in local and global cross-cultural understanding" (p. 5).

A current point of debate among the community of educators directly responsible for the development and implementation of national standards and state-level frameworks related to foreign language is the question pertaining to the purpose and value of studying and speaking a second language. Recently many politicians and educators in states with significant immigrant populations and numbers of speakers of languages other than English have moved to an English-only stance and an English immersion focus for instruction in the schools. Certainly a primary goal in our schools should be enhance students' ability to use English for everyday discourse as well as to help students to use English to achieve academically in all content areas. However, the emphasis on English proficiency should not diminish the value of bilingualism or multilingualism summed up in the introduction of the *Massachusetts World Language Curriculum Framework* (1996). It is stated in this document that, "Multilingualism expands our sense of community. By crossing cultural and linguistic boundaries to talk to one another we gain respect for others and learn about the similarities we share" (p. 7).

Health

The final set of national standards we include is the *National Health Education Standards: Achieving Health Literacy* (1995), which a committee of educators and health professionals developed. The seven standards in health education that students across the grades are expected to have are these:

- Comprehend concepts related to health promotion and disease prevention.

- Demonstrate the ability to access valid health information and health-promotion products and services.

- Demonstrate the ability to practice health-enhancing behavior and reduce health risks.

- Analyze the influence of culture, media, technology, and other factors on health.

- Demonstrate the ability to use interpersonal communication skills to enhance health.

- Demonstrate the ability to use goal-setting and decision-making skills to enhance health.

- Demonstrate the ability to advocate for personal, family, and community health (p. 8).

There are many overlaps between health education and the disciplines of science and physical education. For example, concern for the interaction between the environment and human beings is linked to the disciplines of health and science. Similarly, health education is connected to physical education, especially concerning the belief today that each individual, no matter what his or her age, should maintain a level of physical fitness.

In addition, what a student learns at the elementary level about health should serve as background knowledge for more sophisticated understandings emphasized at the secondary level. For example, at the elementary level, students learn about a variety of causes of pollution (e.g., air, ground, noise, water, and food) in their own communities. At the high school level, students learn how environmental and other external factors affect individual and community health. The emphasis for the older students will be on seeing how, as informed citizens, they can use public health policies and government regulations to safeguard and improve their own lives and that of others in their community.

Finally, discuss with other students in your discipline and with preservice teachers in other disciplines what the implications of these standards are for your preparation as a teacher.

TEACHER AS INQUIRING LEARNER

Look at the standards and the objectives listed for the high school level in your discipline.

- Do you think your classroom experiences and the learning outcomes you were responsible for in high school were shaped by these standards? What understandings, content, and issues did your teachers emphasize in the courses you took? Are there any areas that you feel particularly weak in?

If you are in the arts or physical education, you will find that there are standards documents for you to survey also. Check with individuals in your discipline for the documents they are using, or consult Kendall and Marzano's recent *Content Knowledge: A Compendium of Standards and Benchmarks for K–12 Educators* (2000), available in text format and on the Internet, to find the standards for your discipline.

■ Concerns and Questions About the Standards

These standards and the standards movement itself are not without critics. As some educators and politicians push for a national curriculum, others contend that no national force exists that can make these standards a reality in all schools. We live and teach in a country with an enormous and complex educational system and a student population that is extremely diverse. These factors alone make any attempt to set national standards difficult and challenging.

Another group of critics looks at the range of formats and the number of discrete disciplines developed in the standards movement. These critics are concerned with the sheer number of the standards documents and the implications for what teachers will teach, and what students will learn. Indeed, the expectations for teachers and students to cover these newly created standards do seem staggering.

Finally, educators who have begun to work toward more integration within the curriculum fear that these standards will lead to increased fragmentation in schools. They believe that teachers held accountable within their own discipline for the standards in their field will not have the time to work with their colleagues in other disciplines on integrated curriculum. They believe the time and energy necessary to examine and to validate or change one's own curriculum area using the standards will counter the integrated work with colleagues that has begun to infuse our schools in positive ways.

The national standards are meant to act as goals for their respective disciplines. The standards are *indicators* of what should be emphasized through the curriculum; they are not the curriculum. In most instances, these documents do not designate specific content or subject matter. The content, pedagogy, and resource decisions are left up to individual teachers, departments, and curriculum committees.

Models for Curriculum Development

The national standards have had a profound effect on curriculum development in states, school districts, and publishing companies across the country. In each of the disciplines, classroom teachers and other educators are struggling with which priorities or expectations to focus on, how best to design and implement curriculum that will reflect the standards, and how to assess the outcomes.

In each discipline, individual teachers as well as teams of teachers and curriculum committees are working to interpret the national standards in their discipline in order to turn these standards into viable curriculum that will guide their teaching and their students' learning. Additionally, as a result of the Education Reform Act of 1994, states are developing and disseminating curriculum frameworks for each discipline. Teachers today find themselves needing to demonstrate how the curriculum they develop, and the lessons they carry out, are responsive to the national standards and the state-level curriculum frameworks in their discipline, as well as to district-level guidelines and schoolwide expectations shaped by the demographics and the learning needs of their particular student population. Finally, teachers have to consider the texts and other resources available in their schools to complement the content and the understandings they will emphasize in the curriculum they are adapting or designing for their own students. (See Figure 10.1.)

FIGURE 10.1 Shaping and Designing Curriculum

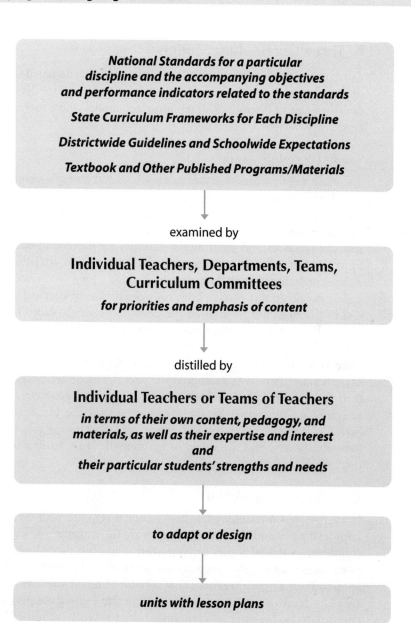

Source: From *Expectations of Excellence: Standards for the Social Studies,* 1994, pp. 111–112. Used by permission of the National Council for the Social Studies.

To demonstrate more clearly how to use the national standards and curriculum frameworks to shape curriculum, we will examine three curriculum models currently used in every discipline and at every level: single discipline, coordinated, and integrated. We briefly describe them in this chapter and then look at them in depth in the following two chapters. And finally in this chapter we will discuss the unit plan and its components, which we also look at in depth in the following chapters.

■ Three Curriculum Models

Curriculum at the elementary and secondary levels is designed and carried out in one of three models: a single discipline model, a coordinated model where parallel work is done in a pair of disciplines, or an integrated model where two or more disciplines are closely interrelated.

Single Discipline Model

The most prevalent model in the middle school and the high school is the *single discipline model*, where teachers teach their subject matter as a separate entity. The advantage is that teachers and students can "cover" a discipline's major topics and study specific topics in the field in depth. The disadvantage is that often students in such classrooms see the content, the processes, and the strategies that they are learning in one discipline as separate from everything else they are doing in school. In addition, students may see their courses as separate from anything they are doing outside school.

Even within this model, however, segregation of curricula from school and the rest of life does not have to be the case. Many single-subject teachers do connect their subject matter to other areas of the curriculum on a regular basis, as well as to applications in everyday life. For example, a middle school teacher of geometry linked what the students were learning about mathematics principles to the arts and social studies. Students examined the prevalence of geometric forms in the architecture of the Greek and Roman civilizations and geometric forms found in the beautiful quilts crafted by the Mennonites and the blankets and pottery of the Navajos. Such an emphasis in content-area classrooms can demonstrate the link between the arts and the world of mathematics in a natural way within the single discipline curriculum model.

Coordinated Curriculum

In *coordinated curriculum*, teachers in one discipline plan their lessons to coincide with lessons in another discipline in order to reinforce and expand student understandings of related topics or issues found in both disciplines. For example, at the same time as an eighth-grade class was studying the American Revolution in social studies, their English teacher chose a book of historical fiction, *My Brother Sam Is Dead* by James and Robert Collier, set in the same time period. Through such a coordinated experience, students used their recently acquired background knowledge from history to evaluate the authors' authenticity in representing a fictional family's experiences during the Revolutionary period. This type of coordinated planning is one of the simplest ways to connect different disciplines and frequently is seen in the middle school setting. For coordinated curriculum to work, teachers across disciplines must communicate with one another about the topics and themes they are covering in their courses.

Coordinated curriculum is not limited to efforts that two different teachers make in different disciplines. An individual teacher can design a lesson or a unit in his or her own area and connect it to related material from another discipline. For example, a science teacher who has created a unit that focuses on weather from a scientific standpoint can extend students' understandings by having students focus on how the weather affects human beings. This extension that focuses on a social studies perspective related to weather could be carried out by having students read informational texts or primary sources about individual explorers who spent time in remote areas with extreme weather conditions, such as the Arctic or the rain forests of Brazil. Students could use their scientific knowledge about weather to understand more fully both the physical and the emotional effects that extreme weather conditions have on human beings who live in or explore such regions of the world.

Integrated Curriculum

The primary emphasis of *integrated curriculum* is on the value of interrelatedness and the importance of finding natural connections among disciplines. The overarching goal of integrated curriculum is to deepen students' understandings of themselves, their communities, and the world rather than to focus on specific discipline-based content or processes.

Let's take an example of coordinated curriculum related to the census and transpose it to an integrated curriculum situation. Content related to the social sciences and the tools of mathematics may be combined in a coordinated curriculum model to help students understand the purpose and use of census data in the United States. If this were an integrated curriculum setting instead, the focus might be on looking at issues related to immigration laws and patterns in the United States. Students could apply their mathematical understandings to examine trends in the census rather than simply trying to understand the collection and use of census data. Students could study recent immigration trends, look at laws about quotas, and learn how actual people have experienced the immigration quotas and laws. The students could read informational books for young adult readers, such as *Illegal: Seeking the American Dream* (P. Anastos & C. French, 1991), *Dan Thuy's New Life in America* (K. O'Connor, 1992), and *Still a Nation of Immigrants* (B. K. Ashabranner & J. Ashabranner, 1993), to learn about the issues immigrants face, especially immigrants in their same age group. Through these nonfiction accounts of young people, students could begin to gain a better understanding of how numbers and statistics are used to make decisions that affect real people. The social studies, mathematics, and English/language arts teachers working within this integrated curriculum model could help students form their own opinions about immigration laws and the use of the census in the United States today. Teachers could encourage students to find avenues to communicate their knowledge and opinions. They might write a letter to the editor of a local newspaper or communicate over the Internet with other individuals who have similar concerns or issues. Through integrated experiences such as these, students would begin to see how the interrelatedness of the disciplines sheds light on real and important questions about their world.

■ The Unit Plan

Curriculum revisions, changes, and additions are an ongoing concern of teachers. Numerous sources might provide an impetus for teachers to engage in planning a new unit or new curricula: courses they take, staff development sessions, changing areas of focus in a discipline, documents like the national standards or state-level curriculum frameworks, and even textbook changes.

Whether your curriculum work is single discipline, coordinated, or integrated, the *unit plan* is a widely used organizational framework for the design of curriculum and the delivery of instruction. Figure 10.2 sets out the typical components of a unit plan, which you may create yourself or which you may find in published material. Earlier in this chapter, you saw in Figure 10.1 that there is an overall relationship between the factors that influence curriculum development, such as the national standards, state curriculum frameworks, and teacher interest and expertise, and the unit plans and lessons that comprise the unit being designed and enacted in classrooms or courses every day.

In Chapter 3 you learned that individual lessons are built on specific content and strategy objectives that guide student learning outcomes. You saw how the lesson plan format we proposed supported the design of instruction in a science lesson focused on

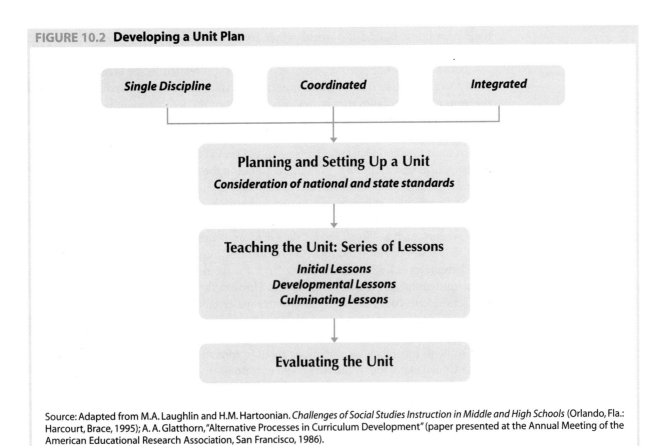

FIGURE 10.2 Developing a Unit Plan

Single Discipline   Coordinated   Integrated

Planning and Setting Up a Unit
Consideration of national and state standards

Teaching the Unit: Series of Lessons
Initial Lessons
Developmental Lessons
Culminating Lessons

Evaluating the Unit

Source: Adapted from M.A. Laughlin and H.M. Hartoonian. *Challenges of Social Studies Instruction in Middle and High Schools* (Orlando, Fla.: Harcourt, Brace, 1995); A. A. Glatthorn, "Alternative Processes in Curriculum Development" (paper presented at the Annual Meeting of the American Educational Research Association, San Francisco, 1986).

nutrition and the importance of interpreting graphs. The content-area lesson example in Chapter 3 was a single component of a larger organizational structure used to design instruction: the unit. The modeling and explaining scripts for mini-lessons on particular strategies found throughout Part Two are another component of content-area unit plans.

Planning and Setting Up a Unit

Once you decide to spend time planning a new unit or course of study in your own discipline or in a coordinated or integrated effort with other teachers, consider these questions:

- How will the new course or unit relate to existing courses in the school's program of study? Is it part of a proposed sequence of courses? Is it intended to relate closely to the content of other courses? (Glatthorn, 1986, p. 10)

- What are the general course or unit outcomes? What general concepts and skills do we hope to develop? (Glatthorn, 1986, p. 10)

- For which group of students is the course or unit primarily intended? (Glatthorn, 1986, p. 10)

- Does this curriculum support the state curriculum frameworks and the national standards in your discipline?

You begin planning a unit by establishing major goals or understandings that are inherent in the topic to be studied. For example, in a unit titled, "Why Study Economics?" intended as an introductory area of study for juniors and seniors in high school, the focus may be on helping students understand the basic premises of economics. The principle that choices in our society are driven by the need to meet unlimited wants with limited resources and that both personal and national economic policies have implications for individuals and for society as a whole is an example of such recurring generalizations in economics (Laughlin & Hartoonian, 1995). These understandings are evident not only in the national social studies standards, but also in many state's curriculum frameworks.

As you plan a unit, you should ask yourself what strategies and skills students will need in order to comprehend the content's major understandings as well as how you will expect students to demonstrate these understandings. In the planning stage of the unit, you should decide on specific concepts, strategies, and skills directly related to the content and goals of the unit. You should emphasize them as well in the lessons through the teaching/learning experiences that occur throughout the unit. For example, in the "Why Study Economics?" introductory unit, the goal should be to help students acquire an understanding of key economic concepts, such as needs and wants and producers and consumers. They might also learn about different economic systems such as capitalism and socialism. Students who have had no prior experience with economic material will need specific literacy strategy instruction and practice. They would need support in order to find and interpret information on economic charts, tables, and graphs and to be able to apply their understandings to current economic issues. Students may require assistance in analyzing data from a number of sources and in using data to make predictions about the issue at hand.

Another important decision in the early planning of a unit concerns determining what materials and resources will complement the area of study. You must take into account the focus of the unit, the disciplines you will incorporate, the needs of the learners, and the availability of resources. When you study the generic unit plan format in Figure 10.2 with the economics unit for high school juniors and seniors in mind, you will probably decide to incorporate some or all of the following types of materials to support instruction:

- A chapter or chapters from a secondary economics textbook.
- A handout entitled "Economic Headlines".
- Editions of local and regional newspapers.
- The film *Very Basic Economics* or the computer program Economics: What, How and for Whom? by Focus Media for demonstration purposes (Laughlin and Hartoonian, 1995, p. 226).

You might want to check back to Chapter 3 for a detailed discussion about choosing materials.

Teaching the Unit: A Series of Lessons

The day-to-day or class-to-class enactment of a unit is made up of a series of lessons using the format we developed in Chapter 3. The lessons themselves are shaped by both the content in a particular discipline (or disciplines), and the literacy strategies needed to understand and use that content. One or more lessons in a unit may be focused on initial ideas, developing ideas, and culminating ideas, determined by the major understandings being pursued, the particular content, and the resources that support the unit, as well as by the learning needs of the students.

Intial Ideas

An *initiating activity* or *introductory lesson* usually begins a unit. The focus in this lesson is on students' generating ideas about the text being used and the topic being studied. The emphasis in the initiating lessons of the unit should be on helping students set purposes for studying the topic using strategies such as making predictions and activating prior knowledge found in Chapter 4. In the initiating lessons, students engage in using tools such as brainstorming, freewriting, and anticipation guides to activate their prior knowledge and generate ideas related to the topic being studied. You should decide on key vocabulary related to the content to explore as part of the generating process.

Developing Ideas

The core of the unit is made up of lessons that emphasize students' interacting with ideas. Students are actively engaged with texts and other resources, and many of the strategies we described in Chapter 5 come into play at this stage in a unit. Therefore, the emphasis in these lessons, which make up the core of the unit, is on students' finding and interpreting important information within the materials they are using. The emphasis should be on students' increasing their understandings of a topic or theme. The reading in various texts and the activities the students are participating in should be focused on students' deepening their understandings. Lessons that incorporate teaching tools such as pattern guides and the DRA are essential. In addition, a teacher may incorporate lessons that emphasize the use of study guides and the value of discussion groups as well as the tools necessary for the interpretation of different types of graphic aids. In these lessons, you should model for students how to use supporting strategies, such as note taking, graphic organizers, and story maps and frames, so that they will better understand the content and concepts they are studying.

Culminating

To bring a unit to culmination, you should ensure that the lessons focus on students' ability to refine or reconstruct their understandings, to organize and revise their ideas, and to connect ideas and information from different sources and other disciplines. At this stage, students can reflect on and find personal meanings in the material they have studied. You can instruct students on the tools they need in order to share their knowledge with others. Students can learn how to write summaries or reviews, give book talks, or design projects that will demonstrate their understandings and their personal interpretations of the content or issues they have studied.

Students often share their culminating experiences or final lessons in a unit with the entire class. During such concluding lessons, students should have opportunities to explain their personal interpretations as well as to compare their individual or small group learning experiences with one another. At this stage in the unit, the emphasis should be on students' collectively having opportunities to revisit, discuss, and even debate the unit's major understandings.

Students should have many opportunities to use their knowledge and to demonstrate their new understandings related to the topic they are studying. For example, students could read their textbooks and survey current newspapers or periodicals such as *Zillions* or *Consumer Reports* for articles related to economics. They could participate in class simulations and discussions about economic issues that are important to them and to their own communities. Students engaged in an economics unit focused on everyday applications of economics could then be expected to explain why the study of economics is important in their lives as teenagers and as citizens of the United States.

Students might be expected to participate in a discussion about the types of important economic choices that leaders in countries around the world must make today. They could focus on recent decisions made in the United States, such as a change in the consumer price index or the rising cost of child care or medical care, which will affect their own lives or those of their family and their community. Students could also discuss such topics as what a change in the availability of natural resources such as lumber or natural gas, widely used in their region of the country, would mean for them personally or for other individuals or companies in their own community.

Evaluating the Unit

Every unit incorporates two types of evaluation: one that is ongoing (formative) and one that is final (summative). Both types should inform teachers about their instruction and students about their learning. *Formative evaluation* takes place when the teacher uses teaching tools and observes student responses during a lesson. Throughout the lessons that make up the unit, teachers can evaluate student learning as students participate in discussions and create various written products. Teachers can assess and give feedback to students as they examine work in progress, such as field notebooks, note cards, or retellings. They can do this while conferencing with an individual student or a group of students engaged in an ongoing study or product development related to the topic being studied. Based on students' and teachers' ongoing, formative evaluation of the students' learning, teachers should revise planned series of lessons so that instruction better matches the students' strengths, needs, and interests that emerge during classroom interactions between student and student and between student and teacher.

Concluding lessons and activities in a unit include within them natural opportunities for evaluation of student learning. In the final evaluation, known as *summative evaluation,* teachers can look at the outcomes or student products in order to assess their instruction as well the students' learning. The focus on evaluation at this stage is often on students' application of their understandings from the course of study or the unit to solving everyday problems or concerns. In a unit like the one on basic economic principles, students could discuss why the states of the former Soviet Union are having such massive economic difficulties since the collapse of communism and the ending of the cold war. Students might consider how this dramatic economic change is affecting the Russian government as well as the day-to-day lives of individual citizens, and they might propose some economic solutions for the future.

A concluding assignment that would be evaluative in nature and would necessitate that the students apply what they have learned about economics to their own lives might be to ask them to bring a current newspaper or magazine article related to economics the following day to share with the class or watch one of the network news programs and report on economic news contained in the newscast. Then the focus of the discussion the next day and the enabling activity would be for the students to think about how economic events influence our (their) daily lives and what some likely consequences are of the events they have heard or read about.

SUMMARY

We began the chapter by focusing on teachers like you.

- **The teacher's role as an adapter and as a designer of curriculum**

Second, we discussed the major force that is affecting the development of curriculum across the disciplines today—the national standards movement—and emphasized the following:

- **Important features of the standards in six major disciplines**

- **Concerns and questions about the standards movement as a whole and the use of the standards documents**

- **The relationship of the national standards to state curriculum frameworks, districtwide guidelines, schoolwide expectations, and individual teacher expertise and preference**

We briefly discussed three models for curriculum development: single discipline, coordinated, and integrated.

Finally, we presented a unit plan structure for teachers to use, both to adapt and to design curriculum for their own courses and learners. We have focused on the components of the unit plan as well as the relationship of the individual lessons you learned about in Part Two to the development of an entire unit. As you begin the following chapters focused on single discipline, coordinated, and integrated curriculum, think about how you will combine the literacy strategies you learned in Part Two of this book and the major understandings of your own content area to create meaningful learning opportunities in the form of units and lessons for your own students.

Inquiry into Your Learning

1. Talk with your cooperating practitioner, supervisor, or instructor to see whether he or she has been involved in some recent curriculum development work. Ask what the impetus was for the work: new standards in the field, reorganization of a department, issues in the community, or something else. Find out if the teacher worked alone, in a team, or as part of a committee, and what role he or she played in the project. Ask how he or she would characterize the experience as a professional and whether he or she implemented this curriculum. If the person has implemented the new curriculum, find out what the outcomes were for the students.

2. Examine the national standards or the state curriculum frameworks in your discipline, particularly at the objectives for the high school level, to note whether there are any explicit applications of literacy within your discipline. Since the focus of this textbook and the course you are now taking is on literacy and learning in your content area, we'd like you to notice how literacy and communication are interwoven in the discipline. Can you find some concrete examples of students' being required to use their reading, writing, listening, and speaking skills and strategies in either the classroom or in real-world applications related to your discipline? How effectively have the developers of these standards helped content-area teachers like you design curriculum for your own students that will enhance both their literacy and communication skills and their content-area knowledge?

Inquiry into Your Students' Learning

1. In this chapter we have discussed three curriculum models that teachers use in schools today. Interview a student at the middle school level and one at the high school level, and ask them to tell you what they are studying in each of their major subjects. Next, ask each of the students whether currently or in the past they have studied a topic from the perspective of two of their content areas (coordinated curriculum). Finally, ask each of the students if they have studied any topic or issue using information and understandings from multiple content areas. If they have participated in coordinated or integrated curriculum, what can they tell you about the advantages or disadvantages they experienced when one teacher or several teachers focused on connections among the content areas in their program of studies? What do the experiences of these students tell you, and how will you use their experiences to inform your future curriculum work when you student-teach or when you have your own classroom?

2. In this chapter we have emphasized how important it is for all content-area teachers to focus on major understandings as well as critical thinking and communication skills within their discipline. We have also stressed the importance of students being able to apply content-area knowledge to their everyday lives.

Interview either a high school or a middle-school-aged student and ask them to tell you in their own words what major understandings or topics are being emphasized in the course/discipline you are planning to teach. Ask this student what types of assignments they have had in their course. Try to determine whether the student has had an opportunity to apply his or her knowledge concretely. Finally, ask the student what he or she has discovered independently or if any specific connections have been made between what he or she is studying in school and what is happening in his or her everyday world.

Reflect on what you have learned from this student and think about how in the future you would want your own students to respond to these questions.

Resources

Books

Jackson, A. W., & Davis, G. A. (2000). *Turning points 2000: Educating adolescents in the twenty-first century.* New York: Teachers College. Provides practical guidelines for teachers of early adolescents with regard to curriculum design, selection and adaptation of standards, and student assessment.

Kendall, J. S. & Marzano, R. J. (2000). *Content knowledge: A compendium of standards and benchmarks for K–12 education* (3rd ed.). Alexandria, VA: Association for Supervision and Curriculum Development. Report of research conducted at Mid-continent Research for Education and Learning (McREL) to consolidate national and state standards in fourteen curriculum areas. For each area, the standards are summarized and then listed in detail for grade groupings. The reports from which the standards were collected are described.

National Association of Secondary Schools Principals. (1999). *Breaking ranks: Changing an American institution.* Reston, VA: National Association of Secondary Schools Principals. Recommends changes for high schools that pertain to the curriculum, environment, time and resources, professional development, leadership, and technology.

Texley, J. & Wild, A. (1996). *National Science Teachers Association: Pathways to science.* Arlington, VA: National Science Teachers Association. Focuses on middle school and high school standards, with suggestions for implementation and assessment across the four science standards and useful classroom vignettes.

Articles

Edmondson, J. (2001). Taking a broader look: Reading literacy education. *The Reading Teacher, 54* (6), 620–629. Emphasizes the need for educators to become more involved politically to ensure that changes in policy reflect their concerns and beliefs. Factors for consideration when reviewing policy proposals are also listed.

Valencia, R. R., & Villarreal, B. J. (2003). Improving students' reading performance via standards-based school reform: A critique. *The Reading Teacher, 56* (7), 612–621. Examines the impact of standards-based school reform in Texas and notes the problems that are evident with such an approach. Also proposes more effective means of change, including preschool education, early intervention, and highly qualified teachers.

Wellinski, S. (2003). Fostering a secondary literacy environment from accountability concerns. *Journal of Reading Education, 28* (3), 38–39. Discusses the need for reading instruction at the secondary level and proposes a framework for supporting this instruction. The framework includes supporting professional development, struggling readers, and a "reading-to-learn" atmosphere.

Web Sites

American Council on the Teaching of Foreign Languages. **actfl.org/public/articles/execsumm. pdf.** General standards for grades K–12 for foreign language that address culture, communication, comparisons, connections to other disciplines and communities—both local and around the world.

National Council of Teachers of Mathematics. **standards.nctm.org/document/index.htm**.Very detailed documentation of the standards for grade groupings in ten different area of mathematics. Sample lesson plans are also provided that address specific standards.

National Association of Science. **www.nas.edu.** Provides the National Science Education Standards for the teaching of science, professional development, and assessment.

National Council for Social Studies. **www.ncss.org/standards/stitle.html**. Proposes general suggestions for furthering the study of social studies and achieving the standards and provides a description of the thematic strands in social studies. Standards, expectations, and examples are not available on-line, but may be ordered on this web site.

International Reading Association. **www.reading.org/advocacy/elastandards/standards.html**. Outlines the twelve standards from the IRA for the English Language Arts. The complete standards are not available on-line, but may be purchased from the on-line bookstore.

CHAPTER 11

Enhancing Literacy and Learning In and Among the Disciplines

KEY CONCEPTS

- single discipline-based courses or programs, p. 274
- coordinated curriculum, p. 274

PURPOSE-SETTING QUESTIONS

1 What are the common concerns that content-area teachers at the middle and high school levels face today? What issues cross subject boundaries?

2 What specific challenges face each of the disciplines today?

3 What particular literacy tools will help students handle challenges inherent in each discipline?

4 Given what you have studied in your courses and what you have seen focused on in the middle schools or high schools with which you have had contact, are there advantages for your students or for you to seek opportunities to coordinate with teachers in other disciplines? Are there particular disciplines or domains within the disciplines (biology or chemistry in science, for example) that have strong connections with your own discipline?

5 What type of scheduling of students and courses, and what sorts of planning do teachers need to do to design and implement the type of coordinated curriculum efforts described in this chapter?

6 Given two sample units, one that demonstrates a single discipline—curriculum at the high school level—and one that demonstrates coordinated curriculum at the middle school level, what are the literacy and learning strategies emphasized in each, and what do you find in these samples that is applicable to your own content area and to your practice as a teacher?

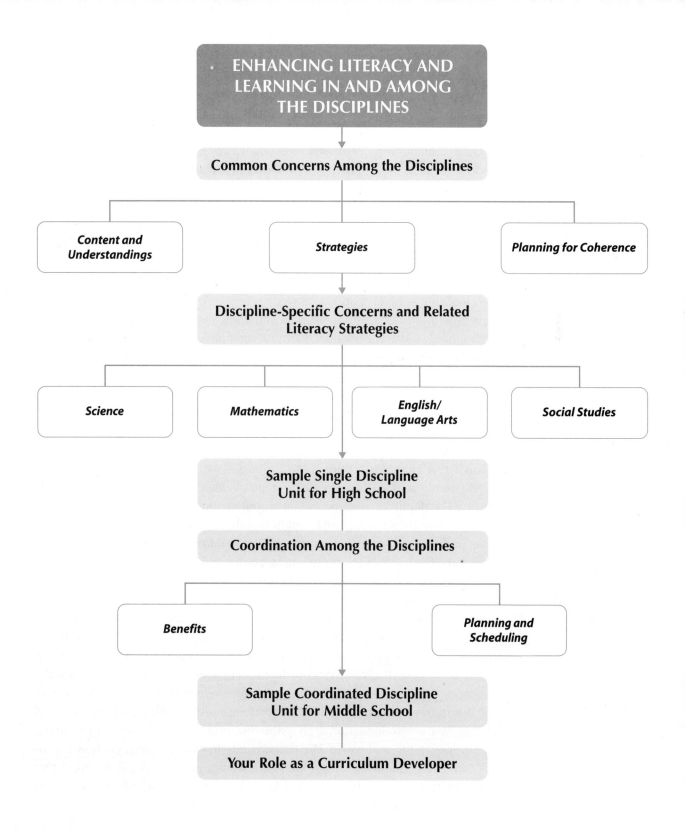

ENHANCING LITERACY AND LEARNING IN AND AMONG THE DISCIPLINES

Common Concerns Among the Disciplines

Content and Understandings

Strategies

Planning for Coherence

Discipline-Specific Concerns and Related Literacy Strategies

Science

Mathematics

English/ Language Arts

Social Studies

Sample Single Discipline Unit for High School

Coordination Among the Disciplines

Benefits

Planning and Scheduling

Sample Coordinated Discipline Unit for Middle School

Your Role as a Curriculum Developer

Most individuals who become middle school or high school content-area specialists do so because they have a strong personal interest in the subject matter associated with a particular domain of a discipline such as biology or chemistry in science or American history or economics in the social sciences. Content-area specialists like you who enter the teaching profession choose to share their materials and knowledge with young people.

In this chapter, we begin by exploring the concerns common to all content teachers, because there are certain key issues that cross subject boundaries. Next we look at some of the specific challenges that particular disciplines pose, and how students can use literacy strategies to meet discipline-specific challenges.

We explore different approaches for designing curriculum and teaching and learning subject matter knowledge. First, we focus on single discipline-based learning because recent data indicates that most middle schools and high schools today are organized around separate disciplines. *Single discipline-based courses or programs* center on domains of knowledge within the social sciences, physical sciences, literature, and the arts that are connected by common principles and concepts as well as vocabulary, rules, and structures inherent within a field. Furthermore, recent efforts directed toward meeting the national curriculum standards (Chapter 10) by both states and individual school districts have given discipline-based curriculum increased attention (Ornstein & Hutchins, 1998).

single discipline-based courses or programs Courses or programs designed to focus on single domains of knowledge within the social sciences, physical sciences, literature, or the arts.

Knowing that students at every stage of development and at every grade level gain depth of understanding about a topic when the disciplines or courses they are studying are brought together in meaningful ways we look at a second model of curriculum referred to as *coordinated curriculum.* This is an approach that focuses on teaching complementary topics concurrently in two different disciplines to the same group of students.

coordinated curriculum Curriculum which focuses on linking two or more discrete disciplines to help students understand a topic more fully.

Finally, no matter what the discipline, the teacher's priority in a classroom should not be to teach subject matter alone; but, rather, to teach students in a manner that challenges their misperceptions and emphasizes their ability to link prior knowledge to new experiences and knowledge. Most important, whether a single discipline or coordinated curriculum model is chosen for the classroom, the emphasis should be on major understandings and big issues in the disciplines, the use of strategies for literacy and learning that we proposed in Part Two, interconnection among the disciplines, and connections from the disciplines to the real world. We demonstrate in two sample units how teachers can teach effectively within their own discipline, and can foster important learning and literacy strategies within both a single discipline and a coordinated curriculum approach.

Common Concerns Among the Disciplines

There is not a text written today focusing on educational pedagogy, policy, or curriculum that does not highlight the need for innovation and educational reform. All educators and many policymakers and parents are asking whether the current view of educational reform evidenced in documents such as the national discipline-based standards, curriculum frameworks, and professional teaching standards will lead to visible, long-lasting changes in our schools and classrooms, as well as tangible benefits for students. Everyone you talk with in education today seems to be either implementing or assessing the impact of the various standards and frameworks and the school restructuring efforts that often accompany them.

This current call for reform emphasizes the need for students to meet higher expectations in problem solving, communication skills, and application of knowledge across the disciplines and the domains of everyday life. Furthermore, recent concerns that teachers, curriculum developers, and subject matter experts have expressed are similar across the disciplines. We do recognize, however, that there are long-standing disagreements regarding the term discipline itself and that scholars and educators within every field are engaged in debating what constitutes the essential structure or the major understandings in their field. Think about the recent standards movement and the documents we discussed in Chapter 10. The clearest example of such dissension within a discipline is in social studies.

The standards movement and its emphasis on identifying essential understandings seems to have exacerbated the differences among the fields commonly associated with the social sciences: history, geography, civics, and social studies. The unfortunate result is that there are now four different sets of standards for social studies, each claiming to be the most necessary standards for the study of social studies. How will middle school and high school teachers decide which set of standards to use as a framework for their own social studies curriculum? This dilemma and similar ones in other disciplines have left individual teachers, departments, school districts, and even publishers trying to decide what to focus on in courses, in curriculum, and in the materials that support these various endeavors.

Table 11.1 shows some of the more prevalent domains or areas of focus being touted as appropriate organizers for courses and curriculum today. Think about this chart and what it says about the dilemma facing educators in secondary schools. What courses were available to you in your own secondary program? How is the content in the discipline you are now studying organized into courses at the college level? If you've looked at a local school district's standards of learning or state-mandated curriculum frameworks and accompanying tests, do you think the courses you are taking match with what you need to know in order to teach your future students?

Beyond the issue of what content to focus on and what domains are central to the development of secondary school programs, educators in each content area are trying to answer three overarching questions in an effort to shape a more responsive curriculum:

- What are the essential understandings in the field of knowledge?

- How do we enhance students' ability to problem-solve, think critically, and apply their understandings of content to everyday life using effective strategies, particularly the literacy strategies of an effective reader and writer?

- How do we ensure time to plan and coordinate these understandings and strategies across each discipline and across the curriculum from level to level and grade to grade in some cohesive fashion?

TABLE 11.1 The Content Domains

Mathematics	Social Studies	Science	Language arts
Mathematics	U.S. history	General science	American literature
Discrete math	World history	Biology	British literature
Algebra	Geography	Chemistry	World literature
Geometry	Civics	Physics	Spelling
Calculus	Economics	Ecology	Writing/composition
	Anthropology	Life science	Grammar
	Political science	Physical science	
	Sociology	Earth and space science	
		Technological science	

STANDARDS ☑ ■ **Content and Understandings**

Each of the standards documents discussed in Chapter 10 emphasizes the importance of big ideas and overarching principles as the cornerstone for the individual discipline. Each of the standards documents is explicitly designed to communicate essential, long-standing, and valuable understandings in their field. Therefore, the discipline-based standards are meant to provide a framework of important understandings from which curriculum can be shaped. The second overarching goal being suggested by each of the standards documents is that all students in our schools receive a quality, equitable education that stresses important understandings in the discipline, thinking and problem solving, and application of content to real-life situations and issues. No matter what courses students take within a discipline, these overarching curriculum goals should be the same.

TEACHER AS INQUIRING LEARNER

In order to understand the dilemma about what to teach in your discipline, examine several texts at a specific grade level in the subject you hope to teach. For example, if you are an English major, look at three anthologies of literature for the tenth grade, or if you are a science major, look at several texts written for high school earth science courses. Examine these texts and ask yourself the following questions:

• Are any topics mentioned in all of these texts or in two out of the three? What fundamentals or

key principles associated with the discipline are explicitly made and covered in depth within each text? What sorts of activities associated with the discipline are emphasized in the activities or the "to-do" sections of the text? What literacy and learning strategies are incorporated into the content-area materials? What everyday applications or career-related examples are provided for students in this text?

As a teacher, you may be in a position to choose specific content from your domain to carry out the national, state, or local curriculum standards or goals. The choices you make will determine the learning experiences you provide and the outcomes of learning for your students. Selecting content carefully helps you keep your focus on the major understandings in your field and also helps you maintain a balance between what is surveyed and what is studied in depth in your discipline.

You may feel overwhelmed when you realize how rapidly your discipline is changing and how difficult it can be to sort through the information explosion affecting every area of your life. Nevertheless, several important principles or guidelines can help you select the content and the understandings to focus on, no matter what your discipline or the level you teach. These guidelines are closely linked to the knowledge you have about your students, the knowledge you have pertaining to materials, and the knowledge you have about strategies to promote literacy and learning discussed in each of the chapters in Part One.

• Choose durable content closely aligned with the main ideas or concepts in a field; avoid minor ideas and trivial details associated with the subject to be studied.

• Think about your particular learners to determine the content and how it is presented with special attention to the life experiences and background knowledge they bring to learning.

• Seek to illuminate and to contextualize the content with data from other fields as well as from students' previous learning (Doll, 1996).

Finally, no matter what your discipline, we think you might find helpful a set of guidelines that the National Science Teachers Association (Texley & Wild, 1996) developed to accompany its curriculum frameworks. We have turned these guidelines into questions you can ask yourself about your own curriculum and the content you focus on:

• Is the content connected to other areas of learning both within the discipline and beyond?

- Does the curriculum provide the necessary tools of the discipline (e.g., math for science, writing for language arts and social sciences)?

- Is the curriculum supported by time, space, and equipment?

- Is the curriculum designed to give diverse learners equal footing and to provide background knowledge when necessary?

- Is the curriculum supported by the faculty and the school community, and has it been assessed and renewed?

■ Strategies

The second issue that teachers in every discipline wonder is how they will enhance their students' independent thinking and use of strategies. Think about the strategies you use on a regular basis to solve problems or to answer questions in your content area. When you read, write, collect data, do research to investigate new topics in your field, or connect past understandings to new knowledge, what strategies do you use? As you explored the strategies detailed in Part Two, did you add some new strategies to your repertoire? This is a good time to review your own learning patterns, the literacy strategies you use regularly, and those you explored as you studied Part Two. You are most likely to be able to model and to explain with credibility to your own students those strategies with which you have had firsthand practice.

We also believe the teacher's role—no matter what the content area—is to explain and model strategic applications of the understandings in a field through "think-alouds" and modeling and explaining scripts like those we explained in Part Two. We think teachers can help their students be more strategic by engaging them in new learning experiences in a coaching mode rather than in a didactic mode. Teachers should use appropriate teaching and assessing tools to support their students and enable them to process content, make knowledge their own, and apply understandings to authentic problems and real-world contexts that have meaning beyond the classroom walls. The major goal in every subject area is for students to explain principles and concepts in their own words and to be able to apply understandings both in and out of school.

■ Planning for Coherence

The third issue teachers in every discipline are dealing with is the lack of coherence in the curriculum from grade to grade and from level to level. Think back to Chapter 1 and our recommendation that you reflect on the essence of your content area and how you will convey that to your own students. What cross-grade opportunities have you seen or have you been able to participate in through a field experience at the middle school or the high school level? When you did your student teaching, did you see your cooperating teacher or mentor work with another teacher in the same discipline? Is there any evidence that the faculty at the institution that you now attend participate in any sort of coordinated work on curriculum? As a new teacher, what opportunities do you think you will have to learn from an experienced teacher?

Teachers at every grade level and in every discipline have very little planning time scheduled during the school day. The usual time structures and schedules in both middle schools and high schools, even when the teachers are organized by discipline, do little to foster discussion and planning of content from grade to grade. Even in middle schools where there are interdisciplinary teams, subject matter teachers at different grade levels rarely meet or plan with one another to create coherence within a discipline from year to year and from grade to grade.

As a beginning or new teacher, we suggest that you seek out colleagues in your discipline, or at least one "buddy" with whom you can discuss the content you are teaching and the teaching and assessing tools you are using in your discipline. We are encouraging our college students to stay in contact with one another via email to maintain the support system they developed during their teacher training. You can begin the curriculum development process in small, manageable increments as you get to know your students, the curriculum, and the context in which you are working. If you focus on assessing your students, becoming familiar with the existing curriculum and materials, and getting to know the community in which you are teaching, you will have a great deal of data to inform your own course development and your day-to-day teaching, particularly after the first year in a setting.

Table 11.2, a guide for curriculum development, was designed for the language arts; however, it can be applied to curriculum development in all disciplines. The

In order to meet various national and state standards and to plan curriculum, teachers need opportunities to meet in teams.
© Michael Zide

examination of existing curriculum, and the careful assessment of one's students can assist you in choosing particular areas of focus in your own discipline to help students arrive at important understandings. The guide can serve as a road map for you and your future colleagues when you are considering curriculum change and development in your own discipline, grade level, department, or school.

Discipline-Specific Concerns and Related Literacy Strategies

This section looks at some discipline-specific concerns and challenges that middle school and high school educators are facing today. We think it is important for you to know about these challenges and to become familiar with content areas other than your own for several reasons. First, we think the knowledge of other disciplines expands your view of education. Second, it provides you with some additional background knowledge to link to your own discipline and your knowledge of pedagogy and practice that you are enhancing in your role as a professional educator. Third, we think it is useful as a classroom teacher to know something about what your students are learning in other disciplines, so that you can connect the content and the strategies of your discipline to other content areas. Fourth, we think that opportunities to learn about the challenges other disciplines face, the focus of Chapter 10, will help you identify opportunities for coordinated and integrated curriculum, the emphasis which is discussed later in this chapter and in Chapter 12. Last, because this text and the course you are taking are focused on literacy learning and helping your students as readers and writers in the disciplines, we have concluded each discipline-based section with a focus on particular literacy strategies we introduced in Part Two. These strategies will help your students deal with the challenges presented by both the subject matter and the resources being used for study in each discipline.

We focus on the concerns found in the four core disciplines that comprise the required curriculum for all high school and middle school students in schools across the country: science, mathematics, English/language arts, and social studies. In addition, we consider courses in foreign or world language and health (and physical education) as well as those in the arts and vocational education, to be very important for students to have a balanced curriculum and to have choices that align with their interests and needs. We have found that many of the concerns as well as the major goals expressed in the health standards are also found in the science standards and existing curriculum. And there are many similarities between foreign or world language goals and those of the English/language arts and even of the social studies. Although we focus on the concerns of the four core disciplines, we think it provides all teachers, regardless of discipline, with valuable and useful insights about their own discipline as well as about the curriculum as a whole, for middle school and high school students.

TABLE 11.2 Curriculum Development Guide

1. *Study Existing Curriculum*

   - Identify basis of existing curriculum—guidebook, adopted text, individual teacher choices.
   - Identify points of excellence and what is working.
   - Identify where there is dissatisfaction.
   - Identify projects or programs that seem most ready and of highest priority for improvement in this setting.
   - Create a list of what in the best of all worlds is desirable for students in this content area.
   - Create a target list for possible changes.

2. *Assess the Community Needs and Interests (Educate While Collecting Data)*

   - Interview parents regarding concerns for their children (be certain to include second-language learners and children with special needs).
   - Conduct informal workshops or information sessions on new curriculum directions.
   - Involve parent volunteers in meetings where they can get firsthand understanding of the change or innovation.
   - Interview representatives of the business community to see their perceived needs for the workforce.
   - Carry out a formal needs assessment of the community.

3. *Assess Students*

   - Determine students' background knowledge and language related to the content area or topic being proposed for study.
   - Determine skills and strategies necessary to carry out the area of study. (For example, in a new area of literature, what writing skills, oral language, and reading skills do students need; what strategies would they be expected to use in studying the new topic or genre; and what skills and strategies would be embedded in the study itself?)
   - Seek information from standardized tests or other tests such as state assessment tools being developed to align with the curriculum frameworks that are given on an ongoing basis in the school or district.
   - Determine what information is available from ongoing student documentation in the form of journals and portfolios and what instruments should be employed to gather specific data.

4. *Assess Faculty Interests and Imperatives*

   - Develop a profile of faculty expertise in the discipline. In language arts, teachers may have expertise and interest in drama, in poetry, or in coaching young writers to write for publication. (Do not assume that discipline teachers have a generic background and broad understandings of their field.)
   - Use study teams to look at innovations or new directions in the field and to report back to their colleagues. Have language arts or social studies teachers investigate the use of media or technology in their field or look at the implications of second-language learning for their discipline and the topics they are teaching.
   - Provide opportunities for teachers to attend institutes or conferences where they can talk and interact with others in their discipline. Especially encourage them to participate in experiences where they can get firsthand experiences with new techniques, strategies, and materials.
   - Identify imperatives in the field such as national standards or state curriculum frameworks that teachers are responsible for. Find ways to address these while at the same time revising the curriculum using the preceding considerations with regard to content, community, and students.
   - Identify the school or curricular conditions that would help teachers more effectively reach the desired curriculum (schedules, resources, etc.).

Source: Adapted from S. Tchudi, *Planning and Assessing Curriculum in English/Language Arts* (Alexandria, Va.: Association for Supervision and Curriculum Development, 1991), chap. 5.

■ Science

For too long, science curriculum across the United States has been a disjointed array of topics and concepts. In many classrooms, students spend at least 50 percent of their time using content-area textbooks (Checkley, 1997; Dillon, O'Brien, & Moje, 1994). In an attempt to give a complete and current view of the field, these texts often do no more than mention a great variety of topics. Furthermore, these texts rarely give teachers using them suggestions about how they might connect these myriad of topics to one another, or how to connect this subject matter to their students' everyday life.

In addition, most science curriculum in the past was focused on scientific processes, models, and procedures, with little emphasis on scientific application to everyday life. Until recently, the major uniformity in the delivery of the science curriculum has been the focus on earth science in grades 8 or 9, biology in grade 10, and chemistry and physics at grades 11 and 12. Although these domains are still recognized as major vehicles for delivery of science education, the emphasis has begun to shift from single domains of study to a focus on key understandings in science that pervade and connect the domains (National Academy of Sciences and National Science Association, 1996). In order to achieve this emphasis on the important understandings of science as a whole, science educators in every field have begun to advocate that elementary, middle, and high school curriculum be focused on students at all levels gaining important understandings about the life sciences, physical sciences, earth and space sciences, and technology, as well as their application to everyday life.

Recent studies have shown that the majority of the public in the United States is scientifically illiterate (Kyle, 1995). Too often students leave their required science courses with limited textbook knowledge about what science is and even less knowledgeable about how it pertains to their own lives. Middle school and high school students need relevant opportunities to use their science understandings to act on issues and challenges in their real world. All students need to understand and be able to apply the advances of science that relate to their lives as consumers. Finally, you and your students have a right to expect science and scientific discoveries to improve your world. At the same time, as citizens of this planet, you and your students also need enough scientific knowledge to monitor the use of science in a world that we all inhabit.

If we believe that basic science understandings are essential in today's world, then scientific literacy goes hand in hand with the communications and literacy strategies we focus on in this text (Allen, 1989). The use of appropriate literacy strategies can provide students with the tools they need to learn science content and to become independent learners who can read and write about these content-based understandings in their academic life and their everyday life.

Many students come to science with limited prior knowledge and misperceptions about facts and principles that explain the universe. Therefore, teachers may find that modeling and explaining how to preview a chapter (as in Chapter 4), or how to use a graphic organizer like a concept map (see Chapter 6), will help students distinguish between important information and supporting details, and unimportant and irrelevant information (Santa & Alvermann, 1991). Since science material is often filled with technical and specific content words, direct instruction on morphemic analysis and common roots in science will help students (see Chapter 5), as will strategies like semantic feature charts (see also Chapter 5), that focus on similarities and differences among concepts or attributes within an area of study in science (Barton, Heidema, & Jordan, 2002).

■ Mathematics

Mathematics suffers from many of the same criticisms and issues as science does. It is rarely connected to other fields or disciplines within the curriculum, and there is very little emphasis on the applicability of mathematics to real life. Mathematics has been taught as a separate core subject offered once a day (like a good vitamin) from the elementary grades through high school. Schools have failed to emphasize the humanizing quality of mathematics and the incredible phenomenon that all cultures have developed some manner of mathematics in order to conduct their daily lives. Human beings have used mathematics to keep records and to allocate resources, and they have always used mathematics to design and construct their dwellings.

Mathematics provides us with language and procedures that help us quantify, measure, compare, and identify patterns useful in all of the other disciplines. Whether we are using a time line in history or a comparison chart showing characters' positive and negative characteristics in literature, we are using mathematical concepts and understandings applied to other disciplines. For example, one middle school unit entitled "Yesterday and Tomorrow" was designed to foster students' ability to observe and think mathematically about things in the world around them. Students focused on examining and learning about change in their community. They used comparative data related to population shifts in their own area to understand how changes in agriculture, industry, and availability of natural resources had affected their community. By studying current population numbers and census figures, the students also began to understand what these numbers meant and what impact they would have on school transportation, and even the size and types of businesses that existed in the community of the present as well as what may be needed for the future. Through participation in a unit such as this one, the students gained firsthand experience using their mathematics understandings and seeing how relevant their understandings are in their everyday lives (Kleiman, 1991).

Whenever students are applying mathematics in various discipline-based endeavors or in everyday life, they need to: perceive symbols, attach literal meaning to numbers and symbols, analyze relationships, and solve word problems (Earle, 1976). Literacy strategies that focus on students' text-based and schema-based connections (the focus of Chapter 6) are particularly useful when doing mathematics. A comprehension study guide that fosters the use of literal and interpretive questions can be used to help students read the graphs and statistical tables present in many content-area materials as well as in newspapers and magazines. Second, many students need assistance in mastering specialized, technical mathematics vocabulary, particularly when it is used in mathematics word problems and in other content areas such as chemistry, economics, or geography. Strategies such as morphemic analysis (Chapter 5), multiple meanings/multiple terms and connotative/denotative meanings (Chapter 5), as well as the use of context clues and glossaries (Chapter 7), help students with the vocabulary demands of mathematics. Finally, auxiliary aids such as text pattern guides and visuals in the form of diagrams or charts (Chapter 7) help students figure out what facts they have and what relationships are present, as well as what processes to use when attempting to solve word problems.

■ English/Language Arts

In the English/language arts curriculum, the major debate is about how best to provide a coherent set of literature experiences that will be both challenging and supportive of students who vary widely by linguistic and cultural background. The depth of the controversy between the "new" (expanded) and the "traditional" (the canon) literature is highlighted by a relevant occurrence in Massachusetts. When the statewide English/Language Arts Curriculum Frameworks were disseminated, participants on the planning and review teams, who represented two very different factions, insisted that two appendixes of "acceptable works" accompany the document. One list included many works written from a multicultural perspective; the other list contained the traditional "great works." With the two lists in hand, Massachusetts teachers and administrators were faced with having to decide which of the two lists to select from, as well as what implications their choices will have for them and for their students.

There is a second set of issues associated with the choice of literary works that teachers make for their students. Advocates of multicultural and contemporary books for middle school and high school students believe that literature exposes students to both tensions among groups and positive interactions between different racial and ethnic groups represented in this country. However, some critics of the newer, more multicultural books built on contemporary themes argue that many of these books place too much emphasis on the negative aspects of race and ethnic relations rather than showing a balance of positive and negative interactions among individuals and groups (Stotsky, 1995).

Although a significant percentage of the literature being used in the schools should be focused on recency and multiculturalism, there is a concern among many English/language arts teachers that traditional readings and authors appear to be slipping out of the curriculum altogether. We believe that the use of some "great works" can challenge students to recognize some of the universals that connect their own personal experiences with those of individuals who lived in other ages and in other cultures. A classical work like Shakespeare's *Hamlet*, which focuses on a young person's dealing with a personal dilemma, can be compared to contemporary realistic fiction such as *Scorpions* (Walter Dean Myers, 1988) or *Park's Quest* (Katherine Patterson, 1988), which also focus on young people facing dilemmas in situations with which students can identify. Rather than seeing literature like Shakespeare's *Macbeth* or Arthur Miller's *The Crucible* as portrayals of people and situations that are unrelated to their lives, you can lead your students to make connections between the past and the present through literature; just as in history they make connections between events happening today and those that took place in the past. Building on the themes of these two works, you can help students identify their own prejudices and see that there are concerns about witchcraft activity today in many areas of the country. In other words, you can help your students see the universality in the human experience and even see how their own lives are connected to those of the characters in the books they read.

The current emphasis in literature is for students of all ages to be exposed to a wider range of literature works (see Chapter 3)—those in "the canon" and those that reflect contemporary relevance and cultural diversity—and to more and varied styles or genres of literature. Students need to be taught how to use story maps as supporting strategies for reading narrative text and to use text pattern guides for understanding the different organizational patterns in the expository or informational texts they will read in all of their content areas (Chapter 7).

Deciding on the particular meanings of words is another challenge for many readers as they meet settings, cultures, and characters very different from themselves in the texts in their literature courses. Students need to learn to be strategic and to learn how to use context clues effectively to deal with new vocabulary and ideas in the books they read for class or on their own as well as when and how they can use the dictionary for determining precise word meanings (Chapter 5). Students also need direct vocabulary instruction and opportunities to apply strategies such as how to discern connotative and denotative meanings in the literature they are reading and how to use vocabulary tools (Chapter 5), such as the dictionary and thesaurus.

Finally, when students read literature, you can assist them in the creation of a discussion web or journal responses (Chapter 6) to help them prepare for expressing their own ideas as they interact with text. You can show them how they can use these webs or journal entries to refine their ideas as they participate in a variety of small group peer-led discussions such as those described in Chapters 6 and 7.

■ Social Studies

There also continue to be pervasive concerns about the current curriculum, materials, and the pedagogy in social studies. *The History Report Card: History Assessment at a Glance* (2001) highlighted how narrow and detail oriented many middle school and high school social studies courses and programs are. The social studies knowledge of many middle school and high school students appears too often to be a collection of unrelated historical facts, dates, and names of famous people. Organizations such as the National Center for History in the Schools have developed standards specifically for history education in grades 5–12. Their emphasis has been to help teachers create learning experiences that will require their students to use their historical understandings to interpret the past, understand the present, and project to the future. Social studies educators from the National Center advocate learning experiences that will involve middle school and high school students in using their historical knowledge to think and problem-solve, rather than to memorize information limited to people, facts, and dates.

There is a movement to expose students to more of the fields of social studies—namely, geography, economics, civics, and political science—and to bring these fields together to help students study real problems and issues. Many educators believe the major goal of all social studies courses and curriculum should be to empower students to become active participants in their communities. Therefore a priority in all social studies classrooms should be students' working to understand why things happened as they did in the past. Teachers should encourage students to reflect on what they can learn from the past to improve their lives and those of others in their communities. In each of the social sciences, teachers should encourage students to think about how issues—such as human rights, affirmative action, and censorship—are dealt with and what impact decisions made today may have on the future (Van Sledright, 1994).

In order to promote students' active involvement in the learning and doing of history and social studies, the pedagogy and materials are changing as well. Even in the early grades, primary sources and oral histories are being used as subject matter, and investigative research is modeled and supported in age-appropriate ways. An emphasis is being placed on students' reading authentic historical materials rather than relying solely on secondary sources. Teachers are modeling for their students concepts like how to find an author's intent in the materials they use (see Chapter 6). Teachers are also helping their students to interpret history, and they are encouraging them to look for cycles and trends as social scientists do, rather than focusing solely on facts and dates (see Chapter 6). Students are also being encouraged to ask questions and to set purposes for their own reading in the social sciences. Strategies such as a KWL chart, a QAR or a DRA, various note-taking techniques, and the use of graphic organizers that social studies teachers model will help students in the middle and secondary grades gain confidence in their ability to use their social studies understandings in the classroom as well as in the real world. In all social studies courses at every level, teachers should encourage students to participate in discussion groups and to write to demonstrate their own learning and understanding.

TEACHER AS INQUIRING LEARNER

In this chapter we have looked at the four primary content areas included in most middle schools and high schools today and have addressed common concerns as well as discipline-specific issues inherent in each. In addition, we have concluded each discipline-specific section with a focus on those literacy strategies from Part Two that will enable you and your students to be more successful readers and writers of the content material. Examine the discipline-specific standards or the frameworks in the state where you now teach. What role does effective communication and literacy appear to play in your discipline's standards document? Furthermore, how are literacy strategies, like those explicitly explained in Part Two, fostered in the performance standards or enabling activities that accompany the state standards (or the national ones if you chose those to examine) for your content area? What are the implications for you as a teacher?

 ## Sample Unit Plans

Sample Single-Discipline Unit for the High School

*I*n Chapters 11 and 12 we have developed sample middle school and high school units to demonstrate the enactment of single discipline, coordinated, and integrated curriculum, respectively. Each of the scenarios, which we developed for this text, represents an amalgam of real classroom events and lessons we have witnessed or heard about and settings and programs that classroom practitioners have described at national and regional conferences that we have attended. These scenarios were also drawn from the goals, performance standards, and vignettes in various national standards documents and curriculum frameworks, as well as from teaching/assessing ideas we have drawn from various books, journals, ERIC documents, and sources on the Internet dealing with curriculum development for specific subject areas. As you read these sample units, imagine yourself participating in these scenarios as a

STANDARDS ☑

middle school or high school teacher working with your own students or as a student teacher working in a classroom doing a field placement.

The high school single discipline unit created for this chapter focuses on science, specifically the domain of geology. The national standards dealing with earth and space science for grades 9–12 emphasize a focus on earth science that will help all secondary students understand local, national, and global challenges to the earth, as well as natural hazards like tornadoes, volcanoes, and floods and the challenges that humans create. We built this sample unit based on the national science standards for the high school level (see both Chapter 10 and Table 11.3), a ninth-grade classroom vignette included in Pathways to Science *(Texley & Wild, 1996), and the literacy and learning strategies we addressed in Part Two.*

An experienced general science teacher wanted to find an interesting way for her students to meet the standards focused on understandings about geology and the origin and the evolution of the earth system. She wanted to enhance the students' awareness about local geology and what the study of earth science means in their own community. In addition, she designed this unit in order to clear up misunderstandings that her students had about the great age of the earth and about the geologic record because she realized that many of her students' only knowledge of the earth came from what they had seen in the science-fiction media, which rely largely on a supernatural or magical approach to how the earth and its layers evolved.

The teacher in this sample used a plan book to write up her ideas for content understandings and strategies to be taught, activities for the students and the teacher to carry out, and resources the students would use. During the planning stage, the teacher reflected on what she had done in the past with this topic, what resources were available to her and the class, and how she could incorporate the new standards into her curriculum.

The outline format we use here for this ninth-grade geology unit is similar to what many teachers use in their own plan books. Each of the components necessary for the development of a unit—the resources, the understandings and strategies, the connections to other disciplines, and the student evaluation—is included in this format. This outline, developed during the planning stage of the unit, would guide the teacher's development of specific lesson plans. Of course, the specific lessons would be determined by particular content in the standards or curriculum frameworks being met by the students' needs and levels of understanding as the unit progresses.

Major Understandings

Students engaged in this unit will develop understandings about the origin and evolution of the earth system and its changes in order to better understand issues and challenges, and how they, as well as other inhabitants of earth, can evaluate the earth and its changes. The students will be engaged in firsthand opportunities to apply and observe processes that geologists use to study such things as constancy and change and evolution and equilibrium in relation to current status and development of the earth's crust. Students will see how these understandings have meaning not only in the science classroom, but also in how they help them make sense of the particular environment in which they now live.

TABLE 11.3 Excerpt from National Science Education Standards

A. Science as Inquiry

B. Physical Science

C. Life Science

D. Earth and Space Science
As a result of their activities in grades 9–12, all students should develop an understanding of these content standards:

1. Energy in the earth system

2. Geochemical cycles

3. The origin and evolution of the earth system
Specific concepts and principles include:

- Geologic time can be estimated by observing rock sequences and using fossils to correlate the sequences at various locations.

- Interactions among the solid earth, the oceans, the atmosphere, and organisms have resulted in the ongoing evolution of the earth system. We can observe some changes such as earthquakes and volcanic eruptions on a human time scale, but many processes such as mountain building and plate movements take place over hundreds of millions of years.

4. The origin and evolution of the universe

E. Science and Technology

F. Science in Personal and Social Perspectives

G. History and Nature of Science

Source: National Science Education Standards. National Academy of Sciences and National Science Association, 1996. Reprinted with permission from *National Science Education Standards*. © 1996 by the National Academy of Sciences, courtesy of the National Academies Press, Washington, D.C.

Resources
Reference Tools

- *Fossils: A Guide to Prehistoric Life,* a nature guide published by Golden Books, for all students to use and share in small working groups.

- Geology resources to accommodate a range of reading levels, such as *Clocks in the Rocks* (Patricia L. Barnes-Svarney, 1991), *Rocks and Minerals* (Tracy Staedter, 1999), and *Rocks and Minerals* (Chris Pelilant, 1992), to provide all students with informational material they can read on their own.

- Other reference tools on paleontology and historical geology from the library.

- Information on geology from the Internet (sources for teachers and students such as **walrus.wr.usgs.gov/ask-a-geologist**).

- A large geologic map.

Artifacts

- Class collection of specimens of fossils[*] from the local area that students sort and label as they are brought into the classroom over a two-week period before the unit was begun.

Science Tools

- Hand lenses, stereo microscopes, old dental tools, toothbrushes and wire brushes to clean and expose the fossils, and glue to fix broken specimens.

Individual Lessons

Initiating Lessons

- As an introduction and motivating activity to the unit, the students collect specimens from the local area over a two-week period.

- Students use their collected specimens and ones that the teacher has and they **ask questions that can frame the guided reading and research** they will do using various natural history guides. Some questions might be:

  What is it [the fossil]?

  What present-day form is it related to?

- Teacher models and explains **how to read diagrams, illustrations, and captions in the guides**[†] and how to connect to the text.

- Students **preview** the format of the guide they are using so they will be able to match their fossil specimens to the appropriate pictorial aid and to gather information from the descriptions in the text.

- Students **recall and review some Latin and Greek root words** they have studied associated with science that will help them understand the vocabulary used in geology; affixes such as *pre-* and *meta-* associated with time and size are examples.

Developing Lessons

- Students **connect graphic information**, such as illustrations and diagrams, to text in the guides they are using.

---

[*] These were built on a collection of geologic specimens the teacher had collected over the years.

[†]Many of the guides tend to be dense in their use of pictorials and graphic aids as well as their use of keys. Therefore, students will need specific modeling and strategy instruction in order to interpret as well as to connect these aids to the brief, highly detailed descriptive text found in most natural history guides.

- Students **connect fossils with graphic aids and text**, to begin the identification process and to answer the questions posed during the collection stage.

- Students individually **find other sources** to clarify and support their identification (the teacher may recommend sources to particular students based on an informal assessment of their needs).

- Students **construct supporting aids**, such as diagrams, sketches, and notes, to organize their findings and to keep track of how certain types of fossils are related to one another (for example, students note which types of fossils are found in certain types of rock).

- Students use their information from these aids to **participate in discussions** related to the three questions posed in the initiating lessons. Students' responses serve as a source of informal assessment.

- Teacher **models the use of a local geologic map, a special type of graphic organizer**, so that students can plot findings about their own specimens and determine in what age and in what environments their fossils were found.

Real-life example of a similar unit: Students in a ninth-grade class in New York state carried out a similar unit and plotted their findings on a geologic map. Among their fossils there were many types of coral, as well as cynobacteria, trilobites, and a starfish, which they then associated with a number of geologic periods ranging from the earliest Precambrian to the Pleistocene eras. The students, with the help of their teacher, also found that their fossils came from many different environments, and they had a firsthand experience seeing the role that glaciers played in altering and shaping the earth's crust (Texley & Wild, 1996).

Culminating Lessons

- Students **prepare a brief written summary** about one type of fossil found in their area to include in a sharing session that will bring all of the students together; students use their own diagrams and drawings as well as those created by other students in their small study groups.

- Whole class discussion focused on the variety of sources and eras of geology represented in their own immediate environment.

- Teacher informally assesses each student's understandings based on the depth and clarity of their individual presentations as well as on their **use of new scientific vocabulary in both their spoken and their written work**.

- Students will **look back and reread what they have written and drawn** to refine their understandings about this topic. At this stage students in small groups decide whether they want to **do further reading or investigations** before creating a final written report supported by drawings and other graphic aids; students will check their report(s) against a **rubric** for creating science reports that they developed in class earlier in the year; a copy of their group's report could be placed into their individual science folders or into their cross-discipline "best works" portfolio.

- In addition to discussing and writing about the fossils they have collected, students may take a **more extensive geologic field trip** in their community to gather more samples, as well as to extend their data pool for drawing conclusions, and for understanding the geologic history of their environment.

- Students **refine** their ideas about this important topic by thinking about how the geologic environment in their area shaped the lives of the local inhabitants. Students **discuss** what building materials are commonly used in the area, such as fieldstone in Pennsylvania or granite in Vermont. They **discuss** constraints that land and rock formations create for the buildings or highways in their area. Students **investigate** the effect that rocks and land formations have had on people's lives or work as well as on the economy where they live.

Student Evaluation

During the Lessons

- Students read and understand text and graphic aids demonstrated by their note taking, drawings, and participation in small group activities and their whole class activities.

- Students match fossils with certain types of rock based on information found in various reference tools and the ability to place the information on a geologic map (a particular graphic organizer used in this unit in the developing lessons).

- Teacher assesses students' appropriate use of new vocabulary words related to the study of geology.

- Students' self-evaluation of their own participation in discussion in both small groups and whole class activities.

After the Lessons

- Students place small group written and illustrated reports into their own science folders or into their cross-discipline portfolio.

- Students evaluate their individual and small group written reports using the rubric for evaluating science reports that the class developed earlier in the year.

- Each student fills in a portfolio assessment sheet that explains why he or she chose the piece for his or her portfolio; the teacher may also complete a response form.

Making Connections Among the Disciplines

Other Possible Areas of Science

- Study of glaciers and their movement as these relate to geological findings.

- Study of volcanoes and the geologic findings in areas where there are ancient volcanoes and where there is more volcanic activity (e.g., Mt. Saint Helens in Washington State).

- Study of major natural hazards such as earthquakes and floods and the interrelationships with the geology of an area (e.g., floods in the midwestern part of the United States, earthquakes in California).

- Study of the relationship of weather and geology (e.g., global warming and the coming of another ice age).

- Links to astronomy and space exploration and the evolving study of Mars and its geology.

- Links to paleontology and the study of dinosaurs.

- Use of resources found on the Internet that would support these explorations such as the specialized web site where students as well as teachers can ask questions about rocks and earth forms, called "Ask a Geologist," (**walrus.wr.usgs.gov/ask-a-geologist**) and the *USA Today* weather site (**www.usatoday.com/weather/wreach.htm**).

Literature

DIVERSITY

- Study the mythology of various cultures to see how the formation of the Earth and various land formations are explained (e.g., Native American, Greek and Roman, Norse).

- Study folktales and tall tales from various cultures to see how they explain the formation of the Earth and various land formations (e.g., Paul Bunyan in the U.S. Midwest; study of the creation myths using sources such as Virginia Hamilton's *In the Beginning*).

Mathematics

- Connect the use of statistics and various types of charts and graphs needed to record geological change.

- Learn about scientific notation and the chemical makeup of various rocks they are studying.

Coordination Among the Disciplines

We demonstrated the value of a single subject teacher connecting his or her individual discipline to others in the sample single-discipline unit you just examined. For the remainder of the chapter, we will look at what occurs when a pair or small group of teachers decide to focus on a shared "big idea" or topic while still teaching in the traditional separate subject configuration. We define curriculum endeavors in which two or more discrete disciplines are linked to help students understand a topic more fully as *coordinated curriculum*. Keep in mind that coordinated curriculum is shaped by the same three guidelines that shaped the single discipline units we explored earlier in this chapter: major understandings and big issues in the disciplines; the use of strategies for literacy and learning that we proposed in Part Two; and interconnections among the disciplines and connections from the disciplines to the real world.

In most efforts toward coordinated curriculum, two teachers in different disciplines seek to help their students gain depth of understanding of a topic in one discipline through the connection, reinforcement, and extension of a second discipline dealing with the same or complementary subject matter. For example, a teacher in a high school general science class on nutrition examining the various nutrients the body needs and how the body uses food throughout the life cycle coordinates with the mathematics curriculum and a focus on the chemical and nutrient balance the body needs. Students practice reading labels on various food packaging and applying the use of measurement terms they learned in mathematics to interpret weight and height tables and calorie charts (Illinois Board of Education, 1998). Coordinating teaching and learning experiences such as this can help diverse learners see how subject matter is related and can be used to solve problems in the real world. In addition, more in-depth exposure to important ideas and the repeated application of understandings in different domains appears to increase students' retention of subject matter, and to increase the likelihood that they will make the knowledge their own and use it in the real world (Ediger, 1998).

Imagine how much more knowledgeable students would be if their high school curriculum included a coordinated unit in which mathematics, biology, and art all looked at symmetry at the same time. In such a situation, complementary views from the different disciplines would enhance the students' understanding of this important concept. Students could learn to use the principles of symmetry in plane and solid geometry as well as see its many everyday applications in the structures around them. They could also learn how useful symmetry is in biology when applied to studying different forms of life—from the smallest protozoa to the largest mammals. Furthermore, students' ability to create and appreciate art works is enhanced with an understanding of symmetry.

Such an emphasis on coordination among the disciplines is not limited to schools and academic settings. There are numerous examples in everyday life of how coordination among professionals in different fields has helped solve problems and challenges. For example, nutritionists are working with neurologists and special educators to determine if a chemical imbalance or allergies might be the cause of, or at least be related to, a number of learning disabilities. Because such coordination occurs in everyday life and in the work world, it is important to look for these opportunities and model coordination in our classrooms.

As you read this part of the chapter, keep the following question in mind. Ask yourself what will be the same and what will be different for you and your future students if coordinated curriculum is the approach to curriculum you use as compared to the usual single discipline model that still pervades most middle schools and high schools.

■ Benefits

Both students and their teachers can benefit from coordinated curriculum experiences. Students benefit from coordinated curriculum because the teaching and learning activities they meet in one subject and those they meet in another complement one another. The experiences students have when different disciplines are connected around an important idea or understanding create a more holistic learning experience than in the usual single discipline delivery model of curriculum. In classrooms where coordination is implemented, what students learn in one discipline becomes background knowledge for the other discipline. Such experiences enhance the likelihood that students will acquire real rather than superficial understandings of important topics and ideas that cross disciplines.

For example, some tenth-grade students in an American history course were studying the Industrial Revolution in the United States. They explored what led up to this era and what it meant for the people who worked in the factories and mills that sprang up across the East and the Midwest. Think about how a coordinated literature unit using historical fiction set in this same time period would be enhanced if the students were studying the same time period in their history class. Think also about how historical fiction that focuses on portrayals of individuals living and working during the Industrial Revolution in America might prompt students to raise questions about the period that perhaps their history text did not cover. The English teacher could use these fictional works to delve into how an author constructs an accurate historical novel and how authors weave fact and fiction into a story to make it compelling. Students could use their own understandings of this period which they acquired from their history course to judge each author's authenticity as well (Norton, 2003).

Such coordination between history and literature could also be an impetus for students to revisit historical sources for verification of the historical information used in the works of fiction. Once students have read a poignant story about a young person like Katherine Patterson's *Lyddie* (1991), they might be curious about the impact

 TEACHER AS INQUIRING LEARNER

Think about your own discipline and the many topics you have studied since you have chosen your subject matter specialization.

- Was each course you took taught as a discrete set of information and understandings to be covered? Were you encouraged to think about the connections of what you were studying to other areas within the discipline, such as the connections between botany and zoology? Were you ever asked to link what you were learning in your discipline to some understanding or some issue in another discipline? Did you have any courses from different disciplines that were taught concurrently or that were linked to one another by the professors teaching them?

If you have personally experienced coordinated curriculum in college or have had the opportunity to observe it in operation in a middle school or a high school where you have done a field experience, you have a model to use when you have your own classroom. If you have not had such an experience, think about a major understanding or an issue in your discipline that could be enhanced by the knowledge and the perspective of a person from another field. If you are a history major, ask an English major if he or she knows of a story set in a particular period that you have an interest in, and compare the impressions of the period your classmate has from literary works with your knowledge of history. If you are a biology major, talk with a health or physical education major, and see what you each know about the human skeletal system and what you each think are the issues for athletes in different sports.

the Industrial Revolution had on real individuals and on their families. Coordinated curriculum work drawing on the social sciences might help the students understand why various laws were enacted during this period that are still in place specifically to protect children and women workers.

■ Planning and Scheduling

Coordinated curriculum efforts at the middle school and high school levels fall along a continuum determined largely by the planning time available to the teachers before and during the unit. In every instance, the amount of actual time available for teacher-to-teacher and teacher-to-student collaboration has much to do with what is feasible given the broader school schedule and organization.

A necessary factor in any of these joint ventures is for the teachers to have planning time together. Planning to develop and to carry out coordinated curriculum helps teachers think about and identify the priorities or big ideas that they hope to convey to their students. When teachers plan for and implement coordinated curriculum, they often are able to solve some of the prevailing issues that stem from an overcrowded curriculum. Such efforts among teachers often lead to more creative use of the physical space and resources in their setting, as well as to a greater variety of ways to meet the learning needs of their students.   There is no one absolute or correct way to set up planning that will work within every context. It is very difficult to do justice to the understandings, strategies, and applications that are the benefits of coordinated curriculum efforts within the typical forty-five-minute class period. Nevertheless, most attempts at coordinated curriculum are carried out by teachers who follow the usual six- or seven-period class schedules and teach a required curriculum; at the same time, they find opportunities to work with other teachers, and to connect their disciplines in new ways.

Numerous variables determine the exact scope and focus of a given effort by teachers of different disciplines to create coordinated curriculum. At the simplest level, two teachers identify complementary content and shared understandings in their individual courses, and they teach these to a given group of students during a semester or marking period. For example, two teachers could arrange the study in geography of the Midwest plains states to occur at the same time that students are reading fictional works such as Patricia MacLachan's *Sarah, Plain and Tall* (1985), or Willa Cather's *My Antonia* (1918/1999), or nonfiction works such as Milton Meltzer's *Driven from the Land: The Story of the Dust Bowl* (2000). The teachers may make varying attempts at explicit connections between the two subjects and the content and understandings at hand. The degree to which they are able to do this depends on the physical structure of their school and classrooms, the length of class periods, the teachers' own planning time, the overall degree of flexibility they have given the other courses in the curriculum, and the broader school schedule.

Teachers who choose to do coordinated curriculum need planning time together before the unit begins and at the very least, some time to check in with one another during the implementation of the coordinated unit. Given the realities of many high schools and even middle schools organized in a team structure comprising discipline-based teachers for each core subject, the only times teachers are assured they can meet and plan are during shared lunch periods or before and after school on their own time. Occasionally two teachers find they have a shared preparation period (often the very time in which their ideas for coordination were sown during informal conversation, as is the case in the sample units you will read about later in this chapter).

The second important variable related to the implementation of a coordinated unit is the scheduling of the students and their teachers and the possibilities during the school day for the teachers and students involved in a unit to work together. In the sample middle school unit detailed next in this chapter, the two middle school content-area teachers are part of a team serving the same groups of students throughout the year. Therefore, the teachers are able to implement both their single discipline curriculum and the newly designed coordinated unit using the class periods that are scheduled back to back each day of the week. Furthermore, these teachers occasionally are able to create a double period to enhance the connectedness of their disciplines. It also creates more opportunities for the students to apply their knowledge at key times throughout the unit without disturbing either the curriculum or the schedules of the other members of their team.

At the high school level, which is still largely organized and scheduled with a priority given to academic departments and the domains within those departments (see Table 11.1), it is most likely that teachers of different disciplines will design their coordinated curriculum for the particular students they have within a period or a common block of time that occurs in a daily or weekly schedule. Such arrangements deal with the reality of the high school schedule, and they enable the teachers and the students to come together at a few key points during the coordinated unit, even if it is only for a culminating activity.

 TEACHER AS INQUIRING LEARNER

We hope you have begun to think about the benefits of coordinated curriculum for yourself as a content-area teacher and for your future students.

• If you believe that your students' learning will be enhanced if you are able to coordinate with teachers at the same grade level or in other disciplines, how will you, as a new teacher, attempt to deal with the usual scheduling and planning dilemmas?

Talk with your classmates and see if you can come up with a list of possible ideas. This is also a good time to engage in discussion with the professor teaching the course you are now taking to see what ideas or suggestions she or he has about coordinating with individuals in other disciplines. You also might want to interview a teacher at the middle or high school level who has had some experience coordinating with colleagues in other disciplines. As you read the rest of this chapter and the sample coordinated units, see if you can add some topics you might consider coordinating with various content in your own discipline.

 **Sample Unit Plans**

Sample Coordinated Discipline Unit for the Middle School

*W*e designed this sample unit to focus on coordination between two members of a typical middle school team: the mathematics and the English/language arts teachers. The mathematics component was inspired by an actual classroom project that one of us had the opportunity to learn about while participating in a university-school partnership grant in a large urban middle school. In addition, we were informed by a variety of literature: Principles and Standards for School Mathematics *(2000) (see Table 11.4), a number of state curriculum frameworks (Illinois Learning Standards, Florida Sunshine State Standards, and New Jersey Core Content Standards), and the findings from the* Third International Mathematics and Science Survey Report *(1997), which focus on geometry and its applications at the middle school level.*

The English/language arts component was based on a chapter in Doing History: Investigating with Children in Elementary and Middle Schools *(Levstik & Barton, 1997) that emphasizes the use of historical fiction to examine connection between history and literature, in particular, the study of the pioneers and the westward movement is often covered in eighth-grade American history courses. This emphasis was also detailed in a unit called "Hats Off and Hats On: A Trip Westward," which was presented by two middle school teachers at an annual National Council of Teachers of English Conference. Finally, one of the author's personal interests in quilts served as an inspiration for this coordinated unit that connected geometry and the English/language arts within a particular period of history.*

How the Teachers Came Together

Two teachers on an eighth-grade team in a large middle school found themselves reflecting on the efforts to create thematic units and to coordinate curriculum in their school. These teachers discussed the benefits of the recent efforts at coordination for their particular team—for both the teachers and the students.

One of the teachers, who taught mathematics, realized that although she was aware of some of the topics and themes that other members of her team had been working on, she herself had been only peripherally involved. She had worked with the science teacher on the team to coordinate some of the mathematics processes she was teaching with the skills and processes the students needed to carry out various science experiments and projects. However, this mathematics teacher and her colleague, the English/language arts teacher, realized that they had never explicitly connected their two disciplines. The teachers wondered if there was some way for them to find a connection between their disciplines that would enhance their students' learning and extend some topic they were already studying in their curriculum. Each agreed to think about their own curriculum and the topics and major understandings that they covered. Then they agreed to meet again in two weeks to see whether they could find a way to coordinate mathematics and English/language arts.

TABLE 11.4 **Excerpt form the Principles and Standards for School Mathematics, Grades 6–8**

Standard 3: Geometry

In grades 6–8, the mathematics curriculum should include the study of geometry so that students can use visualization, spatial reasoning, and geometric modeling to solve problems. All students should:

- Draw geometric objects with specified properties, such as side lengths or angle measures.

- Use two-dimensional representations of three-dimensional objects to visualize and solve problems such as those involving surface area and volume.

- Use visual tools such as networks to represent and solve problems.

- Use geometric models to represent and explain numerical and algebraic relationships.

- Recognize and apply geometric ideas and relationships in areas outside the mathematics classroom, such as art, science, and everyday life.

The Teachers' Goals, Planning, and Scheduling

When the two teachers met a few weeks later, the English teacher shared with the mathematics teacher an idea that she had always hoped to carry out with her students when her class did a unit on historical fiction and letter writing that complemented the study of westward movement in their social studies course. She thought that the students would gain a great appreciation of the period if they created a group quilt. The English teacher explained how important quilts were in many stories, both fictional and real, about families moving West. She told the math teacher about *The Quilt Block History of Pioneer Days* (M. Cobb, 1995), a book that explains various American quilting patterns and how they were created and named for the events of the trip West and for the daily activities of frontier life. The English teacher also thought such a project would give her artistically talented students a chance to shine in a group venture.

The mathematics teacher said that she had not thought about a topic or project as concrete as the one the English teacher mentioned, but that she had done a great deal of thinking about an area in the current mathematics program that needed more emphasis. She pointed out to her colleague that students were not getting enough opportunities to apply the mathematics they were learning to real-life situations. She stated that she was trying to find more ways to have her students apply math beyond the classroom in order to comply with the Principles and Standards for School Mathematics (NCTM, 2000). As she listened to the English/language arts teacher talk about the idea for a quilt, she began to envision the possibility of connecting the geometry she taught with the literature unit focused on historical fiction portraying the western movement.

The two teachers thought that they were on to an exciting idea that had significant possibilities for coordination of their two disciplines. They decided to spend some additional time planning this coordinated venture, which they thought would complement the topics they would already be studying in the spring. In the English classes, they would be studying historical fiction with an emphasis on stories set in the westward expansion period, and in the eighth-grade mathematics classes they would be studying geometry. The two teachers believed that their coordination on a quilt project should come as a culminating project for the respective units they would carry out with their own classes.

The teachers realized that the next step was for them to figure out how they would orchestrate the creation of the quilt and they had to ensure they had the resources they and their students would need. They also wanted to be sure that this project would be more than an art project that was tacked on "for fun." In order to coordinate the quilt project successfully, each teacher decided to review the understandings, the materials, the lessons, and the student evaluation that made up their respective units in mathematics and the English/language arts.

In the next part of this chapter you will see the outline of the literature and geometry units that the students participated in before the two teachers introduced and implemented the coordinated component. Keep in mind that the goal of the quilt project is for the students to refine and extend their understandings and the experiences they had in the individual discipline-based units.

Middle School English/Language Arts Course: Historical Fiction and Letter Writing

Major Understandings

Students understand other people's perspectives through historical fiction focused on the 1880s in America; students learn how experiences shaped people's or characters' lives; they also learn to tell about themselves or a character and to describe unfamiliar settings and situations to a known audience using letters.

Resources

Fiction The teacher uses a collection of tall tales and selections from anthologies to meet the needs of students at various levels, plus four works of historical fiction appropriate for young adolescents (two with female protagonists and two with male protagonists): *My Daniel,* by Pam Conrad (1989); *Brothers of the Heart,* by Joan Blos (1985); *Sarah, Plain and Tall,* by Patricia MacLachlan (1985); and *A Stitch in Time,* by Ann Rinaldi (1994).

The availability of books on tape was important to the selection process, so that the struggling readers in the class could share the content of books appropriate for their age and grade level along with their peers.

Nonfiction The teacher reads aloud to the students "Going West" and "Settling Down" in *The Long Road West* (R. Freedman, 1983), to ensure that they all share background knowledge on the period. Then the students read books about quilts and on making quilts written for adolescents and young adults such as Raymond Bial's *With Needle and Thread: A Book About Quilts* (1996), Kime's *Quilts for Red Letter Days* (1996), and Ellen Howard's *The Log Cabin Quilt* (1996).

Individual Lessons

Initiating Lessons (Chapter 4)

- Students read tall tales that take place in the West to stimulate discussion and to tap their **prior knowledge** and impressions of the West.

- Students create a group **KWL chart** to show what they know and what they want to know about the early West and the westward movement, with a particular focus on the experiences that young people like themselves had.

- The teacher reads to the students and engages them in a **DLTA** using Freedman's *The Long Road West* to focus on problems young people faced traveling west and the comparisons of their lives as young people in the United States today. The teacher also acknowledges the experiences of emigrating today, which some of the students or their parents or relatives have recently experienced.

- The teacher does a **book overview** for each of the four trade books to help students select which book they want to read. The overview contains a discussion of the book cover, any illustrations in the book, and an excerpt chosen about each book to share with the group as a whole. The teacher allows students time to skim the books to make sure their choice is appropriate.

- The teacher creates an **anticipation guide** for each book to help the students set a purpose and to begin reading the book of their choice.

Developing Lessons (Chapters 5, 6, and 7)

- Students participate in **peer-led discussion groups**, making predictions and checking their inferences with a focus on using the anticipation guide that the teacher has created. The students add information to the KWL chart as they find answers to their questions and gain new information about the westward movement.

- Students create individual **character webs** to keep track of the protagonist's feelings, interactions with other characters, and experiences as the story unfolds. They share the information with other students in peer-led discussion groups.

- Students create **graphic organizers** (time lines, route maps, etc.) in order to keep track of details about the place or places where their characters go as they travel west; they share this information in peer-led discussion groups.

- Students keep a **vocabulary journal** of new words or words used in special ways pertaining to the West (e.g., *greenhorns, dugout, prairie schooner, mementos, sentries*).

- Students keep a list of types or forms of writing that the protagonist or other characters in the book use to communicate with others and themselves—for example, journals, diaries, letters, and newspapers.

Culminating Lessons (Chapter 8)

- Students as a class **revisit the KWL chart** they created on the western movement and see what new information they want to add, what they want to change, and what new questions they have.

- Students **compare** the experiences of young people going west across the texts they have read.

- Each student writes a **fictional letter** from the perspective of an individual in the book to someone at home; it includes facts and understandings from the history of the period woven into the information from the book they read and about its setting.

- Students have a **conference** about their letter with a partner using a checklist the teacher developed to guide their revisions in this assignment.

- Each student chooses an event, an episode, or a chapter in the book he or she is reading to do an **oral retelling** to the teacher.

Evaluation of Students

- Students participate in **peer-led discussion groups** (see Figure 11.1).

- Students carry out **peer evaluation** of one another's letters from the character's viewpoint using a written checklist with questions, **praise**, problems, and proposals for the author.

- Students develop and use individual **vocabulary journals**.

- Students create and use graphic organizers such as a semantic map or the character web to check their comprehension and to prepare for writing a fictionalized letter.

- Students **create a letter** written by a character in the book describing a new or unfamiliar setting to a known audience (someone back home).

- Students prepare for and do a **retelling** of a favorite event, episode, or chapter in the book they read that the teacher listens to.

Making Additional Connections Within and Among the Disciplines

English/Language Arts

- Students create a month-long journal written by a young person during a trip west in the 1800s basing it on a book they have read in literature and the information they have about what happened from social studies.

- Students create the front page of a newspaper printed during the 1840s or 1850s, including weather, ads, a main story using the events that occurred in the book they read, and even an advice column for people in the East who are considering the trip west.

FIGURE 11.1 Excerpt from the Form for Student Self-Evaluation in Discussion Groups

	Yes	No	Sometimes
2. Do you state clearly your views about a problem or issue?	X	—	—
3. Do you know how to find the facts?	X	—	—
8. Do you respect the opinions of others?	—	—	X
9. Do you monopolize the discussion or take your turn?	—	—	—
14. Do you change your mind if you find your position is weak or wrong?	—	—	—
15. Are you willing to become informed about alternative positions?	—	—	—

Social Studies

- Students use the computer simulation "Oregon Trail" to problem-solve and to learn more about this time in history. There is a multifaceted web site devoted to the Oregon Trail (**www.isu.edu/trinmich/oregontrail.html/**), and a site that allows them to follow the journey of a group of middle schoolers (**monhome-sw2.k12.wy.us/ot/trail.html**).

- Students view and discuss such videos as *The Donner Party*, one of the specials in the WGBH American Experience Series (Burns, 1997).

- Students learn more about the Native Americans in this part of the country and the experiences they had as the settlers moved West, with a focus on nations, customs, famous leaders, and a better understanding of the Indian experience from the Native American perspective.

- Students learn more about the history and geography of the fifteen states that were settled during this period.

- Students learn about the various ethnic, racial, and religious groups who settled this region. They learn where they came from and why they left their homes.

Mathematics

- Students apply principles of measurement and cost in a simulation of a visit to the general store on the frontier, or in the preparation of the wagon and supplies for the trip west.

Science/Geography

- Students learn about weather occurrences that are more prevalent in the West, such as droughts, dust storms, and tornadoes.

- Students learn about the deserts of the United States (Death Valley) that many of the settlers faced for the first time and compare these deserts to those in other regions of the world.

Middle School Mathematics Course: Geometry

Major Understandings

Students demonstrate that they can reason and problem-solve using various strategies and selecting appropriate computational techniques (e.g., graph paper, dot paper, computers), and students demonstrate that they can communicate their math understandings in written and oral forms.

 Students also understand and apply basic and advanced properties of the concepts of geometry with an emphasis on their combining, subdividing, and changing basic shapes; visualizing geometric shapes in various rotations; and solving real-world problems involving the area of geometric figures.

Resources

Teacher Sources The major teacher resources are the Standards Document of the National Council of Teachers of Mathematics (2000) and the teachers' individual state standards and curriculum documents.

Teacher and Student Sources *Passports to Mathematics, Book 2* (R. E. Larson, L. Boswell, & L. Stiff, 1997), a text designed for middle school students that emphasizes the review and extension of mathematics learned in the elementary grades and new understandings and applications in geometry and algebra.

Individual Lessons

Initiating Lessons

- Students review the names and properties of geometric shapes and participate in a **freewriting** activity in which they respond to this question: "What shape do you think is used most often in society, and why?"

- Students **review the meaning** and use of mathematical concepts and terms: parallelism, perpendicularity, congruence, and similarity. They do some sample applications with various geometric figures and respond to and explain their answers to a set of true-or-false statements, for example, "A square is the only quadrilateral with four congruent sides."

Developing Lessons

- Students **investigate** the idea of area using tangrams of seven common geometric figures (e.g., square, rectangle, parallelogram) and manipulate these figures to understand how these shapes compare to and fit with one another. Students also learn how to compute the area of a parallelogram.

- Students **explore** the idea of similarity and congruence using squares, rectangles, triangles, and parallelograms. They look for real-world examples of similarity and congruence between such things as baseballs and softballs, a photo and its enlargement.

Culminating Lessons

- Students apply their mathematical understandings and organize their ideas to **compare** the area of a single shape and how different shapes fit into a larger surface (e.g., to see how the area of two triangles and a rectangle within a parallelogram compares to the area of the parallelogram).

- In order to apply their knowledge to new situations, students **create** an object for which they have to do calculations and measure fabric or paper in certain shapes (e.g., a kite made up of triangles or a quilt made up of squares).

- Students use their understanding of the principles of geometry and the language of mathematics to **interpret** directions and to carry out word problems.

Evaluation of Students

- Students demonstrate their knowledge of mathematical terms and concepts in a **prewriting** activity.

- Students demonstrate their knowledge of technical vocabulary used in geometry in **discussions**, and when they **explain procedures** during the application activities.

- Students demonstrate their knowledge and understanding in application activities, such as comparing areas and shapes, or creating a kite, a quilt, or other product.

Making Additional Connections Within and Among the Disciplines
Social Studies/Geography

- Students look at the states that were in the original thirteen colonies, and determine their area individually and collectively compared to the United States today.

- Students look at the states that were settled during the westward movement, such as Oregon, Nevada, and Montana, and see how many are in the shapes of parallelograms.

- Students determine the area of these states and draw some conclusions about why, when these territories went for statehood, they had particular boundaries and shapes.

- Students look at a map of their own state and see if they can determine its area as well as that of the county they live in.

Fine Arts

- Students look for and use various geometric shapes within any visuals they create, such as drawings, paintings, sculpture, or models they create at home related to a hobby or a project in school.

- Students create models of real-world objects linked to their studies in science, social studies, and literature.

- Students look at the use of geometric shapes in the architecture found in their community and in fabrics used in clothing.

How the Teachers Carried Out the Coordination of Their Disciplines

Because the two teachers who carried out this unit were part of the team that taught these same students, planning time for the teachers and scheduling of students was already built into the existing structure. In addition, the schedule these teachers and their students had for the spring placed math and English/language arts back to back twice a week. This scheduling arrangement enabled the teachers to allocate some double periods to the quilt project. These longer blocks of time made the project seem more manageable since each student would be designing and then constructing a block for the quilt as well as looking at resources on quilting and conferring with other students and the teachers. An additional advantage of such a coordinated unit is that students had two teachers to answer their questions and to help them design and make their own blocks for the quilt. Because of other units and themes planned for the latter part of the semester, these teachers had only three weeks in which to carry out this coordinated component of their unit.

DIVERSITY   The teachers began the coordinated component of the unit by reading a selection from M. Cobb's *The Quilt Block History of Pioneer Days* (1995) to all of their students. Because of the diversity of the students, especially those with learning disabilities within their classes, the teachers guided their students' listening with a DL-TA. The selection focuses on friendship quilts, which were very popular during the mid-nineteenth century. These quilts were made up of individual blocks stitched and autographed by each family member or friend who worked on the project. Students learned about how friendship quilts were traditionally given to a family at a going-away party in their honor before they left for the West. After the teacher read the selection, the entire class looked at some photographs and samples of quilts. The two teachers found a number of resources on quilting because of the revival of quilting in the United States today. They found books to inform them as adults about this topic, as well as a number of books of fiction (A *Stitch in Time,* by A. Rinaldi, 1994, and *Sweet Clara and the Freedom Quilt,* by D. Hopkinson, 1993) and nonfiction (*With Needle and Thread: A Book About Quilts,* by R. Bial, 1996, and *Quilts for Red Letter Days,* by J. Kime, 1996) about quilts written with a middle school audience in mind.

After the introductory read-aloud activity, each teacher asked the students to make some predictions about why they were learning about quilts at this point in the curriculum. The teacher asked the students to think about whether they saw any connections between quilts and their recent study of quadrilaterals in their mathematics course. Students were also asked this question to see if they could identify any connections between quilts and their study of the western movement through literature. Many of the students made the connection between geometric shapes and quilts once they saw some of the photographs and samples that their teachers had assembled. Some students in the class who had seen a quilt at home or in a museum were able to make a connection between quilts and geometry from their own firsthand experiences. Students who had read books in the *Little House* series or *A Stitch in Time* were able to make some connections between quilts and the westward movement in the United States during the mid-nineteenth century.

The teacher then told the students that they would all participate in making a class quilt to connect their understandings about the westward movement from social studies and literature and their knowledge of geometry. In order to apply their mathematical knowledge about squares and measurement, the students had to figure out how large a block each of them would have to make in order to create a quilt that could serve as a wall hanging for display in the school foyer. Students started by measuring the wall in the school where the quilt would be hung. Then they figured out mathematically, given the number of students in the class, how many blocks of what size they needed to fill the space. They determined that each student could create an eight-inch square for the project.

In order to work on their quilt blocks, the students had to use their literacy skills and strategies throughout the coordinated unit. They had to read and interpret the directions that their teacher provided them about how to design and put together their quilt block. The teachers gave the students a number of choices related to the design of their block and to its construction. Each student was then required to come up with a design for the block that would clearly show something he or she found to be particularly interesting about the westward movement. The teachers suggested that each student design a block that showed a map and the trail that a particular group followed, some memorable scene in the nonfiction or fiction sources they had read, or an adaptation of a quilt pattern like the "broken plate," which told a story about frontier life. Before settling on their final design, the students engaged in using the various resources the teachers had collected, as well as studying some slides provided by the National Quilt Museum and information they found on the Internet about quilts (**www.antiquequilts.com**). Students also took on other math challenges in creating their block. Some students created a block using one of the quilt patterns that pioneers widely used during the 1800s. Many of these patterns the students chose were made up of quadrilaterals they had recently studied in geometry. Patterns like the multiple rectangles in the log cabin pattern and in the rail fence pattern were just two examples of what the students chose to create. Once the students designed their own block for the quilt, they had to figure out the size and shapes of the pieces they needed to fit their design into their own eight-inch block.

Finally, the students were given the option of sewing, gluing, or using an iron-on material, called Wonder Under, to put the pieces together on their individual block. They had to follow directions for the method they chose.

Students had many opportunities to practice their literacy competencies as writers and as speakers in additional activities throughout this coordinated project. All students prepared a brief oral presentation to explain to classmates why they had created their block as they did. To explain the block as a personal statement, all students had to reflect back to what they had learned about the westward movement, what classmates knew, and what new information they had learned from the sources the teachers read and the ones they had read in small groups.

During work time, the teacher encouraged the students to share their rationale for their design and to compare ideas. The students had discussions about how they would arrange their individual blocks to compose the class quilt. As the students shared their ideas, they realized that many of them had been influenced by the hardships that the pioneers experienced and how these experiences contrasted to their own lives in the twentieth century. Finally, in addition to the language arts—related skills and strategies that were enhanced by this project, the students' ability to carry on discussions using the language of mathematics was also enhanced as they talked about the design, size, and color choices they made for their blocks.

Once the group put the quilt together, they came back together once more for a discussion centered on the experience they had as a community in creating something tangible for their school. The teachers focused the discussion on the sense of community that grew as the students worked together. They asked the students if they had any new ideas about the role that quilts played in pioneer life. The teachers also introduced the students to some of the other types of quilts that were important in the history of the United States, such as the brightly colored quilts of the Amish and the story quilts of African Americans. The discussion concluded with the teachers asking the students if they knew of any current projects where people have contributed to a quilt to form a special kind of community. Some students had heard about the AIDS Memorial Quilt, which traveled around the country and was displayed in National Mall in Washington, D.C., for the last time in 1996. Some of the students in this class, which was in the Midwest, knew about the Scrap of Pride Quilt that citizens in northeastern Ohio crafted to commemorate Cleveland's bicentennial, and to demonstrate the diversity of their region's population. Finally, the teachers pointed out that with the enormous current interest in family histories, quilts are considered important artifacts and heirlooms. Some students volunteered that they had quilts from their own family that linked generations past with those in the present and would link their own present with the future.

Your Role as a Curriculum Developer

As a new teacher, or even an experienced teacher, you may be required to use curriculum that other members of your team or other teachers in your department developed. You may also be required to use curriculum that was developed by a districtwide committee, or in some cases, to implement curriculum that has been developed by the state in which you work. Perhaps you will have an opportunity to implement a unit you designed during your teacher preparation program because it is a good match with your learners' needs, as well as with the school or the district's curriculum. We hope that you will look for opportunities to coordinate your content area with others in the school in the same manner in which two teachers did in the sample coordinated middle school unit discussed earlier in this chapter. You can make connections between your own discipline and other disciplines in order to enhance your students' learning, as well as to benefit you as a teacher and as an individual who is always learning from your teaching.

However, as you probably already have learned, the best written plan is simply a road map for action. It is the actual doing of a lesson or a unit that informs you, as the teacher working with real students, how to shape what is on paper to address the needs of your own students. The true challenge of teaching is to ask, "How will I bring worthwhile content and major understandings to all of my students and how will I help them connect those understandings to the real world?"

SUMMARY

In this chapter, which focused on the individual disciplines most prevalent in our secondary schools today, we showed you how theory and practice related to understanding your content, knowing your learners, and being knowledgeable about literacy strategies can come together in coherent single discipline-based, or coordinated units at the middle school or high school level. We have emphasized the common concerns among the disciplines which are centered on how teachers, regardless of their subject matter, help their students:

- **Realize major content understandings.**
- **Become strategic learners.**
- **Experience coherence within the discipline.**
- **Recognize connections between what they are learning in one discipline to other disciplines and to the real world.**

In addition to looking at common concerns, we have explored some of the individual concerns and areas of debate within each of the core disciplines—science, mathematics, English/language arts, and social studies—that prevail at both the middle school and high school levels. We have also emphasized specific prereading, during reading, and after reading strategies, which we also described at length in Part Two, that are useful for students to deal with the literacy challenges found in each discipline. And, finally, we have explored the manner in which coordinated curriculum among the disciplines enhances teaching and learning in the middle school and high school, some of the particular benefits or coordinated curriculum efforts for teachers and students, and the need for careful planning and scheduling that coordinated curriculum efforts depend upon.

In order to assist you in thinking about how to develop curriculum in your own discipline that emphasizes major understanding in the field and lessons that focus on helping students become strategic learners and capable literacy learners, we have provided both a high school science single discipline unit and a coordinated mathematics/English/language arts middle school unit. We believe that both the single discipline and the coordinated sample units in this chapter should help you design meaningful learning opportunities for your own students.

Inquiry into Your Learning

1. Refer back to Chapters 4 through 8. Review your own understandings of the literacy strategies we focused on in Part Two of this text. Look specifically at the graphic organizers at the beginning of each chapter to assist you in your review. Jot down strategies that you use regularly in your discipline. In addition, jot down particular strategies used before, during, and after reading that you have not tried yet which might be helpful to you in the future. Think about which strategies you will need to master so that you can model and explain them to your own students when they are engaged in a topic and need to use a variety of resources to study it.

2. In Part One of this text and again in Chapter 10 and in this chapter, we emphasize that good teaching and learning experiences are created when the needs of the learner, the instructional goals, and the context mesh. Teachers are not unlike their students in that they teach well what they are interested in and confident about. Think about your own discipline and something you would enjoy learning more about. For example, when the middle school English/language arts and mathematics teachers decided to do the quilt project, the literature teacher used this opportunity to build on her own long-term fascination with quilts and to investigate her interest.

   Reflecting on one of your own interests, think about a way in which it could complement or connect with a topic in your discipline. Once you have decided on a topic, find at least three print resources (fiction and nonfiction) that would be appropriate for your students. See if you can identify some artifacts or simulations that would give your students a hands-on experience that would complement the topic. Finally, identify an Internet source where you can exchange ideas with other teachers interested in the same topic, or find an Internet source that would be appropriate for your students to use.

Inquiry into Your Students' Learning

1. Think of a topic or theme that your students have recently been engaged in within your discipline that has many real-world connections (e.g., the current and projected long-term effects of pollution or of global warming). See if the students can generate some connections or applications of the discipline on their own. Then have your students go into their communities to look for more real-world applications of these topics and understandings. Students could gather data from observations of events in their community and through interviews of people in various roles and professions. They could read their local newspaper or listen to the news on television. Finally, you could have your students survey a variety of settings represented in their communities, such as libraries and other cultural institutions, businesses, and government and service agencies to find possible connections and applications of the science, mathematics, social studies, and English/language arts they are learning in school.

2. Interview one student who does well in your content area and one who does not do well. Ask each student a series of questions about his or her experiences as a learner in the discipline. These questions to the two students, and the analysis of their answers, should help you gain some insights about the things you might consider when you are a teacher and planning curriculum for a variety of learners.

You might ask the students what they find difficult and what they find easy in the discipline; you might also ask them to think of what they have found interesting about the content and what was confusing. Ask the students about the sorts of resources they have used; find out which were required in the course and whether there were any resources that they used on their own. Ask them about the kinds of written assignments they have had in their course, and whether they have had to prepare anything for speaking or discussion. You might also want to know about the grouping arrangements they have participated in—cooperative groups, partner work, whole class—and which ones they found most beneficial. Finally, you should ask the students what strategies they use and what sources they find most useful as a learner—books and other print material, audiovisuals, or manipulatives.

This type of information is necessary to collect if you are to know your students better so that you can make conscious choices about the teaching and learning activities that will predominate in your own classroom. This information will also help you design curriculum, whether it be single discipline, coordinated, or integrated, the topic of Chapter 12.

Resources

Books

George, P. S., & Alexander, W. M. (2003). *The exemplary middle school* (3rd ed.). Belmont, CA: Wadsworth. Focuses on the nature of the middle school-aged student, the role of the middle school teacher as adviser, teacher, and team member, and the curricular and organizational parameters necessary for effective middle school education.

Levstik, L. S., & Barton, K. C. (2001). *Doing history: Investigating with children in elementary and middle schools* (2nd ed.). Mahwah, NJ: Lawrence Erlbaum Associates. Designed to help teachers view the study of history from a sociocultural and multicultural context and to build curriculum that fosters in-depth historical thinking using family and personal histories, literature (fiction and nonfiction), and history museums and artifacts in addition to text books.

Stone, R. (2002). *Best practices for high school classrooms: What award-winning teachers do.* Thousand Oaks, CA: Corwin Press, Inc. Provides lesson unit ideas from single discipline educators, with standards discussed for each lesson. Several chapters also address effective ways of incorporating technology into the classroom.

Journals

Barton, M. L., Heidema, C., & Jordan, D. (2002). Teaching reading in mathematics and science. *Educational Leadership, 60* (3), 24–28. Discusses the challenges faced by students when reading a high school math or science text and offers suggestions for teachers to help students interpret the texts. These include activating prior knowledge, identifying ways to approach new vocabulary, and teaching students to recognize the meaning behind different text styles.

Davis, S., & Thompson, D. R. (1998). To encourage "Algebra for All," start an algebra network. *Mathematics Teacher, 91* (4), 282–286. Describes a professional development project for a school district set up so that K–12 teachers could dialogue about weaving algebra principles into the curriculum at all levels.

Science Teacher (September 1998). Entire issue devoted to how the implementation and outcomes of the science standards can be assessed as well as how these are best linked to mathematics and technology and to the teacher's own professional development.

Traill, D. (with the assistance of Harvey, D.). (1998). Team-teaching AP history and English. *Social Education, 62* (2), 77–79. Discusses planning for instruction and gives the coordinated schedule of history themes and English readings.

Web Sites

Eisenhower Clearinghouse. **www.enc.org.** Comprehensive web site focused on math and science for grades K–12. Includes a detailed resource finder that can be accessed by grade level and topic, a monthly update of the twelve most outstanding site and projects, plus current information on the standards, the curriculum frameworks, and recent national and international studies and reports.

Middle Web. **www.middleweb.com**. Focuses on reform in the middle school with relevant news stories, curriculum guides, and tools for teachers that address standards, classroom management, and other issues. The site also highlights high-performing individuals and schools and provides links to other exemplary sites for a wide range of topics.

North Carolina Department of Public Instruction. **www.ncpublicschools.org/curriculum**. Describes the standard curriculum for each content area, with a particularly strong section on social studies. Also provides complementary resources and publications for each content area.

Web English Teacher. **www.webenglishteacher.com.** Provides K–12 English and language arts teaching resources, including lesson plans, videos, biographies, electronic texts, classroom activities, and links to other appropriate web sites.

CHAPTER 12

Integrated Curriculum

KEY CONCEPTS

- **interdisciplinary perspective, p. 316**
- **integrated curriculum, p. 317**
- **theme/thematic study, p. 317**
- **brainstorming, p. 323**
- **webbing, p. 323**

PURPOSE-SETTING QUESTIONS

1 Can I create a working definition and rationale for integrated curriculum that works for me now and that I will be able to use in my career as a classroom teacher?

2 Do I understand what is meant by a thematic approach as it is used in this chapter, and can I find some current themes linked to my discipline using the sources suggested as well as current professional literature in my field and discussions with peers, classroom teachers, and my professors?

3 Do I understand the special importance of preplanning when designing integrated curriculum? How does the model of curriculum development suggested in this chapter compare with the curriculum models introduced in Chapter 11?

4 Do I understand how the types of authentic assessment introduced in Chapter 3 and interwoven throughout Part Three benefit both teachers and students as well as how I might implement some of these in my own discipline?

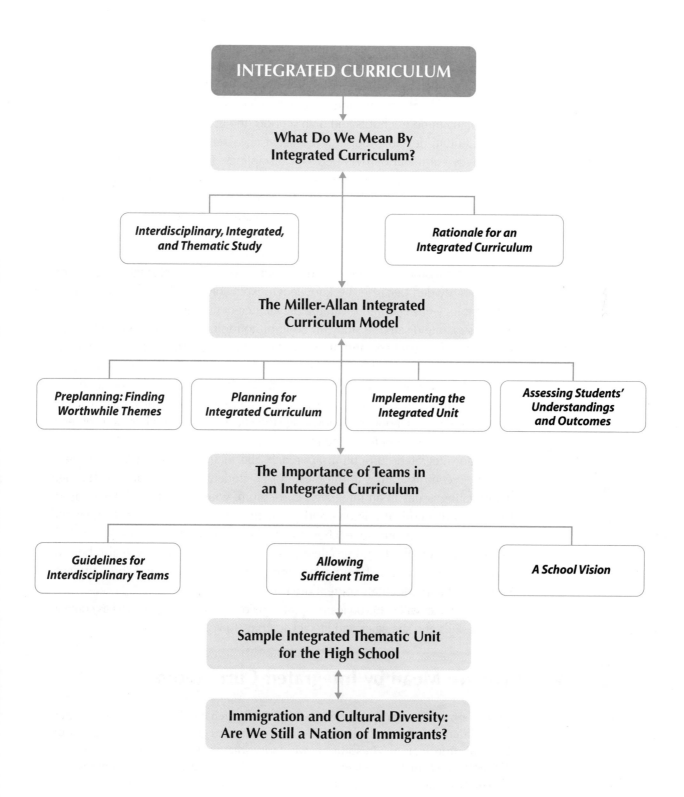

INTEGRATED CURRICULUM

What Do We Mean By
Integrated Curriculum?

Interdisciplinary, Integrated,
and Thematic Study

Rationale for an
Integrated Curriculum

The Miller-Allan Integrated
Curriculum Model

Preplanning: Finding
Worthwhile Themes

Planning for
Integrated Curriculum

Implementing the
Integrated Unit

Assessing Students'
Understandings
and Outcomes

The Importance of Teams in
an Integrated Curriculum

Guidelines for
Interdisciplinary Teams

Allowing
Sufficient Time

A School Vision

Sample Integrated Thematic Unit
for the High School

Immigration and Cultural Diversity:
Are We Still a Nation of Immigrants?

In this chapter, we shift our emphasis from studying discrete discipline-based content and processes to the interrelatedness of the subject areas and a more holistic approach to curriculum design and planning. We look at the issue-based or problem-solving process and content that ignores rigid discipline boundaries.

In many middle schools and high schools, the usual procedures teachers use for curriculum development and the usual class scheduling patterns appear to have placed artificial barriers between disciplines. Barriers even exist between subject matter in related disciplines, such as history and civics or biology and botany. Yet in the real world, experts don't work on issues alone and in discrete forty-five-minute segments. For example, chemists, physicians, social workers, and political activists work together, each lending expertise, to find answers and solutions to the spread and the treatment of AIDS.

In the classroom, teachers' and students' lives are increasingly fragmented and overcrowded because the knowledge explosion and the expanded impact of technology have collided with the prevalence of numerous stand-alone courses and separate discipline study. In addition to too much content in each of the disciplines for teachers and their students to cover adequately, large-scale national assessments like the National Assessment of Educational Progress (2000) show that few middle and secondary school students demonstrate creative or critical thinking skills. Furthermore, there are indications that most students tested cannot apply the knowledge they have gained in school to problems and issues they encounter in the real world.

In an integrated curriculum approach, the focus is on enhancing connections between disciplines and topics and on students' active learning. Through investigating issues in an integrated curriculum, your students will have opportunities to use critical thinking and problem solving. We think that integrated curriculum can encourage teachers to collaborate with other teachers and challenge students to think and problem-solve in an active manner. We also believe that collaboration and shared experiences among teachers and their students can extend and enrich all content-area study.

This chapter will help you learn to foster major understandings as well as content-specific skills and strategies and literacy learning in your discipline.

What Do We Mean by Integrated Curriculum?

In this section we clarify what we mean by integrated curriculum and explain how it is different from single discipline and coordinated curriculum. (Table 12.1 outlines this information.) In addition, we clarify what we mean by the terms *interdisciplinary*, *integrated*, and *thematic*, which are often confused with one another. We also discuss our rationale for including integrated curriculum as an approach in this

TABLE 12.1 **Three Curriculum Design Options**

	Single Subject Departmentalized	Coordinated/Parallel Disciplines	Integrated
Disciplines	Separate disciplines	Teachers in two or more complementary disciplines confer	Teams of teachers from different disciplines work together
	Units have discipline-based objectives		Disciplines serve the problem, issue, theme
Planning	Independent planning and teaching	Together teachers plan to link objectives and activities in own discipline to occur at similar times with that of other disciplines	Teams of teachers collaborate to plan and implement one curriculum
Time schedule	Activities planned for regular class periods	Units taught at the same time of year Little or no change in class time; regular class schedule for each discipline	May remain in usual class periods or combined in blocks for students and teachers May be scheduled for different lengths of time (week, semester, year)
Connections	Often no deliberate attempt to show relationships among disciplines or to connect with other teachers	Two units or topics have complimentary content that connects them Teachers identify related content in their disciplines; however, the connection not always made explicit for students	Focus on problems and issues Disciplines used to solve, to investigate, to provide information

Source: P. S. George, and W. M. Alexander, *The Exemplary Middle School* (3rd ed.) (Belmont, CA: Thomson/Wadsworth 2003), and H. H. Jacobs (ed.), *Interdisciplinary curriculum: Design and implementation.* (Alexandria, VA.: Association for Supervision and Curriculum Development 1989).

part of the text focused on curriculum development and the use of literacy strategies across the disciplines.

■ Interdisciplinary, Integrated, and Thematic Study

As you begin to refine your study about curriculum development in your discipline, you may be confused about the differences among the terms *interdisciplinary*, *integrated*, and *thematic study*. These terms are often used interchangeably because all three refer to cross-discipline study. Acknowledging that no single definition or model for integrated curriculum exists, we will explain working definitions for each of these three important terms that we use throughout this chapter.

Interdisciplinary Perspective

interdisciplinary
perspective Focus
on identifying the
relationship between
disciplines and how
perspectives from
different disciplines
contribute to the
understanding of a
particular topic or issue.

Let us begin with the broadest term, *interdisciplinary perspective* (also referred to as *multidisciplinary* and *transdisciplinary*). Teachers using such a perspective make deliberate attempts to identify the relationship between disciplines and to demonstrate how perspectives from different disciplines contribute to the understanding of a particular topic or issue. When you use an interdisciplinary perspective to shape your curriculum, your students will see how disciplines can work in concert with one another. When we talk about designing curriculum from an interdisciplinary perspective, we identify it as *integrated curriculum*. Integrated curriculum is the heart of this chapter. You will read about integrated curriculum in detail in the next section and will see how to use an interdisciplinary perspective to shape a unit that is built on key content understandings and incorporates appropriate literacy strategies. Before we explain how integrated curriculum is a manifestation of an interdisciplinary perspective, we want to point out that an interdisciplinary perspective can be accomplished within the single subject or coordinated curriculum.

You could accomplish this interdisciplinary perspective in a modified manner as a single subject teacher by bringing in examples from different disciplines or by having your students extend their understandings of a topic they are studying in your discipline by looking at how other disciplines or sources deal with the same topic (our single discipline model in Chapter 11). Furthermore, if you are coordinating the work in your discipline with that of another subject-area teacher, each of you could look at the topic or theme from your own discipline's vantage point and then you could have students see how the information in the two disciplines complements one another. Students could compare and contrast what they learn about the topic from each discipline.

For example, if you were a biology teacher whose class was studying the respiratory system, you might link this topic to a real-world concern, such as the effects of smoking or second-hand smoke on the respiratory system. You might also have your students explore what is being said and written about the benefits of a smoke-free environment. This area of study in science could be coordinated with the social studies teacher's current emphasis on government and the role that lobbyists play in their interactions with legislators. In this manner, students could study recent efforts related to smoking and efforts for and against a smoke-free environment from the vantage point of two separate yet coordinated disciplines.

Before you and the other teachers you are working with engage in time-consuming integrated curriculum planning, you should determine whether exploring interconnections among the particular disciplines will lead to greater insights by your students, and whether knowledge of one content area will actually complement the students' understandings or concepts in another area. All too often curriculum that has been labeled as interdisciplinary has evolved into artificial attempts to connect discipline areas and courses that are present in the existing curriculum. Therefore, when you design your own curriculum, you want to be certain you are emphasizing important understandings and strategies related to the disciplines and that you are not focusing on trivial content or superficially stretched ideas that are not worthy of your own or your students' time and energy.

Integrated Curriculum

integrated curriculum
Study that focuses on issues, problems, or themes.

We use *integrated curriculum* to designate study that focuses on issues, problems, and themes rather than on specific content within preselected curriculum areas or disciplines. The departmentalized structure predominant in secondary schools today gives students a false notion that information is organized into discrete subject areas with very little, if any, connection. When we design integrated curriculum, the emphasis is on helping our students make sense of their world, not on simply studying science or literature or art. When the focus is on issues, themes, and problems rather than on the traditional disciplines or subject areas found in most middle schools and high schools, the expectation is that students will use the concepts and their understandings from the disciplines as tools to learn about and to understand their world.

Too often integrated curriculum is associated with any curriculum approach that moves beyond strictly separate subjects. But truly integrated curriculum is not about doing the same things somewhat differently, such as rearranging the usual course schedule or modifying subject-based tasks or using different methods of assessment. In its purest form, integrated curriculum is created when the entire schedule evolves around projects rather than subjects and when disciplines come into play as resources to be drawn from in the context of the theme and its related issues and activities (Beane, 1995a). The theme, problem, or issue chosen for study should always be the context and the motivation for using a particular discipline and its content, not merely the fact that it is one of the subjects that has to be covered in the curriculum.

We encourage you to incorporate an integrated curriculum unit into your teaching and to experience the benefits for both you and your students. Well-designed integrated curriculum enables you to do the following:

- Capture student interest through focusing on relevant and real topics.

- Surmount overcrowded curriculum because in a single unit you can merge perspectives and skills from several disciplines.

- Gain a new perspective on basic skills as you work to identify the strategies, skills, and content principles that have widespread applicability in both the classroom and in the real world.

- Collaborate with colleagues and find new ways of working in your school and your classroom (Willis, 1992; Drake, 1993).

Thematic Study

theme/thematic study
An emphasis on holistic learning that focuses on the exploration of ideas and issues; a means to achieve integrated curriculum.

We see *thematic study* as a particular means to achieve integrated curriculum, not as an end unto itself. The identification of a theme serves as a tool and an important first step toward integrated curriculum. With well-chosen thematic units, teachers and students have an opportunity to participate in holistic learning at its best (Meinbach, Rothlein, & Fredericks, 2000). Well-chosen themes can lead to the exploration of ideas, can help students pull ideas together, and can stimulate students to form their own interpretations and conclusions. In addition, well-chosen themes create natural connections between the disciplines, as well as between students' in-school and out-of-school lives.

theme
revolution - look up other
countries who
have had a
revolution,

Community theme

In order to create a thematic unit, you should keep in mind that the theme should challenge your learners, should interest you, and should promote powerful linkages among the disciplines. First, you might find interesting themes in existing curriculum or courses that are linked to the usual academics, such as the pioneer experience. With the pioneer experience as your theme, you and your students could focus on a comparison of the pioneer experience in the 1800s and today's pioneering explorations in outer space or in the depths of the ocean. Second, major themes, such as the solar system and space or culture and multiculturism, expressed through the strands in state curriculum frameworks and national standards documents are another rich source for themes that are linked to the existing academic requirements in the schools.

Third, we believe the most compelling source for themes remains the immediate community in which students live. Local concerns and issues like pollution and the effect on water quality or the effect of natural disasters like floods in California or hurricanes and tornadoes in Florida are compelling topics to explore and to use to shape curriculum. Controversial local topics are also good choices because students can investigate using authentic sources they can find in their own communities and that are related to the lives of people they know. Community issues, such as the damage caused by dumping toxic wastes into a previously clean and scenic river can pique your students' interest as well as provide a variety of topics to investigate and study and a natural way to bring the disciplines together in a meaningful way. By interviewing citizens as well as community leaders, your students will see the range of opinions about any controversial issue. An integrated unit shaped by a specific local issue has the advantage of providing immediate relevance and authenticity for both students and their community.

Fourth, in addition to local issues and community-centered issues, students and their teachers might find the themes they wish to explore in more universal problems, such as starvation and other population issues, wildlife protection and extinction issues, and global warming and pollution-related issues. Such issues or problems will have a widespread effect on the students' own lives, and as the adult generation of the next century they should be involved with the solutions for these problems. What better place to start with that problem-solving stance than in the integrated curriculum and authentic experiences with real-life issues in their middle or high school programs?

We also realize that sometimes these local issues touch a nerve. This is especially so when students start asking tough questions of lawmakers and officials in their own communities. We know of an example where a team of teachers and their students were trying to understand what was getting in the way of legislation to support the building of a bicycle path in their community. During the process of their investigation into the issue, the students stumbled on some thorny local politics. The issue became so sensitive that the superintendent of schools asked the teachers not to include this topic in their curriculum in the future. Once you have identified an issue, you should probably discuss the topic with other teachers in your school and community as well as with your principal before you engage in planning and implementing an entire unit of study.

In conclusion, the positive value for teachers and students engaging in thematic study rests on all or some combination of the following outcomes (Fredericks, Rothlein, & Meinbach, 1992):

Possible Outcomes!

- Establishing a clear purpose for students' learning at the outset.

- Emphasizing relationships among areas that contribute to understanding a particular issue or question.

- Applying both content and strategies in meaningful contexts.

- Developing students' ownership as students answer their own questions and see value in their processes for solving problems.

- Enhancing students' learning as they probe, explore, and uncover the aspects of an intriguing issue, problem, or theme.

- Building cooperation between teachers and between teachers and students to create a community of learners.

■ Rationale for an Integrated Curriculum

When you are a teacher at the middle school or high school level, you will want to use integrated curriculum selectively. This model of curriculum development is not a new way to string your existing discipline-based lessons or units together or an approach that should replace the study of significant content or concepts that are central to understanding and applying your discipline. However, when you identify issues of significance or themes that have widespread appeal and durability, you can use them as the core experiences or building blocks for designing an integrated curriculum.

Think about how interesting it would be for you to study a topic or an issue closely related to your discipline in a new way. For example, as literacy teachers and writers, we are very interested in why issues about censorship keep emerging. We ask ourselves what new censorship issues will arise in the next century as we become a more technologically sophisticated society with fewer restrictions on modes of communication. We could examine the censorship issue from a single discipline perspective in language arts. However, we realize that information from other disciplines and different perspectives could help us and students understand this important issue. We could collaborate with social studies teachers who have studied civics and law, or look at censorship issues with email and the Internet by talking with technology experts to see what issues they may have encountered. We could learn about personal and professional real-life, day-to-day experiences that individuals in the community have had with censorship by talking with a librarian, a local newspaper editor, and even school administrators.

Finally, no matter what the form of integration you choose and no matter what portion of the total curriculum you devote to integration, you can ask some questions that will help you decide the merit of this experience for your students and for you and for colleagues. Before you engage in the detailed planning and implementation necessary for quality integrated curriculum, consider your responses to these questions (Jacobs, 1989):

1. How valid are the concepts being fostered within each designated discipline? Is the emphasis on concepts that are important and relevant?

2. How valid is this discipline as a means to explore this theme? Is this a legitimate topic through which to encourage students to use multiple lenses?

3. How important is the central idea? Will it promote flexible thinking and help the students accept multiple views or new ways to solve problems?

4. Will pursuit of this theme enable students to practice an approach to problem solving that will have far-reaching applicability?

The Miller-Allan Integrated Curriculum Model

If you and your colleagues decide to explore curriculum development using an integrated curriculum approach, we hope the impetus will come primarily from the needs and interests of your students and your own need to challenge yourself as an educator. Above all, we hope the interest in some compelling theme, issue, or problem that demands the attention and a team effort by you, your colleagues, and your students is the driving force behind the integrated curriculum you create. In this section we suggest a model for the development of integrated curriculum and some useful ways for you to identify themes that can shape such integrated curriculum. If you and your colleagues attempt to integrate the curriculum, you will have to balance its demands with the many other pulls that are part of your ongoing work as a teacher of a particular subject in a particular setting. However, we believe that well-designed integrated curriculum can help you consolidate some of the components of the already overcrowded curriculum, identify appropriate ways to assess your students, and create clearer links between national, state, and district curriculum frameworks and standards.

Integrated curriculum does not occur automatically; time and teamwork are both necessary. When you decide to explore and then to plan and implement integrated curriculum with other teachers in different disciplines, you and your colleagues may discover that you need training in curriculum design or in team teaching to achieve the goals and benefits you envision for yourselves and your students. Also, you will need support from the administration in order to change the usual scheduling of your teaching and planning time, as well as the instructional time for the students with whom you plan to carry out the unit. You may even decide to plan the unit during one semester and carry it out the following semester or the next year. Teams for designing and implementing integrated curriculum should have the following characteristics as baseline requirements if they are to succeed (Furner, 1995, p. 5):

- Two or more teachers are involved.

- All teachers share common planning time.

- All teachers share the same students.

- All teachers have skill in and are committed to collaboration, consensus building, and curriculum development.

Even when an appropriate theme is identified with clear objectives and purpose, other factors can inhibit the success of an integrated unit. First, if the project is too broad in scope and length or if it necessitates obtaining a large number of new or varied resources, there is a likelihood of failure. Second, if a study involves too many teachers, students, or outside participants, the chances for failure rise. And if administrative and collegial support are not part of the culture of the school, the chances for fully implementing and sustaining integrated curriculum are greatly reduced.

We recognize that there are an increasing number of models designed to help teachers who wish to engage in integrated curriculum planning (Meinbach, et. al., 2000; Cooper and Kiger, 2003). Our recent work with student teachers as well as with practitioners in the schools has led us to a model (set out in Figure 12.1) and a set of steps for the development of integrated curriculum that we will use as we examine integrated curriculum design in the remainder of this chapter.

■ Preplanning: Finding Worthwhile Themes

Thoughtful preplanning can enable you to identify the right theme for both you and your students to study. Recall the four sources for finding a worthwhile theme or question discussed earlier in this chapter: goals in the existing curriculum, strands from the national standards or state curriculum frameworks, local issues, and universal problems and concerns. Three specific approaches for finding and focusing on significant themes begin this section of the chapter. In addition, keep in mind that initiating activities can also help you and your students find and refine worthwhile themes and issues for study.

Martinello and Cook have identified three approaches that are particularly useful in helping you find significant themes or in turning compelling issues or topics into viable themes (Martinello & Cook, 1994). There is the *question-driven approach*, where you and your team could identify themes to be studied by asking, "Given this topic, how would individuals trained in different disciplines go about exploring it?" or "What big ideas are suggested by this topic?" A second approach, known as the *significance approach*, focuses on identifying themes that have the potential for long-term merit. In this situation you and your team could test a theme or question's significance by asking, "Will this theme help students expand their understanding of major issues in the real-world in which they live?" Third, in the *literature-as-source approach*, you can find universal and significant themes in good current young adult fiction and nonfiction by using resources such as *Using Literature in the Middle Grades: A Thematic Approach* (Moss, 1994) or *Books and Beyond: Thematic Approaches for Teaching in the High School* (Gregg & Carroll, 1998). For example, a universal theme is the question of how individual human beings have maintained their nobleness and morality in the face of evil and personal peril in times of tremendous political and societal upheaval. A nonfiction book such as Milton Meltzer's *Rescue: The Story of How Gentiles Saved the Jews in the Holocaust* (1988) or Lois Lowry's 1994 Caldecott winner *Number the Stars* lend themselves to the study of this long-standing universal problem.

Initiating activities such as the ones introduced in Chapter 4 can also help you and your students find and refine worthwhile themes and issues for study. Brainstorming and webbing are two strategies particularly well suited to the initial process of finding a problem or theme for study.

Using Prereading Strategies to Find a Theme

You remember we discussed prereading strategies and activities for your students in Chapter 4. You can use these same strategies to find a significant theme for your unit.

FIGURE 12.1 Miller-Allan Model for Developing Curriculum

1. Preplanning to Identify Theme/Focus
    a. Approaches and activities for finding a significant theme and focus of study
    b. Relation to core curriculum standards and local curriculum requirements

2. Planning
    a. Identifying what students might learn
        • Emphasis on constructing meaning—concepts and ideas
        • Strategies and skills to be learned, enhanced, and applied
    b. Selecting a wide range of resources
        • Print sources—fiction and nonfiction, magazines, primary sources, on-line sources
        • People sources—experts, community leaders, citizens in various roles and specializations
        • Community sources—museums, agencies, businesses
    c. Organizing for implementation
        • Designing teaching-learning events, activites, or lessons that may be initial, developmental, or culminating
        • Outlining a tentative schedule or time line
        • Organizing the setting—arranging the classroom learning space, modifying schedules for teachers and students
        • Seeking support within the school—teachers at other grade levels or in other disciplines; librarians; technology or media specialists; those in the arts; administrators

3. Implementing the Integrated Unit
    a. Activities for initiating the unit (whole class or small group)
    b. Activities for developing the unit (whole class and small groups)
    c. Activities for ending the unit (small groups, pairs, and individual learners)
    d. Formative evaluation guidelines

4. Assessing students understandings and the outcomes of the unit as a whole
    a. Self-evaluation by individual learners; small group evaluation
    b. Sharing with peers and appropriate audiences
    c. Evaluating the team effort and collaborations among students and teachers
    d. Summative evaluation guidelines

Brainstorming and webbing are two strategies particularly well suited to the initial process of finding a problem or theme for study.

brainstorming A learning technique or strategy that involves group discussion to explore a range of ideas or multiple solutions to a problem.

Brainstorming is a highly useful process for beginning to find themes in the pre-planning stage of integrated curriculum development. You and your colleagues can brainstorm many topics or issues arising from multiple sources. You will realize that some of the ideas that surface during your brainstorming will not lead to viable topics or issues for study, while others will appear to be quite viable and worthy of pursuit. The brainstorming process will give you some ideas, as well as questions and resources from which to begin the sorting and prioritizing necessary to shape a thematic study and integrated curriculum.

webbing The use of diagrams or maps to explore the relationships between ideas or concepts.

Additionally, a process like *webbing* is also useful in identifying a major topic and related topics and in determining a viable theme or key question to focus on. Once you have brainstormed interesting and relevant topics, you can select one or two of the most significant ones and categorize the ideas and concepts like the graphic organizer we presented on page 81 in Chapter 4.

➡ TEACHER AS INQUIRING LEARNER

Think about a recent issue or question that has arisen related to your discipline. In pairs or groups of four, talk with some of the other students in this course who are in the same field or discipline to see if they have a similar concern. Next, meet in small groups of three (with students from different disciplines), and talk about the issue or question that you all share. Focus particularly on how different perspectives or different lenses can be used to study an issue or problem. Record these possibilities along with key questions related to the issue that need to be answered. Be certain to discuss how each discipline could help with an exploration of this common issue or question.

■ Planning for Integrated Curriculum

In an integrated curriculum model, students can come to a better understanding of their environment, make decisions, test out assumptions, and develop ownership for the knowledge they are acquiring. Many students, particularly those beyond grade 8, are weak in critical thinking and problem-solving abilities (National Center for Education Statistics, 2000). You can encourage students to become active learners and problem solvers as well as critical thinkers by identifying specific concepts and ideas as well as strategies and skills, by selecting a wide range of resources, and by planning and organizing the schedule and design of lessons and activities that comprise the day-to-day enactment of that curriculum in your own classroom.

Using Strategies to Understand Content

You should provide experiences for your students that help them acquire the strategies they need to deal with current curricula as well as with future academic and real-world problems. For example, students can apply strategies used to solve problems involving size, quantity, or distance in mathematics to a variety of independent problems and projects beyond the mathematics class. And students who have learned to support an argument using either a letter to the editor or a letter of complaint to a town official as a focus of writing in the language arts will know how to use these strategies in the future when they are disturbed by political or environmental issues in their own community.

Many of the strategies we detailed in Part Two foster students' constructing knowledge as well as ownership and independence in their own learning. These strategies not only help your students be more aware of what they already know, but they also help the students confirm, extend, or refute ideas, concepts, and knowledge they have about the issue or theme under study. Before reading strategies such as brainstorming and anticipation guides (described in Chapter 4) help students tap into their background knowledge and the experiences they bring to the unit. At the prereading stage, you can also model strategies to help your students identify a range of resources, including artifacts and people (Martinello & Cook, 2000) that might help them study their issues and find answers to their questions. To aid students during reading, you can select strategies, such as DR-TA or text pattern guides found in Chapter 6, to support students in finding and interpreting important information found in texts as well as in various media and technological sources. Finally, to help your students reflect upon and interpret their knowledge, the focus of Chapters 7 and 8, you may choose to include summarizing or semantic feature analysis charts. Or you may decide to use the KWL variations described in Chapter 4 and extended in Chapter 8.

Selecting Resources and Gathering Materials to Implement the Study

Since your role as teacher is to act as a guide and facilitator in the initial stages of interdisciplinary theme studies, you may select resources that will assist the students with their study, such as an overview of the topic or ones that will highlight different positions or questions related to their issue or theme. You will need to choose enough sources to make the study feasible for the students at the beginning stages as well as to ensure that there are varied sources, especially related to the students' reading levels, available to them for their own investigations. A variety of objects and artifacts, audiovisuals, and print resources as well as technological support, particularly through the Internet, should be available to involve all of the students engaged in the study in meaningful interaction

TEACHER AS INQUIRING LEARNER

In pairs or groups of three or four individuals, discuss the resources that are widely used in your field that you think middle school or high school students should be exposed to and be encouraged to use in classroom and independent investigations—for example, computer simulations, sites on the Internet, references such as atlases or almanacs, or certain science instruments such as microscopes and barometers.

Make a list of some of the resources you use when pursuing work in your discipline or ones that are used in real-world applications of your discipline. Then think about which of these would be especially useful to your own future students. For example, when working with students while pursuing a topic like "Pollution Prevention," your list could include the science text the class is using, which has a chapter on environmental concerns, informational books from the library such as Earth Works Group's *50 Things You Can Do to Save the Earth* (1989), recent newspaper articles, and pamphlets and other documents obtained from the regional EPA center or the Department of the Interior.

and investigations. Keep in mind that the resources you find can influence or change the direction of the students' study as well as the direction of your entire unit.

Searching for resources takes a significant amount of time. Therefore, be certain to build this time into your planning, and enlist the help of the librarian or media specialist, technology expert, and other teachers on your team. Divide up tasks, such as finding resources, by topic or type of material. Reach out into the community to identify a variety of sources—texts, people, and community sources that are available and have relevance for the study. The planning stage is an important time to inform others in the school and the local community at large about the theme or issue that is under consideration.

In this role as facilitator or guide for your students' inquiry, there are some useful questions to consider regarding the resources needed to support the issue or theme (Martinello & Cook, 1994, p. 147):

- Where can I find the most appropriate resources for theme study?

- How do I prepare my students to understand the connection between the questions asked and the type of resources to be used?

- How can I involve my students with the resources so that they can select meaningful data from them?

- How will my students analyze the data they collect by examining these resources? What methods of recording data will they use? What new questions will emerge from the use of these data?

Teachers and students consider a variety of informational sources in order to answer their resource questions
© Susie Fitzhugh

We would add one more question:

- How do I know whether my students have the prereading, during reading, and after reading strategies or the discipline-based skills to use these resources on their own?

Organizing for Implementation

We recognize that to a large degree in elementary schools, teachers have a great deal of autonomy and make decisions about how to shape the day and to weave in disciplines, content, and strategies. At the other extreme, in most high schools, teachers have little to say about their own schedule or those of their students. Most often in the high school, the arrangement to accommodate the different disciplines and the numbers of students is a departmentalized structure, with teachers grouped together who teach in the same discipline area. The usual department structure tends to lead to rigidity and lack of integration among subject areas, as well as to barriers between teachers' and students' working together. The department structure also reinforces the notion that knowledge is compartmentalized by the separate disciplines. The goal to create integrated curriculum fosters cross-discipline mini-departments between and among teachers of different disciplines.

At the middle school level, however, we are finding increasing numbers of teams of teachers working together to create and implement comprehensive academic programs for specific groups of students at a single grade level. In fact, 86 percent of the "schools for excellence" designated by the U.S. Department of Education were made up of small teams of four to five different subject-area teachers working with the same students in the same building area and planning together what their students would study across disciplines.

No matter what the organization or scheduling decisions are in your school, they should be flexible enough to align with the curriculum priorities and the themes and topics being studied—those that are mandated and those that a particular group of teachers creates to serve the academic and future needs of a particular population of middle school or high school students. Scheduling arrangements should accommodate interconnections of the disciplines as well as coordination among teachers and their students.

When the administration supports teachers' scheduling days, weeks, and even semesters, creatively and flexibly to meet the needs of their students and to complement the subject matter, often the best teaching and learning ensues. Students and their teachers benefit from flexibility in the schedule because differences in learning needs cannot be met more effectively and different types of content and resources can be used. For example, when there is the possibility of longer time periods than the usual forty-five minutes per subject, accommodations can be made for large group instruction, lab experiments and computer simulations, small group work, and individualized or independent study opportunities for students.

■ Implementing the Integrated Unit

Teachers need to model and provide many opportunities for students to engage in their own learning (National Association of Secondary School Principals, *Breaking Ranks*, 1996). The activities you develop and the learning environments that you create for your

Think about the schedule you followed when you were a middle school (or junior high school) and high school student.

- Did the schedule make sense to you? Did you feel your schedule added continuity to your academic experience, or did it tend to reinforce the separation of the disciplines from one another and from your everyday life? Did you ever get confused by the schedule or have trouble fitting in both the requirements and choices you wanted, such as art or orchestra? Did you ever have a period longer than forty-five or fifty minutes for a given course? Did you ever participate in a class or a course that two teachers from different disciplines taught?

Now that you have reflected on your own experiences, think about what you have observed recently as a student teacher at the middle school or the high school level.

- Did you have any difficulty getting accustomed to the schedule of the classes you taught or getting to know who your students were, much less their abilities and their needs?

Talk with classmates in your same discipline and with classmates in other disciplines who are interested in teaching at the same grade level as you are to see what their experiences have been related to the scheduling of classes.

students should give them opportunities to think critically when they are presented with an issue or problem that they have to clarify or sort out. Your students should have a number of opportunities to compare and contrast information from different sources, as well as to find patterns and relationships. They should be helped to synthesize information when they try to brainstorm solutions to problems, when they make predictions and attempt to confirm these predictions, and when they create a model, a diagram, or a plan to explain something they have discovered or developed to others.

Throughout the implementation stage of a unit, you can provide choices for your students to help them gain confidence in their own decision-making ability and to experience alternate routes to solving problems. First, you should continuously model and support the strategies you want students to use. Second, if you want your students to develop problem-solving abilities and be able to apply both strategies and skills, you should provide opportunities for them to gather and analyze data on their own. And finally, you should foster opportunities for your students to share their findings with the community in the form of information and service. Encourage the community to regard the school as a place where problems and issues that affect everyone are being investigated and as a place where they can raise questions and issues to inform the curriculum.

Many of the strategies we explained in Part Two are useful in helping students deepen and extend their ownership of content and the concepts and ideas from different disciplines related to an issue being studied. These strategies also foster connections between students' current understandings of data and their implications for future situations in the real world.

■ Activities for Generating Ideas or Initiating the Unit

In any content area, when your students' background knowledge is activated, their learning is enhanced.

When planning your daily lessons in your integrated unit, you'll want to use generating activities such as brainstorming and webbing to introduce your unit and to create a common initiating activity for all students. Webs and other graphic organizers are particularly useful in integrated curriculum because they enable teachers and students to examine how different disciplines explore an issue or question. When individual students or small groups share their graphic organizers, differences of opinion and additional questions about a topic often surface. Such differences or contradictions related to a topic frequently come to be the basis for the investigations that students pursue during the interacting phase of the unit.

During the initiating phase of a unit, students should begin to use the resources you have collected during the preplanning stage. You may choose to adapt the tasks and materials to meet the individual needs of different learners in your class. You may decide to use tools such as the anticipation guides described in Chapter 4 to help your students use new texts or resources.

At this stage, you can also model previewing and predicting as strategies (Chapter 4) for your students to use with their texts. If you have introduced these strategies to your students earlier and your informal assessment during this phase shows that the students are not using them effectively, you should remind the students or review the procedures with the content at hand. You may also need to enlist the aid of resource staff members such as the reading specialist, a resource teacher for learning disabled students, or the English as a Second Language teacher to help the students complete activities and to use resources supporting the integrated curriculum unit.

Activities for Interacting with Ideas or Developing the Unit

While your students are grappling with new information they have found in the resources you provided, comparing this information to prior knowledge, and integrating new information with prior information, they are transforming their thinking on a subject and interacting with ideas. Overall the emphasis at this stage is on helping students find what is important related to the topic, issue, or theme they are studying, as well as how ideas and concepts connect.

Each student should be guided to look for the important big ideas in text they are reading, videos they are viewing, and technology they are interacting with. You should also encourage your students to find supporting details related to the major ideas from a number of sources at this stage. Do not overlook the value of a core text or set of readings for the entire class to use. DRAs, comprehension guides, and text pattern guides are particularly useful tools to assist students at this stage in their work.

As students find important information that is directly related to the questions, they might need the supporting strategies **of constructing auxiliary aids**, such as the note-taking graphics we introduced in Chapter 7. They may need to learn how to record data and how to organize various pieces of data from their own search. By introducing your students to different formats such as note taking, math notations, oral recordings, and graphic organizers, as well as schematic representations, you can continue to give them tools useful for demonstrating their thinking in classrooms as well as in the real world.

You will notice that there is much fluidity at this stage in the unit. Students are working with and interacting with various peer groups and alone. Strategic learners will continue the task with little or no guidance. You can support the nonstrategic learners with teaching tools that will introduce them to appropriate strategies. You and your colleagues who are working on an integrated unit will also find yourselves in a variety of roles as you model particular strategies for the entire class or a small group, confer with small groups who are engaged in discussions or working with certain resources, and helping individual students interact with the text and the content they are attempting to understand and to use on their own.

Activities for Ending the Unit

At this third stage, which is the focus of Chapter 8, you should ask strategic learners to view the theme or topic as a whole. For this reason, much of the work at this stage centers on opportunities to bring the entire group or class together. Students may review the thinking they did at the prereading stage of the unit. They can identify what similarities or contrasts among data have been uncovered by their classmates and what new information has been found. The most useful strategies at this stage are **categorizing ideas and summarizing**, which were described in detail in Chapter 8. Encourage students to reflect on the different ideas and views they have been exposed to in order to draw conclusions about the topic or issue. At this stage, you can instruct and help students add to the notes or outlines they have created in the interacting stage of the unit. Because the emphasis is on taking time to review, reflect on, and revisit information, you should plan for sufficient time for individuals, pairs, and small groups to refine and reconstruct the ideas they have developed during the earlier stages of the unit.

By writing drafts, summaries, and graphic organizers, students at this stage often refine their purpose or revise their thinking about a topic. As students summarize their findings in these ways, you will notice where there are missing pieces of information and where there are conflicting views or opinions. You should encourage your students to revisit text that they have previously studied and to seek additional sources that might answer their new questions or solve a dilemma that has arisen.

If the problem your students pursue is to have authentic implications, they must have opportunities to communicate their findings to others whom it affects. Therefore, you should encourage students to share the results of their investigations with others in their immediate setting, like the students at their own grade level or their entire high school population, others in the field or profession that deals with the issue or topic studied, or others in the broader community in which they live. They can do this in the form of pamphlets, how-tos, speeches, or panel presentations as well as letters to the editor of a local newspaper or articles for a school newspaper. Each of these communications provides a powerful culminating activity for your students, as well as a means for them to influence appropriate audiences, in school and in the larger community, in a real way.

■ Assessing Students' Understandings and Outcomes

Students who are working with integrated curriculum units should have many opportunities to engage in interactive and meaningful assessment authentically related to the issue they are studying. They should state and support their conclusions or opinions; critique something they have read, seen, or heard; or establish criteria for a situation or an event based on their firsthand experience.

During the planning stage of the unit, you and the other teachers you are working with can identify assessment tools and criteria for performance that correspond to the objectives of the unit. As you recognize the students' different learning needs and their use of different strategies, you should encourage the students to demonstrate their understandings through a variety of modalities—for example, interviews, observations, and a wide variety of written forms like journals, logs, outlines, and drafts. Students will also demonstrate their understandings of the theme, issue, or problem when using various project-related assessment tools like checklists and inventories, as well as through their creation of videotapes and audiotapes and their participation in the visual and performing arts.

Multifaceted Assessment and Integrated Curriculum

A multifaceted approach to assessment will enable each student to demonstrate understanding in appropriate and meaningful ways. You and the other teachers in the team can use the various formats your students develop, such as pamphlets and how-tos, letters to the editor and to town officials, and displays and models, to evaluate your students' individual and collective understandings of the theme or issue focused on in the integrated unit. Through authentic school- and community-based activities, students will be able to see the impact their investigations might have on their own lives and others they know. In addition to teacher evaluation and feedback, students need opportunities to engage in self-evaluation of their learning using the criteria or rubrics developed to go along with their projects.

Looking at students' work in progress (as seen in the teaching/assessing tools covered in Chapters 4 through 8), teachers and the students get a more complete picture of how effectively students are gaining new understandings and using their skills and competencies. In particular, students' work done individually or that done with a partner or small group provides many rich opportunities for both teachers and learners to assess understandings and progress. Students' individual works in progress, such as math calculations to solve a word problem, drafts of lab reports in science, story maps or learning logs to record impressions and understandings of a chapter book in literature shows their understanding during the development of the unit. Likewise, a student's participation in a group discussion, a lab experiment with a partner, or feedback during peer writing conferences provides valuable data to both the student and teacher.

Teachers can use data from ongoing assessment of their students to add to and to modify groupings they planned at the beginning of a unit. Teachers view individual students' work in progress and the day-to-day work of the class as the data for evaluating their students' learning as well as material for shaping and revising their own ongoing modeling and explaining and direct instruction. Anecdotal records and observations are very important tools for the teacher at this stage. For example, a teacher's collective observations of several pairs of students struggling as peer editors with an effective paragraph structure may lead the teacher to develop a mini-lesson focusing on the structure and purpose of introductory and concluding paragraphs in expository writing.

Another benefit of the assessment associated with integrated curriculum that benefits teachers and ultimately the students is the information that teachers share about how well the students as a group and individual students are grappling with the major concepts and content of the unit. In other words, teachers in one discipline may learn about a student's strategies (or lack of strategies) from their observations, interviews, and conferences with students in their discipline that will be useful to other teachers on the team as they organize groups or carry out instruction for the class as a whole or attempt to meet an individual student's needs. Often specialists such as the reading specialist, the English as a Second Language teacher, or the special needs teacher can offer insights and suggestions from their ongoing assessment of the students they work with to support learning by all students involved in the integrated unit.

Teachers involved in collaborative planning and implementation often create criteria that work across the disciplines and therefore align their assessment procedures and their evaluation of students. The development of criteria across disciplines helps teachers strengthen and clarify the overarching goals of the curriculum, the purpose of their teaching, and the measures of accountability for their students. For example, a team of high school teachers adopted a generic rubric for writing research papers across disciplines to be used in an integrated unit connecting English/language arts, history, and the arts. The teachers discussed what was necessary at the high school level to qualify as a quality research paper and provided the students with a generic rubric (shown in Table 12.2), which the students could continue to use and to refine throughout their high school experience.

The Role of Portfolios in Integrated Curriculum

The role that portfolios play in integrated curriculum highlights the relationship between authentic assessment and instruction and the emphasis on process learning within a realistic framework. Collectively, portfolios are a powerful source of data from which a teacher or team can assess the outcomes of their instruction and the activities in their content-area classroom, as well as the development and implementation of the unit as a whole.

Portfolios may differ in purpose, in format, and in use. They may be as individual as the students who create them. Regardless of whether the portfolio is the *collection type*, with many works in progress as well as finished products, or a *showcase portfolio*, with carefully selected works meant to represent the student's best work for a unit, a semester, or an entire academic year, it may be constructed for a single discipline or across disciplines.

Lastly, no matter what the precise format or purpose, portfolios that accompany integrated curriculum as well as single or coordinated discipline work that make up any given student's school experience should meet clear guidelines that are articulated by the teachers and understood by their students. Portfolios should be (Mc Millan, 1997, p. 232):

- Based on specific learning targets.

- Systematic and well organized.

- Built on preestablished guidelines for selecting content and for the evaluation of work samples.

- Demonstrative of student engagement in selection of products as well as reflective of their work.

- Inclusive of student-teacher conferences to review progress, identify areas of improvement, and facilitate student reflection.

TABLE 12.2   Rubric for a High School Research Paper

Criteria for Writing Component

	Distinguished	Proficient	Not Proficient
Thesis	Clearly defined and sustained throughout	Stated	Unclear or unidentifiable
	Topic effectively limited	Attempt to limit topic	No attempt to limit topic
Development	Topic thoroughly developed throughout with specific examples to support thesis	Topic developed General supporting evidence	Topic not developed clearly Unnecessary information
Organization	Highly organized plan with effective transitions	Logical organization, but with inconsistent transitions	No organizational plan
	Superior introduction and conclusion clearly relate to whole	Introduction and conclusion relate to whole	No attempt to create unity No transitions
Research	Four or more qualified sources cited appropriately	Three qualified sources cited	Fewer than three qualified sources cited
	Bibliography includes three or more types of sources (books and interviews, for example)	Bibliography includes two types of sources (books and interviews, for example)	Bibliography includes only one type of source
Mechanics	Superior editing (fewer than four total errors in paper) in the following areas:	Careful editing (no more than one error per page) in the following areas:	Careless editing (more than one error per page) in the following areas:
	• punctuation • capitalization • spelling	• sentence structure • run on/fragment • verb usage	• subject/verb agree • pronoun usage • point of view • manuscript form

The greatest benefit that portfolios provide to students is the student's own metacognitive reflection on the knowledge gained, the strategies that worked, and the pride and motivation he or she experienced while carrying out the varied tasks and creating the different products in the unit. By participating in the setting of criteria for judging the merit of their work, selecting which items will be representative of them as a student, and carrying out self-evaluation and reflection on the items themselves and on their process as a learner, students participating in portfolio assessment gain a new depth of understanding and a new sense of ownership that extends beyond any single assignment and beyond the particular unit or content. Therefore, although portfolios may be included in both single discipline or coordinated discipline settings, we include them with integrated as well because reflection on process and product, which is an important aspect of the portfolio approach, aligns closely with integrated curriculum's emphasis on students' achieving ownership of their learning and on their competency as problem solvers and critical thinkers.

TEACHER AS INQUIRING LEARNER

Review the different types of data collecting (assessment) sources we set out in this chapter as well as the teaching/assessing tools we examined in Chapters 4 through 8.

- How many of the sources we discussed and explained have you had firsthand experience with either as a student or as a teacher?

List the types of data collecting you are familiar with and the examples you remember producing yourself or seeing students produce in the classes where you have observed or student taught. Compare your list with someone who is in the same discipline, and see if you have any assessment tools

in common. Decide whether these assessment tools have particular relevance to your field and the sorts of activities an individual who is a scientist, a historian, or an economist uses daily at work. Now compare your list with that of someone in another discipline and see which tools are the same and which are different. Choose one assessment tool to focus on.

- What can you learn about students from this assessment tool? How do you think a good student's performance would differ from a poor student's? What criteria would you use to judge students using this tool?

The Importance of Teams in an Integrated Curriculum

We have indicated throughout this text that no one model of curriculum design or instruction is consistently appropriate for a single teacher or group of teachers. Nevertheless, we do believe that the team approach is absolutely necessary in order for the interdisciplinary connections of an integrated curriculum to work. Quite simply, cooperation among teachers of different disciplines is essential.

Teachers who have participated on effective teams often mention significant changes for themselves as professionals in terms of their own heightened sense of competence in decision making. Many teachers say that the support of the team enabled them collectively or individually to work more effectively with the administrators, parents, and counselors who are also involved with their students. Among the benefits teachers mention are these:

- More approaches to deal with an overcrowded curriculum.

- More opportunities for student individualization and less isolation for students.

- More support to deal with external demands, such as standards for their students and professional expectations for themselves.

- More resources (human) to deal with the increasing diversity and heterogeneity in the student populations found in their schools and classrooms.

- More opportunities collectively and individually to work effectively with other constituencies: administrators, parents, and counselors.

- More opportunities as a group to do in-depth planning and creative problem solving beyond what any one individual could have achieved alone.

■ Guidelines for Interdisciplinary Teams

In order to design and develop the kind of integrated curriculum that we have described

TEACHER AS INQUIRING LEARNER

Determine whether there are any teams of teachers working on curriculum in the middle school or high school where you are doing your field-based experience. Also consider whether your own college or department offers any integrated courses or programs. Many undergraduate colleges now offer programs focused on community service-learning, which is often interdisciplinary in nature. For example, in our college, a team of social studies, science, and technology faculty worked on a new course, entitled Interdisciplinary Curriculum for the Middle School, which emphasizes many ways in which the disciplines can be interconnected as well as how technology is integrated across the curriculum.

Interview a teacher who is a member of a team. Find out what the stimulus was for the team to be created and what its major purpose is. Ask the individual to describe what the advantages are for him or her personally as an educator and what the advantages are for the students. Be sure to ask if there are any disadvantages or weaknesses in the model for him or her personally or for the students. Record your findings, and then share them with other students in your class who have talked with individuals in other disciplines and in different settings.

- Have your classmates found some of the same advantages and some of the same frustrations with team teaching that you have found?

at the beginning of the chapter, we believe a team approach is the most useful structure. Just like any other team situation, there are rules or norms that maximize the possibility that a curriculum team can succeed as an entity and that a successful integrated unit will be the result of their work together. Certain guidelines for team building seem to help maximize the potential for success at the beginning of the team unit building process. Too often when teachers who are each experts in their own domains come together, they do not attend to the early stages of team building that are highlighted in these guidelines, and their efforts are minimized or even doomed from the beginning. You might even use these same guidelines when you and a group of your classmates set out to do a collaborative class assignment in the future (Maurer, 1994).

Guidelines for Collaborative Curriculum Building

1. Start with an aim to clarify your purpose and arrive at a unified sense of the reason for doing this project together.

2. Make decisions by consensus, not by majority, and be able to admit that conflict may exist.

3. Work toward and value active listening that will lead to understanding differences.

4. Gain administrative support for the team and its work.

5. Pilot a few lessons as a first step, and examine the results.

6. Solicit, examine, and value feedback from parents, administrators, and students both during and at the culmination of the project.

7. Place the goals and purpose of the team as the focus of each individual's participation, while honoring the other memberships and responsibilities a member may have.

■ Allowing Sufficient Time

Once you and a group of colleagues decide to pursue integrated curriculum and use the team model, the single most important factor that appears to determine whether a team will succeed is their awareness and acceptance of the amount of time collaboration takes (see Figure 12.2). Teaming to achieve integrated curriculum appears to be an evolutionary process. Before any real curriculum development work can be done, the team members need time to organize the working structure of the team and to decide on the various roles for the participants. In essence, just like with a sports team you have participated on, in order to function as a unit, teachers need time to get to know one another and to build community among themselves. They need time to get to know one another's strengths and interests that can be brought to bear on the project at hand.

In the early stages of integrated curriculum, it is important for the team to take the time to disseminate information about the project on an ongoing basis in order to gain the support for and the understanding of the goals and the outcomes within the school, the district, and the community. Once the interdisciplinary thematic study is launched, the plan is in place, and the implementation of instruction has begun, team members need time to meet in order to assess and revise their instruction. Team members also need time throughout the implementation to meet with other constituencies such as administrators, parents, and community representatives as well as to contact and work with people and agencies outside the school to further the particular theme or topic.

Finally, team members and students participating in the study need time to assess the outcomes in terms of student performance and learning to determine the effectiveness of the unit to see how effectively it is meeting the designated goals and outcomes related to the issue or theme under study. The effect of the team effort on the participants, both the teachers and their students, should also be continuously evaluated.

In addition to the importance of time and all of its implications, if teachers are going to attempt to do things differently instructionally and organizationally, they need incentives that will explicitly confirm the commitment of the administration while at the same time support the changes they are attempting. Such things as relief from some usual building assignments, block or cohort programming with other team members, and classroom coverage for interventions and training opportunities seem to make the most significant difference to the teachers who are engaged with their colleagues in

FIGURE 12.2 Time Allocation and Integrated Curriculum

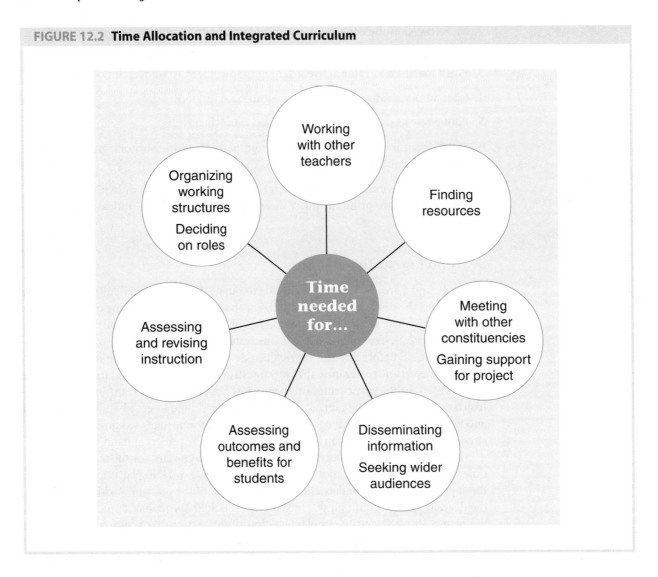

designing and implementing integrated curriculum (Beane, 1995a). Finally, teachers need to have the support and understanding of the administration and their colleagues that the first attempts with integrated curriculum are pilots from which everyone—the administration, the teachers, and the students—can benefit and learn. These teachers need to be able to show other teachers in their school, especially those in their departments, that their success can be reasonably replicated in other classrooms.

■ A School Vision

All of the benefits of teaming and the development of integrated curriculum in middle schools and high schools will be fruitless unless they are part of systemic planning and commitment by a number of constituencies: the teachers in the team and their other grade-level or discipline-based colleagues, the building-level administration, and even the central administration. In order to support integrated curriculum, a school community needs to develop a school vision that places value on integration and connectedness across the disciplines, teacher involvement in and commitment to the vision, administrative support for teaming, and planning time and in-service for the teachers who will design and implement the integrated curriculum. If the schools in which you work are going to be transformed by integrated curriculum, there must be commitment to the development and maintenance of a variety of internal structures like the scheduling of students and courses, planning time for teachers, and the reallocation and the addition of resources to foster this approach. No matter how appropriate the theme you have chosen and how carefully you and your colleagues have pursued the preplanning and planning steps of designing integrated curriculum, if the structures are not in place to support your teaming with other teachers and alternative scheduling for your students, you and your colleagues will not be able to change our schools and the learning opportunities for your students with integrated curriculum. Integrated, interdisciplinary curriculum and the challenges and promises it offers to middle school and high school teachers and their students is at its very core school reform. "Though far from a panacea . . . the interdisciplinary [integrated] model is still the most powerful and appropriate way to reconstruct our classrooms [today and for the future]" (Panaritis, 1995, p. 628).

 SAMPLE UNIT PLANS

Sample Integrated Thematic Unit for the High School

*Y*ou will now have the opportunity to see how a team of teachers at the high school level planned, implemented, and assessed an issues-based integrated curriculum unit. You will learn what the impetus was for the chosen topic, and you will see how the team of teachers used the Miller-Allan Model for Developing Curriculum (refer back to Figure 12.1). You will also get a clear sense of how teachers in different disciplines worked together to support one another, their students, and the unit as a whole. A planning web accompanies the thematic unit. The web shows the activities explicitly described in the text as well as some additional connections that could be made to other disciplines. These additional suggestions would allow teachers like you to tailor the unit to meet specific learning needs and interests of their own students more effectively, as well as to meet the particular curriculum frameworks in their state or the guidelines in their districts.

"Immigration and Cultural Diversity: Are We Still a Nation of Immigrants?"

DIVERSITY

I mmigration and cultural diversity is a timely and significant theme for the development of integrated curriculum at the high school level. It is important that young people realize that questions about immigration, assimilation, and cultural pluralism are not unique to those of us living now but are in fact long-standing questions embedded in our history as a nation founded by immigrants. An additional impetus

STANDARDS ☑

for focusing on this theme in an interdisciplinary, integrated manner in the curriculum is the fact that these issues are emphasized in national standards documents like

Expectations for Excellence: Curriculum Standards for the Social Studies (National Council for Social Studies, 1994) and in many of the recent state curriculum frameworks, especially those focused on history and the social sciences and on foreign or world languages (Massachusetts Department of Education, 1996).

Applying the Miller-Allan model (refer back to Figure 12.1) for the development of an integrated issues-based unit, a group of ninth-grade teachers created a four-week unit entitled, "Immigration and Cultural Diversity: Are We Still a Nation of Immigrants?" These teachers were particularly interested in this issue because they and their students, as well as the rest of their community, faced these concerns on an ongoing basis. The ninth graders had come from two different middle schools in their district. Therefore, the teachers believed that an integrated unit at the beginning of the school year would foster understanding of one another, create a more cohesive academic setting for the students, and give them a chance to deal firsthand with a significant historical and social issue affecting their own lives.

Preplanning

The collaboration in this unit was prompted by a ninth-grade history teacher's desire to find a compelling way to introduce his students to a newly required two-year sequence of American history courses (colonialism to 1865 and 1865 to the present). The issues immigrants face and questions those already living in a community ask were interesting and real for this teacher because his own community was facing an influx of new immigrants. In addition, this teacher had recently attended a session at a social studies conference that focused on the importance of using relevant subject matter and attention to social issues that students in high schools today would be expected to deal with as adults.

This teacher wondered if he and his colleagues could create an integrated unit in which the students examined the status and implications of immigration today in the United States. To explore the feasibility of connecting a number of disciplines around this issue, the social studies teacher asked a group of his ninth-grade teaching colleagues in different content areas (English/language arts, mathematics, science, and foreign language) to meet for a brainstorming session. The teachers came away from this meeting with an interest in the proposed theme, a commitment to reflect on the role their own discipline could play in its study, and a decision to meet again to develop a planning map similar to the one developed for the middle school unit described earlier in the chapter. The outcome of their second meeting can be seen in the thematic map in Figure 12.3.

Planning

The discussions led the teachers to realize that exploring this issue would enable them to pursue some curriculum goals they held in common for their students. The teachers next developed four overarching objectives and learner outcomes to guide their own work and that of the students who would be engaged in the integrated unit:

- An awareness of patterns of emigration to the United States from other lands, with particular focus on the countries and reasons that people are coming here

FIGURE 12.3 How the Disciplines Work Together

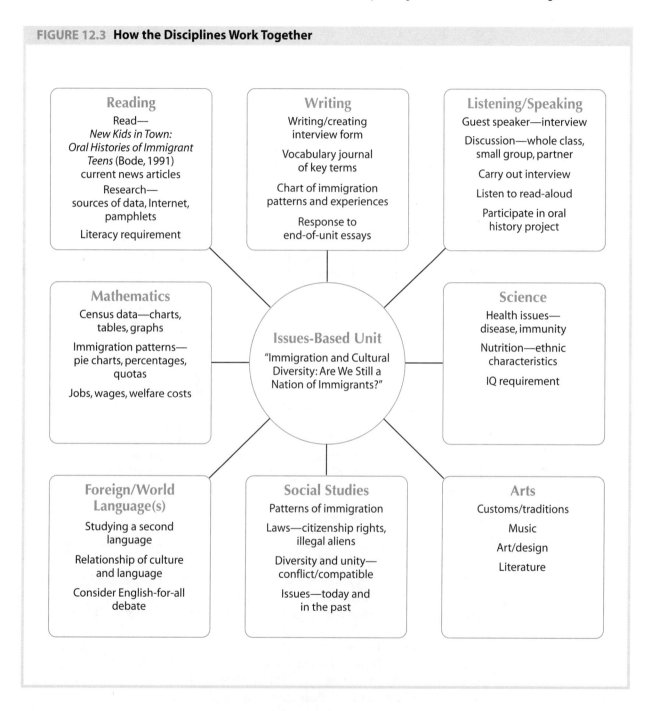

today (drawing on history, geography, and economics).

- An understanding of the topics that are most often debated in relation to immigration: costs for schooling, health care, and welfare needs; implications of the variety of languages and cultures present in the United States today; and economic implications, especially with regard to competition for jobs between immigrants and citizens.

- An understanding of the principles and laws pertaining to citizenship rights in the United States and the rights and benefits of legal immigrant residents.

- Refinement and extension of the students' research skills and their use of technology for research as well as their critical writing and speaking skills and a focus on evaluating a variety of sources on one topic with differing viewpoints expressed.

At the preplanning stage, the teachers also spent time selecting a range of resources to meet the learning needs and levels represented by the students in their ninth-grade class. They also selected a range of sources appropriate for research on the theme they chose for their unit. The English teacher identified fiction works, such as Sandra Cisneros' *The House on Mango Street* (1991), Fran Leeper Buss' *The Journey of the Sparrows* (1993), and Maureen Crane Wartski's *A Long Way from Home* (1982), and nonfiction works such as Janet Bode's *New Kids in Town: Oral Histories of Immigrant Teens* (1991). The social studies teacher contributed such resources as a public issues series developed by the Social Science Education Consortium and the Lucent Overview series focusing on social, political, and environmental issues and written for middle and high school audiences. The teachers located specialized research tools such as almanacs and yearbooks and sources on the Internet to support the development of this unit. In addition, they selected media sources such as recent feature stories and editorials in the local newspaper, as well as films, videos, and television documentaries. Finally, the teachers did some research on their own community to find out about its ethnic makeup represented by its clubs and churches, specialized stores, or restaurants as well as census information related to its ethnic and cultural background. They contacted local government officials as well as the school administration to find out about current issues related to immigration that they were knowledgeable about.

Implementing

Activities for Initiating the Unit

The history teacher began the unit with a role play in which he played his grandfather from Latvia who came to the United States in 1910 at the age of ten. During the role play, the students learned why his grandfather came to the United States, what his native country was like then, how he traveled and who he traveled with, and what his initial experiences were like. The other content-area teachers and the students who were participating in the unit were asked on a volunteer basis to share where their families came from and why they had come to the United States. The students began a **chart** to show the countries represented in their community and the reasons they or their ancestors came to the United States. Many similar reasons for emigrating emerged. This whole class activity identified similarities between the students who were born in the United States and their classmates who were the newer immigrants.

Following this discussion, the teacher showed a cartoon on the overhead and asked the students to define the words *immigrant* and *emigrate,* highlighted in the cartoon

FIGURE 12.4 Cracker's Barrel

Source: Cobblestone (1982). Peterborough, N.H.: Cobblestone Publishing Company, Reprinted with permission of the artist.

(see Figure 12.4). They listed several other words and phrases: *assimilation, pluralism, diversity, equality, the American way,* and *melting pot* and *salad bowl.* Using a **vocabulary chart** such as the one introduced in Chapter 5, the teacher asked the students to write their own definitions of the words or phrases that they thought they knew. The students

---

FIGURE 12.5 Immigrant Interview Questions

1. What country did you come from?
2. Why did you immigrate?
3. What difficulties did you have when you first arrived?
4. Was the United States what you expected?
5. How much did it cost you to come here?
6. Who was your sponsor? *or* Who did you know here?

Source: Adapted from L.S. Levstik and K.C. Barton, *Doing History* (Mahwah, N.J.: Erlbaum, 2001).

---

got together in small groups of three to four to share what they knew and thought about these words and phrases. Finally, the teacher asked the students to consider how these words and concepts applied to them personally and to their community. These two activities set the stage for the teachers to pose the key questions for the unit: "Are we still a nation of immigrants?" or "What is the immigrant experience today?"

The before reading activities laid the foundation for the students to decide on questions they would ask someone in their own family or someone in their community who had emigrated recently. With the teacher's support, the students created an interview form that contained what they considered to be the most important questions (see Figure 12.5).

Activities for Interacting with Ideas or Developing the Unit

Using the interview questions that the class generated, the teachers decided to arrange a group interview to sharpen the students' questioning abilities and to give them an opportunity to practice their listening and their note-taking skills before they interviewed an individual on their own. One of the teachers asked a Cambodian couple who had recently immigrated to their community to come to the class in order to share their experiences and to be interviewed.

While the students were preparing for their interviews, and realizing that there were various ability levels and language levels among the students in the class, the English teacher decided to do a read-aloud of *The House on Mango Street*, a young adult novel about the immigrant experience. She chose this story for its overall literary value as well as the fact that it shows a young person's perspective on how the immigrant experience can be both positive and negative. After some discussion of the story, the teacher suggested that the students create a list of positive and negative immigrant experiences in the book to which they could add the firsthand experiences being shared by the people they were individually going to interview.

Each student was independently reading the nonfiction accounts of young people like themselves coming to the United States found in *New Kids In Town: Oral Histories of Immigrant Teens* (Bode, 1991). The book focuses on why each of these young persons came to the United States, whom they came with, and what experiences they are having as recent immigrants. The students in the class were encouraged to share their thoughts and impressions with a partner and to record these discussions on a **discussion web**. The students added the positive and negative aspects of the immigrant experience they found in these personal accounts to the class chart they had begun earlier in the unit.

Throughout this phase of the unit, students refined their knowledge of the vocabulary and the key concepts identified during the prereading phase of the unit. All students kept a **vocabulary journal** in which they recorded clarifications and ideas related to the terms *immigration, diversity, assimilation,* and *pluralism.*

As the students read with their partners and discussed current news articles in their local newspaper, they became increasingly curious about U.S. citizenship laws and how census data were collected and used in the United States. The mathematics, science, and social studies teachers helped the students research these areas of interest. This research component of the unit, triggered by real questions and concerns, enabled the students to use a variety of community-based sources other than texts: newspapers, Internet sources focused specifically on immigration issues on the Immigration Home Page (**www/bergen.org/AAST/Projects/Immigration**) and on a web site focused on immigration issues at the University of California at Davis (**heather.cs.ucdavis.edu/pub/Immigration/Index.html**), and on the web site maintained by the Elis Island Foundation (**www.ellisisland.org**), as well as informational pamphlets and brochures such as the Department of the Interior's *Guide to Citizenship.* The social studies teacher created **study guides** for the students to use to find answers to their questions using some of the specialized resources they identified during the preplanning stage. The mathematics teacher helped the students contact local government representatives to gain current information about how the census data were being used in their community. This teacher helped the students use **graphs and charts** to interpret the census data. The students also learned how the census data were used to allocate funds for services to community agencies such as schools for programs like Title I and free lunch or breakfast programs for children of school age. Another group of the students, prompted by a recent newspaper article, "Undercurrent of Anger as Immigrants Gain Jobs" (*Boston Globe,* March 9, 2003), explored a prevalent economic concern in communities such as theirs with large influxes of new immigrants. The students wanted to find out what the real impact was on the availability of jobs in their own community.

Throughout the month, all students kept a collection portfolio that contained their written reflections related to the key questions, their personal vocabulary journals, and other supporting materials that demonstrated their meeting the learning goals of the unit. Furthermore, the data in these portfolios (as well as what was not there) helped the teachers identify individuals or groups that needed coaching, conferencing, or direct instruction. The portfolios were the most helpful sources for teachers to use in order to individualize the learning experiences for the variety of ninth-grade students in their classes. They provided the teachers with a source of data useful in selecting resources, strategies, and grouping patterns to help each student gain the most from this integrated unit.

Activities for Refining Ideas or Ending the Unit

As they moved into the final phase of this unit, the teachers wanted to ensure that each student had individually grappled with the issues and questions posed at the beginning of the unit. Second, they wanted the students to see that the immigrant issue had persisted since our earliest settlements. The teachers wanted the students to use these

FIGURE 12.6   **Final Individual Response Questions**

Question #1: Place yourself on these two continua.

Views of the United States

Refuge for the Oppressed .... *America for "Americans"*

Views of National Character

Strength through Diversity .... *Strength through Unity, Assimilation*

Consider what has most influenced your placement on the two continua. Has your own view changed since we began the unit, and if so, how? Finally, do you think Americans will ever reach agreement on these issues? Why do you think it is so difficult to reach agreement on these issues?

Question #2: Reflect on both the positive and the negative experiences immigrants face or have faced in the American culture. Think about a person proud of their ethnic/cultural heritage or a person who wants to hide their foreign background. How would that person react to specific immigrant experiences? Would the individual you are thinking about have a different viewpoint if he or she had settled in another part of the country? If they settled in our community how would they react? If they came here as a child or teenager, would they react differently?

Source: Adapted from Social Science Education Consortium (1988). *Immigration: Pluralism and National Identity.* (Boulder, CO: Social Science Education Consortium.)

questions—"Are we still a nation of immigrants?" and "What is the current immigrant experience?"—and their new understandings about immigration as a framework for the upcoming study of American history from the colonial days to the present, which was the statewide social studies requirement for the ninth and tenth grades.

The teachers designed two culminating activities for this unit: an individual activity and a group project that extended the unit into the real life of their community. First, each student was to write an individual opinion piece based on research throughout the unit, discussions of readings with partners, and the information he or she learned in small research groups and from whole class discussions (see Figure 12.6). The students chose one of the two essay questions designed by the team of content-area teachers involved with the unit.

Because the integrated unit on immigration coincided with the town's year-long centennial celebration, the students and their teachers decided to pull the information they had learned about their community and its immigrant groups together into an oral history project. Finally, the students used their newly acquired knowledge about their community and its ethnic heritage to help the town's board of selectmen and the town's historical society plan and implement a Heritage Pride Day for their town's special celebration.

Assessing Students' Understandings and the Outcomes of the Unit as a Whole

Each of the essays was written for a certain purpose. The essays were a response to one of the questions designed to demonstrate students' critical-writing ability, their knowledge of the vocabulary and concepts dealt with in the unit, their ability to express their personal opinion, and their ability to assimilate and use data from a variety of sources.

The second culminating project, the group oral history, allowed the students to focus on the ethnic makeup of their community, which they had learned about through their investigations using the census data as well as through their personal interviews with a variety of individuals living and working in the community.

SUMMARY

This chapter concludes the part of the text devoted to the development of curriculum and the enhancement of literacy learning across the disciplines. In this chapter, we have emphasized:

- **The role of integrated curriculum.**
- **The interrelationships among disciplines to solve problems and issues and to explore significant themes.**

We began the chapter by explaining our definition for integrated curriculum and pointed out where there is confusion in the terminology. Then we provided a rationale for pursuing this form of curriculum development and collaboration with colleagues in different disciplines.

We presented a refinement of the unit plan model we introduced in Chapter 10 and implemented in Chapter 11, designated the Miller-Allan Model for Developing Curriculum. This plan has four components:

- **Preplanning and finding significant themes.**
- **Planning the unit, with emphasis on working with colleagues, scheduling, and finding resources.**
- **Implementing the unit with emphasis on the content understandings and literacy learning using teaching/assessing tools.**
- **Assessing the unit with an emphasis on the role of portfolios in evaluation and the benefits for both teachers and students.**

Since integrated curriculum involves working collaboratively with other content-area teachers over time, we include some guidelines for teachers working in interdisciplinary teams. We also provide some recommendations for teams of teachers to consider in order to ensure that their setting will support and accommodate the curriculum they have designed.

Finally, we concluded this chapter with a sample integrated at the high school level. The unit shows in detail how the content-area teachers and their students used the Miller-Allan Model for Developing Curriculum in order to study a significant real-world issue.

Inquiry into Your Learning

1. Think about the themes of the sample high school unit in this chapter. Now consider your own discipline, courses you have taken, and real-world occurrences with which you are familiar. Look at the planning web on page 339 on immigration and decide what you could add from your academic or personal experiences to extend this integrated learning map.

2. Look at the national standards or curriculum frameworks in your discipline. Identify one or two topics or understandings in your field that you think you could link to one or more other disciplines. Discuss the possibilities with peers who are subject matter specialists in other areas to get their ideas and reactions.

Inquiry into Your Students' Learning

1. The issues or problems that face the students' own communities are a rich source of integrated curriculum themes. Have your students survey their community for issues by reading the newspaper, listening to the local news station, and talking with friends and neighbors as well as officials in law enforcement, education, or community service positions. Help the students identify areas of concern like recreation, the environment, civil and political rights, health, education, and job- and employment-related issues. Once the students have had a chance to survey their community, see whether the students have come up with similar or related concerns. If so, discuss with the students how they could explore these issues in any one of or in a combination of the disciplines that make up their school's existing curriculum.

Resources

Books

Dickinson, T. S., & Erb, T. O. (1997). *We gain more than we give: Teaming in middle schools.* Columbus, OH: National Middle School Association. Provides useful historical background for the team teaching concept, case studies that describe different models for teaming, and, most important, guidelines for the design, implementation, and evaluation of effective teams at the middle school level.

Drake, S. M. (1998). *Creating integrated curriculum: Proven ways to increase student learning.* Thousand Oaks, CA: Corwin Press, Inc. Explores using interdisciplinary and transdisciplinary approaches in teaching and suggests effective ways of incorporating standards into the curriculum.

Lowery, R. M. (2000). *Immigrants in children's literature.* Boston: Peter Lang. Examines the representation of immigrants in children's literature with regard to race and class issues in three waves of immigration to the United States: 1820–1899, 1900–1964, and 1964–present. The criteria used for assessing the texts are explained in detail. It is recommended that educators use similar criteria when selecting classroom material.

Meinbach, A. M., Fredericks, A., & Rothlein, L. (2000). *The complete guide to thematic units: Creating the integrated curriculum* (2nd ed.). Norwood, MA: Christopher-Gordon Publishers, Inc. Discusses methods for designing and completing thematic units and authentic assessment. Also provides detailed units for primary and intermediate grades with supplemental literature and extension activities for each unit.

Roberts, P. L., & Kellough, R. D. (2000). *A guide for developing interdisciplinary thematic units* (2nd ed.). Upper Saddle River, NJ: Merrill. Suggests guidelines for implementing an interdisciplinary unit from selecting a theme and setting goals to final projects, assessment, and reflection. Sample interdisciplinary units and lesson plans are provided. Appendix contains templates for teacher self-assessment when planning, conducting, and reflecting on a unit.

Tchudi, S. (1993). *The astonishing curriculum: Integrating science and the humanities through language.* Urbana, IL: National Council of Teachers of English. A collection of essays focused on the role that language plays in connecting science and the humanities in the real world and the classroom. These essays highlight K–12 courses and projects that have fostered learning of language, science, and technology.

Journals

Howes, E. V., Hamilton, G. W., & Zaskoda, D. (2003). Linking science and literature through technology: Thinking about interdisciplinary inquiry in middle school. *Journal of Adolescent and Adult Literacy, 46* (6), 494–504. Results of teacher research conducted with fifth to eighth graders that examined two methods of connecting literature, science, and technology in the classroom. Students created web sites based on different elements of their local environment.

Schug, M. C. (1998). The dark side of curriculum integration in social studies. *Social Studies, 89* (2), 54–57. Focuses on myths associated with the benefits of curriculum integration at the secondary level and offers useful cautions for teachers who are thinking about integration, as well as a chart for planning curriculum integration.

Vars, G. F., & Beane, J. A. (2000). *Integrative curriculum in a standards-based world. ERIC Digest.* Champaign, IL: ERIC Clearinghouse on Elementary and Early Childhood Education. (ERIC Document Reproduction Service No. ED441618). Discusses integrated curriculum planning with regard to state standards and tests. Provides "integrative standards" proposed by three national education groups to meet these needs.

Web Sites

Anthony D. Fredericks. **www.afredericks.com.** Provides specific ideas for an integrated curriculum with activities and questions that support critical thinking. Also gives annotations for books by Anthony Fredericks that address social studies, science, language arts, and general school curriculum.

Scholastic. **teacher.scholastic.com/immigrat/tguide. htm.** Describes a unit dealing with immigration. Lesson plans, objectives, assessment tools, and materials, including photos, oral histories, charts and graphs are provided. Also indicates which of the national standards are met in completing this project.

CHAPTER 13

Continuing to Grow as a Reflective Professional

KEY CONCEPTS

- classroom inquiry, p. 351
- teacher researcher, p. 351
- teaching log or journal, p. 355
- field notebook, p. 356
- double-entry journal, p. 356
- cooking the data, p. 358

PURPOSE-SETTING QUESTIONS

1 What is meant by professional teaching standards, and how do they apply to you now and in the future?

2 What is meant when we say that schools should support a *community of learners?* Perhaps you have heard this term used with regard to your students and the culture of the classroom you create. What do you think a community of learners for teachers is and why do you think it is important for beginning teachers as well as a veteran teachers to be a part of this community?

3 Have you ever heard about classroom inquiry? What do you think we mean when we say another role we'd like to add to your repertoire of choices is that of a teacher researcher?

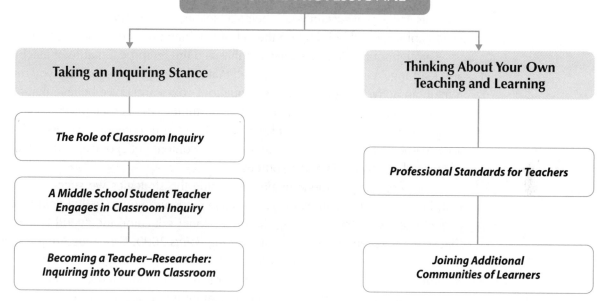

CONTINUING TO GROW AS A REFLECTIVE PROFESSIONAL

Taking an Inquiring Stance

The Role of Classroom Inquiry

A Middle School Student Teacher Engages in Classroom Inquiry

Becoming a Teacher–Researcher: Inquiring into Your Own Classroom

Thinking About Your Own Teaching and Learning

Professional Standards for Teachers

Joining Additional Communities of Learners

As you approach student teaching, you are about to embark on a career that will sustain and fulfill you for more than thirty years. You will certainly experience tired feet, mounds of student papers and lab reports to correct, satisfaction when a struggling student "gets it," and exciting work opportunities with colleagues as well as challenges from new mandates, new curriculum, and new students. What will sustain you is being a lifelong learner. This will happen if you keep exploring and building on the act of teaching and the art of teaching.

 Throughout this text, we have emphasized the reciprocal nature of teaching and learning. We have also emphasized that to be an effective teacher, you must remain an active, ongoing learner throughout your career. We believe that as a preservice teacher, you have had many opportunities to become informed about the act of teaching, which includes knowledge of your content area (discipline), your learners, and your growing repertoire of content pedagogy and knowledge of curriculum materials and resources.

By engaging in the activities and using the strategies we suggest in this text, in combination with your other course work and your ongoing field-based experiences, you are becoming the professional educator, the "good teacher," that so many recent reports, such as *Turning Points* 2000: *Educating Adolescents in the 21st Century* (2000) and *Breaking Ranks: Changing an American Institution* (1999) have touted. These reports as well as the standards documents discussed in Chapter 10 and new credentialing initiatives across the nation are focused on you as the next generation of teachers who will provide the leadership for our schools.

In this text we suggest many in-class inquiry activities and simulations to help you focus on the activities, the questioning, and the problem solving required of an educator who will teach in the future. We hope these opportunities have helped you try on your role as a teacher and have given you many tools for your future in the classroom.

Furthermore, we have suggested you share your experiences as a learner as well as a teacher with peers (colleagues) in the same discipline, with peers interested in students at the same level (middle school or high school), and even across disciplines. We began this focus on connections with others in your profession in Chapter 1 to encourage you to see yourself as part of a community of educators, and in this chapter we extend these ideas by focusing on some of the broader professional communities that we hope you will join.

Finally, we have focused on your learners and your role as an effective teacher of literacy and learning in your particular discipline. We have also mentioned repeatedly how ongoing learning is necessary to meet the challenges of changing schools in a diverse society. As you read this concluding chapter, you may want to ask some questions that are focused on yourself as both a learner and a teacher.

Taking an Inquiring Stance

As you prepare to be a teacher, your ideas about teaching and learning have probably been shaped by your own experiences as a student as well as by the courses you have taken and your field experiences in a middle school or a high school. As you have thought about the pedagogy, strategies for learning literacy, and content and assessment tools you have learned about recently, have you ever wondered where these ideas came from? Even if you have not explicitly been told, no doubt you have already been influenced by an array of educational research including large scale studies like the National Assessment of Educational Progress (2000), basic or laboratory research, and applied educational research focused on classroom and teaching practices. This later form of research, when practice-driven and initiated by teachers in their own classroom settings, is referred to as teacher research or *classroom inquiry*.

classroom inquiry
Collecting and analyzing data in a systematic way in order to answer questions about one's own students and classroom practices.

■ The Role of Classroom Inquiry

At the core of classroom inquiry or teacher research is a teacher's goal to understand his or her own teaching practice rather than to prove that a specific teaching practice works. Teacher research or classroom inquiry is done primarily for the teacher's own continuous learning (discussed at the beginning of this text in Chapter 1) and to enhance the learning of his/her students. Effective teachers have always sought to learn from students, as well as to use new teaching tools to improve their students' learning and understanding. However, what is different about being a *teacher researcher* is that these teachers collect and analyze their data in an organized, systematic manner in order to answer questions about their classrooms and their classroom practices. Rather than relying on hunches and impressions about the effects of their classroom practices, teacher researchers follow focused plans to produce findings, and to draw conclusions about classroom practices.

teacher researcher A classroom teacher or specialist who studies what they are doing in a systematic way and uses the results to inform their own practice.

Throughout this text, and especially in Part Two where we examined the literacy strategies and teaching tools, we have encouraged you to approach your teaching with an inquiring stance. We have advocated that you try out many of the teaching/assessing tools we have discussed with a small group of learners at a grade level or within a discipline in which you hope to teach. In doing this, we suggest you continue to ask yourself about your practice as a teacher as well as about your students' learning. For example, after we introduced you to a pattern guide to be used with a new resource in your discipline in Chapter 8 or a categorization chart to organize information from sources in Chapter 7, we suggested you try these strategies yourself as a learner and then with your own students.

In addition, we have suggested in the Teacher as Inquiring Learner activities embedded in the chapters and the Inquiry into Your Learning and Inquiry into Your Students' Learning activities at the conclusion of each chapter that you continue to think about and learn more about your discipline, your teaching methodology (especially your use of teaching tools), a variety of curriculum materials and resources, and, most important, your learners. We have done this by:

(handwritten margin note: Promote teacher reflection, questioning, research)

- Asking you throughout the chapters to question, analyze, and reflect on the understandings and the philosophy you have pertaining to your field or discipline.

- Encouraging you to think about how you use literacy strategies to learn from different resources.

- Asking you to assess your own background knowledge, your perceptions and beliefs, and your values in order to understand yourself as both teacher and learner.

- Suggesting that you think about how different students respond to a topic being studied, such as girls versus boys, the strongest students in the content area versus the weaker ones, the students who have some background knowledge and the ones who have little or none.

While taking this questioning stance integral to the multifaceted role of a teacher, you have been engaged in reflecting on your own actions in the classroom. (Schön, 1983). Without knowing it, you have been doing what is currently being referred to as "classroom inquiry" and have begun to take on the characteristics of a teacher researcher.

■ **A Middle School Student Teacher Engages in Classroom Inquiry**

A student in our middle school program wrote a summary of the classroom inquiry she carried out in the eighth-grade classroom where she did her student teaching. This example, set out in Figure 13.1, shows the evolution of an inquiry question and demonstrates the dynamic nature of the inquiry process. It also clearly demonstrates how carrying out classroom inquiry can help teacher researchers understand their classroom, as well as inform them for the future in a way that can help them and their students. In this example, you can see the question that the student teacher framed, the tools she used to gather her data, how she analyzed her data, and what outcomes and inferences she drew from this inquiry. Finally, you can see how naturally this inquiry fits with her ongoing teaching practice with this particular class, and why she thinks the results will serve to inform her practice as a middle school teacher in the future.

■ **Becoming a Teacher Researcher: Inquiring into Your Own Classroom**

In order to be a teacher researcher, the most important ingredient is finding a question, a puzzle, or a dilemma you want to answer or solve that is evident from your ongoing practice. To date we have suggested literacy strategies and teaching/assessing tools for you to learn about and for you to try yourself and with your own students. We have guided your question asking and inquiry and your reflection on your practice.

We believe that good teachers are those who keep asking questions about their students, their own teaching/assessing practices, the resources they are using, and the strategies, skills, and content they are presenting to their students. When you are doing inquiry in your own classroom, we hope you realize that interesting questions won't appear in some perfectly obvious and neat form, nor will they come from some outside sources. Questions come from the surprises, the puzzles, and the concerns you experience in your own classroom.

FIGURE 13.1 **Summary of Classroom Inquiry**

Classroom Inquiry Question

What techniques can I use to interest females in science and eliminate gender differences in participation and interest?

Plan to Answer Question

Who: One class consisting of seventeen eighth graders—twelve boys and five girls

Focusing on different methods of assessing class participation and looking for changes in the amount that each student participates. My goal is to empower the girls to participate more often and to encourage the boys to participate more selectively.

Documenting the inquiry goal by taking notes and making observations myself, and by designating certain students to keep a daily tally sheet (students will be given a sheet that asks them to record *positive participation* (relevant questions or comments), *negative participation* (irrelevant answers or comments), and *beyond negative participation* (put-downs or rudeness of other types) of the members of the group by gender.

Changes Made to Question and/or Plan Along the Way

Deciding to make this goal more of a class effort rather than a teacher-led project. The method of assessment I used was completely student generated. I realized that my original plan to use multiple methods of assessment was too far reaching, so I decided to focus on and analyze only one method. Students were responsible not only for devising a system of assessment, but also for keeping that system in check on a daily basis.

At the end of each class, I delegated a student to go around the room with a class list, asking each person what he or she thought his or her score for the day should be on a system decided by students: *check +* if they participated twice with a thoughtful, relevant comment; *check* if they participated once in an appropriate manner, and *check −* if they didn't participate at all or participated inappropriately.

What Did You Find Out? What Did You Learn?

First, I learned that students at this level become more involved and invested in a project like this when they themselves are responsible for making and following through with the basic ground rules. Second, eighth graders are also more likely to cooperate when they know they are being assessed, or graded.

I also gained some insight into adolescent psychology, in particular when I introduced the project and had the girls and boys each fill out a large Idea Sheet. (This sheet asked each gender group separately why they did or did not participate to date, what could be done, and what they thought the student teacher could do to change what currently existed.) Two things struck me from the sheets: the girls did not feel intimidated by the boys, and the boys perceived themselves as more secure than the girls. I didn't feel that either was true, but it was interesting to consider how the students wanted to be perceived.

What Is a New Question You've Discovered?

Will such a method of student-generated assessment work as well in a class with students of more diverse abilities?

Would introducing this idea at the beginning of the school year create students more willing to participate on their own, without assessment, by the middle or end of the year?

What Would You Do Next Time?

Next time, depending on the makeup of the class, I might choose to discriminate between participators and nonparticipators, rather than specifically between boys and girls. I might also attempt to videotape certain classes in order to determine how often I call on certain students and what effect that has on participation.

Developed by J. P. Walker, May, 1997

Source: Julie P. Walker, Lesley College Clinical Intern, Middle School Master's Program, May 1997.

We have worked with our own student teachers and with experienced teachers in order to support their classroom inquiry and to help them become teacher researchers. Both student teachers and experienced teachers we have worked with have followed a three-step model of classroom inquiry:

1. Finding or framing a question

2. Deciding what data or information they already have and what additional data they need to collect to answer their question

3. Knowing when the analysis or study of data has provided them with answers to their questions that will help them understand their teaching and the students in their classrooms

Finding and Framing a Question

We ask our student teachers to look at the journals they have been required to keep during the first several weeks of their student teaching. We ask experienced teachers to look over journals, conference notes, or anecdotal records they have kept as part of their ongoing classroom record keeping. The teachers in each of these groups are likely to find within their reflections some wondering or question about a particular student, a group, or a teaching practice that keeps worrying or annoying them. Looking at these raw notes often leads them to find that some patterns emerge or that certain puzzles or surprises stand out from the rest of their notes. We suggest at this stage that they create a tentative question related to the topic, the issue, or the student or students that intrigues them. Question stems (see Figure 13.2), like the ones we offer the teachers we work with who are carrying out an inquiry project, might also help in your classroom inquiry. We also suggest to our students at this stage, whether they are experienced teachers or student teachers, that they share their question with a partner and take some time to talk about their questions in an effort to clarify what they are really interested in.

We give our students, experienced teachers and student teachers alike, the plan shown in Figure 13.3, which is designed to help teacher researchers keep focused on their question and to make the inquiry process reasonable and doable within the normal flow of classroom life. Once you decide on a question, we recommend that you use a working plan to guide your data collection and analysis.

FIGURE 13.2 Sample Question Stems for Classroom

What is the role of . . . . . ?
How do . . . . . ?
What procedures . . . . . ?
What happens when . . . . . ?
Do (does) **X** change **during/over time/after** . . . . . ?

FIGURE 13.3   Working Plan for Classroom Inquiry

- What is your question?
- Who is involved?
- When will the activity occur?
- What is to happen?
- Would it be helpful to know what the students already know, think, or feel? If so, how will you find that out?
- How will you know you've answered your question? *or* What data will you collect to answer your question?

---

teaching log or journal
A place for teachers to record thoughts and observations related to their teaching.

Although you may be tempted to use classroom inquiry to help all of your students, we recommend to the teachers we work with that they limit their sample or select only a few students to study. We recommend that they select a single student, perhaps the most puzzling one for them, or that they select a high, an average, and a weaker student to compare in the use of a new strategy or content-area material. They may also choose a few contrasting students who differ by gender, regular education or special education placement, or ones who are more verbal or less verbal, to observe carefully as they are engaged in ongoing classroom practice.

TEACHER AS INQUIRING LEARNER

Perhaps when you student teach or when you do a field placement, you will be advised to keep a journal or log to record the most significant events of your day or your week. You may share these with your cooperating teacher, with your supervisor, or with other students in your seminar in an attempt to understand your perceptions and your concerns as a teacher in training.

We believe a *teaching log or journal* is one of the best tools for any teacher, whether new or experienced, to think about classrooms and to find questions that can shape future classroom inquiry as well as to inform future teaching practice. Look back at your own log to see how many of your observations were related to your discipline, your own teaching, the materials you were using or were trying to use, and your students and their differences and needs.

For example, perhaps you will find that you often mention your concern with a specific student's lack of attention or failure to participate in group discussions, or perhaps you are concerned about an ELL student's inability to read and comprehend a required social studies textbook. Perhaps you have ended your entry with questions such as, "How can I help this student? or "Are there materials available on tape for the two students who are struggling with the reading level of the major resource?"

Finally, discuss your findings with another student in your discipline or at your level, to see whether she or he has similar questions about pedagogy, students, or even about the content-area material.

Deciding on Data Collection

Rather than trying to use new data collecting tools, we recommend you take classroom inquiry as an opportunity to look more systematically at what you are already doing and what data are readily available in your classroom. You should look for available data in the field notebook you began when you were determining your question, your notes as you used various teaching/assessing tools with your students, and the evidence of your students' learning found in their ongoing work and their culminating projects and products.

First, we recommend that in addition to relying on student work, teacher researchers sharpen their own observational and listening skills in order to collect data from ongoing classroom interactions more effectively. Many teacher researchers keep a *field notebook* in which they jot down observations, comments, and questions they have during the day that are related to the question they are probing, the students they are focused on, or the strategy they are studying. They may write notes to themselves and keep these in a notebook. Daily or weekly the teacher researcher can look over these notes and write reflections or interpretations about what is occurring in the class in what is often referred to as a *double-entry notebook* (Figure 13.4). Although such double-entry notebooks are not the only means for collecting and analyzing rich, ongoing classroom data, we feel they are one of the most effective tools a teacher researcher, no matter what the discipline or the level he or she is teaching, can use. In addition, you may have anecdotal notes that you kept as you observed individual students or groups in process within your classroom, and notes you keep during writing or reading conferences and workshops or during group discussions or cooperative group work. All of these are rich sources of data that are readily available.

For example, a teacher whose question was, "What is the best method for grouping ninth-grade students for cooperative science activities: assigning groups or allowing them to choose their own groups?" recorded observations over several days to note which students were participating consistently in the recently formed cooperative learning groups. When the teacher carefully looked at her field notes at the end of the week, she realized that the two students with learning disabilities with whom she was most concerned had each volunteered an answer twice during the small group sessions, whereas neither had ever voluntarily responded during previous whole class discussions.

Second, you have used various teaching/assessing tools like those described in Part Two to meet the learning needs of your students. Teacher researchers undoubtedly use these tools to inform their own practice as a teacher as well as to help their own students judge themselves as learners. Now these teacher researchers can look at these sources of data more closely and more systematically than they have before. They can organize and analyze the data in new ways to answer a specific question they have framed about their own ongoing practice and can use their analysis and its implications to inform future practice.

Finally, we advise experienced teachers and the student teachers with whom we work to look at what student work (writing samples, projects, reading lists, lab reports, and field notebooks) and what assessment data (test results, rubrics, checklists, and portfolios) are available as part of their and their students' regular classroom routine. These products will show what literacy strategies students are using effectively as readers

field notebook
A place to record direct observations of what you are seeing in a setting where you are carrying out inquiry.

double-entry journal
A journal kept when doing inquiry that includes both raw data and interpretations and questions.

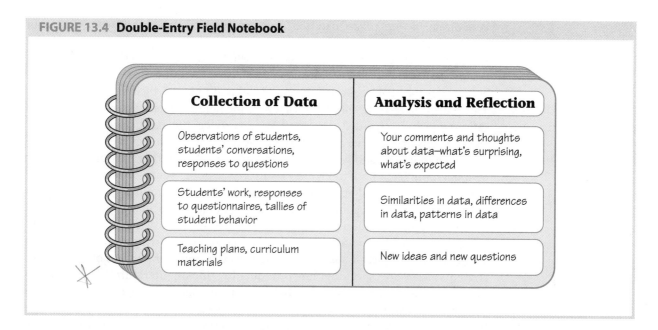

FIGURE 13.4 **Double-Entry Field Notebook**

Collection of Data

Observations of students, students' conversations, responses to questions

Students' work, responses to questionnaires, tallies of student behavior

Teaching plans, curriculum materials

Analysis and Reflection

Your comments and thoughts about data—what's surprising, what's expected

Similarities in data, differences in data, patterns in data

New ideas and new questions

and writers and what content understandings they have acquired, as well as where there is need for additional or new teaching and learning.

TEACHER AS INQUIRING LEARNER

Although we recommend that you as a beginning teacher researcher you put your energy and time into using the teaching/assessing tools in your classroom for the data when you do your inquiry, at some point you may want to try some other tools teacher researchers use. Several of the most widely used and accessible tools for collecting data in one's own setting are interviews, surveys, sociograms, videotapes and audiotapes (Hubbard & Power, 1993; Anderson, Herr, & Nihlen, 1994).

- Have you ever been a respondent to any of these forms of data collecting tools as a student in middle school, high school, or college? Have you seen your cooperating teacher or supervisor or a college instructor use any of these tools to collect data about students and about students' learning? Do you think the information from these tools helped the particular teacher work more effectively with his or her students?

Analyzing and Interpreting Data

So much of what an experienced teacher does is on-the-spot decision making about individual students, groups, pedagogy, and even resources based on their reflection in action. Teachers revise a lesson on the spot based on the cues they are receiving from their learners. We know that this is something in which you will gradually build confidence; at first you will feel wedded to that lesson plan that you have spent so much time writing and planning. Eventually, you will focus less on what you are doing in a lesson and more on what your students are doing and how that informs you about their thinking and learning.

Periodically as you collect data that you have decided will inform your classroom inquiry question, you should look over your field notes and some of your data samples and take the time to do freewriting. Ask yourself, "What is emerging?" "What could this mean?" Teacher researchers do this careful reflection on action on a regular basis aided by the data they have collected during the second phase of their classroom inquiry. This process of looking with a critical eye at the notes you have taken and the observations you have recorded is referred to as *cooking the data* (Hubbard & Power, 1993). At this stage teacher researchers are engaged in a discovery process in which they are trying to understand what the data means and whether they have answered their own question. Look back to Figure 13.4 to see the double-entry notebook that many teacher researchers find very useful for collecting and sorting data and impressions associated with their ongoing classroom work and their particular inquiry question.

cooking the data
Analysis and interpretation of available raw data.

We remind the experienced teachers and the student teachers we work with to look for patterns or characteristics that are naturally occurring in their classroom settings. For example, we suggest that these teachers look for patterns of behavior of students who are speaking most frequently during literature circles in the English/language arts courses or those participating most appropriately during discussions and debates in social studies courses. We also suggest they look for evidence that students are using various graphic organizers (webs or semantic feature charts) or other study aids on their own with content-area materials.

Student teachers gain a great deal from sharing their data analysis and findings from inquiry projects with their peers as well as with cooperating teachers and supervisors.

© Elizabeth Crews

In addition, as the teachers look over their own field notes or their students' ongoing work samples, we remind them to look for surprises and puzzles in the data. For example, a teacher may ask why a usually quiet student chose to participate more on a given day than he or she had in the past. Asking oneself, "Does the student have more background knowledge on this topic or is the composition of the group more conducive to the student's willingness to participate?" might yield some useful information for the future. Finally, we encourage teachers to reflect constantly on their teaching plans (both lessons and units), as well as on their curriculum materials, in order to generate new ideas and questions to inform their classroom practice.

Thinking About Your Own Teaching and Learning

In order to be the continuous learner we discussed in Chapter 1 and to meet the standards of the profession throughout a career of teaching, teachers need time devoted to learning about new initiatives like the national discipline-based standards, changes in subject matter relevant to their discipline, and teaching/assessing tools designed to enhance student learning. Teachers at every level and in every discipline need time to find and to develop resources to support the teaching and learning activities that will make up the daily fabric of their own classrooms. You too will have these needs as you attempt to meet the myriad of expectations placed on you as a teacher and curriculum developer trying to create relevant and long-lasting learning experiences for your own students.

■ Professional Standards for Teachers

STANDARDS ✔️ Just as there are standards for the disciplines that are meant to guide the development of curriculum and quality of instruction, there are also standards being developed for teachers who are the primary agents for school reform and the major developers of curriculum in schools today. Three areas are being focused on to establish quality within the teaching profession. First, standards are being proposed for institutional or program accreditation, whereby an institution's program or program for the preparation and entry of individuals into the field of education is approved or accredited by a state, regional, or national agency responsible for teacher education. If you have not already done so, you might want to look at your institution's course catalog or program booklet provided. Can you determine which agency or agencies accredit your teacher education program?

Second, once you have successfully completed your program of study and one or more field-based experiences, such as student teaching or an internship, you will receive your first credential or certificate to teach. This certificate is granted most often by the department of education in the state in which your college or university is located. As of 2003, most states require a passing score on a teacher test, which usually focuses on communication skills and subject matter knowledge, in addition to the successful completion of an accredited program at a college or university before one can become credentialed as a teacher.

Finally, as a result of concerns about the quality of teaching in our schools and equitable opportunities for all students, states have individually designed rigorous recertification programs for in-service teachers in all fields. A number of states and professional organizations have also joined together to establish national performance standards and tests of competence for beginning and experienced teachers. The developers of these standards believe that such unified professional standards will create a teaching force that is capable of producing comparable, quality instruction for all students across the country.

Recommendations related to the preparation of teachers, qualifications for entry into the teaching profession, and guidelines for continuation in the field of education have many similarities.

■ Joining Additional Communities of Learners

In addition to the community of learners you create in your own classroom, we hope that throughout your career you will participate in two other communities of learners:

- The other teachers in your discipline, your grade level, or your team who are your most immediate colleagues.

- The larger professional community in which you have entered as a content-area specialist.

These will offer you a wider community of learners to interact with in order to create a collective knowledge base about teaching practice, content, and students. In order to break the isolation of working alone and focusing only on your own classroom and students, collaboration and conversation with other teachers, especially those who know the same student population and the same school setting, are essential. What can be more credible than hearing about the effectiveness of a teaching/assessing tool or a grouping procedure from a colleague who teaches down the hall or who works in the same discipline in another district? We hope that as you go from your role as student teacher to being a professional in the field, you continue to question and learn from your teaching, and that you share your triumphs as well as your puzzles with other professionals throughout your teaching career.

We encouraged you to seek out peers and colleagues as you considered the literacy and learning strategies we emphasized in Part Two and the application of those strategies within a range of disciplines we explored in Parts Two and Three. We hope you have begun to see yourself as a member of a community of learners and that you will continue to seek out colleagues when you become an in-service teacher with your own students and your own classroom. If a new text or a new set of frameworks is introduced for your content area, we hope you will approach their implementation with a questioning stance. In other words, we hope that you will always attempt to identify how well these changes match with your students' needs, as well as what literacy strategies and teaching tools you will need to introduce students to in order to complement the demands of new material or new understandings.

We also hope you will become part of the broader professional community associated with either your discipline, such as the National Council of Teachers of Mathematics, or with your level, such as the National Middle School Association. As a beginning teacher, it is easiest to become connected to this type of professional organization by maintaining a membership and a subscription to a journal in your field. Many national and state-level professional organizations also have web sites so that you can be constantly connected to a broader professional community of educators and learners. These resources will help you continue to think and to learn from teachers in your field who may have similar students, similar content, and similar settings.

We recommend that you seek out a local or regional organization for teachers in your discipline, such as the New England Association of Teachers of English or the Bay Area Association of Teachers of Mathematics. We believe that membership and participation in such professional organizations will give you many opportunities to learn about new teaching techniques and resources, keep up with standards and frameworks for your students and credentialing and licensing issues that may affect you, and share ideas and concerns with colleagues across a broader professional base than just those in your own school or district.

CONCLUSION TO THIS BOOK

We have built this book on some very specific premises related to being an effective teacher, and we believe that in doing so we have given you a tall order to fill as you become a teacher. In essence we have said you need to be:

- A teacher and a learner.
- A participant and an observer.
- A facilitator and a coach.
- A developer of curriculum and a critic of content/materials.
- A collaborator and an evaluator.

Throughout this text we have prompted you to try out literacy strategies for yourself as a learner in your own discipline, and to try these strategies and teaching/assessing tools with your own students. We have asked you to reflect on the effectiveness of these strategies and tools with different students and with different resources. Furthermore, we have often recommended that you share and compare the outcomes of your learning and your teaching with peers, other preservice teachers, and experienced teachers in the schools where you are doing your field placement. We have challenged you to reflect on your own actions and experiences as a teacher in order to see what works for you and your particular students in your discipline and in the context in which you find yourself, and not merely to believe us as the authors of this text.

We hope you will continue to question and reflect on what you are doing as a middle school or high school content-area teacher. We also hope you will continue to ask yourself questions about your learners, your content, and your pedagogy. We believe your own ongoing learning in the profession is dependent on thoughtful reflections and your willingness to revise and to revamp your practices. As Linda Darling-Hammond (1994) said at an annual conference of the American Association of Teacher Educators, "We are at a moment in education when we are re-evaluating the entire educational system, teachers and students within it and developing a paradigm in support of more professional learner-centered teaching." Almost a decade later, we concur with Darling-Hammond and believe that a teacher, by the nature of the profession, no matter what the discipline or level, must be engaged in continuous learning.

Throughout the text, we have also reminded you about the many choices you will have as a teacher, for both yourself and your students. We have not offered you these choices to confuse or confound you. Rather, we have done this to challenge you to review your current situation regularly and to consider everything you have learned as a teacher, as well as all that is in your repertoire, before making educational decisions. If you do this, you will be able to revise and reshape your role as teacher, your classroom organization, the teaching tools you use, and the resources you choose based on the learners who are before you.

We have filled this text with examples of strategies, teaching tools, and sample content-area lessons and units. We have invited you to add your own examples from your discipline and from your grade levels along the way. We believe that you will be able to take the understandings of your discipline and understanding your students, and your newly enhanced pedagogy, particularly your knowledge of literacy and learning strategies and use them effectively and reflectively as a capable, professional middle school or high school teacher who will guide the students and shape the schools of the twenty-first century.

Resources

Books

Campbell, D. M., Cignetti, P. B., Melenyzer, B. J., Nettles, D. H., & Wyman, R. M. (2001). *How to develop a professional portfolio: A manual for teachers* (2nd ed.). Boston: Allyn and Bacon. Step-by-step guidelines for collecting artifacts and organizing a portfolio based on standards from the Interstate New Teacher Assessment and Support Consortium. Examples of possible portfolio contents provided. Describes effective portfolio maintenance for those in a teaching position, in a job search, or in a teacher preparatory program.

Hubbard, R. S., & Power, B. M. (1993). *The art of classroom inquiry: A handbook for teacher-researchers.* Portsmouth, NH: Heinemann. Describes a clear set of steps for teacher researchers to follow in order to carry out classroom inquiry from finding and framing a question to analyzing and using data to inform one's own practice.

Hubbard, R. S., & Power, B. M. (1999). *Living the questions: A guide for teacher researchers.* York, ME: Stenhouse Publishers. Notes the importance of teacher research and provides guidelines for question development, data collection and analysis, publishing, and reflection. Also suggests sample projects and strategies for resource and time management.

Lieberman, A., & Miller, L. (Eds.). (2001). *Teachers caught in the action: Professional development that matters.* New York: Teachers College. Discusses professional development in the context of school reform and proposes using inquiry and assessment to strengthen teaching. Case studies in professional development and school reform provided.

Journals

Slavin, R. E. (2003). A reader's guide to scientifically based research. *Educational Leadership, 60* (5), 12–16. Suggests criteria regarding what to look for and what to avoid when assessing the validity of research articles. Also contains a brief explanation of different types of research studies.

Stremmel, A. J. (2002). Teacher research: Nurturing professional and personal growth through inquiry. *Young Children, 57* (5), 62–69. Provides a definition for teacher research and discusses the value of active participation in research conducted in a real life context.

Wolf, K., & Sui-Runyon, Y. (1996). Portfolio purposes and possibilities. *Journal of Adolescent and Adult Literacy, 40* (1), 30–37. Emphasizes that the purpose of a portfolio should determine its form and describes three models, each with a different purpose, and their strengths and limitations.

Web Sites

PEAK Learning Systems™ Educators Resource Center. **www.new-teacher.com/portfolio.html.** Provides an outline for the organization of a portfolio, discusses what potential employers wish to see in a portfolio, and makes suggestions for items to include. Links to other related web sites are present.

Scholastic. **www.teacher.scholastic.com/professional/ futureteachers/professional_port.htm.** Discusses what should be included in a portfolio and suggests possible presentation formats.

References

Afflerbach, P., & Vansledright, B. (2001). Hath! Doth! What? Middle graders reading innovative history text. *Journal of Adolescent & Adult Literacy, 44* (8), 696–707.

Albright, J., Purohit, K., & Walsh, C. (2002). Louise Rosenblatt seeks *QtAsnBoi@aol.com* for LTR: Using chat rooms in interdisciplinary middle school classrooms. *Journal of Adolescent & Adult Literacy, 45* (8), 692–705.

Alexander, P. A., Jetton, T. L., Kulikowich, J. M., & Woehler, C. A. (1994). Contrasting instructional and structural importance: The seductive effect of teacher questions. *Journal of Reading Behavior, 26* (1), 19–45.

Alexander, P. A., & Judy, J. E. (1988). The interaction of domain-specific and strategic knowledge in academic performance. *Review of Educational Research, 58* (4), 375–404.

Alexander, P. A., & Kulikowich, J. M. (1994). Learning from physics textbooks: A synthesis of recent research. *Journal of Research in Science Teaching, 31* (9), 895–911.

Allan, K. K., & Miller, M. S. (1995*). Purposeful reading and writing: Strategies in context.* Fort Worth, TX: Harcourt Brace.

Allen, S. (1989). *Writing to learn in science* (ERIC Documentation Reproduction Service NO. ED 362 883).

Almasi, J. F. (1995). The nature of fourth graders' sociocognitive conflicts in peer-led and teacher-led discussions of literature. *Reading Research Quarterly, 30* (3), 314–351.

Almasi, J. F., O'Flahavan, J. F., & Arya, P. (2001). A comparative analysis of student and teacher development in more and less proficient discussions of literature. *Reading Research Quarterly, 36* (2), 96–120.

Alvermann, D. (1994). Trade books and textbooks: Making connections across content areas. In L. M. Morrow, J. K. Smith, & L. C. Wilkinson (Eds*.), Integrating language arts: Controversy to consensus* (pp. 51– 69). Needham Heights, MA: Allyn & Bacon.

Alvermann, D. E., O'Brien, D. G., & Dillon, D. R. (1990). What teachers do when they say they're having discussions of content area reading assignments: A qualitative analysis. *Reading Research Quarterly, 25* (4), 296–321.

Alvermann, D. E., Smith, L. C., & Readance, J. E. (1985). Prior knowledge activation and the comprehension of compatible and incompatible text. *Reading Research Quarterly, 20,* 420–436.

Alvermann, D. E., Young, J. P., Weaver, D., Hinchman, K. A., Moore, D. W., Phelps, S. F., Thrash, E. C., & Zalewski, P. (1996). Middle and high school students' perceptions of how they experience text-based discussions: A multicase study. *Reading Research Quarterly, 31* (3), 244–267.

American Association of University Women. (1992*). The AAUW report: How schools shortchange girls.* Washington, D.C.: AAUW Educational Foundation.

American Council on the Teaching of Foreign Languages. (1999). *Standards for foreign language learning in the 21st century.* Yonkers, NY: American Council on the Teaching of Foreign Languages.

American Institutes for Research. (1998*). Gender gaps: Where schools still fail our children.* Washington, D.C.: American Association of University Women Educational Foundation.

Ames, R., & Ames, C. (1991). Motivation and effective teaching. In L. Idol & B. F. Jones (Eds.), *Educational values and cognitive instruction: Implications for reform* (pp. 247–271). Hillsdale, NJ: Erlbaum.

Anderson, G. L., Herr, K., & Nihlen, A. S. (1994*). Studying your own school: An educator's guide to qualitative practitioner research*. Thousand Oaks, CA: Corwin Press.

Anderson, R. C. (1994). Role of the reader's schema in comprehension, learning and memory. In R. B. Ruddell, M. R. Ruddell, & H. Singer (Eds.*), Theoretical models and processes of reading* (4th ed.) (pp. 469–482). Newark, DL: International Reading Association.

Anderson, R. C., Reynolds, R. E., Schallert, D. L., & Goetz, E. T. (1977). Frameworks for comprehending discourse. *American Educational Research Journal, 14*, 367–382.

Armbruster, B. B. (1984). The problem of "inconsiderate text." In G. G. Duffy, L. R. Roehler, & J. Mason (Eds,), *Comprehension instruction: Perspectives and suggestions* (pp. 202–217). New York: Longman.

Armbruster, B. B., Anderson, T. H., & Ostertag, J. (1987). Does text structure/summarization instruction facilitate learning from expository text? *Reading Research Quarterly, 22*, 331–346.

Aronson, E. (1978). *The jigsaw classroom*. Thousand Oaks, CA: Sage.

Atwell, N. (1998*). In the middle: New understandings about writing, reading, and learning* (2nd ed.). Portsmouth, NH: Heinemann.

August, D., & Hakuta, K. (Eds.). (1998). *Educating language-minority children*. Washington, D.C.: National Academy Press.

Baker, J. (2002). Trilingualism. In L. Delpit & J. K. Dowdy (Eds.). *The skin that we speak*. (pp. 49–61). New York: New Press.

Baldwin, R. S., Ford, J. C., & Readence, J. E. (1981). Teaching word connotations: An alternative strategy. *Reading World, 21* (2), 103–108.

Ball, A. F. (1992). Cultural preference and expository writing. *Written Communication, 9* (2), 501–532.

Ball, D. L. (1991). Research on teaching mathematics: Making subject-matter knowledge part of the equation. In J. Brophy (Ed.), *Advances in research on teaching* (Vol. 2, pp. 1–48). Greenwich, CT: JAI Press.

Barnes, D., & Todd, F. (1995). *Communication and learning revisited*. Portsmouth, NH: Boynton/Cook, Heinemann.

Barton, M. L., Heidema, C., & Jordan, D. (2002). Teaching reading in mathematics and science. *Educational Leadership, 60* (3), 24–28.

Baumann, J. F., Edwards, E. C., Font, G., Tereshinski, C. A., Kame'enui, E. J., Olejnik, S. F. (2002). Teaching morphemic and contextual analysis to fifth-grade students. *Reading Research Quarterly, 37* (2), 150–176.

Bausch, L. S. (2003). Just words: Living and learning the literacies of our students' lives. *Language Arts, 80* (3), 215–222.

Bean, T. W., & Rigoni, N. (2001). Exploring the intergenerational dialogue journal discussion of a multicultural young adult novel. *Reading Research Quarterly, 36* (3), 232–249.

Beane, J. A. (1995a). Curriculum integration and the disciplines of knowledge. *Phi Delta Kappan, 76* (8), 616–622.

Beane, J. A. (1995b). Introduction: What is a coherent curriculum? *Yearbook for the Association of Supervision and Curriculum Development.* Alexandria, VA: ASCD.

Beck, I. L., McKeown, M. G., Hamilton, R. L., & Kucan, L. (1997*). Questioning the author: An approach for enhancing student engagement with text.* Newark, DL: International Reading Association.

Beck, I. L., McKeown, M. G., & Kucan, L. (2002). *Bringing words to life: Robust vocabulary instruction.* New York: Guilford.

Beck, I. L., McKeown, M. G., McCaslin, E. S., & Burkes, A. M. (1979). *The rationale and design of a program to teach vocabulary to fourth-grade students.* Pittsburgh: University of Pittsburgh, Learning Research and Development Center.

Bergen County Academies Academy Projects Database. (n.d.) *The American Immigration Home Page.* Retrieved April 2, 2003 from *bergen.org/AAST/Projects/Immigration*

Bernhardt, E. (2003). Challenges to reading research from a multilingual world. *Reading Research Quarterly, 38* (1), 112–117.

Blachowicz, C. L. S., & Fisher, P. (2000). Vocabulary instruction. In M. Kamil, P. B. Mosenthal, P. D. Pearson, & R. Barr (Eds.) *Handbook of Reading Research, Vol. 3* (pp. 503–523). New York: Macmillan.

Bloom, A. (1987). *The closing of the American mind.* New York: Simon & Schuster.

Bos, C. S., & Anders, P. L. (1990). Interactive teaching and learning: Instructional practices for teaching content and strategic knowledge. In T. E. Scruggs & B. Y. L. Wong (Eds.), *Intervention research in learning disabilities* (pp. 166–185). New York: Springer-Verlag.

Bos, C. S., & Anders, P. L. (1990, Winter). Effects of interactive vocabulary instruction on the vocabulary learning and reading comprehension of junior-high learning disabled students. *Learning Disability Quarterly, 13,* 31–42.

Bos, C. S., Anders, P. L., Filip, D., & Jaffe, L. E. (1989). The effects of an interactive instructional strategy for enhancing reading comprehension and content area learning for students with learning disabilities. *Journal of Learning Disabilities, 22* (6), 384–390.

Boston Public Schools. (1996). Citywide learning standards and curriculum frameworks. Boston: Boston Public Schools.

Boyd, M. P., & Rubin, D. L. (2002). Elaborated student talk in an elementary EsoL classroom. *Research in the Teaching of English, 36* (4), 495–530.

Bransford, J. D. (1994). Schema activation and schema acquisition: Comments on Richard C. Anderson's remarks. In R. B. Ruddell, M. R. Ruddell, & H. Singer (Eds.), *Theoretical models and processes of reading* (4th ed.) (pp. 483–495). Newark, DL: International Reading Association.

Brown, A. L., & Day, J. D. (1983). Macrorules for summarizing texts: The development of expertise. *Journal of Verbal Learning and Verbal Behavior, 22,* 1–14.

Brown, D. E. (1992). Using examples and analogies to remediate misconceptions in physics: Factors influencing conceptual change. *Journal of Research in Science Teaching, 29* (1), 17–34.

Bruce, B. C. (2002). Diversity and critical social engagement: How changing technologies enable new modes of literacy in changing circumstances. In D. E. Alvermann (Ed.), *Adolescents and literacies in a digital world,* (pp. 1–18). New York: Peter Lang.

Buikema, J. L., & Graves, M. F. (1993). Teaching students to use context cues to infer word meanings. *Journal of Reading, 36* (6), 450–457.

Callahan, M. (2002). Intertextual composition: The power of the digital pen. *English Education, 35* (1), 46–65.

Carnegie Commission Task Force. (1986). *A nation prepared: Teachers for the 21st century*. Report of the Task Force on Teaching as a Profession. New York: Carnegie Corporation.

Carnegie Council on Adolescent Development. (1990). *Turning points: Preparing American youth for the 21st century*. Report of the Carnegie Council on Adolescent Development's Task Force on Education of Young Adolescents. New York: Carnegie Corporation.

Carr, E., & Ogle, D. (1987). KWL Plus: A strategy for comprehension and summarization. *Journal of Reading, 30,* 626–631.

Chall, J. S., Jacobs, V. A., & Baldwin, L. E. (1990). *The reading crisis: Why poor children fall behind.* Cambridge, MA: Harvard University Press.

Chang, J-M. (2003). Multilevel collaboration for English learners: An Asian American perspective. In G. G. Garcia (Ed.), *English learners: Reaching the highest level of English literacy,* (pp. 259–285). Newark, DL: International Reading Association.

Checkley, K. (1997). International math and science study calls for depth not breadth. *ASCD Education Update, 19* (1) 1, 3.

Christoph, J. N., & Nytstrand, M. (2001). Taking risks, negotiating relationships: One teacher's transition toward a dialogic classroom. *Research in the Teaching of English, 36,* 249–286.

Cochran, J. F., De Ruiter, J. A., & King, R. A. (1993). Pedagogical content knowing: An integrative model for teacher preparation. *Journal of Teacher Education, 44,* 263–272.

Collins, A., Brown, J. S., & Newman, S. E. (1989). Cognitive apprenticeship: Teaching the craft of reading, writing, mathematics. In L. B. Resnick (Ed*.), Knowing, learning, and instruction: Essays in honor of Robert Glaser* (pp. 453–494). Hillsdale, NJ: Erlbaum.

Committee for Economic Development. (1987). *Children in need: Investment strategies for the educationally disadvantaged.* New York: Committee for Economic Development.

Conard, S. (1984). *On readability and readability formula scores.* Ginn Occasional Papers: Writings in Reading and Language Arts, no. 17. New York: Ginn.

Cooper, J. D., with N. C. Kiger. (2003). *Literacy: Helping Children Construct Meaning* (5th ed.). Boston, MA: Houghton Mifflin.

Crawford, L. W. (1993). *Language and literacy learning in multicultural classrooms.* Needham Heights, MA: Allyn & Bacon.

Daniels, H. (2002). *Literature circles: Voice and choice in book clubs and reading groups,* (2nd ed.). Portland, ME: Stenhouse.

Darling-Hammond, L. (1991). The implications of testing policy for quality and equality. *Phi Delta Kappan, 73,* 220–225.

Darling-Hammond, L. (1994, February 17). *Standards for teachers.* 34th Charles M. Hunt Memorial Lecture, AACTE 46th Annual Meeting, Chicago.

Delpit, L. D. (1988). The silenced dialogue: Power and pedagogy in educating other people's children. *Harvard Educational Review, 58,* 280–298.

Delpit, L. (1995). *Other people's children: Cultural conflict in the classroom.* New York: New Press.

Dillon, D. R., O'Brien, D. G., & Moje, E. B. (1994). Literacy learning in secondary school classrooms: A cross-case analysis of three qualitative studies. *Journal of Research in Teaching Science, 31* (4), 345–362.

Dillon, J. T. (1994). *Using discussion in classrooms*. Philadelphia: Open University Press.

Dole, J., Duffy, G. G., Roehler, L. R., & Pearson, P. D. (1991). Moving from the old to the new: Research on reading comprehension instruction. *Review of Educational Research, 61* (2), 239–264.

Doll, R. C. (1996). *Curriculum improvement: Decision making and process* (9th ed.). Needham Heights, MA: Allyn & Bacon.

Dornan, R., Rosen, L. M., & Wilson, M. (1997). *Multiple voices, multiple texts: Reading in the secondary content areas*. Portsmouth, NH: Boynton/Cook Publishers.

Drake, S. M. (1993). *Planning integrated curriculum: The call to adventure*. Alexandria, VA: Association for Supervision and Curriculum Development.

Duffelmeyer, F. A. (1994). Effective anticipation guide statement for learning from expository prose. *Journal of Reading, 37* (6), 452–457.

Duffelmeyer, F. A., Baum, D. D., & Merkely, D. J. (1987). Maximizing reader-text confrontation with an extended anticipation guide. *Journal of Reading, 31* (20), 146–150.

Duffy, G. G., & Roehler, L. R. (1989). Why strategy instruction is so difficult and what we need to do about it. In C. B. McCormick, G. Miller, & M. Pressley (Eds.), *Cognitive strategy research: From basic research to educational applications* (pp.133–154). New York: Springer-Verlag.

Duffy, G. G., Roehler, L. R., Sivan, E., Rackliffe, G., Book, C., Meloth, M. S., Vavrus, L. G., Wesselman, R., Putnam, J., & Bassiri, D. (1987). Effects of explaining the reasoning associated with using reading strategies. *Reading Research Quarterly, 22* (3), 347–368.

Eagleton, M. B., & Guinne, K. (2002). Strategies for supporting student Internet inquiry. *The NERA Journal, 38* (2), 39–47.

Earle, R. A. (1976). *Teaching reading and mathematics*. Newark, DL: International Reading Association.

Ediger, M. (1998). Designing the curriculum. (ERIC Documentation Reproduction Services ED 336 198.)

Eeds, M., & Wells, D. (1989). Grand conversations: An exploration of meaning construction in literature study groups. *Research in the Teaching of English, 23* (1), 4–29.

Elbow, P. (1973). *Writing without teachers*. New York: Oxford University Press.

Englert, C. S., Raphael, T. E., Anderson, L. M., Anthony, H. M., & Stevens, D. D. (1991). Making strategies and self-talk visible: Writing instruction in regular and special education classrooms. *American Educational Research Journal, 28*, 337–372.

Evans, K.S. (2002). Fifth-grade students' perceptions of how they experience literature discussion groups. *Reading Research Quarterly, 37* (1) 46–69.

Featherstone, J. (1995). Letter to a young teacher. In W. Ayers (Ed.), *To become a teacher: Making a difference in children's lives* (pp. 11–22). New York: Teachers College.

Fecho, B. (2000). Critical inquiries into language in an urban classroom. *Research in the Teaching of English, 34*, 368–395.

Fecho, B. (2001). "Why are you doing this?": Acknowledging and transcending threat in a critical inquiry classroom. *Research in the Teaching of English, 36* (1), 9–37.

Figueroa, R. A., & García, E. (1994). Issues in testing students from culturally and linguistically diverse backgrounds. *Multicultural Education, 2* (1), 10–9.

Finders, M. J. (1997). *Just girls: Hidden literacies and life in junior high.* New York: Teachers College.

Fine, M. (1991). *Framing dropouts: Notes on the politics of an urban high school.* Albany: State University of New York Press.

Fink, R. (1995–96). Successful dyslexics: A constructivist study of passionate interest in reading. *Journal of Adolescent & Adult Literacy, 39* (4), 268–80.

Flavell, J. H., Miller, P. H., & Miller, S. A. (1993). *Cognitive development.* Englewood Cliffs, NJ: Prentice Hall.

Frayer, D. A., Frederick, W. C., & Klausmeier, H. H. (1969). *A science for testing the level of concept mastery* (Working Paper No. 16). Madison, WI: University of Wisconsin Research and Development Center for Cognitive Learning.

Fredericks, A. D., Meinbach, A. M., & Rothlein, L. (1992). *Thematic units: An integrated approach to teaching science and social studies.* New York: HarperCollins.

Fry, E. B. (1977). Fry's readability graph: Clarifications, validity, and extension to level 17. *Journal of Reading, 21,* 242–252.

Fulwiler, T. (1987). *Teaching with writing.* Portsmouth, NH: Boynton/Cook, Heinemann.

Furner, J. (1995). *Planning for interdisciplinary instruction: a literature review.* Tuscaloosa, AL: University of Alabama College of Education. (ERIC Document Reproduction Service No. ED 385 515.)

Gambrell, L. B., & Almasi, J. F. (1994). Fostering comprehension development through discussion. In L. M. Morrow, J. K. Smith, & L. C. Wilkinson, *Integrated language arts: Controversy to consensus* (pp. 71–90). Needham Heights, MA: Allyn & Bacon.

García, E. (2002). *Student cultural diversity: Understanding and meeting the challenge* (3rd ed.). Boston: Houghton Mifflin.

García, G. E. (1991). Factors influencing the English reading test performance of Spanish-speaking Hispanic children. *Reading Research Quarterly, 26* (4), 371–391.

García, G.E. (1998). Mexican-American bilingual students' metacognitive reading strategies: What's transferred, unique, problematic? In T. Shanahan & F. V. Rodiquez-Brown (Eds.), *National Reading Conference Yearbook, 47,* (pp. 253–263). Chicago: National Reading Conference.

García, G. E., & Nagy, W. E. (1993). Latino students' concept of cognates. In D. J. Leu & C. K. Kinzer (Eds.), *Examining central issues in literacy research, theory, and practice* (pp. 367–373). 42nd Yearbook of the National Reading Conference. Chicago: National Reading Conference.

García, G. E., & Pearson, P. D. (1994). Assessment and diversity. In L. Darling-Hammond (Ed.), *Review of research in education* (Vol. 20, pp. 337–391). Washington, D.C.: American Educational Research Association.

Garner, R. (1987). *Metacognition and reading comprehension.* Norwood, NJ: Ablex.

Garner, R., & Alexander, R. (1989). Metacognition: Answered and unanswered questions. *Educational Psychologist, 24* (2), 143–158.

Garner, R., Gillingham, M. G., & White, C. S. (1989). Effects of "seductive details" on macroprocessing and microprocessing in adults and children. *Cognition and Instruction, 6,* 41–57.

Gaskins, I., & Gaskins, E. T. (1991). *Implementing cognitive strategy teaching across the school: The Benchmark manual for teachers.* Cambridge, MA: Brookline Press.

Gee, J. P. (1996). *Social linguistics and literacies: Ideology in discourses* (2nd ed.). Bristol, PA: Falmer Press, Taylor & Francis Group.

Geography Education Standards Project. (1994). *Geography for life: National geography standards.* Washington, D.C.: Geography Education Standards Project.

George, P. S. & Alexander, W. M. (2003). *The exemplary middle school* (3rd ed.). Belmont, CA: Thomson/Wadswoth.

Gersten, R., Fuchs, L. S., Williams, J. P. & Baker, S. (2001). Teaching reading comprehension strategies to students with learning disabilities: A review of the research. *Review of Educational Research, 71* (2), 279–320.

Glatthorn, A. A. (1986). *Alternative processes in curriculum development.* Paper presented at the Annual Meeting of the American Educational Research Association, San Francisco.

Goatley, V. J., Brock, C. H., & Raphael, T. E. (1995). Diverse learners participating in regular education "Book Clubs." *Reading Research Quarterly, 30* (3), 352–380.

Goerss, B. L., Beck, I. L., & McKeown, M. G. (1999). Increasing remedial students' ability to derive word meaning from context. *Journal of Reading Psychology, 20,* 151–175.

Gollnick, D. M., & Chinn, P. C. (2001). *Multicultural education in a pluralistic society.* New York: Merrill/Macmillan.

Goodlad, J. I. (1984). *A place called school.* New York: McGraw-Hill.

Gordon, C. J., & Macinnis, D. (1993). Using journals as a window on students' thinking in mathematics. *Language Arts, 70,* 37–43.

Grant, R. A., & Wong, S. D. (2003). Barriers to literacy for language-minority learners: An argument for change in the literacy education profession. *Journal of Adolescent & Adult Literacy, 46* (5), 386–394.

Gregg, G. P., & Carroll, P. S. (1998). *Books and beyond: Thematic approaches for teaching literature in high school.* Norwood, MA: Christopher-Gordon Publishers.

Grossman, P. L. (1991). What are we talking about anyway? Subject-matter knowledge of secondary English teachers. In J. Brophy (Ed.), *Advances in research on teaching* (Vol. 2, pp. 245–264). Greenwich, CT: JAI Press.

Guthrie, J. T., & McCann, A. D. (1996). Idea circles: Peer collaborations for conceptual learning. In L. B. Gambrell & J. R. Almasi (Eds.), *Lively discussions! Fostering engaged reading* (pp. 87–105). Newark, DL: International Reading Association.

Guthrie, J. T., & Wigfield, A. (1997). *Reading Engagement: Motivating readers through integrated instruction.* Newark, DL: International Reading Association.

Guzzetti, B. J., (2001). Texts and talk: The role of gender in learning physics. In E. B. Moje & D. G. O'Brien (Eds.), *Constructions of literacy: Studies of teaching and learning in and out of secondary schools,* (pp. 125–146). Mahwah, NJ: Erlbaum.

Guzzetti, B. J., & Williams, W. O. (1996). Gender, text, and discussion: Examining the intellectual safety in the science classroom. *Journal of Research in Science Teaching, 33* (1), 5–20.

Haggard, M. R. (1982). Vocabulary self-collection strategy: An active approach to word learning. *Journal of Reading, 27,* 203–207.

Haggard, M. R. (1986). The vocabulary self-collection strategy: Using student interest and world knowledge to enhance vocabulary growth. *Journal of Reading 29,* (7), 634–642.

Hare, V. C., Rabinowitz, M., & Schieble, K. M. (1989). Text effects on main idea comprehension. *Reading Research Quarterly, 24,* 72–88.

Harmon, J. M. (2002). Teaching independent word learning strategies to struggling readers. *Journal of Adolescent & Adult Literacy, 45* (7), 606–615.

Harris, K., & Pressley, M. (1991). The nature of cognitive strategy instruction: Interactive strategy instruction. *Exceptional Children, 57,* 392–404.

Harste, J., Short, K., with Burke, C. L. (1988*). Creating classrooms for authors: The reading-writing connection.* Portsmouth, N.H.: Heinemann.

Hartman, D. K. (1995). Eight readers reading: The intertextual links of proficient readers reading multiple passages. *Reading Research Quarterly, 30* (3), 520–561.

Henning-Stout, M., James, S., & Macintosh, S. (2000). Reducing harassment of lesbian, gay, bisexual, transgender, and questioning youth in schools. *School Psychology Review, 29* (2), 180–192.

Herber, H. L. (1978). *Teaching reading in the content areas* (2nd ed.). New York: Prentice Hall.

Hidi, S., & Anderson, V. (1986). Producing written summaries: Task demands, cognitive operations, and implications for instruction. *Review of Educational Research, 56* (4), 473–493.

Hill, M. (1991). Writing summaries promotes thinking and learning across the curriculum—but why are they so difficult to write? *Journal of Reading, 34* (7), 536–539.

Hirsch, E. D., Jr. (1988). *Cultural literacy: What every American needs to know.* New York: Random House.

Hollon, R. E., Roth, K. J., & Anderson, C. W. (1991). Science teachers' conceptions of teaching and learning. In J. Brophy (Ed.), *Advances in research on teaching* (Vol. 2, pp. 145–185). Greenwich, CT: JAI Press.

Hubbard, R. S., & Power, B. M. (1993). *The art of classroom inquiry: A handbook for teacher researchers.* Portsmouth, NH: Heinemann.

Hynds, S. (1997). *On the brink: Negotiating literacy and life with adolescents.* New York: Teachers College Press.

International Reading Association and National Council of Teachers of English, Statement on readability. (1984). Newark, DL: International Reading Association.

Illinois State Board of Education. (1998). *Integrated nutrition education.* Curriculum guide developed for the Illinois State Board of Education (ERIC Document Reproduction Services No. ED 231 505).

Jackson, A. W., & Davis, G. A. (2000). *Turning Points 2000: Educating Adolescents in the 21st Century. A Reprot of the Carnegie Corporation.* New York: Teachers College Press.

Jacobs, H. H. (Ed.) (1989). *Interdisciplinary curriculum: Design and implemention.* Alexandria, VA: Association for Supervision and Curriculum Development.

Jiménez, R. T. (2003). Literacy and Latino students in the United States: Some considerations, questions, and new directions. *Reading Research Quarterly, 38* (1), 122–128.

Jiménez, R. T., García, G. E., & Pearson, P. D. (1996). The reading strategies of bilingual Latina/o students who are successful English readers: Opportunities and obstacles. *Reading Research Quarterly, 31* (1), 90–112.

Johnson, D. D., & Pearson, P. D. (1984). *Teaching vocabulary* (2nd ed.). New York: Holt.

Johnson, D. W., Johnson, R. T., & Holubec, E. J. (1990). *Circles of learning: Cooperation in the classroom* (3rd ed.). Edina, MN: Interaction Book Company.

Joint Committee on National Health Education Standards. (1995). *National health education standards: Achieving health literacy.* Washington, D.C.: American Cancer Society.

Jones, M. G., & Wheatley, J. (1990). Gender differences in teacher-student interactions in science classrooms. *Journal of Research in Science Teaching, 27* (9), 861–874.

Kendall, J. S., & Marzano, R. J. (2000). Content knowledge: A compendium of standards and benchmarks for K–12 education (3rd ed.). Alexandria, VA: Association for Supervision and Curriculum Development.

Kleiman, G. M. (1991). Mathematics across the curriculum. *Educational Leadership, 49* (2), 48–51.

Knapp, M. S., & Woolverton, S. (1995). Social class and schooling. In J. A. Banks & C. A. M. Banks (Eds.), *Handbook of research on multicultural education* (pp. 548–569). New York: Macmillan.

Kozol, J. (1991). *Savage inequalities: Children in America's schools.* New York: Crown.

Kuhn, M. R., & Stahl, S. A. (1998). Teaching children to learn word meanings from context. *Journal of Literacy Research, 30* (1), 119–138.

Kyle, W. C. (1995). Scientific literacy: Where do we go from here? *Journal of Research in Science Teaching, 32* (10), 1007–1009.

Langer, J. A., Bartolome, L., Vasquez, O., & Lucas, T. (1990). Meaning construction in school literacy tasks: A study of bilingual students. *American Educational Research Journal, 27,* 427–471.

Laturnau, J. (2003). Standards-based instruction for English language learners. In G. G. Garcia (Ed.), *English learners: Reaching the highest level of English literacy,* (pp. 286–306). Newark, DL: International Reading Association.

Laughlin, M. A., & Hartoonian, H. M. (1995). *Challenges of social studies instruction in middle and high schools.* Orlando, FL: Harcourt Brace.

Laverick, C. (2002). B-D-A strategy: Reinventing the wheel can be a good thing. *Journal of Adolescent & Adult Literacy, 46* (2), 144–147.

Lee, C. D. (1993). *Signifying as a scaffold for literary interpretation.* Urbana, IL: National Council of Teachers of English.

Lee, O., & Fradd, S. H. (1998). Science for all, including students from non-English-language backgrounds. *Educational Researcher, 27* (4), 12–20.

Lee, S. J. (2001). More than "model minorities" or "delinquents": A look at Hmong American high school students. *Harvard Educational Review, 71* (3), 505–528.

Lerner, J. (2003). Learning disabilities: *Theories, diagnosis and teaching strategies* (9th ed.). Boston: Houghton Mifflin.

Leu, D. J., Jr. (2002). The new literacies: Research on reading instruction with the internet. In A. E. Farstrup & S. J. Samuels (Eds.), *What research has to say about reading instruction,* (pp. 310–336). Newark, DL: International Reading Association.

Leu, D. J., Jr., & Leu, D. D. (1997). *Teaching with the Internet: Lessons from the Classroom.* Norwood, MA: Christopher-Gordon Publishers, Inc.

Levstik, L. S., & Barton, K. C. (1997). *Doing history: Investigating with children in elementary and middle schools.* Hillside, NJ: Erlbaum.

Lewis, C. (2001). *Literacy practices as social acts: Power, status and cultural norms in the classroom.* Mahwah, NJ: Erlbaum.

Lexile Framework for Reading (*www.lexile.com*).

Lounsbury, J. H. (Ed.) (1992). *Connecting the curriculum through interdisciplinary instruction.* Columbus, OH: National Middle School Association.

Lozauskas, D., & Barell, J. (1992). Reflective reading. *Science Teacher, 59* (8), 42–45.

Luke, C. (2002). Re-crafting media and ICT literacies. In D. E. Alvermann (Ed.), *Adolescents and literacies in a digital world* (pp. 132–146). New York: Peter Lang.

Maloch, B. (2002). Scaffolding student talk: One teacher's role in literature discussion groups. *Reading Research Quarterly, 37* (1), 94–112.

Mandler, J., & Johnson, N. (1977). Remembrance of things parsed: Story structure and recall. *Cognitive Psychology, 9,* 111–151.

Manning, M., Manning, G., & Long, R. (1997). *The theme immersion compendium for social studies teaching.* Portsmouth, NH: Heinemann.

Many, J. E., Fyfe, R., Lewis, G., & Mitchell, E. (1996). Traversing the topical landscape: Exploring students' self-directed reading-writing-research processes. *Reading Research Quarterly, 31* (1), 12–35.

Martinello, M. L., & Cook, G. E. (1994). *Interdisciplinary inquiry in teaching and learning.* New York: Macmillan.

Martinello, M. L. & Cook, G. E. (2000). *Interdisciplinary inquiry in teaching and learning* (2nd ed.). Upper Saddle River, NJ: Merrill.

Massachusetts Department of Education. (1996). *World languages curriculum frameworks.* Malden, MA: Massachusetts Department of Education.

Maurer, R. E. (1994). *Designing interdisciplinary curriculum in middle, junior high, and high schools.* Needham Heights, MA: Allyn & Bacon.

McDiarmid, G. W. (1991). What teachers need to know about cultural diversity: Restoring subject matter to the picture. In M. M. Kennedy (Ed.), *Teaching academic subjects to diverse learners* (pp. 257–270). New York: Teachers College Press.

McDiarmid, G. W., Ball, D. L., & Anderson, C. W. (1989). Why staying one chapter ahead doesn't really work: Subject-specific pedagogy. In M. C. Reynolds (Ed.), *Knowledge base for the beginning teacher* (pp. 193–205). New York: Pergamon Press.

McDonald, J. P. (1992). *Teaching: Making sense of an uncertain craft.* New York: Teachers College Press.

McMahon, S. I., & Raphael, T. E. (Eds.), with Goatley, V. J., & Pardo, L. S. (1997). *The book club connection: Literacy learning and classroom talk*. Newark, DL: International Reading Association.

McMillan, J. H. (1997). *Classroom assessment: Principles and practices for effective instruction*. Needham Heights, MA: Allyn & Bacon.

McMillan, J. H. (2001). *Classroom assessment: Principles and practices for effective instruction* (2nd ed.). Boston: Allyn & Bacon.

Meinbach, A. M., Rothlein, L., & Fredericks, A. D. (2000). *The complete guide to thematic units: Creating integrated curriculum*. Norwood, MA: Christopher Gordon Publishers.

Meyer, L. (1991). Are science textbooks considerate? In C. M. Santa & D. E. Alvermann (Eds.), *Science learning: Process and applications* (pp. 28–37). Newark, DL: International Reading Association.

Michaels, S. (1981). Sharing time: Children's narrative styles and differential access to literacy. *Language in Society, 10,* 423–442.

Miller, G. A., & Gildea, P. M. (1987). How children learn words. *Scientific American, 257* (3), 94–99.

Minami, M., & Ovando, C. J. (1995). Language issues in multicultural contexts. In J. A. Banks & C. A. M. Banks (Eds.), *Handbook of research on multicultural education* (pp. 427–444). New York: Macmillian.

Moffett, J. (1983/1968). *Teaching the universe of discourse*. Boston: Houghton Mifflin.

Moll, L. C. (1992). Bilingual classroom studies and community analysis: Some recent trends. *Educational Researcher, 21* (2), 20–24.

Montgomery County Public Schools Web Site Evaluation Form. *(www.mcpsk12.md.us/department/isa/elit/mid/websiteevalform.htm#criteria)*

Moran, C. E., & Hakuta, K. (1995). Bilingual education: Broadening research perspectives. In J. A. Banks & C. A. M. Banks (Eds.), *Handbook on multicultural education* (pp. 445–462). New York: Macmillan.

Morrell, E., & Duncan-Andrade, J. M. R. (2002). Promoting academic literacy with urban youth through engaging hip-hop culture. *English Journal, 91* (6), 88–91.

Moss, J. F. (1994). *Using literature in the middle grades: A thematic approach*. Norwood, MA: Christopher-Gordon Publishers.

Munoz-Plaza, C., Quinn, S. C., & Rounds, K. A. (2002). Lesbian, gay, bisexual and transgender students: Perceived social support in the high school environment. *High School Journal, 85* (4), 52–64.

Myer, B. J. F., Brandt, D. M., & Bluth, G. J. (1980). Use of top-level structure in text: Key for reading comprehension of ninth-grade students. *Reading Research Quarterly, 16,* 72–103.

Nagy, W. E., & Herman, P. A. (1987). Breadth and depth of vocabulary knowledge: Implications for acquisition and instruction. In M. G. McKeown & M. E. Curtis (Eds.), *The nature of vocabulary acquisition* (pp. 19–35). Hillsdale, NJ: Erlbaum.

Nagy, W. E., & Scott, J. A. (2000). Vocabulary processes. In M. Kamil, P. B. Mosenthal, P. D. Pearson, & R. Barr (Eds.), *Handbook of Reading Research, Vol. 3* (pp. 269–284). New York: Macmillan

National Academy of Sciences and National Science Association. (1996). *National Science Education Standards.* Washington, D.C.: National Academy Press.

National Association of Secondary School Principals. (1996). *Breaking ranks: Changing an American institution.* Report of the National Association of Secondary School Principals in partnership with the Carnegie Foundation for the Advancement of Teaching on the High School of the 21st Century. Washington, D.C.: National Association of Secondary School Principals.

National Center for Educational Statistics. (2002). *nces.ed.gov.pubs2002/snf report/table 05.asp* Retrieved April 16, 2003.

National Center for Educational Statistics. (2002). *Digest of Educational Statistics. nces.ed.gov//pubs2002/digest2001/tables/dt108asp.* Retrieved August 23, 2002.

National Center for Educational Statistics (2000). National Assessment of Educational Progress. Washington, D.C.: U.S. Government Printing Office.

National Center for Educational Statistics. (2001). *History report card: History assessment at a glance.* Washington, D.C.: U.S. Government Printing Office.

National Center for Educational Statistics. (2000). *Math report card for the nation and the states.* Washington, D.C.: U.S. Government Printing Office.

National Center for Educational Statistics. (1996). *The condition of education.* Washington, D.C.: U.S. Department of Education.

National Commission on Excellence in Education. (1983). *A nation at risk: The imperative for educational reform.* Washington, D.C.: The National Commission of Excellence in Education.

National Council for the Social Studies. (1994). *Expectations of excellence: Curriculum standards for social studies.* Washington, D.C.: National Council for the Social Studies.

National Council of Teachers of English and International Reading Association. (1996). *Standards for the English Language Arts.* Champaign, IL, and Newark, DE: National Council of Teachers of English and International Reading Association.

National Council of Teachers of Mathematics. (1989). *Curriculum and evaluation standards for school mathematics.* Alexandria, VA: National Council of Teachers of Mathematics.

National Council of Teachers of Mathematics. (2000). *Principles and standards for school mathematics.* Reston, VA: National Council of Teachers of Mathematics.

Nelson-Barber, S., & Estrin, E. T. (1995). *Bringing Native American perspectives to mathematics and science teaching. Theory into Practice, 34* (3), 174–185.

New London Group. (1996). A pedagogy of multiliteracies: Designing social futures. *Harvard Educational Review, 66* (1), 60–92.

Nichols, S.L. (1999). Gay, lesbian, and bisexual youth: Understanding diversity and promoting tolerance in schools. *The Elementary School Journal, 99* (5), 505–519.

Nieto, S. (2002). *Language, culture, and teaching: Critical perspectives for a new century.* Mahwah, NJ: Erlbaum.

Nieto, S. (1996). *Affirming diversity* (2nd ed.). White Plains, NY: Longman.

Nilsen, A. P., & Nilsen, D. L. F. (2002). Lessons in teaching of vocabulary from September 11 and Harry Potter. *Journal of Adolescent & Adult Literacy, 46* (3), 254–260.

Norton, D. E. (2003). *Through the Eyes of a Child: An Introduction to Children's Literature* (6th ed.) Upper Saddle River, NJ: Merrill/Prentice Hall.

Nystrand, M., & Gamoran, A. (1991). Instructional discourse, student engagement, and literature achievement. *Research in the Teaching of English, 25,* 261–290.

Nystrand, M., Wu, L. L., Gamoran, A., Zeiser, S., & Long, D. (2001). Questions in time: Investigating the structure and dynamics of unfolding classroom discourse. CELA Research Report Number 14005. *cela.albany.edu/nystrand01–5/index.html.* Retrieved October 30, 2002.

Oakes, J. (1992). Can tracking research inform practice? Technical, normative, and political considerations. *Educational Researcher, 21* (4), 12–21.

Ogbu, J. U. (1993). Differences in cultural frame of reference. *International Journal of Behavioral Development, 16* (3), 483–506.

Ogle, D. M. (1986). KWL: A teaching model that develops active reading of expository text. *Reading Teacher, 39,* 564–570.

Ogle, D. M. (1996). Study techniques that ensure content area reading success. In D. Lapp, J. Flood, & N. Farnan (Eds.). *Content Area Reading and Learning: Instructional Strategies* (2nd ed.) (pp. 277–290). Boston: Allyn & Bacon.

Oldfather, P., & Dahl, K. (1994). Toward a social constructivist reconceptualization of intrinsic motivation for literacy learning. *Journal of Reading Behavior, 26* (2), 139–158.

Olsen, L. (1997). *Made in America: Immigrant students in our public schools.* New York: New Press.

Orellana, M. F., Reynolds, J., Dorner, L., & Meza, M. (2003). In other words: Translating or "para-phrasing" as a family literacy practice in immigrant households. *Reading Research Quarterly, 38* (1), 12–34.

Ornstein, A. C., & Hunkins, F. P. (1998). *Curriculum: Foundations, Principles and Issues* (3rd ed.) Boston: Allyn & Bacon.

Palinscar, A. S., & Brown, A. L. (1984). Reciprocal teaching of comprehension-fostering and comprehension-monitoring activities. *Cognition and Instruction, 2,* 117–175.

Palmatier, R. A. (1973). A notetaking system for learning. *Journal of Reading, 18,* 36–39.

Palmer, R. G., & Stewart, R. A. (1997). Nonfiction tradebooks in content area instruction: Realities and potential. *Journal of Adolescent & Adult Literacy, 40* (8), 630–641.

Panaritis, P. (1995). Beyond brainstorming: Planning a successful interdisciplinary program. *Phi Delta Kappan, 7* (8), 623–628.

Pappamihiel, N. E. (2002). English as a second language students and English language anxiety: Issues in the mainstream classroom. *Research in the Teaching of English, 36,* 327–355.

Paris, S. G., Lipson, M. Y., & Wixson, K. K. (1983/1994). Becoming a strategic reader. In R. B. Ruddell, M. R. Ruddell, & H. Singer (Eds.), *Theoretical models and processes of reading* (4th ed., pp. 788–810). Newark, DL: International Reading Association.

Paterson, P. O. (2000). The role of text in peer-led literature circles in the secondary classroom. In T. Shanahan & F. V. Rodriguez-Brown (Eds.), *49th Yearbook of the National Reading Conference,* (pp. 235–251). Chicago: National Reading Conference.

Pearson, P. D., & Gallagher, M. C. (1983). The instruction of reading comprehension. *Contemporary Educational Psychology, 8* (3), 317–344.

Pearson, P. D., & Johnson, D. D. (1978). *Teaching reading comprehension.* New York: Holt.

Peresich, M. L., Meadows, J. D., & Sinatra, R. (1990). Content area cognitive mapping for reading and writing proficiency. *Journal of Reading, 33* (6), 424–432.

Perkins, D. N., & Salomon, G. (1989). Are cognitive skills context-bound? *Educational Researcher, 16* (1), 16–25.

Perry, T. & Delpit, L. (Eds.). (1998). *The real Ebonics debate: Power, language and the education of African-American children.* Boston: Beacon Press.

Porter, A. C. (1994). National standards and school improvement in the 1990's: Issues and promise. *American Journal of Education, 102* (4), 421–449.

Portes, A., & Zhou, M. (1994). Should Immigrants Assimilate? In *Public Interest, 116,* (Summer, 1994), p.18. Retrieved April 2, 2003 from University of California at Davis database *heather.cs.ucdavis.edu/pub/Immigration/Portes.html.*

Pressley, M., Goodchild, R., Fleet, J., Zajchowski, R., & Evans, E. D. (1989). The challenges of classroom strategy instruction. *Elementary School Journal, 89* (3), 301–342.

Raphael, T. E. (1986). Teaching question answer relationships, revisited. *Reading Teacher, 40,* 516–522.

Ravitch, D. (1995). National standards and curriculum reform. In A. C. Ornstein & L. S. Behar (Eds.), *Contemporary issues in curriculum.* Needham Heights, MA: Allyn & Bacon.

Readence, J. E., Bean, T. W., & Baldwin, R. S. (1989*). Content area reading: An integrated approach.* Dubuque, IA: Kendell/Hunt.

Reid, T. R. (2003). The Serpas. *National Geographic, 203 (5), 55.*

Rex, L. A. (2001). The remaking of a high school reader. *Reading Research Quarterly, 36* (3), 288–314.

Reyes, M. de la Luz (1992). Challenging venerable assumptions: Literacy instruction for linguistically different students. *Harvard Educational Review, 62,* 427–446.

Richgels, D. J., McGee, L., Lomax, R. G., & Sheard, C. (1987). Awareness of four text structures: Effects on recall of expository text. *Reading Research Quarterly, 22,* 177–196.

Rief, L. (1992). *Seeking diversity: Language arts with adolescents.* Portsmouth, NH: Heinemann.

Robinson, F. (1961). *Effective study.* New York: Harper & Row.

Rong, X. L., & Brown, R. (2001). The effects of immigrant generation and ethnicity on educational attainment among young African and Caribbean Blacks in the United States. *Harvard Educational Review, 71* (3), 536–565.

Rosenblatt, L. M. (1994). The transactional theory of reading and writing. In R. B. Ruddell, M. R. Ruddell, & H. Singer, *Theoretical models and processes of reading* (4th ed.) (pp. 1057–1093). Newark, DL: International Reading Association.

Rosenshine, B., & Meister, C. (1994). Reciprocal teaching: A review of the research. *Review of Educational Research, 64,* 479–530.

Rowe, M. B. (1974). Relation of wait-time and rewards to the development of language, logic, and fate control: Part one, Wait-time. *Journal of Research in Science Teaching, 11,* 81–94.

Rubinstein-Ávila, E. (2003). Facing reality: English language learners in middle school classes. *English Education, 35* (2), 122–136.

Ruddell, M. R., & Shearer, B. A. (2002). Extraordinary, 'tremendous', 'exhilarating', 'magnificent': Middle school at-risk students become avid word learners with the vocabulary self-collection strategy (VSS). *Journal of Adolescent & Adult Literacy, 45* (5), 352–363.

Rutherford, F. J., & Ahlgren, A. (1990). *Science for all Americans: A project 2061 report on goals in science.* New York: Oxford University Press.

Sadker, M., & Sadker, D. (1994). *Failing at fairness: How America's schools cheat girls.* New York: Charles Scribner's.

Sanders, N. M. (1966). *Classroom questions: What kinds.* New York: Harper & Row.

Santa, C. M., & Alvermann, D. E. (1991). *Science learning: Processes and applications.* Newark, DE: International Reading Association.

Sarroub, L. K. (2001). The sojourner experience of Yemeni American high school students: An ethnographic portrait. *Harvard Educational Review, 71* (3), 390–415.

Schmidt, D. (1985).Writing in math class. In A. R. Gere (Ed.), *Roots in sawdust: Writing across the disciplines* (pp. 104–116). Urbana, IL: National Council of Teachers of English.

Schön, D. A. (1983). *The reflective practitioner.* New York: Basic Books.

Schunk, D. H., & Zimmerman, B. J. (1997). Developing self-efficacious readers and writers: The role of social and self-regulatory processes. In J. T. Guthrie & A. Wigfield (Eds.), *Reading engagement: Motivating readers through integrated instruction* (pp. 34–50). Newark, DL: International Reading Association.

Schwartz, R. M. (1988). Learning to learn vocabulary in content area textbooks. *Journal of Reading, 32* (3), 108–118.

Scott, J. A., & Nagy, W. E. (1997). Understanding the definitions of unfamiliar verbs. *Reading Research Quarterly, 32* (2), 184–200.

Short, K. G. (1992). Researching intertextuality within collaborative classroom learning environments. *Linguistics and Education, 4,* 313–333.

Shulman, L. S. (1986).Those who understand: Knowledge growth in teaching. *Educational Researcher, 15* (2), 4–14.

Shulman, L. S. (1987). Knowledge and teaching: Foundations of the new reform. *Harvard Educational Review, 57* (1), 1–22.

Seidenstricker, L. S. (2000). Student engagement in literature discussion: An exploratory investigation into small-group peer-led and large-group teacher-led interactive structures. In T. Shanahan & F. V. Rodriguez-Brown (Eds.), *49th Yearbook of the National Reading Conference* (pp. 252–265). Chicago: National Reading Conference.

Sills-Briefel, T., Fisk, C., & Dunlop. V. (1996/1997). Graduation by exhibition. *Educational Leadership, 54* (4), 66–71.

Simpson, M. L. (1986). PORPE: A writing strategy for studying and learning in the content areas. *Journal of Reading, 29,* 407–414.

Singer, H. (1992). Friendly texts: Description and criteria. In E. K. Dishner, T. W. Bean, J. E. Readence, & D. W. Moore (Eds), *Reading in the content areas: Improving classroom instruction* (3rd ed.) (pp. 155–170). Dubuque, IA: Kendall Hunt.

Singer, H., & Donlan, D. (1992). Learning-from-text guide. In K. D. Wood, D. Lapp, & J. Flood (Eds.), *Guiding readers through text: A review of study guides* (pp. 31–33). Newark, DL: International Reading Association.

Slavin, R. E. (1988). Cooperative learning and student achievement. In R. E. Slavin (Ed.), *School and classroom organization.* Hillsdale, NJ: Erlbaum.

Sleeter, C. E. (1997). Reflections on my use of multicultural and critical pedagogy when students are white. In C. E. Sleeter & P. L. McLaren (Eds.), *Multicultural education, critical pedagogy, and the politics of difference* (pp. 415–438). Albany, NY: State University of New York Press.

Sleeter, C. E., & Grant, C. A. (1991). Race, class, gender, and disability in current textbooks. In M. W. Apple & L. K. Christian-Smith (Eds.), *The politics of the textbook* (pp. 78–110). New York: Routledge.

Smith, M.W., & Wilhelm, J. D. (2002). *"Reading don't fix no Chevys: Literacy in the lives of young men.* Portsmouth, NH: Heinemann.

Social Science Education and Consortium. (1988). *Immigration: pluralism and national identity.* Boulder, CO: Social Science Education Consortium.

Sosenke, F. (1994). Students as textbook authors. *Mathematics Teaching in the Middle School, 1* (2), 108–111.

Speigel, D. L. (1987). Using adolescent literature in social studies and science. *Educational Horizons, 65,* 162–164.

Stahl, S. A., Hynd, C. R., Britton, B. K., McNish, M. M., & Bosquet, D. (1996). What happens when students read multiple source documents in history. *Reading Research Quarterly, 31* (4), 430–456.

Stahl, S. A., & Fairbanks, M. M. (1986). The effects of vocabulary instruction: A model-based meta-analysis. *Review of Educational Research, 56* (1), 72–110.

Stahl, S. A., & Vancil, S. J. (1986). Discussion is what makes semantic maps work in vocabulary discussion. *Reading Teacher, 40* (1), 62–67.

The Statue of Liberty–Ellis Island Foundation, Inc. (2000). *Ellis Island Online.* Retrieved April 2, 2003 from *www.ellisisland.org.*

Steffenson, M. S., Joag-Dev, C., & Anderson, R. C. (1979). A cross-cultural perspective on reading comprehension. *Reading Research Quarterly, 15,* 10–29.

Stein, N. L., & Glenn, C. G. (1979). An analysis of story comprehension in elementary school children. In R. Freedle (Ed.), *New directions in discourse processing* (pp. 53–120). Norwood, NJ: Ablex.

Stotsky, S. (1995, April). Changes in America's secondary schools. *Phi Delta Kappan,* 605–612.

Suárez-Orozco, C., & Suàrez-Orozco, M. M. (2001). *Children of Immigration.* Cambridge: Harvard University Press.

Suárez-Orozco, M. M. (2001). Globalization, immigration, and education: The research agenda. *Harvard Educational Review, 71* (3), 345–365.

Taylor, B. M. (1980). Children's memory for expository text after reading. *Reading Research Quarterly, 15,* 399–411.

Taylor, B. M., & Beach, R. W. (1984). The effects of text structure instruction on middle-grade students' comprehension and production of expository text. *Reading Research Quarterly, 19,* 134–146.

Tchudi, S. (1991). *Planning and assessing the curriculum in English/language arts.* Alexandria, VA: Association for Supervision and Curriculum Development.

Tchudi, S. (1993). *The astonishing curriculum: Integrating science and the humanities through language.* Urbana, IL: National Council of Teachers of English.

Terner, J. et al. (1988). Biographic sources in the sciences. In *Library of Congress Science Tracer Bulletin.* Washington, D.C.: National Center for Science and Technology (ERIC Document Reproduction Services ED 393 727).

Texley, J., & Wild, A. (1996). *National Science Teachers Association pathways to science.* Arlington, VA: National Science Teachers Association.

Thelen, J. N. (1984). *Improving reading in science* (2nd ed.). Newark, DE: International Reading Association.

Tinajoro, J. V., & Hurly, S. R. (1997). Literacy instruction for students acquiring English: Moving beyond the immersion debate. *Reading Teacher, 50,* 356–359.

U.S. Department of Education, Office of Special Education Programs. (2001). *Children and youth with disabilities served by selected programs 1991–2000.* Washington, D.C.: U.S. Department of Education, Office of Special Education Programs.

Vacca, R. T., & Vacca, J. A. L. (2002). *Content area reading* (7th ed.). New York: Longman.

Van Sledright, B. A. (1994). *"I don't remember—the ideas are all jumbled in my head": 8th graders' reconstruction of colonial American history.* Paper presented at the AERA Annual Meeting, New Orleans, LA (ERIC Document Reproduction Services ED 393 727).

Van Sledright, B. A., & Kelly, C. (1998). Reading American history: The influence of multiple sources on 6 5th graders. *The Elementary School Journal, 98* (3), 239–266.

Warren, A. R., & McCloskey, L. A. (1997). *Language in social contexts.* In J. B. Gleason (Ed.), The development of language (pp. 210–258). Needham Heights, MA: Allyn & Bacon.

Weinstein, S. (2002). The writing on the wall: Attending to self-motivated student literacies. *English Education, 35* (1), 21–45.

Wepner, S. B., Valmont, W. J., & Thurlow, R. (Eds.), (2000). *Linking Literacy and Technology: A Guide for K–8 Classrooms.* Newark, DE:IRA.

White, T. G., Graves, M. F., & Slater, W. H. (1990). Growth of reading vocabulary in diverse elementary schools: Decoding and word meaning. *Journal of Educational Psychology, 82* (2), 281–290.

White, T. G., Sowell, J., & Yangihara, A. (1989). Teaching elementary students to use word-part clues. *Reading Teacher, 42,* 302–308.

Whitin, P. E. (1996). Exploring visual response to literature. *Research in the Teaching of English, 30* (1), 114–140.

Wigfield, A. (1997). Children's motivations for reading and reading engagement. In J. T. Guthrie & A. Wigfield (Eds.), *Reading engagement: Motivating readers through integrated instruction* (pp. 14–33). Newark, DL: International Reading Association.

Willis, S. (1992, November). Interdisciplinary learning: Movement to link the disciplines gains momentum. *ASCD Curriculum Update*, 1–8.

Wineburg, S. S. (1991). On the reading of historical texts: Notes on the breach between school and academy. *American Educational Research, 28* (3), 495–519.

Wineburg, S. S., & Wilson, S. M. (1991). Subject-matter knowledge in the teaching of history. In J. Brophy (Ed.), *Advances in research on teaching* (Vol. 2, pp. 305–347). Greenwich, CT: JAI Press.

Winograd, P. N. (1984). Strategic difficulties in summarizing texts. *Reading Research Quarterly, 19,* 404–425.

Wolf, D. P., & Reardon, S. F. (Eds.). Access to excellence through new forms of student assessment. In J. B. Baron & D. P. Wolf (Eds.), *Performance-based student assessment: Challenges and possibilities.* Chicago: National Society for the Study of Education and University of Chicago Press.

Wood, K. D. (1988). Guiding students through informational text. *Reading Teacher, 41* (9), 912–920.

Wood, K. D., Lapp, D., & Flood, J. (1992). *Guiding readers through text: A review of study guides.* Newark, DL: International Reading Association.

Name Index

Subject Index